Symbolic Interactions

Symbolic Interactions

Social Problems and Literary Interventions in the Works of Baillie, Scott, and Landor

Regina Hewitt

Lewisburg
Bucknell University Press

Associated University Presses
2010 Eastpark Boulevard
Cranbury, NJ 08512

Library of Congress Cataloging-in-Publication Data

Hewitt, Regina, 1959–
    Symbolic interactions : social problems and literary interventions in the works of Baillie, Scott, and Landor / Regina Hewitt.
        p. cm.
    Includes bibliographical references and index.
    ISBN 0-8387-5639-5 (alk. paper)
1. Scottish literature—19th century—History and criticism. 2. Scott, Walter, Sir, 1771–1832—Political and social views. 3. Baillie, Joanna, 1762–1851—Political and social views. 4. Landor, Walter Savage, 1775–1864. conversations. 5. Literature and society—Great Britain—History—19th century. 6. Social problems in literature. I. Title.
    PR8552.H49 2006
    820.9'3552—dc22

                                            2005024412

Contents

Preface

IN THIS STUDY, I CONSIDER HOW DRAMAS BY JOANNA BAILLIE, NOVELS by Walter Scott, and *Imaginary Conversations* by Walter Savage Landor perform a kind of social work comparable to the work undertaken by Jane Addams and other "Settlers" who developed an interventionist sociology in the pre-disciplinary era before theory and practice were separated. Using concepts of "symbolic interaction" that have evolved from the works of Addams and George Herbert Mead, as well as from subsequent practitioners, I examine the ways in which the literary works encourage their audiences to sympathize with others, renovate traditional roles and experiment with new roles within their communities, avoid entrapment in inherited social structures, and carefully reform social relations.

My chapters illustrate the writers' interventions through a series of examples organized around the social problems with which they and the later social workers were especially concerned—problems in programs for criminal justice, relief of poverty, and political participation. By juxtaposing the approaches of the writers with those of the social workers, I use one field to comment on the other (and vice versa) in a manner that encourages cross-disciplinary thinking. Such thinking is important to my study because, while focusing on the specified problems and intervention in Romantic-era literature, I also argue that disciplinary divisions have contributed to social problems in our time. By separating literature from lived experience, they have discouraged Romanticists from treating texts as symbolic resources (to use a term from Norman Denzin's "Social Work in the Seventh Moment")[1] that can enrich social programs, and they have discouraged social workers and scholars of literature from collaborating to enlist symbolic resources in efforts to help people change their situations. These negative consequences are evident even in the attitude of Jane Addams, who both embraced and repudiated literature. Through the textual and contextual analysis of Addams's reading of De Quincey that frames my study, I attribute the tension in her attitude toward literature to the pressures of disciplinarity that increased during her career.

Post-disciplinary efforts, such as those by Paul Hamilton, David Haney, and Frederick Burwick, to account for and overcome aesthetic isolation have taken strides toward bringing literature and lived experience closer together.[2] Those works, however, tend to theorize their goals in philosophical terms. My attention to social work and symbolic interaction offers an alternative approach to the problem. By identifying a common starting point in Romantic-era writing for the mobilization of symbolic resources, I encourage Romanticists to explore and promote the interventionist potential of literary work.

Because the chapters juxtapose a good deal of materials from different eras and fields, it may be helpful to begin with a detailed overview of the argument. I therefore devote the remainder of the preface to a chapter-by-chapter summary designed to serve as an orientation to the study.

In chapter 1, I begin with Jane Addams's (mis)reading of De Quincey's *English Mail-Coach* in order to introduce the contradictory attitudes about the social functions of literature that have limited its use for social problem solving. After correlating the limits with the rise of disciplinarity, I point out how the decline of disciplinarity offers opportunities to reconnect literature with social applications. Elaborating on the particular opportunities offered by the trend in Romantic-era scholarship toward contextual reading, I note how revisionist views of Joanna Baillie and Walter Scott call for further study of their political positions. I posit that a larger context of social engagement, which subsumes the political, gives us new insight into their works. Concomitantly, I note that revisionist scholarship has not yet paid comparable attention to Walter Savage Landor, and I attribute that neglect to lingering disciplinary constraints. I bring Landor into this study in order to show how his work can be read in post-disciplinary times, to compare his fictionalizing of history with Scott's, and to contrast the political focus of his *Imaginary Conversations* with the broader social orientation in Baillie's and Scott's works (which I do in chapters 6, 7, and 8). In the remainder of chapter 1, I define the concept of "symbolic interaction" that I use to illuminate Baillie's and Scott's social engagement. After a brief history of "symbolic interactionism" (as it came to be called) from the works of Addams and George Herbert Mead in late nineteenth-century Chicago to the "interpretive interactionism" of Norman Denzin in the present day, the chapter identifies four "signal traits" (constructionism, performativity, personal agency, and pragmatism) of this orientation that have affinities in the works of Baillie and Scott. The chapter previews some of the analyses of their works in terms of these traits that appear in the subsequent chapters.

The subsequent chapters center on exemplary problems and interactionist ways of solving them. In each chapter, I show that the literary works offer neither an escape from social problems nor solutions to be accepted or rejected; instead, they suggest lines of inquiry through which spectators at plays or readers of novels can work toward solutions. They encourage their audiences to treat literary and lived experience analogously. It is this sense of equivalence, available during the Romantic period and becoming available again in this post-disciplinary era, that we lost during the disciplinary age. Through the following examples, I seek to recover and develop that equivalence.

Chapter 2 centers on the problem of criminal justice, prominent in England and Scotland during Baillie's and Scott's time and in Chicago during Addams's and Mead's. In Romantic-era England, reformers sought the declassification of many capital crimes that had made execution a common penalty; in Scotland, which did not share England's legal system, the issue of capital punishment aroused national pride as Baron Hume, a legal commentator whom Scott admired, used reference to the smaller number of executions in Scotland to promulgate an idea of his country as the more compassionate society. In Chicago, Addams and Mead worked for the elimination of capital punishment, the creation of a separate juvenile court system, the use of psychiatric evaluations, and the replacement of the norm of "punitive justice" with an approach that interactionists continue to study as "integrative social control." This chapter contextualizes Baillie's and Scott's works with respect to the problem of punitive justice and argues that they move toward (and encourage their audiences to move toward) the more sympathetic, integrative ideal. In particular, I consider Baillie's attention to sympathy, to legal professionals, and to scenes of execution in the *Introductory Discourse* to her *Series of Plays* on the passions. I argue that her advocacy of a merciful ideal not yet common in her society aligns her with "humanity-mongering" reformers of her time. Since many of her plays deal with capital punishment, I single out her most extensive treatment of the topic in *Rayner* for analysis here; I pair that example with Scott's most extensive treatment in *The Heart of Midlothian*. Like Addams and Mead, Baillie and Scott recognized that overcoming fear of the criminal and learning to sympathize with the humanity of lawbreakers are preconditions for mitigating punitive justice. Though Scott was less able than the others to overcome his fear, his positive emphasis on sympathetic discretion within the legal system complicates any view of him as merely a conservative upholder of law and order.

Further, like Baillie's construction of a merciful ideal, it opens up lines of compassionate inquiry that even conservative thinkers can pursue.

Chapter 3 is devoted to four plays (*The Dream, Henriquez, The Stripling,* and *The Homicide*) by Baillie that deal with capital crimes. By analyzing the plays, I further align Baillie with reform efforts and interactionist approaches to justice. Specifically, I show how she habitually directs attention to the humanity of the prisoner and the inhumanity of punitive justice, creating opportunities for spectators to critique the interactions that define criminality. She exposes the failures in interpretation and sympathy through which social relations disintegrate while also suggesting the constructive, integrative tendencies of less selfish thoughts and emotions. Since my examples are drawn from both plays in the passions series and plays classified as "miscellaneous," I argue that the overarching goal of promoting a "more just, more merciful, more compassionate" society (as she states in the *Introductory Discourse*)[3] spans this division in her works.

In chapter 4, I turn to the problem of poverty. Debates over reforming the Poor Laws occurred repeatedly during the Romantic era, pitting advocates of efficient, new workhouses against advocates of decentralized personal care. Just as Scottish nationalists referred to the Criminal Code to idealize Scottish society as more humane than English society, so they referred to the Scottish decentralized approach to poor relief as kinder than England's. The tension between impersonal efficiency and personal involvement evident in the Romantic-era Poor Law controversies appears likewise in later approaches to social work. Against programs for charity visiting, in which distant social workers intruded on poor families they did not know, Addams promoted the Settlement ideal, in which social workers moved into poverty-stricken areas and became helpful neighbors. Significantly, they provided as much intangible as tangible relief. They brought together residents of different ethnic and economic backgrounds in ways that eased tensions among immigrant groups and allowed people to experiment with different roles and to envision changed social relations. Contemporary interactionists and social workers continue to seek ways to use symbolic resources to promote social change. The emphasis on social responsibility on the part of privileged people and social cooperation at all levels, which are common elements in defenses of the Old Poor Laws and the Settlement Movement, revises any simple categorization of the former as reactionary and the latter as progressive. The affinities between the two therefore call for a reassessment of Scott's advocacy of the Old Poor Laws. Looking at his characterization of the beggar Edie Ochiltree in *The Antiquary,* his criticism of elite selfishness in *The Bride of Lammermoor,* his projection of social cooperation in the Roseneath section of *The Heart of Midlothian*, and statements about personal charity in his letters, I argue for a revised understanding of Scott's paternalism. Instead of finding his position conservative and condescending, I find it moving toward an interactionist view of social relations that requires mutual respect among different groups.

Chapter 5 continues to explore the problem of poverty by comparing Baillie's presentation of Lady Griseld Baillie as a role model for women in her time with Addams's analysis of charity visitors and Settlement residents. Though finding Baillie's and Scott's views of charity compatible with each other regarding personal involvement, I see them diverging over the extent to which they expect poor people to suffer for the sake of collective order in a society controlled by an irresponsible elite. Whereas Scott accepts the necessity of self-sacrifice on the part of the poor in such situations, Baillie cannot countenance it. I believe that that difference between them lies at the heart of the differences in their presentations of old, poor women who are thought to be witches in *The Bride of Lammermoor* and *Witchcraft*. I develop that contrast in an intertextual reading of those two works along with Addams's related story of "The Devil Baby at Hull-House."

In chapter 6, I consider the problem of political participation that led, by the end of the Romantic era, to the reorganization of Parliament as a more representative body. Drawing on Charles Tilly's argument for "popular contention" as the catalyst for this reform,⁴ I show how Landor's *Imaginary Conversations* among historical figures strategically present contention as a normal mode of interaction in the past and thus encourage its continuation in the present. I explain this use of history in terms of interactionist ideas about how we create the past as a problem-solving exercise in the present. Though Landor's *Conversations* endorse an egalitarian treatment of others that overcomes elite selfishness, they also rely on conflict in ways that can interfere with community building. Their oppositional mode favors political over social goals; inverse proportions are favored by Baillie's and Scott's works. For an additional contrast between Landor's political and Scott's and Baillie's social goals, I analyze Landor's imaginary conversation between Romilly and Perceval on the topic of capital punishment, which approaches that issue with greater attention to regulation than to sympathy or integrative control. The other conversations I select involve mainly seventeenth-century figures so as to facilitate comparison with Scott's use of history, which I undertake in the next chapter.

Chapter 7 presents the contrasting view of popular contention informing Scott's and Baillie's works. Analyzing *Redgauntlet* and *Woodstock*, I posit that Scott prefers "temporizing" to "contending," an approach that works toward the gradual correction of abuses of power instead of the direct confrontation of them. Regarding the use of the past to solve present problems, I argue that Scott takes a deferential approach to history and tradition even as he transforms them to manifest the supportive social relations he idealizes. Scott's approach to history itself exemplifies the co-operative and temporizing mode. A similar preference for cooperation over contention is evident in Baillie's drama *The Election*. A comedy on hatred in the passions series, the play reduces political contention to selfish quarreling. Like Scott, Baillie uses subtle transformations of the past to set precedents for new social relations in the present. I examine her procedure in *Constantine Paleologus* and *The Family Legend*, plays that would turn the tide of history away from aggression, domination, and revenge.

In chapter 8, I return to the problem of disciplinarity with which I opened the study. Looking at nineteenth- and twentieth-century editions of the *Imaginary Conversations*, I track how the "need" to separate fact from fiction, which was not perceived by Romantic-era readers but imposed by the disciplinary system, grew into a monumental precondition for reading this work. The *Imaginary Conversations* were not readable within the modern disciplinary system because Landor's conflations of fiction and history could not be untangled or explained away as easily as could Scott's, whose work could still be accommodated, though not favored, within this system. A landmark critique of disciplinarity by interactionist David Maines assesses the system in narrative terms that I adapt in the remainder of the conclusion: the story of disciplinarity is driven by a plot that denigrates "human utterance" and elevates quantification.[5] I use this plot to explain not only why such effort was expended on separating fact from fiction in Landor's and Scott's works but also why additional effort has been expended on valorizing the extracted "literary" component. When literature had to be distinguished from lived experience, the literary had to be assigned unique value—or dismissed. Romanticists took the former approach; Jane Addams, the latter. Returning to Addams's account of her reading of De Quincey, I find the plot of the devalued human utterance behind her denial of the positive influence that De Quincey's text clearly asserts and exerts. I conclude that post-disciplinary scholarship is ready to reunite Addams with De Quincey, lived with literary experience. By showing how the works of Baillie, Scott, and Landor participate in social problem solving, my work furthers the movement of Romantic-era studies out of aesthetic isolation and into the social world.

Acknowledgments

For permission to quote extensively from the 1976 reprint of
the 1851 edition of Joanna Baillie's *Dramatic and Poetical Works*, I am
grateful to the publisher, Georg Olms, in Hildesheim, Germany. In the
absence of a complete modern edition, this reprint remains an essential resource for scholarship on Baillie.

For permission to include in this book portions of my work on Bail-
lie, Scott, and Landor that first reached print as articles, I am grateful to
the publishers of the journals in which they appeared. Specifically, portions connecting Baillie with Addams appeared in "Joanna Baillie at
Hull-House: A Working Hypothesis for Disciplinary Reform," *Studies in
Symbolic Interaction* 27 (2004): 113–49, which I use here by permission of
Elsevier; portions on Baillie and Scott appeared in "Scott, Baillie, and the
Bewitching of Social Relations," *European Romantic Review* 16 (2005): 341–
50, which I incorporate here by permission of Taylor and Francis; portions on Landor appeared in "Landor, Shelley, and the Design of History," *Romanticism on the Net* 20 (Nov. 2000), <http://users.ox.ac.uk/~scat
0385/20hewitt.html>, which I use by permission of Michael Eberle-Sina-
tra, and in "On Reconciling Past and Future: Some Effects of Landor's
Imaginary Conversations," *Studies in Symbolic Interaction* 24 (2001): 273–97,
which I use by permission of Elsevier.

I developed the ideas that became this book over many years in the
supportive environment created by e-mail dialogue and conference ses-
sions with colleagues from the Nineteenth-Century Studies Association
(NCSA), the North American Society for the Study of Romanticism
(NASSR), and the Society for the Study of Symbolic Interaction (SSSI).
These encounters, both virtual and "real," repeatedly introduced me to innovative ways of thinking about these writers and about interaction, and
they energized me to continue my research. I received generous advice
about legal research from Anthony Simpson at the Lloyd Sealey Library,
John Jay College of Criminal Justice, and I was cordially welcomed and

assisted at the Biddle Law Library of the University of Pennsylvania by Joseph Parsio and other librarians.

Special thanks should go to Frederick Burwick, Norman Denzin, Karl Kroeber, Robert M. Ryan, Carl Woodring, and the late Stanford Lyman, whose inspiration and advice were crucial to this project even when they originated at earlier times and in different contexts. More immediately, Norman Denzin exemplified editorial open-mindedness in allowing me to rethink and revise my work for *Studies in Symbolic Interaction*. Thanks are due also to Kathy Charmaz and the late Donna Darden, who kindly encouraged me to tell the story of Addams and De Quincey that frames this book; to Victoria Myers, who graciously shared with me her work-in-progress on Baillie; to Joseph Kestner, who offered insightful comments on my work-in-progress on Landor; to William Heim and William Scheuerle, who led my search for editions of Landor's works to a happy conclusion; and to Christine A. Retz and Marianne Grace, who expertly and tactfully edited the manuscript.

Symbolic Interactions

1

Introduction:
Conceptualizing Symbolic Interaction

> [A]t the very moment of looking down the East London street [at the impoverished inhabitants] from the top of the omnibus, I had been sharply and painfully reminded of "The Vision of Sudden Death" which had confronted De Quincey one summer's night as he was being driven through rural England on a high mail coach.

WITH THE ABOVE EVOCATION OF A ROMANTIC-ERA TEXT, JANE ADDAMS begins to explain how she developed the commitment to social welfare that led to the founding of Hull-House. Continuing, Addams recounts the appearance of the lovers' gig in the path of the runaway mail-coach and elaborates on De Quincey's attempt to prevent a collision:

> De Quincey tries to send them a warning shout, but finds himself unable to make a sound because his mind is hopelessly entangled in an endeavor to recall the exact lines from the "Iliad" which describe the great cry with which Achilles alarmed all Asia militant. Only after his memory responds is his will released from its momentary paralysis, and he rides through the fragrant night with the horror of the escaped calamity thick upon him, but he also bears with him the consciousness that he had given himself over so many years to classic learning—that when suddenly called upon for a quick decision in the world of life and death, he had been able to act only through literary suggestion.

Following this assessment of De Quincey's conduct, Addams analogizes his failure to act quickly and effectively to save the lovers with her and her peers' failure to relieve the sufferings of the poor: "[t]hat is what we were all doing, lumbering our minds with literature that only served to cloud the really vital situation spread before our eyes." She concludes: "[i]t seemed to me too preposterous that in my first view of the horror of East London I should have recalled De Quincey's literary description of the literary suggestion which had once paralyzed him."[1]

As a Romanticist concerned with the social functions of literature, I find Addams's rejection of De Quincey troubling. That the pursuit of social work should depend on the repudiation of literature seems to anticipate attacks on the Romantic ideology in our own time and to launch them with devastating effect.[2] Yet, as we have worked out through the many considered responses that McGann's criticism provoked, Romantic-era writers and the scholars who study them play multiple and varied roles in society, including roles that could be labeled "social worker," "sociologist," or "activist." Moreover, even if Addams is right to suspect De Quincey's social conscience, her account advances an astonishing misreading of his text. In his version of the mail-coach incident, laudanum, not literature, retards his ability to act; the "literary suggestion" provides the sudden, inspiring breakthrough that helps him find his voice.[3] Addams's interpretation inverts the value of literature in De Quincey's account, making it negative instead of positive. How, I wondered, could Addams have made so egregious a mistake? This book evolved to answer that question.

A provisional answer is that she did not make a mistake at all. If, as Marilyn Butler has argued, "literature lives by seeming to express the experiences and interests of its readers,"[4] then De Quincey lived for Addams by provoking her thoughts about the social responsibilities of the culturally privileged. Addams used De Quincey's text to explore issues, reflect on values, reach self-consciousness, and set goals for herself and her peers. Her productive (mis)reading demonstrates the use of literature for problem solving and value inquiry that bears out claims for imaginative writings advanced by De Quincey himself as well as by other Romantic-era figures from Joanna Baillie to William Wordsworth. Such use is further demonstrated by Addams's eagerness to stage dramas and host reading groups at Hull-House, incorporating literature into the methods of social work practiced there.[5] A better question, then, to ask about Addams's (mis)reading is why was it so important to her to distance herself from literature, to deny the power in lived experience[6] it clearly had for her.

The answer to that question lies in the gulf between humanistic and scientific cultures that widened to nearly unspannable size between the early nineteenth and early twentieth centuries.[7] To develop credible and effective ways of promoting social welfare, Addams had to associate her work with the scientific culture privileged in the rising discipline of sociology, in government policy making and administration, and in legal systems, and she had to dissociate it from the humanistic culture that was increasingly perceived as escapist, elitist, idealistic, or naïve. We see the result of this separation in the tensions between what Addams says about reading and how she uses reading. Not only in her treatment of De Quincey but in characteristic statements such as "while I may receive valuable suggestions from classic literature, when I really want to learn about life, I must depend on my neighbors,"[8] she pulls back from equating literary with lived experience and from fully acknowledging the importance of the former in her work for social change. Taking account of Addams's situation provides an answer to the question about her puzzling interpretation of De Quincey. She projected onto his text the negative ideas about literature that were prominent in her culture, and by distancing herself from him, she distanced herself from those attitudes that she feared would prevent her from contributing to the good of her society.

Understanding Addams's ambivalence toward literature[9] as a function of disciplinarity is now possible because we have entered a post-disciplinary age. Instead of shying away from literary experiences, much social work is now cultivating them. Some practitioners see their work as helping people tell different stories or script different plays about their lives.[10] Shannon Jackson has even redefined the social work done at Hull-House itself as "reformance," i.e., the performance of social change.[11] Seeing social workers turn to literature for qualitative or humanistic methodologies to replace scientific, bureaucratic, and rationalistic controls, I am struck by a need for greater reciprocity from Romanticists, for it is in Romantic-era writing that we can find qualitative inquiry taking shape as resistance to quantitative reduction. To be sure, many recent studies have shed light on the social and political involvements of the period's writers, expanded the canon of writers we deem significant, revised our view of the importance of the theater and the novel in comparison with poetry during this age, and changed our sense of the relationship between public and private spheres, but no study has considered how any writing from the period may be a kind of social work or interventionist sociology, how it promotes value inquiry and social consciousness through what might be termed "symbolic interaction" in both literary and lived experience.

Without reference to social work or symbolic interaction (a concept I explain in detail later in the introduction), existing scholarship has investigated the pursuit of value inquiry and social responsibility in the writing of this era. I would single out three studies as exceptionally important in this regard—David Haney's *The Challenge of Coleridge*, Frederick Burwick's *Mimesis and Its Romantic Reflections,* and Paul Hamilton's *Metaroman-ticism.*

Haney grapples with a problem related to the one I perceive in Addams's reading of De Quincey. Specifically, he identifies a reductionistic binarism in much thinking about literature that results in "either/or" interpretations: readers see texts as either aesthetic and therefore not connected with ethics or as didactic and therefore not aesthetic. Haney draws on Coleridge's drama criticism to correct this condition. Coleridge's criticism can do so because it focuses on the need for spectators to actively interpret rather than passively imitate what they see. The interpretive challenge Haney educes from Coleridge leads him to contemporary philosophy and to more complex ways to think about oppositions between aesthetics and ethics, self and other, past and present.[12] My present study shares Haney's aim of wanting to overcome the gap between the aesthetic and the ethical, though I figure it in terms of the literary and the social.

Correcting the belief that Romantic-era thinkers divided the aesthetic from the cognitive, Burwick reveals that such divisions arose with late nineteenth-century aestheticism (and thus, I observe, at a time crucial for the development of Addams's thought). Romantic-era thinkers, on the contrary, saw art as bringing mind and matter together and thereby facilitating self-consciousness; they took "mimesis" to be an imitation of the mind perceiving the world, making it a concept of connection rather than disconnection. Further distancing Romantic-era literature from theories of aesthetic escapism, Burwick argues that Schelling and others used the concept of "art for art's sake" as a strategy to avoid institutional control, not as a means to avoid cognitive and/or social engagement. My conviction that Addams's misreading of De Quincey stems from a culturally conditioned separation of disciplinary, epistemic and cognitive categories is influenced by Burwick's work.

Finally, Paul Hamilton's *Metaromanticism* seeks a way to make the hypothetical freedom of Schiller's aesthetic state operable in the "real" world. According to Hamilton, Schiller envisioned ideal political configurations by abstracting their patterns of interaction (though he does not use that term in any privileged sense) from their historical instantiations. He thus made the ideal available in different times and places, but he left it inchoate in art: he had no effective way to communicate it.[13] Hamilton turns to Habermas to find the missing means of communication and thus to bring the promise of harmonious free play among independent entities into practice under existing conditions of postcolonial diversity. My study joins in Hamilton's quest to connect imagined ideals with lived experience, but I see a wider channel of communication in works known as "symbolic interactionism"—a way of studying, interpreting and (re)constructing society that developed from the efforts of Jane Addams, George Herbert Mead, and other pioneers of pre-disciplinary sociology in Chicago.

The need for a study of Romantic-era writing as social work arises not only from post-disciplinary interest in qualitative methods but from new questions about Romantic-era writers prompted by new perspectives on them. This situation is especially apparent in the cases of Joanna Baillie and Walter Scott. Though we now recognize Baillie as a significant presence for this period and treat her *Introductory Discourse* to *A Series of Plays* on the passions with almost as much familiarity as Wordsworth's *Preface* to *Lyrical Ballads*, we do not adequately understand her claims to be using drama to promote a "more just [and] more merciful" society, nor have we fathomed how or whether these claims apply to all her plays or what idea of justice she held.[14] In the case of Scott, we now attach significance to disjunctions in his writing and thinking that we used to overlook or incorporate into unified explanations. We are now more inclined to see him grappling with value conflict in his representations of British rule and Scottish identity, logical explanations and legendary knowledge, historical research and antiquarian indulgence, but we often leave him in the midst of political contradiction without fully educing a social agenda from his work.[15] Furthermore, no recent study asks what made it possible for Baillie, who identified herself with the Whigs, and Scott, who identified himself with the Tories, to have been so intellectually compatible that Baillie could refer to Scott as her "only political correspondent."[16] I posit that their compatibility stems from a social agenda that takes them beyond party politics.

The case of Walter Savage Landor inverts the pattern of scholarly attention evident in the cases of Baillie and Scott. Whereas publications, editions, performances, and special issues of journals herald rising interest in Baillie and Scott, very little notice is being taken of Landor.[17] That neglect is unfortunate because his *Imaginary Conversations* shares with Scott's novels and Baillie's historical plays many of the characteristics—such as manipulation of fact and fiction, past and present—that are most open to revaluation from a post-disciplinary standpoint. Landor, moreover, was committed to republican government, which brings him into instructive contrast with Scott and Baillie. Landor's thought, I posit, stayed more narrowly focused on politics than did Scott's or Baillie's, yet his *Imaginary Conversations* serve social purposes that go beyond the partisan agenda for which they were designed. The study of Landor complements the study of Baillie and Scott, making the social dimensions of their works more readily apparent and furthering our knowledge of the diversity and complexity of Romantic-era writing.

My purpose in this study is to educe the constructive social agenda from Baillie's and Scott's works by reading them through the lenses of social work and interactionist sociology. Through the perspectives, concepts, and vocabulary of these latter ways of knowing, we can see how their dramas and fictions adjust social relations by provoking interpretation, criticism, and response. Concomitantly, I read Landor's *Imaginary Conversations* through an interactionist view of the construction of history that reveals the social function of his political work. Treating political behavior as one kind of social interaction, I show how the writers' varied manipulations of history arise in response to the activity of political claims making but diverge in their assessment of it. Finally, I return to the disciplinary issues that divided De Quincey from Addams, literary from lived experience. I show how the disciplinary divisions of modern knowledge systems conditioned how we could study Baillie, Scott, and Landor, and I argue that post-disciplinarity offers us greater opportunities to rejoin the literary and the social in their work and in ours.

Though I address the topic of politics in chapters 6 and 7, it may be helpful to say something in this introductory chapter about Baillie's and Scott's positions because they are so closely associated with the political parties from which I would separate them. Without denying that these affiliations were part of their identities, I see them both as keenly aware of the inadequacy of political responses to social problems and eager to pursue more comprehensive interventions. Both would, I maintain, gladly join Ravenswood in consigning "Whig" and "Tory" to the coffeehouse and opening up justice to all.[18]

As a woman, Baillie was not a political participant in her society, though, as Anne Mellor has shown, lack of enfranchisement did not keep women from having important public voices. In fact, Mellor argues, evidence of women's participation in the public sphere demands that we revise the dichotomy of public and private and recognize the importance of a "social sphere that mediates between" the two.[19] I take the social sphere as not only mediating but subsuming; I treat it as a larger category that contains the political and private. Social interaction by women and men alike can precipitate change that may have political and/or domestic consequences. Letters by both Baillie and Scott show their interest in this larger arena where the welfare of a whole community or of humankind takes precedence over the satisfaction of partisan groups. Writing to Scott, Baillie stated: "Who comes into power and who goes out I am not at all concerned about, but as it may affect the good of the country"; writing to Baillie, Scott opined: "There is no difference except in words and personal predilections between the candid and well informed of both parties."[20]

National barriers around political participation may have oriented Baillie and Scott toward the social sphere. Numerous scholars have correlated Scotland's lack of political autonomy with the flourishing of its philosophical, legal, and social culture as thinkers and writers who might have been more caught up in politics turned to other areas.[21] Both Baillie and Scott struggled to balance British and Scottish identities, and I suggest that their awareness of differences between political and national identities also correlates with an awareness of differences between political and social spheres. Though I do not doubt Ian Ward's thesis that Scott turned to Toryism as "a way of life, not a political creed" because he feared revolution and "hated political factions,"[22] I find it necessary to look outside of Toryism—or patriarchy or paternalism—to fathom how Scott transformed the political and traditional anchors of this thought. To me, Toryism as "a way of life" implies the need to put politics in social perspective.

In the remainder of this introduction, I explain the bodies of knowledge I mean by "social work," "interventionist sociology," and "symbolic interactionism" on which I draw to educe the social functions of Baillie's, Scott's, and Landor's works. In the ensuing chapters, I create a series of intertextual configurations that show how the selected writers on one hand and the selected social workers and interactionists on the other have approached similar social problems—specifically, problems of criminal justice, poverty, and political contention. In examining these configurations, I address how each approach intervenes in the given situation, opening up ways to change the relationships among the people involved. I say "intervenes" rather than "solves" to avoid the suggestion of settling an issue once and for all. According to interactionist ways of thinking, problem solving is an ongoing activity: solutions provisionally modify a situation, which remains open to further change. I see Baillie and Scott as contributing to the process of problem solving rather than as proffering definitive solutions, and I see what Landor took to be a definitive solution as an ongoing process.

I stress similarities between the Romantic era and later figures but not without acknowledging significant differences. The procedure of intertextual reading or strategic juxtaposition, which is a way "of enabling texts from radically separate textual orders to illuminate each other and then distilling historical and human insight from their resonances, intersections, and divergences," is itself an example of a qualitative method that Mary Louise Pratt has singled out as counter to "unreflective empiricism."[23] It is masterfully employed by David Haney in *The Challenge of Coleridge*, which juxtaposes Coleridge's ideas with those of more recent philosophers, especially Ricoeur and Levinas, to grapple with the ethics of interpretation. By connecting writers with social workers, I bypass the disciplinary norms that separated them throughout most of the last century; those norms include the expectation of linearity itself, for which I substitute the principle of affinity. In the conclusion, I argue that it is now possible to rejoin even Addams and De Quincey. Though I do not claim that Baillie, Scott, and Landor anticipated interactionism, I am aware of anachronism in reading them in interactionist terms. Anachronism, however, as Jerome Christensen has observed, can be a catalyst for change, prompting "the emergence of unrecognized possibility."[24] By my anachronistic view of Baillie, Scott, and Landor, I encourage the recognition and renewal of the social functions of their work.

Symbolic Interaction(ism): Concept, History, Context

Like "Romanticism," "symbolic interactionism" eludes definition. It is a dynamic way of thinking about social processes that cannot and should not be reduced to any one fixed outline of premises. Nevertheless, certain elements or concerns, which I call "signal traits," are prominent in the works of its proponents, and these traits can serve as descriptive guides to this way of thinking. The name "symbolic interactionism" was given to this "perspective and method" in sociology by Herbert Blumer, who developed it from work begun by George Herbert Mead at the University of Chicago at the turn of the twentieth century. It is useful to distinguish between "symbolic interactionism" as a specialized view of human conduct and "symbolic interaction" as a term for that conduct itself. Without the "ism," the phrase has non-specialized implications, which I exploit in this study.

For people who are unfamiliar with the specialized usage or for those trained in literary specializations, "symbolic interaction" suggests an interpretive encounter between readers and writers or readers and texts. It suggests the overload of meaning often said to elevate symbolic texts over allegories, and it evokes thoughts of interpretation as performative, as an embodying and enacting of meaning. Except for the textual basis, these non-specialized connotations coincide with the specialized usage, for the strongest signal trait of symbolic interactionism is its view of social reality as consisting of interpretive encounters. Taken literally, symbolic interaction belies the separation between literary and lived experience that disciplined thought between the Romantic era and our own time.[25] Serendipitously, it furnishes my study with a single term through which to embrace predecessors and later figures. Since the phrase, in a non-specialized sense, would be intelligible and acceptable to many Romantic-era writers as a descriptor of their work, I consider "symbolic interaction" a "sensitized concept" for this study. In interactionist research, sensitized concepts mediate between different levels of meaning involved in studying a situation. Instead of imposing a technical term on their subjects, interactionists try to adapt a term from those used or understood by the people they observe. The adapted or "sensitized" concept joins the meaning of the behavior for the actors with its meaning for the observer. Though the observer sees more levels of meaning than the actors, the sensitized concept maintains a respect for the meanings acceptable to the actors.[26] In observing symbolic interaction in Romantic-era writing, I strive to add levels of meaning to a concept that would be intelligible to Baillie, Scott, and Landor.

Before looking further at the signal traits of interactionism, it is necessary to reflect briefly on its history. Though not named until later, symbolic interactionism emerged in the ideas and practices of George Herbert Mead, who had joined the Philosophy Department at the University of Chicago in 1894 at the invitation of John Dewey. Interactionism thus evolved along with philosophical pragmatism, with which it shares some concepts and concerns. Interactionism permeated the Sociology Department through the interdisciplinary exchanges common in the early days of the university, and as disciplinary walls began to harden, it lodged primarily in sociology, where it evolved into a way of studying and understanding social processes. Most interactionists cite Herbert Blumer's distillation of three key ideas from Mead—agency, constructionism, and interpretation—as the core around which symbolic interactionism grew.[27] According to Blumer, Mead's greatest insight was his recognition of "human beings . . . as persons constructing individual and collective action through an interpretation of the situations which confront them."[28] Interactionism's commitment to this insight guaranteed that it would never quite be at home in a discipline favoring structural determinism, totalizing theories, statistical methods, and large demographic samplings.

Proponents of more deterministic sociologies often charged symbolic interactionism with failing to deal with social structure at all and failing to formulate theories about its individual case studies. Responding to such criticisms, Lyman and Denzin, among others, explain that they are misplaced. Interactionism does indeed grapple with social structures, classes, hierarchies, and systems, and it draws conclusions that apply to more than individual cases, but it treats structures and theories differently from the way the critics think they ought to be treated. Instead of examining only how structures exert pressures on people's lives, interactionists also examine how people accept, resist, or otherwise respond to such pressures and how they alter structural relationships by doing so. Instead of privileging the explanatory power of theories or principles in the abstract, interactionists work with a pragmatic skepticism about disembodied knowledge; they generalize in ways that remain faithful to the cases they have studied.[29] My earlier example of the "sensitized concept" illustrates this point. Throughout much of the twentieth century, symbolic interactionism occupied a counter-disciplinary position, always threatened by scientific dominance and always reviving to challenge that force. The fluctuations in its status are captured in Gary Alan Fine's descriptively titled article "The Sad Demise, Mysterious Disappearance, and Glorious Triumph of Symbolic Interactionism."[30]

Recently, the "glorious triumph" has been affirmed by David Maines, who notes that the ideas of this once-marginal orientation have been moving ever closer to the center of sociological inquiry as traditional disciplinary and epistemic divisions have been called into question.[31] Now, even the National Science Foundation's Program in Sociology recognizes a need to study "not only . . . the structural and material features of our social world, but also the underlying ideational structures—for example, notions of justice, purity, danger, sexual respectability, and equality. These must be examined in order to better understand meaning systems that govern peoples' 'rational choices.'"[32] New branches of the discipline, such as postmodern existential sociology, join symbolic interactionism in centering on the ability of the self to create meanings within and in spite of the confines of "immediate circumstances."[33] Appropriately, given interactionists' openness to change, proposals for reshaping symbolic interactionism itself abound. Most notable are Denzin's proposal for a merger with culture studies along with his refiguring of interactionism as "interpretive." Following both of these directions, interactionism would become more critically aware of the textual nature of social reality, more insightful about the complex interrelations between private and public experiences, and more committed to finding solutions for social problems.[34]

From an academic standpoint, the preceding few paragraphs give a well-rounded history of symbolic interactionism, but telling the history as only academic omits a significant feature of interactionist practice—its involvement with social work. Pioneering research by Mary Jo Deegan into early Chicago sociology has revealed an interventionist character that was sacrificed to disciplinary norms of objectivity. In its predisciplinary form, sociology included social work. The fields were not separate. Mead, Dewey, and other Chicago faculty members worked with Jane Addams, Sophonisba Breckinridge, and other Hull-House Settlers both to gain knowledge of urban conditions and to improve them. Addams herself presented papers to the American Sociological Association and was published in *The American Journal of Sociology*. According to Deegan, interactionism and interventionism cannot be separated: Mead conceptualized people as actors who change structures because he was involved with reform movements; Addams saw better communication as a solution to structural problems because she had an interactionist orientation.[35] This atmosphere of collaboration did not last long into the twentieth century. Pursuing scientific prestige, academic sociology dissociated itself from interventionism and reduced social work to an ancillary profession. In disciplinary history, Jane Addams was demoted "from sociologist to social worker."[36] Deegan implies that, because of this demotion, it is condescending to refer to Addams as a social worker, but I mean no slight by using the term. On the contrary, I would prefer to rehabilitate the term and extend it to all involved in both social research and social intervention.

In light of Deegan's discoveries, the history of symbolic interactionism should include Addams and Hull-House as well as Mead and the University of Chicago. The inclusion is all the more warranted since interactionism is now coming full circle in seeking applications in social work. In addition to presenting interpretive interactionism, along with the merger of symbolic interactionism and culture studies, as programs for social change, Denzin has extrapolated an agenda for social work that helps people use "symbolic resources" to resist the roles and stereotypes imposed on them and to create better roles and identities for themselves.[37] To complete this section on interactionism, then, I turn to Addams and Hull-House.

As part of the Settlement Movement, Hull-House occupied the same kind of counter-institutional position with respect to organized charity as symbolic interactionism occupied with respect to disciplinary sociology. At the end of the nineteenth century, two models for what would become "social work" were operating in the public sector: the dominant model was represented by the Charity Organization Society (COS) and the Charity Organization Movement that it spread throughout Britain and America; the other model came from Toynbee Hall and the Settlement Movement that it inspired in Britain and America.[38]

Founded in 1869 to rationalize and coordinate programs that subsidized the poor, the COS aspired to a "science of charity": it would send "case workers" or "visitors" into the houses of the poor to assess their needs and determine what measure of assistance, if any, to provide. Advocates of the system praised it for channeling resources where they were most deserved—for example, by separating disabled people who could receive pensions under the Poor Laws from people who could be helped toward employment—and they endorsed visiting as a way that comfortable members of society could show personal concern for less comfortable members. Critics of the system, especially those in the Settlement Movement, saw the COS as a self-serving bureaucracy that withheld more assistance than it authorized, and they saw visiting as impersonal surveillance.[39] In contrast, the Settlement Movement brought comfortable members of society into poor neighborhoods as residents, not as visitors. Settlers lived beside the poor, sharing cultural and material resources with them. As both Shannon Jackson and Mina Carson emphasize in their studies of Settlement houses, settling was process-oriented. The Settlers did not so much provide relief from specific hardships as develop supportive social relations. Committed to the idea that people could and should continually improve each other's lives, Settlers implemented a model of cooperative social organization that, for Carson, merged Victorian notions of character building with "new theories of personality development and social interaction propounded by academics like John Dewey, Charles Horton Cooley and Simon N. Patten."[40] To this list, Carson might have added, as Jackson does, George Herbert Mead.[41]

Addams modeled Hull-House after Toynbee Hall, the London house credited with being the first Settlement, which she visited in 1888. She and her coresidents furnished it with their own fine possessions and opened the doors to the poor people they habitually called "neighbors."[42] They hosted reading groups for adults and preschool and after-school programs for children. They started a theatrical club that eventually turned into an internationally known troupe. Expanding into other buildings, they started a soup kitchen, which became a café, and realizing that "cleanliness is an expensive virtue," they made available public baths.[43] In following the Settlement approach, Addams was also deliberately not following the COS model, which she found insensitive and ineffective. She wrote: "Even those of us who feel most sorely the need of more order in altruistic effort and see the end to be desired, find something distasteful in the juxtaposition of the words 'organized' and 'charity.' . . . [W]e distrust a little a scheme which substitutes a theory of social conduct for the natural promptings of the heart, even although we appreciate the complexity of the situation."[44] Because Addams knew her neighbors as people, she knew that they perceived organized relief as impersonal, condescending, and demeaning. She sympathized with one neighbor who had told visitors not to warm her feet with anything except an old jacket that had belonged to her deceased son because "it's warmer yet with human feelings than any of your damned charity hot-water bottles."[45] In this example, Addams shows an awareness of the value of symbolic resources over material resources, and she derives that awareness from her participation in her neighbors' lives.

The participatory nature of the relationship between Hull-House Settlers and neighbors has been explored by Shannon Jackson, who draws on performance theory to explain what the Settlers accomplished. Going farther than Carson in her emphasis on process, Jackson argues that the Settlers achievement "cannot be measured in terms of what it completes" because their greatest achievement lies in the process by which they constructed new social identities and relationships.[46] Coining the term "reformance" for this performance of social change, Jackson claims that Hull-House created spaces for "cross-class and cross-cultural" interactions that could not occur in traditional settings. At Hull-House, immigrant groups that elsewhere regarded each other with suspicion, and younger and older generations of immigrants who disagreed about assimiliation, could set aside their conflicts, join each other in shared experiences, and learn to overcome their habits of hostility toward each other. Just as importantly, Settlers who came mostly from comfortable families met people who did not have such advantages, and these disparate groups learned to reject their stereotypes of each other. Indeed, the fact that these interactions were "reciprocal," changing the "selves" of the Settlers as much as they changed the lives of their neighbors, leads Jackson to defend the Settlement Movement from the charges of elitism that have sometimes been leveled against it. For critics such as Standish Meacham, the Settlers used cultural ideals to exert a self-serving control over a subject population, but as Jackson counters, this view overlooks the way in which Settlement life destabilized the hierarchies and assumptions of all involved.[47]

Though reformance does not depend on writing, acting, or viewing plays in any literal sense, dramas were often staged at Hull-House, and Jackson examines how these theatrical activities furthered the Settlement agenda of cooperation and assimilation.[48] Given her interest in establishing reformance as a way of life at Hull-House, Jackson says less than one might expect about Addams's claims for drama in a more literal sense. Those claims, along with comparable statements by Mead, warrant further investigation for the ways in which they trace social change to a symbolic starting point. The play, an enactment of a literary text, becomes part of the lived experience of the spectators as they interpret, respond to, and continue interacting as a result of its promptings. Addams's and Mead's treatments of drama reconnect literary and lived experience more directly than Addams was willing to do in her reflections on other genres. Furthermore, their confidence in drama to script social change reconnects them with their Romantic-era predecessors. Like Baillie, they believed that drama could educe sympathetic propensities and lead to a more compassionate society. These dramatic claims resound with even more meaning when they are considered along with the theatrical metaphors that inform symbolic interactionism itself. Mead and all subsequent interactionists use the concept of role-taking to describe the process by which human actors develop selves and relationships with others.

From even this brief history, we can see signal traits of symbolic interactionism that direct us back toward Romantic-era writers as much as forward toward postmodern sociologists. In addition to the first trait of defining reality in terms of interpretive construction, symbolic interactionism defines selves and societies in performative terms, social relations in personal terms, and social responsibility in pragmatic terms. These signal traits can also help us identify a constructive social agenda by which to gauge Baillie's, Scott's, and Landor's works. I outline that agenda below.

INTERPRETIVE CONSTRUCTIONS

Joanna Baillie's *Introductory Discourse* to the first volume in her *Series of Plays* on the passions is now often taken as an agenda for her goals as a dramatist. That procedure seems warranted, since the *Discourse* introduces not only the given volume but the two others in the series published in 1802 and 1812 as well as plays in the series not published until 1836. Attention to the *Discourse* has focused on the concept of the passions, and this focus predominates in analyses of exemplary plays. Again, the procedure seems warranted by the nature of the material being introduced, yet it leaves us to wonder about the relationship between the passions plays and the "miscellaneous" plays published in 1804 and in the 1836 volume (along with the other plays in the passions series). Baillie's preface to the *Miscellaneous Plays* of 1804 calls them "pieces of a different kind" prompted by her desire to "vary [her] employment," but in explaining their difference, she refers to their independence from the design of the passions series, not necessarily from the content of that series.[49] In content, the miscellaneous play *Rayner* may well be construed as a play on the passion of sympathy, and it actually follows up on the points in the *Discourse* about sympathetically observing prisoners before execution more fully than any play in the series until *The Dream* in 1812. The distance between the passion plays and the miscellaneous plays is further shortened when we consider Baillie's annoyance with reviewers who criticized the passion series for unnaturally isolating emotions from each other—an isolation, she says, she never meant to imply.[50] If the *Discourse* might well be introducing a miscellaneous play, and if the passion plays were not meant to separate emotions, we must ask what larger purpose spans Baillie's works.

I posit that the larger purpose involves observing situated behavior, whether or not a predominant passion is in the spotlight. The terms of symbolic interactionism can help to clarify this purpose. Specifically, the *Discourse* and the plays, irrespective of their classification, focus on interpretive behavior that constructs selves and societies. We see this focus in the *Discourse*'s emphasis on the circumstantial development of passion and on the effects of observation, and we see it in each play's representation of a world constructed by interpretive encounters.

Distinguishing Baillie's plays from other tragedies that present the "mind under the domination of strong and fixed passions . . . seemingly unprovoked by outward circumstances," the *Discourse* announces Baillie's intention to show the "gradual steps that led [the protagonist] into the [passionate] state." The purpose of this presentation is to show "stages" when the "foe" or "enemy" passion might yet have been resisted and a different world constructed.[51] These statements treat the situation—the passionate "state" in which the protagonist ends up—as an accumulation of interpretive blunders. But the situation is a construct that did not have to be. Neither character nor situation has determining force. They are mutually determining, and the characters are actors who could respond differently if they attached different meanings to what was happening and thereby change the course of emerging events.

To grasp the significance of this attention to the interplay between structure and meaning, it is helpful to see Baillie approaching an interactionist view of structure. For interactionists, social structures are patterns of interactions that have become reified in the laws, customs, rituals, and routines of a given community.[52] These structures channel ongoing interaction into the familiar patterns, but they have to be redefined when new situations arise that do not fit in.[53] Explanations of how such redefinition occurs vary, but interactionists agree that the process involves the adjustment of structure—i.e., accumulated meaning—by new meaning. In fact, David Snow argues that interactionists should expand on Blumer's perspective and method by paying more attention to how meanings become part of social structure. Greater insight in that area would lead to greater insight into how the "claims-making actions" of social movements change things and how "cognitive and affective changes can be significant products" of social movements, products as important as legislation and other material and measurable effects.[54] This emphasis on the process of change as an act of interpretation is relevant to Baillie because it is in her sense of structure as a series of adjusted meanings that she approaches interactionism. It is not simply that she sees humans as free agents; rather, she realizes that action is not just an expression of character or "attitude"[55] but a response to a situation and moreover a response that depends on the meaning the actor gives to the situation. The most obvious example of this view in Baillie's work is furnished by *The Dream*, a play on fear that portrays its protagonist as courageous in combat but terrified of execution. I look at this play in detail in chapter 3.

Reference to defining the meaning of a situation alludes to an interactionist idea that has circulated so widely as now often to appear disconnected from its source, but it was Mead's colleague W. I. Thomas who posited that "if men define situations as *real*, they are real in their consequences."[56] Baillie's plays dramatize this proposition. They stage the real consequences of the situations that emerge from their characters' interpretations of events. Moreover, they stage them for purposes that are compatible with interactionist research. Interactionists usually study what a person's definition of a situation allows him or her to do, irrespective of whether that definition has validity apart from the situation. A line of inquiry opened up by Stanford Lyman illustrates this approach. Instead of worrying about the validity of Marx's historical dialectic, for instance, Lyman would ask what responses it provokes: "Does the communist cell member believe that the party must undertake actions to overthrow the government by force and violence now, before the word about the death of the Marxist discourse becomes public knowledge? Or does he or she believe that all is lost and the party should cease and desist from any and all insurrectionary activity?"[57] Through Baillie's plays, spectators can study what characters can and cannot do as a consequence of the ways they have defined their situations. The *Introductory Discourse* encourages assessment of the characters' situated behaviors onstage, in "literary" experience, as well as of people's behavior offstage, in "lived" experience.

According to the *Discourse*, spectators are to learn from the characters' interpretive blunders how to interact more successfully in their own situations.[58] For my purposes, that point is best examined in the section on the signal trait of performance. In this section, I wish to look further at the *Discourse*'s connection between behavior and circumstances. The early part of the *Discourse* deals with observing people in lived experience, which, it maintains, "sympathetic curiosity" leads us to do. In this context, as in the literary context I examine above, what is observed is situated behavior, not character in itself: we want "to know what men are in the closet as well as the field, by the blazing hearth, and at the social board"; we want to watch the prisoner on the scaffold or "to lift up the roof of his dungeon."[59] The implication of this situating is that character develops in and through circumstances and that learning about human behavior necessarily involves learning about social situations and symbolic interactions. But there is another significant point to be made about the reference to the prisoner on the scaffold. In addressing the motives for watching public executions, the *Discourse* rules out all but the positive one of learning how humans can cope with extreme circumstances.[60] As I argue at length in chapter 2, this representation can be better understood as an interpretive construction: it does not describe the motives that usually prevail in such situations; it creates a prevailing motive that redefines the situation in ways that rule out unwanted ones. The rationale for Baillie's doing so and for my reading Baillie as doing so comes from the context of criminal justice reform I posit in chapter 2.

To continue this section, I turn to Scott. To state that Scott engaged in interpretive construction is in some ways to state the obvious, especially in light of studies by Burwick, Chandler, Christensen, Ferris, Malley, Maxwell, Mayer, and Robertson.[61] Yet questions persist about how Scott defined the structures of the past, how he adjusted them to accommodate new meanings, and what his procedures enabled him to do. Symbolic interactionism can shed some light on these matters, particularly because Mead devised an extensive explanation for how and why "every generation rewrites its history."[62] As I consider at greater length in chapters 6 and 7, in connection with both Scott's and Landor's historical interactions, Mead saw the revision of the past as a regular step in the process of responding to emerging events. Briefly, when an emergent event does not fit the familiar pattern of ongoing interaction, one way to "repair" a break in the continuity of experience is to alter the pattern of the past so that a "new past" connects with the new event.[63] But if Mead's work illuminates the process of historical revision, it still leaves obscure the reasons why an avowedly conservative figure like Scott apparently regarded social structures, including the structure of history, as available to be altered by new meanings.

I suggest that Scott's sense of the malleability of structure arises from a sense of social responsibility that exceeded his politically conservative position.[64] Without denying that Scott's paternalistic ideas have ties to politics or that paternalism can be used "to defend authority" in the ways Christopher Whatley details,[65] I posit that Scott took the personal responsibility involved in paternalistic relations more literally than the inherited structure could accommodate. Consequently, he opened up this structure to dimensions now known as an "ethic of care." Though more usually associated with women writers and feminist thinking (especially that of Carol Gilligan), care-centered social thought does not divide exclusively along gendered lines.[66] Indeed, its successful development depends on its crossing such categorical divisions between people. As Erin McKenna argues, care-centered models of society that perpetuate opposition between "masculine" and "feminine," or even between "self" and "other," do not adequately conceptualize the social self. A successful conceptualization would break through the "either/or alternatives of ethics as it has been."[67] Setting aside gender divisions, I associate Scott with comprehensively caring relations suggested by studies of both paternalism and law in his time.

First and most generally, Roberts credits Burke and Scott with launching a "paternalistic revival" but argues that Burke's political focus made the movement inadequate to deal with social problems.[68] Treating Scott only in passing, Roberts moves on to study varieties of paternalistic thinking that broadened the paradigm in Victorian applications. Secondly and more specifically, Farmer's and Riggs's studies of the Scottish legal system during the Romantic era reveal an emphasis on crime as a failure to perform one's social duties; they reveal further that Scottish legal professionals took pride in dealing with criminals more mercifully than their English counterparts and in attending to the criminal's state of mind and motives. These characteristics are especially evident in Baron Hume's (so called to minimize confusion between him and his uncle, the philosopher David Hume, whose first name he also shares) *Commentaries on the Law of Scotland*, first published in 1797 and greatly admired by Scott.[69]

Such legal studies would certainly account for Scott's gaining a broader social vantage point than his political commitments would allow. Though he never fully broke free of political restraints, he did in his writing experiment with ways to give new meaning to paternalistic and patriarchal structures. In what Beiderwell and James Kerr have seen as his selective valorizations of old regimes, Scott creates worlds that differ from the traditional models on which they are based.[70] In these reconstructions, Scott not only develops his social vision but engages in social criticism of any elite[71] that failed to uphold an ethic of care. This criticism is especially keen in *The Bride of Lammermoor*, which I treat in chapter 4 in connection with the Poor Laws.

Before *The Bride of Lammermoor*, which I consider a dystopian novel, Scott published *The Heart of Midlothian*, a novel with a utopian section that helps us to distinguish between his political and social visions. Though Roseneath exhibits a patriarchal structure, the interaction that occurs there involves a reciprocity beyond what one would expect in traditional societies. I find it problematic, therefore, to classify it by its political structure. If structures are accumulated meanings, and if new meanings change existing structures, then the altered structure should be defined by its altered meanings rather than by the traces of its earlier ones. Hierarchical structures that admit more widely responsible social relations are no longer the "same" structures.[72] Scott's social vision is entangled in what David Zaret calls the "paradox of innovation"—"a common development in which individuals do not acknowledge the innovative behavior in which they participate."[73] In spite of his politics, Scott was touched by reformist trends toward lessening social and economic disparities.[74] Though he always opposed reform measures, his efforts to revive old ways of being socially responsible resulted in a vision of less disparate hierarchies.

More radical structural alterations are accomplished by Landor's *Imaginary Conversations*. Uninhibited about criticizing inherited ideas, Landor reconstructs history, changing it from a narrative of sustained patriarchal control to an episodic succession of republican activities. Though the *Imaginary Conversations* raise such social questions as how leaders can emerge in a society that rejects any elitism through which leadership can be defined, the episodic nature of the work precludes extended attention to such questions. Always alert to prevent anyone from becoming dominant, the speakers must check each other and move on to other topics. The limits of the conversations in this regard suggest the limits of politics in general with respect to social problems. As Roberts notes in dealing with paternalism, something more than its political form was needed to solve social problems.[75]

Performing Selves and Societies

Due especially to the work of Catherine Burroughs, we now see Baillie's work as caught up in negotiations over gender roles. Recovering the history of closet drama during the Romantic era, Burroughs reveals how the closet stage could serve as an alternative performance space for women, one that mediated between public and private spheres and allowed them to practice, or challenge, the gender roles they were expected to take in society. Contextualizing Baillie within this history, Burroughs illuminates

Baillie's association with the closet as both a positive and negative outcome of her struggles to be represented in the masculine world of the public theater. Furthermore, Burroughs reads Baillie's early plays as about "how characters comply with or rebel against prescribed gender and sexual identities in both private and public settings."[76] Such efforts to modify conventions governing who can perform what roles in what spaces participate in the activity of "reformance," which is, as I have indicated above, the term Jackson uses for the performance of social change at Hull-House.

Symbolic interactionism can help us find further significance to role-taking in Baille's plays because it treats role-taking as the means by which people develop social and self-consciousness. Baillie's confidence that "sympathetic curiosity" about others would prepare people to fill the roles of judges, magistrates, and advocates can be better understood in light of interactionist ideas about the development of a "social self." In chapter 2, drawing on work by interactionist Candace Clark, I deal specifically with the sequence of role-taking and sympathizing. In this section, I address the concept of role-taking more broadly.

Symbolic interactionists treat all human behavior as performative. They reject the notion of an essential or autonomous being in favor of a concept of a self "as a set of shifting identities" that develops by taking the roles of others.[77] Baillie's emphasis on situated behavior, addressed above, also aligns her with the anti-essentialist view. Moreover, a note in the *Introductory Discourse* rejects gender essentialism in favor of a notion of learned and situated behavior: "I believe there is no man that ever lived, who has behaved in a certain manner, on a certain occasion, who has not had amongst women some corresponding spirit, who on the like occasion, and *every way similarly circumstanced*, would have behaved in the like manner."[78] My view does not necessarily contradict Aileen Forbes's position on the passions as an essential part of human nature for Baillie: Baillie may approach a distinction between biological beings and social selves that allows her to see emotions—or gender—as parts of the biological being that require social development. Insofar as Forbes argues that Baillie "constructs passions" as the "secret of humanity" that her plays then reveal, her ideas are compatible with mine on Baillie's participation in the social development of human nature.[79]

A distinction between biological and social being is the starting point for Mead's concept of role-taking. His position is most lucidly presented by Dmitri Shalin: "the 'self' [is] an emergent property of the human body transformed by social interactions to a point where it grows conscious of its multiple presence in different systems and uses this awareness to conduct itself intelligently."[80] Role-taking proceeds as a "conversation of gestures" between people. When one encounters another, one imagines the other as gesturing toward the self, and the self as interpreting and responding to the gesture. To complete this process, one must put oneself in the place of the other in order to read the gestures as "significant symbols" and consider appropriate responses.[81] Through this process, people become aware of themselves as acting beings, and they become aware of what others expect of them. They may not always fulfill those expectations, either because of misunderstandings or deliberate refusal, but the process is the means by which social relations of any kind occur.[82] The importance of this point cannot be overemphasized: as Hans Joas stresses, the process of role-taking is the only universal in Mead's thought.[83]

Though interactionism does admit conflict, Mead concentrated on the conciliatory and problem-solving potential of role-taking. For Mead, the mind as well as the self emerges through interaction. Mind becomes the activity of "practical minding" by which individuals gain the ability to participate in group life.[84] Mindfulness curbs eccentricity, but, as Shalin stresses, it does not require conformity. In fact, the individual "mind's activity has . . . a pervasive impact on society": it "makes personal experience available to others and compels the group to look at the world in a new way."[85] Because role-taking makes one mindful of others, Mead linked it to social change: "the way a community comes to realize a social evil is by taking the role of another individual who is subject to injustice."[86] Mindfulness was also the key to social change for Addams, who held that "much of the insensibility and hardness of the world is due to the lack of imagination which prevents a realization of the experiences of other people."[87] Both Mead and Addams thought that mindfulness could be facilitated by the theater, for drama provides the "imagery of others" through which spectators can "think from all points of view."[88] By recognizing others' perspectives or imagining others' experiences, people learn alternatives to their own narrow views, and multiple perspectives provide ways around oppositional relations, dichotomous positions, and binary thinking. Baillie's confidence in drama to promote a more just and more merciful society—a construct that coordinates two usually opposed concepts—shares in Mead's and Addams's hope to restage social relations.

Theatrical performances at Hull-House at least partly realized Addams's wishes. In *Twenty Years at Hull-House*, Addams credits classic tragedies and plays about assimiliation with easing tensions among immigrant groups by helping them to respect each other's cultural heritage and to see that they had problems in common as minorities and outsiders in America. Works by Shaw, Galsworthy, and Ibsen were also performed, and Addams praised them highly. They inspired her to assert that "the stage may become a pioneer teacher of social righteousness" because plays can "expose the shams and pretenses of contemporary life and . . . penetrate into some of its perplexing social and domestic situations."[89] They can even set social change in motion by prompting people to reject and replace the moral principles underlying current systems. In Addams's words, "[M]uch of our current moral instruction will not endure the test of being cast in a lifelike mold, and when presented in dramatic form will reveal itself as platitudinous and effete." If people can become critical of prevailing norms, they can look for alternatives, and thus the stage can become "a reconstructing and reorganizing agent of accepted moral truths."[90] Addams's sense of the efficacy of drama was shared by Mead, who praised Galsworthy's play *Justice* for illuminating the "discrepancy between legal justice and social good."[91] Through the "imagery of others" provided by the drama, and in the provisional environment of the theater, spectators can experiment with interactions they might resist in more conventional settings.

Addams's and Mead's comments on drama are notable for their emphasis on a critical response from the audience. Though I develop this point about responsiveness in a later section on pragmatism, I would point out here that responding to theatrical experience, like responding to others in lived experience, should not be confused with merely copying or pretending to take on another identity. Mead stated that the term "imitation" is not really suitable in reference to role-taking, and he preferred descriptions of one gesture "calling out" another.[92] Mistaking imitation for response has sometimes resulted in the dismissal of arguments about the social value of drama or, more broadly, of literature. David Haney's work on Coleridge's theater criticism admirably corrects such mistakes by subordinating the drama's "representational function" to its "hermeneutic challenge."[93] Drama—and I would add, despite Addams's reservations, literature—becomes available for social work when its meaning moves off the stage and off the page.

Since the concept of performance does not depend on the genre of drama, it is scarcely necessary to justify turning to Scott's novels under this heading;[94] nevertheless, the generic classification is worth considering because of its impact on our understanding of Scott's—and Landor's—works. Genre itself may be best understood as performative—an insight I derive from Robert Mayer's analysis of the relationship between history and fiction in Scott's work. Mayer concludes that the division between history and fiction cannot be maintained epistemically; it can only be enacted: the novel is both history and fiction because we read it as both.

To follow up on this conclusion in interactionist terms, we would ask what putting a given work in a generic category allows us to do. The answer is often that it allows us to discipline the work. According to Denzin, generic categories are "socially and politically constructed categories . . . too often used to police certain transgressive writing forms." For that reason, he refuses to "distinguish among literary, nonliterary, fictional and nonfictional text forms" in identifying modes for interpretive interactionism."[95] An example of this policing function can be found in the fate of Landor's *Imaginary Conversations*. As I detail in chapter 8, this work became unreadable when it could not be disciplined according to the standards of history or literary criticism, and as I show in chapter 6, it is now readable by new standards.[96] That Scott did not suffer the same fate as Landor is probably due to the deferential stance he projected toward history in many of his notes and prefaces, which effected his literary classification.

Unsettling our classification of Scott is part of the achievement of Chandler's *England in 1819*. Opening up the "dramatism" in the novels, Chandler examines how the *Bride of Lammermoor* sets scenes, providing both a "context for dramatic exchange" and a "spectacle of human conflict."[97] In dealing with the *Bride* in chapter 4, I concentrate not on scene setting but on role-taking. I posit that a particular kind of role-taking, which Mead called taking the role of the "generalized other," figures in Scott's efforts to construct socially responsible communities. For Mead, the "generalized other" is a symbol or personification of a community to which members gradually learn to respond. Adults can be said to be socialized into a community when they have identified with the attitudes and values of most other members sufficiently to experience the community as if it were a person calling on them to take up certain duties and responding to them in kind.[98] For Scott, such a figure is formed by the traditional roles, such as the Master of Ravenswood or the Laird of Abbotsford, that each new generation is called on to fulfill. The responsibility to live up to the role remains, whether or not each predecessor did so. The concept of a role model who is all previous holders of the role but no one of them in particular serves as a tool for both criticism and encouragement. Scott's representations of Lady Ashton, the old Lord Ravenswood, and other selfish members of elite groups show his awareness of and objections to abuses of power. His reconstructions of previous social systems can be accomplished only if elite members really fulfill roles as caretakers, guardians, and leaders of the community; there is no room for self-indulgence in the system. Many of his novels, especially *The Bride of Lammermoor*, are highly critical of elite figures who fail in their traditional responsibilities, and they attempt to awaken younger elite characters to the nature of the role they should take in the community in terms that can be understood as the gesture of a "generalized other."

In Landor's *Imaginary Conversations*, role-taking has a more sharply critical function. Encouraging vigilance against tyranny and skepticism about authority, the *Conversations* challenge readers to check all gestures that might facilitate the ascendancy of one person or faction over others. While the *Imaginary Conversations* thus promote an egalitarianism that overcomes selfishness, they also accept an either/or pattern of opposition that limits their scope of possible responses to others or possible definitions of situations.

PERSONALIZING RELATIONS

I return to the concept of the "generalized other" because its nature as an implied person is important in Scott's view of social relations as well as in symbolic interactionism. Though Mead does present the generalized other as an abstraction and the ability to deal with it as an abstract thought process, he says that "at any moment the process may become personal."[99] In other words, social relations remain relations between people—societies are "societies of selves"[100]—and while people do not simply take the roles of specific individuals, their more abstract and general interactions still depend on, share in, and take meaning from the personal origin. I quote Mead at some length on this point not only to present his idea but to call attention to his dramatic metaphor: "Until this process [of role-taking] has been developed into the abstract process of thought, self-consciousness remains dramatic, and the self which is a fusion of the remembered actor and this accompanying chorus is somewhat loosely organized and very clearly social. Later the inner stage changes into the forum and workshop of thought. The features and intonations of the dramatis personae fade out and the emphasis falls upon the meaning of the inner speech, the imagery becomes merely the barely necessary cues."[101]

Mead's notion of social relations as personal performances gives us a way to understand Scott's emphasis on personal roles in nonpolitical terms. Instead of focusing on the embodiment of power or authority, we can see Scott's attachment to patriarchy and paternalism as a preference for personalized relations over such abstractions as contracts, rights, principles, and statutes. Or, moving as I propose from a political to a legal frame of reference to account for Scott's social development, we can see his confidence in personal judgment arising from the emphasis in Scottish law on the court's discretionary power, a concept on which I elaborate in chapter 2. Irrespective of how we judge Scott's political choices, we can acknowledge a human social vision behind them. A desire to make social relations personal and caring has also sometimes led symbolic interactionists to make some startling political choices. Mead, for example, took "paternalistic sponsorship of workers" as an indication of "democratic citizens . . . be[ing] responsible for each other."[102] Though Addams did not share this view, she did argue that government cannot be effective in the abstract; it can only be effective in personal terms. That is why, she maintained, corrupt aldermen continue to stay in power with community approval: they personalize a government which is otherwise meaningless to constituents. Addams wanted people to transfer their personal attachment to unworthy role models to the government, which actually did provide more care than they realized.[103] It is not my purpose to defend Scott's politics. I wish, rather, to reveal the diverse social concerns that can subsume them. To clarify Scott's sense of personal commitment, I examine in chapter 4 a series of letters he wrote, including one to Baillie, that show his own efforts to take a responsible role toward the poor in his community. Contrastingly, the *Imaginary Conversations* reveal the impersonality of political contention that aims to eliminate differences among citizens.

Improving social relations by improving personal interactions is also of central concern to Baillie. More skeptical than Scott of patriarchal and paternalistic models, she concentrates on the need to revise given roles and stereotypes. The *Introductory Discourse* sets up this pattern. It begins by noting the habit of classifying people into character types, but it then shows that habit as insufficient to satisfy our curiosity about others. To do justice to others, one must recognize them as persons and recognize one's connection to them. The *Discourse* associates this recognition with the transformation of self and society. Her remarkable claims for the results of sincerely exercised "sympathetic curiosity" include self-knowledge ("in examining others we know ourselves"); altered patterns of interaction ("we cannot well exercise this disposition without becoming more just, more merciful, more compassionate"); a conviction that "kindness" can and should prevail in the world; and respect for self and others ("It [sympathetic observation] teaches us, also to respect ourselves, and our kind; for it is a poor mind, indeed, that . . . learns not to dwell upon the noble view of human nature rather than the mean").[104] It is difficult to take these claims literally partly because they assign cognitive and emotional causes, at a personal level, to widely social effects. Such causality defies the solidity of material structures and the power of impersonal forces.

I suggest that we can credit Baillie with more than wishful thinking by treating her claims as precursors to interactionist agendas. Addams, Mead, and Denzin have all treated the development of a social—or socially aware—self as vital for a more just and compassionate world. To emphasize the ways in which these interactionist proposals resound Baillie's, I address their terms below.

Personal transformation underwrites Addams's creation of a "social ethics" that would counter "selfish" behavior and change both self and society. Addams defines selfishness as a delusion of difference from others, which leads to seeking preferment and to associating only with people who seem most like oneself. Addams would counter this insularity by having people take seriously the "moral obligation" to avoid selfishness by seeking broadening experiences. Realizing a connection between self and others is the starting point for "actual Justice," which, Addams wrote, "must come . . . by broadened sympathies toward the individual man or woman who crosses our path."[105]

In an essay published in the 1920s amid worries about lingering hostilities from World War I, Mead connected sympathetic curiosity about others with the success of social cooperation in general and cooperative institutions such as the World Court and the League of Nations in particular. Mead begins by positing that "a journalism that is insatiably curious about the human attitudes of all of us is the sign of the times." He continues: "The other curiosities as to the conditions under which other people live, and work, and fight each other, and love each other, follow from the fundamental curiosity which is the passion of self-consciousness. We must be others if we are to be ourselves."[106] These remarks establish the basis for the international cooperation he wants to see succeed. Regarding cooperation in general, he states: "If we can bring people together so that they can enter into each other's lives, they will inevitably have a common object, which will control their common conduct." The greatest obstacles to bringing people together are "those fixed attitudes of custom and status in which our selves are embedded." Mead hopes that passionate curiosity about others will overcome these obstacles and connect people in more broadly sympathetic ways. The World Court and the League of Nations have a chance to "sketch out common plans of action if there are national selves that can realize themselves in the collaborating attitudes of others."[107]

More recently, in setting the agenda for interpretive interactionism, Denzin assigned a prominent place to "epiphanies" or "turning-point experiences" during which an individual realizes that his or her "personal troubles" are part of "larger . . . public issues." Interpretive research promotes awareness of each person as a "universal singular," and it takes that awareness as the starting point for finding solutions for the issues that trouble people's lives; moreover, it takes "the individual case [as] the measure of the effectiveness of all applied programs."[108]

Surely Baillie deserves to be named in the prehistory of such thinking.

Baillie's plays follow up on her claims for the benefits of sympathetic curiosity by directing its operation. To yield the results that Baillie projects, the "propensity" has to be developed; without conscious effort, it functions only "in a passing and superficial way." To go beyond this basic level, people must "reason and reflect" on their observations, and according to the *Discourse*, "they may be easily induced to do both . . . [by a] mode of instruction . . . that . . . lays open before them, in a more enlarged and connected view, than their individual observations are capable of supplying, the varieties of the human mind."[109] To this end Baillie devoted her dramas. The next section of the *Discourse* runs through the advantages and disadvantages of directing sympathetic curiosity by other modes of writing, including philosophy, history, poetry, and novels, until it reaches the conclusion that drama, because of the immediacy of its representations, is best suited to the given task. In short, the *Discourse* treats drama as a means of working through social problems. I elaborate more on how it can do so in the next section.

Pragmatic Responses

By "pragmatism," I mean the orientation toward treating knowledge as situated and instrumental rather than abstract and theoretical that is characteristic of both Scottish law during the Romantic period and of symbolic interactionism throughout its history.[110] The pairing is not so unusual as it may at first appear since Anthony Blasi and Shalin have noted the influence of Scottish Enlightenment philosophy on Mead.[111] A pragmatic view of knowledge leads to a preference for problem solving over theory building. Though this preference is often construed as an opposition to theory, a more nuanced distinction places pragmatism in opposition only to "grand theories," i.e., totalizing schemes in which knowledge appears to transcend historical circumstances.[112] Pragmatists do indeed reject such abstractions of knowledge.

This skepticism about theory guaranteed that pragmatism would exist at the margins of our disciplinary system, which until recently, fetishized theory. To count as knowledge, ideas had to transcend circumstances and be generally applicable in a variety of times and places. The most obvious example of this epistemic bias is the rise of the natural sciences and their scientific method to preeminence among the disciplines. Their purported ideal of objective knowledge cast a shadow over all particularized ways of knowing — or, to describe this occurrence another way, as Amanda Anderson and Joseph Valente do in their introduction to *Disciplinarity at the Fin de Siècle*, the scientific impulse to determine and generalize was internalized in all fields as the constraining part in a dialectic of constraint and freedom, with freedom being the "pragmatic" impulse to act. The "slippage between the epistemic and the pragmatic" was and continues to be constitutive of our intellectual territories.[113] The mere fact that the dialectic can be stated as an opposition between the epistemic and the pragmatic reveals the tendency to regard pragmatism as not-knowledge. Our new openness to variation in ways of knowing makes it possible to credit the works of Romantic-era writers with an interventionism that could not be fully explored when literature had to be distinguished from the scientifically and theoretically grounded pursuits of social work and sociology.

Baillie and Scott themselves show a pragmatist bent in deciding to carry out their work primarily through literary forms, or "hybrids" of literary and historical forms, instead of theoretical exposition.[114] Baillie's plays and Scott's novels serve as something like case studies for particular problems, though I use "case" more generally than Chandler, who makes the "case" the "cognitive form" of Scott's novels.[115] I will have more to say about the relationship between Chandler's reading of the novels in terms of cases and casuistry and my reading of them in terms of symbolic interaction later in this study. In this section, my purpose is to present attention to individual cases as an alternative to theory. By their treatment of problems on a case-by-case basis, in the particular situations of novels and plays, Scott and Baillie engage in pragmatic inquiry. I suggest that Scott's avoidance of theories and abstractions stems directly from the bias against theory and abstraction in Scottish law and that Baillie's stems indirectly from the same source. In contrast, the overarching principle of political contention moves Landor's *Imaginary Conversations* away from situated behavior.

As I detail in chapter 2, drawing on scholarship by Farmer and Riggs, Scottish legal professionals were proud that their system relied more on case law and judiciary discretion than did England's. The dearth of statutes made a notable difference in capital crimes, for England's "bloody code" of hundreds of offenses punishable by death did not extend to Scotland. The differences were celebrated in Baron Hume's *Commentaries on the Law of Scotland*, which Scott admired and, according to David Hewitt's analysis, relied on in portraying the crime of "mobbing" in *The Heart of*

Midlothian. Hewitt quotes a passage about Hume from Scott's *Memoirs* that I find significant for an understanding of Scott's own pragmatic, interpretive, and constructive undertakings. In the relevant passage, Scott reflects on how the

> law, formed originally under the strictest influence of feudal principles[, had been] . . . innovated, altered and broken in upon by the change of the times, of habits and of manners untill it resembles some ancient castle, partly entire, partly ruinous, partly dilapidated, patched and altered during the succession of ages by a thousand additions and combinations, yet still exhibiting, with the marks of its antiquity, symptoms of the skill and wisdom of its founders and capable of being analyzed and made the subject of a methodical plan by an architect who can understand the various stiles of the different ages in which it was subjected to alterations.[116]

The image of the law as always being reconstructed as circumstances warrant accords not only with Hume's emphasis on the adaptability of Scottish law but with Scott's procedures for adapting historical structures and traditional roles to present needs. Moreover, the procedure of always adding to the building but never demolishing any of it implies a respect for one's predecessors that enhances Scott's commitment to personalized relations.[117]

Though Baillie is usually associated with medical rather than legal studies, she is likely to have been familiar with the salient aspects of Scottish law because of the cultural and national importance attached to them.[118] Medical and legal interests also sometimes collided during the Romantic era over the use of the bodies of criminals for medical research, as Dwyer and Myers have noted.[119] Baillie's acquaintance with Scott may certainly have increased her legal awareness, and she does demonstrate knowledge of Scottish and English laws concerning marriage, divorce, and property in her letter dated October 24, 1837 to Andrews Norton.[120] Even more significantly and earlier in her career, her *Discourse*'s singling out of judges, magistrates, and advocates among those who would be better able to "fulfil [their] duties" by cultivating sympathetic curiosity shows an interest in legal affairs.[121] Baillie's plays are notably preoccupied with justice, crime, and punishment, particularly capital punishment, and her treatment of these matters, which I address in later chapters, is often consistent with Baron Hume's emphasis on the legal obligation to control one's passions and to think of the welfare of others.[122]

Apart from legal matters, evidence of Baillie's preference for problem solving over theory building can be found in her comments on the work of

Harriet Martineau, who is now, after the work Susan Hoecker-Drysdale, widely regarded as the first woman sociologist.[123] In the above-referenced letter to Andrews Norton, Baillie expresses admiration for the "descriptive part" of Martineau's *Society in America*, which she goes so far as to call "marked with genius & often with good feeling," but she complains about the "political discussions, always referring to abstract principles"; she compares these discussions with "the old diversion of steeple hunting where one was obliged to go in a direct line to a certain object, over walk & house-tops or whatever else might intervene."[124] Baillie's impatience with Martineau's theorizing shows a pragmatist, interactionist preference for working with situated behavior. Such a preference led Mead to trust problem solving over theorizing to bring about social reform. In his words, "[a] conception of a different world comes to us always as the result of some specific problem that involves readjustment of the world as it is, not to meet a detailed ideal of a perfect universe, but to obviate the present difficulty."[125]

In keeping with this specificity, I situate Baillie's, Scott's, and Landor's works with respect to particular social problems detailed in the body of this study. But more broadly, Baillie and Scott might be said to be working through the problem of locating the self in society. To them, social relations were perplexing, in the pragmatist sense of that term. In that sense, embedded in Addams's phrase about drama as "penetrat[ing] into . . . perplexing social and domestic situations" that I quoted above, perplexity signals a cognitive and emotional puzzle to be worked out through value inquiry and adjustment.[126] The plays and novels show characters grappling with the perplexities of human relations, sometimes well and sometimes poorly. Borrowing the phrase from Haney, I see each work issuing a "hermeneutic challenge" to its audience to evaluate the interactions in the text or on the stage, determine how the representations connect with their own experience, and adapt the meaning to work through problems in those connected situations.

As I stressed above, this response is not mere imitation or acceptance of a "moral" from the story. In the terms of Baillie's *Discourse*, it is a process of reasoning, reflecting, analogizing, and "call[ing] up in the mind." In the terms of interpretive interactionism, it is a process of "naturalistic generalization," through which people compare their own experience to the experiences represented.[127] Denzin calls the result of the process "thick interpretation," a counterpart to the text's "thick description." Though thick description is most often associated with narrative, what matters for the process is not the generic classification of the text but the fullness of its content. Works that enable people to compare experiences are "performative writing[s]." Unlike the concept of generalization as a universal principle or an abstract result that has predominated in our thinking, naturalistic generalization does not aim to transcend personal experience but to juxtapose numerous personal experiences in ways that are "uniquely adequate" for the needs of the people involved.[128] Naturalistic generalization can be a source of "epiphanies," the connections between public and private described above.

Interpretive interactionism closes the gap between literary and lived experience by acknowledging that the former can be as conducive to epiphanies as the latter. The reason for this equivalence is the fictiveness of shared experience. As Denzin argues forcefully, we have no direct access to the thoughts, feelings, and perceptions of others. We know them through symbolic mediations, and we always respond to our readings of their gestures, our sense of their meaning.[129] From a different disciplinary starting point, Haney reaches a consonant conclusion in his view that texts and persons can be situationally, albeit not ontologically, equivalent.[130] Acknowledging this equivalence actually fosters a greater respect for the uniqueness and integrity of every person than does the presumption that we can know them. Like Scott's respectful attitude toward preceding builders of the legal castle, a respectful attitude toward all others honors the integrity of those with whom we would construct relationships.

As we have seen from Addams's reading of De Quincey, the assumed difference between literary and lived experience has kept us from fully pursuing the implications of literature as social work. Because Baillie, Scott, and Landor were yet undisciplined, they could hold the opposite assumption and enter fully into the pursuit. Now that our knowledge systems are catching up to them, we can and should readily explore the symbolic interactions performed by these writers. This study sets out on that endeavor.

2
The Problem
of Criminal Justice

In the *Introductory Discourse*, Baillie elaborates on the operation of sympathetic curiosity by examining what motivates people to watch public executions. Her choice of example follows precedents set by the Enlightenment philosophers with whom she has been linked,[1] yet her reference is more than a conventional illustration. For one thing, it oversimplifies attitudes observably present (according to historical research[2]) in crowds at executions and in scenes in her plays themselves. For another, it introduces a preoccupation with capital punishment that recurs in plays she wrote throughout her career and that spans the division between "miscellaneous" plays and those in the "passions" series. Coupled with the *Discourse*'s singling out of judges, magistrates, and advocates as the spectators most in need of cultivating sympathetic curiosity,[3] Baillie's references to capital punishment seem designed for applications in criminal justice reform. The topic of capital punishment is less pervasive throughout Scott's canon, since, as Beiderwell points out, "legal execution[s] in . . . the world after 1688" occur in only two novels,[4] but the treatment of the topic in *The Heart of Midlothian* has a depth and breadth that warrants not only the attention Beiderwell gives it but further study in connection with criminal justice reform.

In raising questions about capital punishment, Baillie and Scott grapple with a cause of considerable perplexity in their time and a matter that remains troubling in ours. That attitudes and practices were changing during the Romantic era is evident from the steady decline in the use of the death penalty over the first three decades of the nineteenth century. In England, the decline was influenced by reformers' agitations for changes in the "Bloody Code" that listed more than two hundred offenses, including such acts as shoplifting and sheep-stealing, as capital crimes. Many of these crimes were indeed declassified by legislation passed during the 1820s and 1830s.[5] In Scotland, where the independent legal system had no equivalent code, the decline stemmed from judicial discretion, which Scottish legal professionals often touted as evidence of their system's superiority to England's.[6] In both countries during the Romantic era, executions became a social problem that led people to question the justice, mercy, and humanity of their ways of treating lawbreakers. According to some scholars, the trend toward restricting the death penalty to exceptionally serious crimes does show an increased willingness to sympathize with prisoners and an inclination to weigh lawbreakers' intentions more heavily than their acts when judging and sentencing them.[7]

A century later and an ocean apart from Britain, Hull-House reformers continued this trend toward "humanizing justice" (as Addams called it) with proposals for eliminating all death sentences, for using psychiatric evaluation in judging lawbreakers, and for creating a separate court system for juveniles.[8] That these efforts to achieve what might be called "integrative social control" involved establishing sympathetic relations between lawbreakers and law keepers becomes clear in light of Candace Clark's interactionist study of the operation of sympathy in contemporary American society.[9] Interactionist thinking about social relations, including relations of social control, helps us to see that reform efforts are not only about attaining a specified goal — declassification of theft, for instance — but about the ongoing process of responding to transgression. Segregative responses protect an existing social structure by excluding, eliminating, or punishing any behavior that challenges it. Integrative responses may also be protective, but they are open to adjusting a given structure to meet challenges posed to it. While segregative approaches aim at deterrence by making people afraid of the consequences of committing crimes, integrative approaches work more positively toward prevention by making people want to uphold community standards. Baillie's and Scott's works facilitate this shift away from deterrence and toward prevention.

Little is known about Baillie's attitude toward capital punishment apart from her plays. In a letter to Margaret Holford Hodson dated July 26, 1840, she mentions that she is reading the memoirs of Sir Samuel Romilly, the sponsor of significant, albeit defeated, bills for the declassification of many capital crimes in 1808–11, but she does not specify what interests her about Romilly.[10] Contextualizing Baillie's *Introductory Discourse* with respect to arguments in English law for and against mitigation of punishments, Myers concludes that Baillie's position is "equivocal."[11] While I concur that Baillie's position "does not reduce to a political platform,"[12] I do find her work in touch with broader reform efforts. Surprisingly, given his well-known support for the death penalty and excessive punishment for political discontents (emphasized, or perhaps overemphasized, in John Sutherland's biography[13]), Scott's work also favors integrative social control. In the most focused study of Scott and criminal justice published to date, Bruce Beiderwell finds Scott "ambivalent" about the widespread use of capital punishment and argues that punishments in his novels are meant to usher in a government so just that it will be unopposed and therefore will no longer need to punish.[14] While I also see Scott as pursuing a goal of prevention, I suggest that he looked to the Scottish legal system, in which officials had great discretionary power in deciding individual cases, for a practical and interactive way to adjust social relations so as to restrict transgression and hold punishment indefinitely in abeyance.

In this chapter, I situate Baillie's and Scott's most extensive treatments of capital punishment—her *Introductory Discourse* and *Rayner*, his *Heart of Midlothian*—in the context of relevant legal practices[15] and consider how the works grapple with questions about social control raised in this context. Insofar as they prompt viewers and readers to confront the perplexities of just social relations, these literary interventions contribute as much to the process of criminal justice reform as do the activities of petitioners, judges, prosecutors, and legislators.

Legal Justice, Social Good, and Sympathy

By the Romantic era, England surpassed neighboring British, European, and American countries in the number of crimes classified as capital offenses (more than 200) and in the number of people hanged for them (7,000 in London between 1770 and 1830).[16] In contrast, Scotland had approximately 40 capital crimes and 23 executions between 1767 and 1797.[17] Among reasons for England's dubious distinction are unwarranted confidence in the example of execution to deter others from committing crimes and excessive zeal for legislating remedies to social problems. The latter is perhaps the more surprising factor. The high number of capital crimes was not a legacy from earlier and presumably more violent centuries but a creation of relatively recent years. In *The Province of Legislation Determined*, David Lieberman traces the multiplication of statutes, including criminal statutes, to the Glorious Revolution when Parliament's lawmaking powers were affirmed. From that time on, Parliament embraced its legislative role by passing more and more laws.[18] In one respect, this activity inaugurated a trend toward participatory government that eventually made Parliament more responsive to citizens' claims. I address that trend in chapter 6. In other respects, however, the multiplication of criminal statutes impeded the legal system's ability to maintain a just order. Almost any instance of localized poaching, vandalism, or misconduct was likely to be met by the passing of a law criminalizing the given specific behavior. Once cases governed by these statutes were tried in court, they set precedents that influenced judgments in future cases.[19] As a result, the English legal system was burdened by an excessive number of capital cases, and it faced the dilemma of either consistently upholding the law by mercilessly executing petty offenders and thus establishing a repressive order or inconsistently granting exceptions and thus undermining the credibility of the law.

Though many executions were carried out, many exceptions were also granted. Home Office records examined by Gatrell show 1,300 petitions for mercy granted between 1812 and 1822, with that number doubling by the 1830s.[20] Because officials often looked for ways to avoid hanging nonviolent criminals, the number of executions actually decreased while the number of capital statutes increased. Scholars differ over the significance of this pattern. Gatrell concedes that it does show some discretionary leniency in the system, but he points out that many petitions for mercy were denied. Finding discretion more operative, Peter King argues that the legal system effectively compensated in practice for its harshness in theory by various strategies of withholding charges and arranging acquittals.[21] Even if the English system functioned with a good deal of discretion, the contradiction between statute and practice was perceived as problematic, and reform efforts began by seeking to reconcile the two: reformers wanted many crimes declassified so that courts would not hesitate to convict and punish with milder sentences and thus realign the law as stated with the law as practiced.[22]

An alternative approach to the problem of crime and capital punishment was taken in Scotland. Because Scotland kept its own legal system even after its union with England, the multiplication of capital crimes in England did not apply in Scotland. Consequently, Scotland experienced less conflict between the theory and practice of the law, but that consequence did not follow only from the smaller number of capital crimes. It followed from the acceptance of discretion as an integral part of the system, not merely a compensatory principle. Scholarship by Riggs and Farmer details how Scottish legal professionals embraced discretion and flexibility as the distinguishing features of their system and how they used them to decrease their imposition of death sentences without crisis or legislation.[23] This occurrence is important for an understanding of Walter

Scott, a legal professional with a strong attachment to the Scottish system; it is also important as a frame of reference for Baillie.

A landmark event in Scottish legal history occurred in 1797 when David Hume, nephew of the philosopher and instructor of Walter Scott at the University of Edinburgh, published his *Commentaries on the Law of Scotland respecting the Description and Punishment of Crimes*.[24] According to Farmer, Hume deliberately exaggerated differences between Scottish and English laws, shaping the former into a symbol of cultural and national identity.[25] The features that Hume emphasized were the discretion and flexibility that followed from the Court's "declaratory power," i.e., the power to decide what behavior is and is not criminal, the extent to which it threatens a community, and the appropriate way to counter that threat.[26] Few points of law were governed by statute in Scotland. As in England, common (or case or customary) law provided guidelines, but in contrast to the English practice of treating cases as separately binding precedents, Scottish practices treated them as a collectively suggestive pattern. Similarly, Scottish law seldom prescribed particular sentences for particular crimes. It stratified its court system according to the maximum penalties that could be imposed by judges in each tier and then left judges free to sentence by "individuation, or . . . making the punishment fit the circumstances of the case and the culprit."[27] Judges were not the only officials expected to exercise discretion. The procurator fiscals and advocates-depute responsible for assigning cases to the various courts acted on their "hypothesis of guilt and a judgement . . . of what the minimum sentence should be." Prosecutors were free to "restrict the pains of the law"—i.e., ask for a lenient sentence—when presenting their cases.[28]

Discretionary power was thus institutionalized within the Scottish system, which therefore experienced no crisis of disparity between theory and practice. Hume and his followers distrusted statutory law because of its abstraction and remoteness from "experience"; they thought that relying on statutes subjected individual cases "to the fallacious conjectures of human wisdom before the event."[29] Abuses of power undoubtedly arose in a system licensing so much individual decision making,[30] and by understanding this system, we can more readily see why Baillie would single out legal professionals as those most in need of ethical instruction. In Riggs's estimation, the strength of the system lay in its adaptability: it could meet the challenge of social change, including the change in community attitudes toward the death penalty.[31]

Changes in public opinion regarding capital punishment are relatively easy to document with reference to petitions and jury verdicts, as Gatrell and Riggs do, but relatively difficult to explain. No single factor adequately explains the emergence of marked disapproval of the death penalty during the Romantic era, just as no single factor adequately accounts for the larger, pan-European trend away from displays of severely punitive power toward more subtle penalties and surveillance of which it is part.[32] A single factor may nevertheless predominate in the experience of individuals living through a certain transition, and attention to that factor can thus reveal a good deal about how those people perceived and responded to the trend. For Baillie and for Scott, as for groups of English reformers and Scottish professionals, the predominant factor was sympathy.

Much scholarship addresses the cultural value of sympathy that evolved from Scottish Enlightenment philosophy,[33] but interactionist research gives us the greatest insight into how the process of sympathizing constructs and reconstructs social relations. In her study of sympathy in contemporary America, Candace Clark argues that people decide whether to give or withhold sympathy in individual cases based on the "feeling rules" or "sympathy logic" of their culture. All societies have conventions about who deserves sympathy. At this time in American society, for example, the rules weigh luck against responsibility: people who seem to have caused their own troubles are deemed less sympathy-worthy than victims of circumstances beyond their control. These rules are complicated, however, by a widespread "belief in a just world." Because this belief makes the idea of undeserved suffering unacceptable, people often try to resolve the contradiction between a just order and unjust experiences within it by blaming victims or trivializing the extent of their sufferings.[34] When people give sympathy according to the rules of their culture, they affirm its logic, its values, its existing patterns of relations. But people can give sympathy in violation of those rules, and when they do so, they can precipitate social change. Because sympathy involves so much complex interaction that can reinforce or alter social relations, Clark compares the process to a drama that "allows us to define or rehearse our notions of morality."[35] Extending this comparison, one might say that the process of sympathizing opens cognitive and emotional spaces for new relationships and that it thus describes the social work performed by Baillie's plays and Scott's novels.

The process of sympathizing that Clark delineates warrants further attention for its connection with social problem solving and social justice. To begin with, it solves the problem of the alienation between the self and others that Addams termed "selfishness" and Mead, "hedonism." It does so through the activity of role-taking that sets it in motion. In the tradition of Addams and Mead, Clark indicates that a person must imagine being in a sufferer's place, imagine how he or she would think and feel in that situation, before sympathizing becomes possible. After this first step, the process of sympathizing continues through the use of the feeling rules described above and the resolution of the "cognitive-emotional dissonance" that often arises when one's thoughts or feelings about a victim diverge from the thoughts or feelings suggested by the rules.[36] Of course, the first step is easier to take when the sufferer resembles the self or is in a predicament that the self has experienced. Less familiar others are more perplexing. Putting oneself in their places "takes effort and skill" and the abandonment of stereotypes. It sometimes also needs the help of a "sympathy broker" or "sympathy entrepreneur"—Clark's terms for intermediaries who can point out to potential sympathizers why a victim's plight deserves compassion within the logic of the given culture.[37] In difficult cases, role-taking and applying feeling rules become more like problem-solving exercises, and working through them accomplishes a fuller development of the social self. Addams and Mead associated the ability to sympathize with those unlike the self or to see an unexpected resemblance between the self and others with the ability to correct injustice in both personal relations and in social structures. Actually, Addams, like many later interactionists, makes no sharp distinction between micro- and macro-level relations. Because social structure is made up of personal interactions, a change on the small scale has an impact on the large scale. In Addams's words, "justice must come by trained intelligence, by broadened sympathies toward the individual man or woman who crosses our path."[38]

Recent work on social movements confirms this sense of social change beginning with the cognitive-affective experience of sympathy. For example, Jane Mansbridge finds "sympathetic consciousness" necessary for members outside an oppressed group to perceive that group's situation as unjust and to advocate liberation.[39] Furthermore, Jeff Goodwin, James M. Jasper, and Francesca Polletta argue that downplaying cognitive-emotional factors in analyzing social change perpetuates the rationalist-materialist bias of twentieth-century disciplinarity, and they call for a return to pre-disciplinary openness to intangible factors.[40] Such revisionist views of what Clark calls the "social force" of sympathy[41] invite reexamination of that power in Romantic-era contexts.

In the context of Romantic-era movements against capital punishment, sympathy had the following effects. First, the vogue, stemming from Hume's and Smith's philosophy, for the cultivation of sentiment led middle class people to attend executions, visit prisons, and collect portraits and other artifacts of convicts on the grounds that "one had to *witness* others' suffering" in order to learn to sympathize.[42] While Gatrell does not find this sensibility itself sufficient for reform, he does credit it with closing the distance between law keepers and lawbreakers on which harsh punishment depends; harsh punishments are more easily carried out against "social others" who are presumably not like the law abiders.[43] In light of interactionist research, we can associate the practices of those cultivating sensibility with the first step in the process of sympathizing and in changing social relations—the step of taking the roles of unfamiliar others. Secondly, among active reformers, so-called humanity-mongers used narratives of prisoners' sufferings in petitions for mercy in individual cases and in arguments that the criminal code was unjustly harsh.[44] We might see humanity-mongers as sympathy brokers who helped middle- and upperclass people discard stereotypes about lawbreakers and discover them as human beings like the law keepers themselves.[45] Such mediation seems especially important in considering Gatrell's assertion that reform was impeded by the "cramped imaginations" of judges who could not recognize the humanity of nonelite people.[46] Finally, Gatrell believes that reformers, numerically a small group, succeeded because they "exaggerated" popular sympathy for their cause.[47] In other words, they *constructed* the attitude that more people did eventually adopt and that did change the social system. If we bring this awareness of sympathy in Romantic-era criminal justice reform to bear on Baillie's works (as I do in the next section), her singling out of legal professionals and her preoccupation with executions become specifically and urgently meaningful. Baillie appears as a sympathy broker, constructing humane attitudes toward lawbreakers.

Though organized campaigns for declassifying capital crimes were not necessary in Scotland, efforts to bring more sympathy and humanity into the system are nevertheless evident. Riggs's research clearly shows that legal professionals and jurors did not find death sentences to be appropriate penalties for most crimes during this period: potentially capital cases were assigned to courts that could impose only lesser sentences; prosecutors "restricted the pains of the law" in almost all cases, and juries refused to convict when they did not. In fact, Riggs argues that "prosecutors effectively abolished the death penalty for crimes other than murder" through a systematic use of their discretionary powers.[48] That sympathy in some way influenced this change is evident from judicial attention to the concept of humanity. In one case, for instance, a judge praised "the humanity of the Public Prosecutor" who chose not to seek capital punishment.[49] Scottish professionals were openly proud of the "relative leniency" of their sentencing and their care in distinguishing insanity from criminality.[50] According to Hume, "reason and humanity" dictate that the insane receive "an entire exemption from any manner of pain" for their actions.[51] Scott brings this attitude to the fore in his treatment of Madge Wildfire.

Concomitantly, Scottish law gave extraordinary attention to the matter of criminal intent and the crime of "culpable homicide."[52] Predictably, this charge was attractive because it offered more reasons for leniency than did a charge of murder, and controversies over whether "killing with provocation" ought to be classified in this category imply a search for ways to sympathize with prisoners as human beings who behaved in understandable ways. Hume wrote: "[W]e cannot as men be insensible to the wide difference between that homicide which has no incentive but wickedness of heart, and that which is in retaliation only of grievous and alarming injuries suffered upon the spot." He continued: "[N]o more on this than on other occasions, can we, in judging of human conduct, put the feelings of human nature out of question on views of policy."[53] Surprisingly, however, culpable homicide was used to hold more lawbreakers accountable for more actions. It encouraged convictions not only in cases where a charge of murder would surely bring a jury verdict of "not guilty" at all but in cases where a death followed from someone's acting "without that caution and circumspection which may serve to prevent harm to others."[54] According to Farmer, the preference for and expansion of the charge of culpable homicide over murder inverted the relationship between action and intention in legal judgments. Instead of referring to states of mind for help in judging actions, the court came to refer to actions for help in judging states of mind. Intention became more important than outcome in these cases. Farmer interprets this trend as evidence of "a greater degree of social intervention on the part of the courts"; criminal law was becoming concerned with "build[ing] character and teach[ing] social behaviour" by focusing on "duties and responsibilities."[55] This more socially aware way of judging forms a significant context for Baillie's plays, especially *The Stripling* and *The Homicide*, as well as for Scott's valorization of judicial discretion in *The Heart of Midlothian*. Though his criticism of the law condemning Effie in that novel has been widely noted,[56] his openness to interventionism has not been fully explored.

While a Foucauldian reading of the trend toward holding people responsible for each other would posit that it set up a culture of surveillance, an interactionist approach allows for more positive implications. It suggests the emergence of a socially ethical culture in which the concept of mind is, as it was for Mead, the concept of minding—a culture in which people are expected to put themselves in the places of others and respond sympathetically. This kind of culture relies more on integrative than segregative social control: it attempts to bring lawbreakers back into society or, preferably, prevent crime from occurring by making potential lawbreakers feel too attached to the community to violate its standards. As

Clark explains, sympathy exerts social control "by creating obligation": a rule breaker who receives lenient treatment may feel grateful, relieved, and obligated to embrace, respect, or at least conform to the standards of the people who were kind to him or her. The rule breaker thus becomes attached "to the very society whose rules were violated."[57] Insofar as it values conformity, integrative control can undoubtedly be a stifling force, yet it has the potential to liberate society from a narrowly punitive sense of justice.[58] That potential is best explained with reference to the work of Mead and Addams, who fervently believed in it.

Mead's essay on "The Psychology of Punitive Justice" explains that conflicts between "legal justice and social good," between "retribution" and "prevention" will remain insoluble until we recognize the "emotional attitudes" represented by these abstractions. "We do not respect law in the abstract," he wrote, but in personal relations: the law to us is the police officer who protects us, the community that embraces us.[59] An element of fear also exists with this love of community, for as the law can protect and unite, it can also divide and exclude. It can "cut off from the world to which [they] belong" those people whose acts depart from community norms. To people within the community, the transgressor appears as an "enemy," one toward whom they direct a hostile attitude, and this "hostility toward the lawbreaker . . . unit[es] . . . the community in the emotional solidarity of aggression."[60] When courts impose severe penalties, they further draw the community together against the criminal, but the unity depends on the maintenance of hostility. Far from threatening society, crime holds society together—so much so that the need for a criminal justice system may be independent of its effectiveness in dealing with crime.[61] What is needed, in Mead's view, to prevent crime—or, on a larger scale, war—is a way to draw people together without hostility. Mead found the juvenile court system a promising alternative to punitive justice because it directed hostility away from the lawbreakers themselves and toward the conditions that discouraged them from having a positive relationship with the community. The goal was to solve the problem of the conditions so that a positive relationship among people could go forward.[62]

In Addams's analysis, retribution fails because destitute and desperate people romanticize crime, seeing execution as a heroic death superior to "prosaic life in prison." Further, capital punishment makes law abiders inhumane and self-righteous or, alternatively, dishonest and cynical if horror at the penalty leads judges and juries to acquit people who have clearly broken the law. For Addams, this dysfunctional system of penalizing criminals, whether on the local level of the Chicago courts or the global level of the Sacco and Vanzetti case, shows society drawing together out of fear. It is fear of the criminal that makes people want retribution. Hence, the criminal justice system depends on and perpetuates the fear that draws people together in protective unity. The solution for Addams is "immunity from fear"—and that comes from creating a non-oppositional relationship between the lawbreaker and the group. Addams's efforts to learn how things look from the other's point of view, evident in her insight into fantasies of criminal heroism as well as into different understandings of law among different national groups, move toward this interactionist solution.[63]

An earlier plea for sympathetic prevention of social unrest can be found in Harriet Martineau's remarks on Peterloo in *A History of the Thirty Years' Peace*. Martineau made the following observations about the sentencing of Orator Hunt's associates: "It certainly appears that the prisoners were treated with kindness and respect by the great men they had to deal with, from the home secretary to the police officials, when the parties were brought face to face. If they could have known each other better beforehand—their feelings, ideas, and interests—perhaps there would have been no Six Acts on the one hand, or Spa-fields and Manchester meetings on the other."[64] Though Baillie and Martineau ultimately differ in their approaches to social problem solving (as I explain in chapter 4), Martineau's sense of the change in social relations that could come about if people would recognize each other's humanity further contextualizes Baillie's— and Scott's—work. Baillie's plays participate in efforts to achieve sympathetic social relations that run, episodically, from the Scottish courts to Hull-House. Most notably, her sense that social change depends on understanding the passions sets a striking precedent for Mead's argument that reform must begin with "emotional attitudes." Scott's *Heart of Midlothian*, which offers an analogue for Mead's certainty that law and justice must be personal relations and not abstractions, is also caught up in a search for a more sympathetic society, despite the fear of the criminal that sometimes overwhelmed him and later made him notoriously unsympathetic to the victims of Peterloo.[65] With these contexts in mind, I turn to Baillie's and Scott's works.

From the *Introductory Discourse* to *Rayner*

Among reasons for seeing Baillie as engaged in social work that subsumes the distinction between the plays on the passions and the miscellaneous plays is the connection between the passion series' *Introductory Discourse* and the miscellaneous play *Rayner*. *Rayner* explores in such depth and breadth the problem of capital punishment raised in the *Discourse* that it seems designed to follow up on that document. Though Baillie may have planned to treat capital punishment in *De Monfort*, the tragedy on hatred published at the same time as the *Discourse*, that play is too concerned with the thoughts and feelings leading up to De Monfort's killing of Rezenvelt to do more than allude to the punitive consequences. The only direct reference to capital punishment occurs when De Monfort asserts, after he has committed the crime, "But I am human still," and his sister responds with the promise, "Yea, on the scaffold, if needs must be, I never will forsake thee" (5.2.48, 71–72).[66] Though the statements make a thought-provoking point about the humanity of the criminal, the play does not pursue the point since De Monfort's death obviates the matter of punishment.[67] Not until *The Dream*, published in 1812, did Baillie take up this topic extensively in the passions series, though passing allusions to it, such as the use of execution to terrorize prisoners in *Ethwald II*, the tragedy on ambition published in 1802, occur in the interim. The miscellaneous play *Rayner*, published in 1804, however, dramatizes and investigates the effects of watching executions broached in the *Introductory Discourse*.

If we read the *Discourse* with awareness of the humanity mongering that was changing the criminal justice system during the Romantic era, we can recognize its attributions of sympathetic motives to watchers of executions as strategic assertions. Like reformers who exaggerated popular sympathy for their cause,[68] Baillie *constructs* an attitude that more people did eventually adopt. Although she acknowledges the possibility of unsympathetic curiosity, she denies that it motivates most witnesses to executions: "[i]t cannot be any pleasure we receive from the sufferings of a fellow-creature which attracts such multitudes of people to a public execution." I suggest that Baillie's habitual reliance on the adjective "sympathetic" to modify "curiosity," along with her denial of negative motives, narrows the focus of the *Discourse*, placing other kinds or functions of curiosity outside of its scope.[69] In place of negative motives, Baillie substitutes the desire for a fuller understanding of human nature. Spectators want to learn how a person copes with the ordeal of facing execution: they go "to see a human being bearing himself up under such circumstances, or struggling with the terrible apprehensions which such a situation impresses"; they focus on his demeanor—"whether he steps firmly; whether the motions of his body denote agitation or calmness." This same wish lies behind the curiosity of those who cannot bear to attend the execution but who want to hear an account of it from the eyewitnesses. Since the curiosity is directed toward the ways in which the prisoner copes with the situation rather than toward the actual death, Baillie concludes that it would be better satisfied if people could "lift up the roof of [the]dungeon . . . and look upon the criminal the night before he suffers, in his still hours of privacy," for then consciousness of being watched would not influence the individual's behavior.[70]

These assertions are remarkable not only for filtering out negative motives for watching executions but for ignoring the positive ones officially attached to the spectacle. Law keepers routinely justified public executions with reference to their deterrent value. They were supposed to impress spectators with the power of the law and frighten them into compliance. Scott examines this justification in *The Heart of Midlothian*, considering how sympathy for the prisoner can sometimes interfere with it but also vividly depicting what Mead called the "solidarity of aggression" against the convict.[71] Baillie, however, writes the deterrent value out of the *Discourse*. There is no solidarity of aggression in her crowd or even the romanticizing of the criminal that Adams detected. There is only the wish to solve the perplexity of human nature and the possibility that that wish can be satisfied by some means other than witnessing an execution.[72] With the construction of this attitude, the *Discourse* renders capital punishment obsolete as a means of social control and points toward sympathy as an alternative means of regulating human relations. It moves from deterrence by segregative means toward prevention by integrative means.

The *Discourse* justifies scrutiny of others on the ground that it is morally beneficial to the observer and to society as a whole. First, it teaches observers what they might and should be capable of when they face "distressing and difficult situations" in their own experiences, for by "examining others we know ourselves."[73] Juxtaposed with Baron Hume's definition of crime and the duty of "self-command," Baillie's statements, indeed her whole aim of promoting the control of passion, take on specific social applications not otherwise apparent to present-day readers. According to Hume, in defining crime, "the law always supposes that the delinquent has infringed, in some respect, those duties which he owes to the community."[74] Among those duties, Hume placed control of passion. In a lengthy paragraph introducing the conditions under which homicide may and may not be excusable, Hume expatiates on the topic of emotional reactions and restraint. People, he writes, "are subject to the feeling of resentment on injuries," but they are also capable of moderating their reactions. By practicing self-control,

> even the feeling [of resentment] itself may . . . be chastened and subdued: so that the very things which [a person] does in self-defence, shall

be done calmly and with temperance, and less out of anger or revenge, than from considerations of justice and necessity. *To gain this state of self-command is part of every man's duty*; . . . and so far to fall short of it, as mortally to avenge any insult or injury not attended with danger to one's life, and not impossible to be repelled and chastised by gentler means, — this is certainly criminal excess.[73]

Hume dwells on the need to make emotional control a habit because of the "great frequency of . . . scenes of provocation" to resentment. And because provocation is so frequent, the law must punish, albeit not with death, homicides committed by people who *should* have been able to control their emotions under the circumstances.[76] Given this legal application for restraint of passion, the project Baillie launched with her *Discourse* becomes more clearly a problem-solving project. By encouraging spectators to view "scenes of provocation," learn what emotional controls people can achieve, and apply the lesson to themselves, Baillie promotes the performance of self-control and the focus on duties to the community that prevent crime.

It is worth noting that the lessons to be learned by watching people in distressing situations are to be applied to the self through the processes of analogizing and reflecting that I compared earlier to Denzin's "naturalistic generalization"; these processes of imagining a connection between the cases of others and one's own experience are likewise expected of people watching the plays. The connection is remarkable in both the lived and literary examples of gatherings at the scaffold because of Baillie's underlying assumption that law-keeping observers can see the criminal as a person *like* themselves. As we know from interactionist studies, that view is difficult to obtain.[77] It requires putting oneself in the place of an "other" whose identity as a convicted criminal distances him or her from those who have not broken or have not been condemned for breaking the law. Recognizing this common humanity overcomes the distance between the observer and the unfamiliar other and thus allows for the development of the observer's social self. Closing the distance also allows for a sympathetic response to the prisoner, which is the opposite of the response projected in the official justification. Deterrence depends on keeping a distance between lawbreakers and law keepers. It assumes that the latter can put themselves in the place of the former only by imagining themselves as criminals, and it expects them to recoil from that frightening "otherness" and identify with a law abiding community that excludes the criminal. But because Baillie's observers see the criminal's humanity, they do not base social relation on conflict between "good" and "bad" people. Instead, they find "more . . . kindness than . . . cruelty" in the world; they develop more "respect" for themselves and others, and they actively respond to others in ways that create "more just, more merciful, more compassionate" social relations. Or, to adapt words from Addams, they advance justice by responding with broadened sympathy to the individual man or woman or crosses their path.[78]

Rayner presents spectators with an opportunity to observe paired contrasting examples of attitudes toward criminals—a sympathetic one, that, as Michael Gamer has noted, illustrates the behavior Baillie projected in the *Introductory Discourse,*[79] and an unsympathetic one that exposes the hostility in punitive justice. In addition, it shows behavior that falls between the two extremes. On the whole, the scenes pose a "hermeneutic challenge" (to use Haney's phrase) to readers or viewers of the drama and offer them the opportunity to consider and possibly adjust the sympathy logic of their culture.

The sympathetic behavior is exhibited by the crowd waiting outside a court to learn whether Rayner will be found guilty of murder. While waiting, they tell each other about the bearings of other prisoners they have witnessed. As is consistent with the construction in the *Introductory Discourse,* they focus on the humanity of the prisoners. They agree that "it is a piteous thing" for "a human creature [to] be thus thrust out of the world by human creatures like himself" (3.1.402). They listen to an account by one of their number who has witnessed an execution. According to the witness, who "paid half a dollar for a place near the scaffold," "it would have made any body's heart drop blood to have seen him [the prisoner] when he lifted up the handkerchief from his eyes, and took his last look of the day-light, and all the living creatures about him" (402). When Rayner does appear, the crowd displays sympathy toward him by insisting that his guards let him comfort his intended wife, who has fainted. Rayner himself claims that a right to comfort Elizabeth "is permitted [him] by ev'ry sense of human sympathy," which is "a power stronger than law or judgment" (403). The unsympathetic behavior is exhibited by the two executioners hired to carry out the sentence against Rayner. In what the stage direction calls a "vain-glorious manner," they boast about the high-ranking men they have killed and revel in their own celebrity status (5.1.412–13). They care about their own power, not about justice.

Between these two extremes lies the behavior of a would-be witness to Rayner's execution—the stock comic figure of a "clown"—whose humane attitude, surprisingly, in light of the *Introductory Discourse,* prevents him from learning to watch executions. Feeling inadequate because he has never seen an execution, he pays the jailor for a place near the scaffold, but he is horrified at the prospect. "Poor man! Poor man!" he exclaims repeatedly, referring to the prisoner. "I shall think of him many a night after this before I go to sleep. . . . [W]hat terrible things there be in this world if a body does but think of them" (5.1.413). Upon meeting the executioners, he refuses to shake hands or drink from the same cup with them, yet when the jailor wants to refund his money and give his place at the scaffold to someone else, the clown refuses, saying, "I have a huge desire to see how a man looks when he is going to have his head cut off, and I'll stay for the sight tho' I should swoon for it" (413).

As the clown's stated desire makes clear, the scene indulges in some parody of the *Introductory Discourse*, in which sympathy draws spectators to execution scenes, but it raises serious questions about the correspondence between observing and sympathizing as well. Here, familiarity has desensitized the executioners; in contrast, the clown's highly developed sympathy makes him want to avoid the sight, but he cannot break through the cultural conditioning that leads him to believe he should watch. He has not gone beyond the "representational function" (to rely again on Haney's terminology) of the spectacle, so he only imitates the convict's suffering.[80] A more interpretive approach is taken by the crowd waiting for Rayner at the jail, for they move on from identification to intervention in arranging for him to comfort Elizabeth. This move shows that they are not putting themselves in the place of law keepers but in the place of the prisoner, yet they have not so far distanced themselves from the given order as to question the use of capital sentencing that has aroused their sympathy. To rise to that level of questioning is to meet the "hermeneutic challenge" posed by this drama.

Meeting that challenge requires the practices treated in the *Discourse* as analogy, extension, and reflection—or by Denzin as "naturalistic generalization" and "thick interpretation."[81] Spectators should evaluate what they see onstage in comparison with aspects of their own experience that the representation "will naturally call up in the mind."[82] For Romantic-era audiences, the scenes I have just examined could not fail to suggest the trials and executions regularly occurring in their society as well as the attendant crowds and accompanying legal and moral controversies. The scenes would also evoke other literary representations, for audience members are likely not only to have observed these spectacles firsthand but to be familiar with ballads, stories, dramas, newspapers, and other documents dealing with them. Spectators must connect the new element in their experience—*Rayner*—with these existing aspects of their experience[83] and reflect on how *Rayner* confirms, expands, or contradicts their understanding of just social relations. They must make Rayner's case personally meaningful for them and then bring this meaning into play in interactions with others in their culture.

To elaborate on just one way that *Rayner* may prompt revision of attitudes toward and practices of social control, I return to the dialogue between the executioners. Because this scene may be dismissed for pandering to the popular taste for caricatures of executioners that Gatrell finds common during the eighteenth and nineteenth centuries, it is important to realize that its alliance with popular culture contributes to its effectiveness. There are two factors to consider. First, as Gatrell points out, caricatures and comedy surrounding executions betray anxiety about the practice: laughter can be a coping mechanism.[84] Secondly, as Denzin argues, popular culture shows us the predominant concerns of people in a given society.[85] By asking her audiences to reflect on these caricatures, Baillie can be both a manipulator of popular culture and a facilitator of serious inquiry.[86]

These axe-wielding and bloodthirsty executioners emphasize the brutality of capital punishment that was perhaps not so openly displayed in the bloodless method of hanging that was the standard sentence in England and Scotland during the Romantic era. Decapitation belonged to the remote British past or the very recent French Reign of Terror. It had ceased to be a standard sentence in Scotland early in the seventeenth century, and it was reserved in England for matters of treason, as demonstrated by the decapitation, after hanging, of the Cato Street conspirators in 1820.[87] In *Rayner*, as in most of Baillie's plays involving executions, decapitation is the usual sentence. The method fits the vaguely remote settings she favors. With the exception of her history plays *Constantine Paleologus* and *The Family Legend*, Baillie often sets her dramas in some distant time and place—a fourteenth-century Swiss monastery (*The Dream*), in and near Zamora during the thirteenth century (*Henriquez*), in Germany along the borders of Poland and Silesia (*Rayner*)—but unlike Scott, she minimizes the specificity. According to her explanation, in the preface to the second volume of plays in the passions series, of her reasons for setting *Ethwald* in Mercia "towards the end of the Heptarchy," these placements are strategic. They link her personal, imaginative work with lived, shared, public experience, but they allow her to shape circumstances according to her "design" without "disturbing or disarranging" received ideas about the given historical era.[88] As a result, the plays encourage analogizing between a present time and place and past ones.[87] The unfamiliar settings make the plays perplexing and arouse interpretive effort. More familiar representations—a hanging in nineteenth-century England, for example—might arouse only whatever habitual response dominated spectators' attitudes to the cases they encountered. By having to connect an apparently unfamiliar representation with the familiar, spectators can discover unexpected resemblances that cause them to question practices they had taken for granted. In the case of the executioners in *Rayner*, a connection between past and present practices may awaken spectators to brutality in their own time to which they had become inured.

So far, I have addressed only crowd scenes revolving around the main plot of *Rayner*, but that main plot itself deals with a sympathetic intervention that prevents an execution. Rayner has been wrongly convicted of a murder committed by Count Zaterloo. He is saved from execution by Ohio, a former slave now employed as a servant at the prison. The sympathy that develops between Rayner and Ohio — not principles of law — prevents injustice in this play.

The sympathy between these two characters testifies to the transformative power of role-taking, for their relationship begins with hostility. On the night before the scheduled execution, Ohio tries to steal Rayner's cloak, reasoning that the garment is of more use to the living than the dead (5.2.414). Waking, Rayner at first reacts angrily, but when Ohio expects Rayner to beat him in retaliation, Rayner takes pity on him, giving him the cloak and adding, "I know thee now; thou art the wretched negro / Who serves the prisoners; I have observ'd thee. / I'm sorry for thee; thou art bare enough, / and winter is at hand" (5.2.114). Instead of thinking only from his own point of view, Rayner has thought from the point of view of the other, putting himself in the place of the cold and oppressed servant, then responding to relieve that suffering to the extent that he can. Rayner's unexpected sympathy elicits a similar response from Ohio: "Ha! Art thou sorry that the negro's cold? / Where wert thou born who art so pitiful?/ I will not take thy cloak, but I will love thee. / They shall not cut thy head off" (414). Ohio actually carries out this promise by sabotaging the scaffold so that it collapses on the executioner, delaying the proceedings long enough for a messenger to arrive with Rayner's pardon, issued because the real murderer confessed (5.4.418–19).

In some sense, this contrived ending is disappointing because of the way it renders the development of the social self as if by time-lapse photography. It speeds up a complicated transformation that would not, we expect, happen so quickly or linearly. But this scene has been prepared by one earlier in the play that dramatizes another aspect of the *Discourse*, a scene in which Baillie "lift[s] up the roof of the dungeon" and allows us to see and hear Rayner as he ponders his fate. Observing Rayner, we overhear a soliloquy that shows an already developed or developing sociality. Rayner's fears of death are fears of disembodiment and disconnection from others. For Rayner, human life is social life; death, individual isolation:

> Who but would shrink form this? [i.e., becoming
>   "unbodied spirit," previous line]
> It goes hard with thee,
> Social connected man; it goes hard with thee
> To be turned out into a state unknown,
> From all they kind an individual being. (5.2.414)

Rayner's sense of social self, of individual being as necessarily bound up with others, and of isolation as the worst fate a person can suffer underlies his ability to sympathize with others. Earlier scenes, moreover, establish that his sympathy is not elitist: in Maureen Dowd's view, Rayner's kindness to his servant Herman approaches "egalitarianism."[90] With this preparation, we should be less surprised to see that he can put himself in the place of an unfamiliar "other"—a person of a difference race—at the end of the play. Even if the ending remains oversimplified, it does not diminish the play's "hermeneutic challenge." Insofar as it still prompts spectators to consider how predatory relationships might be transformed by sympathy and what benefit might follow from cross-racial and cross-class role-taking, it has the potential to improve social relations.[91] A similar potential was realized, according to Addams, when drama improved relations among immigrant groups at Hull-House.

A horror of being cut off from humanity—or, in Mead's phrase, "cut off from the world to which [they] belong"[92]—is typical of Baillie's imprisoned characters. Irrespective of their guilt, they fear segregative control. Thus, the guilty De Monfort fears being "out from the pale of social kindred cast" (5.4.99) as much as the innocent Rayner fears disembodiment and disconnection from others.[93] The attention to a social or human connection that is not broken by committing a crime further evidences the "humanity mongering" and "sympathy-brokering" potential of Baillie's work. The character in *Rayner* who *is* socially disconnected—the murderer Count Zaterloo—is disconnected more by his selfish attitude than by his criminal act. The contrast between Rayner and Zaterloo, which Baillie's preface indicates she deliberately contrived,[94] is most evident in the way they regard others. Zaterloo and Rayner are in parallel circumstances insofar as Zaterloo, in hiding, also faces death, for he was wounded while committing his crime. Zaterloo thinks primarily of himself. Knowing that his confession can prevent Rayner's execution, he nevertheless delays sending it until he is sure he will not recover and will therefore suffer no repercussions from admitting his guilt. The preface deflects some blame from Zaterloo by showing his attitude to have been conditioned by his "absurdly indulgent mother" (389), who is even responsible for some of the delay in sending the confession (5.4.417). Nevertheless, Zaterloo's suffering arouses little sympathy from spectators because it fits so easily into what Clark calls a "just world" scenario: Zaterloo seems to deserve to suffer because he cares insufficiently about the suffering of others.

By arranging both the rescue of the innocent Rayner and the death of the guilty Zaterloo, the play satisfies spectators' desire to believe in a "just world" while making the means to that end something other than official prosecution. This retention of the value of retribution outside of the criminal justice system is typical of Baillie's plays: it recurs, for instance, in the deaths of Osterloo in *The Dream* and Annabella in *Witchcraft*, and though it seems at first inconsistent with reformist thinking, it is actually conducive to the value inquiry necessary for reform to occur. Value inquiry is, after all, an investigation of competing goods; it is seldom merely the substitution of one value for another.[95] An exception, of course, may be Percy Shelley's approach to the problem of justice, for Shelley's essay "On [really, "Against"] the Punishment of Death," like his preface to *The Cenci*, calls for the categorical rejection of punitive values and the substitution of conciliatory ones.[96] But Shelley's approach leaves behind those who cannot fully make this conversion; thus, it is difficult to adapt to the slow, cumbersome process of compromise by which reform usually occurs. Baillie's approach does not require such certainty, and thus it is more adaptable.

An additional comparison between Baillie and the other canonical Romantic poet to have written about capital punishment, William Wordsworth, further illuminates the way in which Baillie's work conduces to value inquiry. Taking the opposite position from Shelley, Wordsworth's *Sonnets Upon the Punishment of Death*, published to protest the declassification of many capital crimes during the 1830s, supports the extreme penalty. The reasons given include the sense that victims deserve more sympathy than criminals; that vigilantism flourishes when official prosecutions of crimes are weak; that execution is more merciful than life imprisonment or exile; and that the death sentence may lead some prisoners to religious conversion, repentance, and salvation.[97] The definitiveness of the position taken in the sonnets closes off inquiry in ways that are surprising and disappointing compared with Wordsworth's more characteristically ambiguous works. Reader response is limited to assent or objection, with the latter predominating from the first criticism by "weak-minded humanitarians" (in Wordsworth's own phrase) to recent analysis by Sharon Setzer, who admits a "bias" against it.[98] It takes an exceptionally accomplished reader like William Galperin to find unintended irony in the sequence and to advance a contextual reading in which the sonnets encourage a questioning of authority. They expose, he argues, the arbitrariness of authority that justifies the notions of duty and punishment in the sequence.[99] Following Galperin's work, the sonnets become more readily available for value inquiry, but Baillie's plays are more fully available, especially to readers to have contradictory thoughts and feelings about the topic, because they more freely explore the conflicts at issue.

Baillie's plays acknowledge the competing values of justice and mercy—as does the *Introductory Discourse,* which calls for a society that is both "more just" and "more merciful."[100] To approach the goal of making the institutions of law and order more merciful without making them less just, the plays show the institutions as already flawed as embodiments of justice: they are riddled with vengeful officials, false accusations, and excessive suffering; justice exists literally outside of those official bodies. *Rayner* makes it possible to be critical of punitive norms without entirely rejecting the value of retribution, and thus they make it possible for even conservative spectators to consider modest changes to the system, such as the declassification of many capital crimes or an expansion of the court's discretionary powers. At the same time, they do not close off opportunities for more radical reconceptualizations of justice that might include the elimination of all death sentences.

THE HEART OF MIDLOTHIAN

It may be disorienting to turn from *Rayner* to *The Heart of Midlothian,* for at first glance, the narrative seems more intent on reinforcing the sympathy logic that distances law keepers from lawbreakers than in revising it. Only in the case of Madge Wildfire does the narrative stress recognizing the captive's humanity. In the cases of Wilson, Porteous, Meg Murdockson, and Effie Deans, as well as in reflections on the appearance of the gibbet in the landscape, fear dominates the presentation. These scenes surely project much of what Ian Ward refers to as Scott's "almost pathological dread of civil unrest"[101] into the novel, yet they show that fearful state of society as itself pathological. As Beiderwell has pointed out, the deterrent function of capital punishment that is accepted by narrative assertion early in the novel is undermined by interactions later in the novel: most of the witnesses to Meg Murdockson's execution do not know why she is being punished. Once rules have been broken, sympathy for the offender can seldom heal the social breach. After all, to cite another example from

Beiderwell, it's the crowd's sympathy for Wilson that leads to their brutality toward Porteous.[102]

Of course, sometimes it is possible that leniency toward a rule breaker such as Effie would reconnect her to her community,[103] and Scott valorizes the discretionary power—explicitly the power that the monarch has but implicitly, as I argue below, the power the court *should* have—that can spare her life. For Scott, the damage done by rule breaking can never be reversed, though it can and should be repaired on a case-by-case basis as he and many of his contemporaries believed it was in the Scottish courts of his day. But Scott saw rule breaking itself—or the potential for rule breaking—as a social problem that must be addressed before it occurs. Deviance to him suggested a failure in one's sense of obligation to others. Beiderwell defines Scott's interest in prevention as a political vision of a just state,[104] but it is also only a small step away from Hume's definition of crime as a failure to fulfill existing duties. In fact, the extension to inchoate duties may be seen as an example of the "declaratory power" by which Scottish judges could recognize new crimes.

As Farmer emphasizes, the declaratory power is controversial because it can so clearly be used in enforce conformity, but Farmer also points out that it is seldom used, and when it is invoked, it is usually to cover a variation of an already familiar crime.[105] Hume gives an example and defense of this power in the case of the "sending of an incendiary or threatening letter." According to Hume, the Scottish judge who was able to declare that act a crime upon its first appearance and sentence the sender to transportation prevented this kind of activity from becoming as widespread in Scotland as in England; he thus also prevented people from seeing a need to make this act a capital crime. Hume contrasts the Scottish situation with that in England, where the activity became widespread before legislation making it a crime could be passed; the legislation consequently appeared as a response to a "flagrant and alarming" trend and made the crime a capital offense. For Hume, then, the power of a judge to recognize and classify certain behaviors as criminal does more to discourage them than does the example of harsh punishment. He argues that England undermined its ability to prevent crime with its excessive number of harsh statutes that it then handled with an "infinite number of pardons and commutations of punishment."[106] Hume's line of thinking could clearly serve as a springboard for Scott's interest in preventing crime by declaring community standards and encouraging people to fulfill their roles within those guidelines.

To explain this interest in interactionist terms, one would see deviance as an inability or refusal to take the role of others, to imagine how one's behavior responds to their gestures, and to care about the effects of one's responses on others. Rule breaking thus becomes an unsympathetic, selfish, or hedonistic response that shows indifference to the suffering one's acts might cause. In a "just world" scenario, it would "deserve" to be met with fear, segregation, or equivalent lack of sympathy. But it is preferable to prevent such failures. The time to bring sympathy into social relations is before rule breaking occurs, when it can create the sense of obligation that inclines people to embrace, respect, or at least conform to a community's standards and that thus effects integrative social control.[107] On the whole, Scott's work is devoted to fostering respectful interactions that would prevent rule breaking from occurring.

For Scott, the effort to achieve social integration is no small and finite task but an act of continuous reconstruction that must be carried out by people of all ranks in society. People must build onto their communities as scholars and professionals must, in the figure I have quoted from Scott in the introduction, add onto the castle of law. In chapter 4, I examine the community built in Roseneath; in this chapter, I examine factors that threaten to destroy community in the main plot of the novel. Specifically, I concentrate on Scott's portrayal of the fearful social relations created by lawbreaking and punitive responses to it. Following Ian Ward, I read *The Heart of Midlothian* as Scott's "critique of English law" in particular and of "law in general,"[108] but instead of focusing on Scott's pursuit of a new constitution, as Ward does, I focus on Scott's pursuit of an interactive solution to the problem of entrapment in legal and social structures.

The most direct connection between harsh punishments and fear of the lawbreaker as a threat to the community—indeed, to the idea of social order itself—is made during Effie's trial. Everyone involved perceives the statute against infanticide as exceptionally harsh. Effie's and Jeanie's predicaments arouse the sympathy not only of the crowd gathered for the trial, who "all, even the very rudest and most profligate, were struck with shame and silence" when Jeanie and David Deans arrive, but of the judge who "repeatedly wip[es] his eyes during the proceedings" (213, 232).[109] But the spectators' sympathy has been superficial; they "soon forg[e]t" the emotion of the moment and lapse back into the selfish or self-protective behavior that the narrator finds "natural to the degraded populace of a large town" (212). The judge's fear of lawlessness, which is greater than his sympathy, leads him to defend the statute and the capital sentence despite his sense of their injustice in this case. The judge's fear is aroused by Effie's lawyer's criticism of the given statute as "entitled to no favourable construction" (233), which implies that the court should somehow have the discretion to disregard or alter it in this case. The judge decides that an exception cannot be made because, he states: "[t]he present law, as it now stood, had been instituted by the wisdom of their fathers, to check the alarming progress of a dreadful crime; when it was found too severe for its purpose, it would doubtless be altered by the wisdom of the legislature; at present it was the law of the land, the rule of the court" (234). Rather than risk disruptions of collective order manifested by crime—or unofficial challenges to the law—the judge is willing to live with the rule—even tyranny—of indiscriminately punitive statutes.

To readers familiar with the conditions of English and Scottish law when this novel was published in 1818, such lines about the "wisdom of the legislature" must ring with irony. As I have indicated above, England was then trying to declassify numerous capital crimes created by injudicious legislation, and Scotland was quite effectively reducing its use of capital punishment through the court's discretionary power. Moreover, Scott calls attention to the long delay in legislative mitigation of the infanticide statute by noting that the capital sentence was changed to banishment in 1803 (528 n23)—a century after Effie's case. The irony is compounded by the association, which Ward points out, of this statute with English law,[110] though it was technically a Scottish statute dating from before the Union. I suggest that what makes the infanticide law an "English" law is its statutory nature and that the novel's criticism of it is a criticism of the privileging of any statutory law over common law.[111] Whereas Scottish officials could not exercise discretionary power in cases governed by statute, they could exercise it in cases involving common law, and they were taking national pride in doing do as early as 1797 when Hume first celebrated the practice in his *Commentaries*. The injustice in *The Heart of Midlothian* is caused by a lack of discretion. Thinking and feeling people cannot act justly toward Effie because they are trapped in a legal structure. The statutory approach to law fetishizes law in the abstract. The common law approach, especially as taken in Scotland where individual precedents did not weigh heavily, treats law as more flexible: it is a device for solving problems in social relations, and it must be continuously realigned with the values of the community using it. The injustice of Effie's execution is ultimately prevented by an act of discretion, the pardon by the monarch, but the novel clearly invites readers to see that the case should never have gone so far.[112] Scott raises the possibility that the legal system should be exclusively a common law system and always subject to the discretionary power of its judges.

Although such a proposal has political and nationalist implications that reinforce Andrew Lincoln's reading of the *Heart* as Scott's "passive resistance" to the English governance of Scotland he publicly endorsed,[113] I believe that Scott's position stems more from social than political concerns. The valorization of the law in the abstract, like the fear of lawlessness that follows from it, involves a misunderstanding of social structure (or at least what is a misunderstanding from an interactionist standpoint). It assumes that structure transcends human action and that it does and should determine what people can do. For Scott, as for later interactionists, structure is simply the accumulated interactions of a society: it is always in a process of being reshaped by ongoing activity. The problem of structural entrapment—of being bound by "past chains of agency" (to repeat the definition of structure I quoted from Lachmann in the previous chapter)—that the novel poses invites readers to rethink social relations, and the emotions and values informing them, in very thorough and extensive ways. Like spectators of *Rayner*, readers of *The Heart of Midlothian* cannot rest content with its representations but must rise to the interpretive challenge of connecting them to other lived and literary experiences and discovering how the addition reforms their knowledge.

The interpretive challenge of the novel comes not only from the cognitive-emotional dissonance represented in and aroused by Effie's trial, but by the fears, mixed feelings, anxieties, and contradictions surrounding other scenes of execution. For instance, chapter 2 contains what looks like a narrative endorsement of public executions as the narrator questions the relatively new practice of locating the scaffold near the prison and eliminating the procession to a distant site:

> The mental sufferings of the convict are indeed shortened. He no longer stalks between the attendant clergymen, dressed in his grave-clothes, through a considerable part of the city, looking like a moving and walking corpse, while yet an inhabitant of this world; but, as the ultimate purpose of punishment has in view the prevention of crimes, it may at least be doubted, whether, in abridging the melancholy ceremony, we have not in part diminished that appalling effect upon the spectators which is the useful end of all such inflictions, and in consideration of which alone, unless in very particular cases, capital sentences can be altogether justified. (28)

But this acceptance of the deterrent function of the spectacle is subverted not only later in the novel, by the ignorance of the crowd at Meg Murdockson's hanging on which Beiderwell has remarked, but in this same early chapter that begins with a reference to the "victims of justice"; furthermore, the sense of the "fright with which the school-boys" saw the gibbet is offset by the implication of thrill seeking in Mrs. Howden's description of the children's truancy from school in order to watch Wilson's hanging and her comment that her granddaughter "had just cruppen to the gallows' foot to see the hanging, as was natural for a wean," when the shooting started (48). In this society, children are socialized to watch executions, but the lessons they are supposed to learn are not clearly delineated.

The reactions of adult observers are governed by self-interest, as the narrative analysis of differing attitudes toward Wilson and Porteous make clear. Though "in most cases," the "populace [through] good-nature . . . forgets the crime of the condemned person, and dwells only on his misery" (28), this general goodwill prevails, according to the narrator, only "where [spectators'] own prejudices are not concerned" (32). In the latter cases, self-interest either increases or decreases sympathy. It increases it for Wilson because many of the spectators can or wish to put themselves in his place as a smuggler who is resisting English tax law in Scotland and as a generous person who helps his cohort to escape (32). It decreases it for Porteous because spectators cannot or do not wish to put themselves in his place as an overzealous English authority figure. They display these feelings with different responses. They want to see Wilson "rescued at the place of execution" (32) — a maneuver actually planned but foiled by mistiming. They want to see Porteous hanged. In his case, they assemble "to glut their sight with triumphant revenge" (40), and when the official spectacle is delayed, they take matters into their own hands and carry out the sentence on their own. The differences are significant not only for showing opposite courses of action devolving from the same sympathy for Wilson that Beiderwell has observed but also for casting doubt on the function of sympathy after lawbreaking has occurred.[114] According to the narrative analysis of these cases, sympathy for the lawbreaker does not necessarily evidence the development of the social self or a humane outlook; it still may express narrow interests. More broadly improved social relations require the overcoming of self-interest at an earlier stage.

The novel suggests that, after rule breaking has occurred, sympathy for rule breakers is best left to the discretion of the legal system. This possibility is raised by the case of Madge Wildfire, who should be saved by a humane magistrate from a hostile mob. The keeping of order by the execution of wrongdoers may actually be parodied in the crowd's treatment of Meg Murdockson and Madge Wildfire as witches,[115] for that crowd is motivated by a fear that is unmasked as superstition. Explaining why the crowd seizes Madge after the hanging of her mother, the narrator states ironically that "their wisdom imputed to witchcraft" (393) a recent epidemic among cattle in the area. Led by "butchers and graziers cheifly"

(392–93), i.e., by those whose interests were most directly affected by the loss of the cattle, they turn Madge into a scapegoat for their misfortune, inventing her identity as a witch so as to make her available as an object to punish and on which to project their anger, frustration, and sense of injustice. Yet the "injustice" of their loss is clearly not Madge's fault, and their behavior exemplifies Mead's remark that punitive justice unites a group in the "solidarity of aggression."[116]

Against this superstitious hostility, Scott pits a view of Madge as mentally ill. This view is held by the narrator, who calls her "the poor maniac," and by Archibald and Jeanie, who try to rescue her: "'She is mad, but quite innocent; she is mad, gentlemen,' said Archibald, 'do not use her ill, take her before the Mayor'" (393). This confidence that officials will act mercifully toward Madge is consistent with the Scottish legal system's exempting the mentally ill from punishment, and it is associated in the novel, as in the courts themselves, with humane thinking and feeling: Archibald is characterized as "a man of humanity" (393), and Jeanie's concern for Madge is presented as "a matter of humanity" (394).[117] Insofar as there is an institutional alternative—consignment to a workhouse—to the crowd's scapegoating of Madge for Archibald to seek, the novel shows the humanizing of the legal system and valorizes discretionary power. When not impeded by statutes, legal professionals may practice broad interventionism that creates a place for people who do not fit in existing social spaces.[118] The official protection of the mentally ill has the potential eventually to change less educated perceptions of them in ways that will make superstitious fear obsolete.

Scott's revealing the superstition behind the crowd's construction of Madge's "crime" of witchcraft parodies the official construction of Effie's "crime" of infanticide. Both crimes are the projections of fearful groups seeking to protect themselves from perceived threats to their social order. If parody is criticism by imitation, then the construction of the imaginary crime of witchcraft imitates and criticizes the construction of the imaginary crime of infanticide, for as the novel repeatedly points out, Effie's crime does not have to be proved by the existence of a body or any confirmation that Effie killed her baby. The crime is constructed by the imaginative projection of fearful lawmakers. The novel repeatedly refers to the constructive power of the law.[119] It is the "doctrine of constructive crime" that the more technically interested spectators at Effie's trial discuss (213), and it is the interpretive matter of "favourable construction" that Effie's lawyer uses in his unsuccessful attempt to force a reconstruction of the law in this case (233). The officials in this system treat the law with superstitious awe, essentializing it, allowing it to tie their hands in Effie's case. For them, its principles transcend individual circumstances. The transcendent quality is likewise invoked by Reuben Butler in his effort to prevent the hanging of Porteous, for he tells the mob that "it is murder even in a lawful magistrate to execute an offender otherwise than in the place, time, and manner which the judges' sentence prescribes" (69). While these comments, which accurately paraphrase Hume on the matter of how sentences are to be carried out,[120] hold out the supra-individual nature of the law's construction as a safeguard against individual abuse of power, the novel shows that in practice, the act of constructing has given way to the guarding of the given structure. If social relations are to improve, those officially responsible for social control must have the discretionary power to modify the law by human—and humane—interaction.

Mrs. Saddletree actually voices this pragmatic solution to structural entrapment. Told by her husband that the crime of which Effie is accused is a murder of the law's own creation, she replies: "if the law makes murders . . . the law should be hanged for them" (55).[121] By turning the power of the law back on itself, Mrs. Saddletree suggests the renovation necessary to make the law serve the community. People in this case *should* have had the power to act on their better judgment. Support for reining in statutory law can be educed from Hume. It follows from the stance he took on an historic controversy concerning the distinction between willful and "casual" homicide (i.e., accidental killing or killing in a "hot quarrel"). During the seventeenth century, some question had arisen as to whether the distinction, which had been part of ancient Scottish law, had been abolished or had expired with the Reformation because the ancient distinction relied upon an accidental killer's being given sanctuary, a practice discontinued with the Reformation. Though the distinction continued to be honored figuratively, no new law had been created to supply a new procedure. Hume concludes that the distinction cannot be abolished indirectly, as a result of the elimination of sanctuary; abolition would require a law directing addressing the two kinds of killing. Maintaining that "reason and humanity" require that deliberate and accidental killing be separated, Hume adds "and our Judges, as long as they have it in their power, will properly refuse to believe, that the Legislature could intend to pass so barbarous a law" as would equate malice with accident.[122] Hume's addition about the judges' refusal to believe what goes against "reason and humanity" suggests that the discretionary power ought to be able to overrule even statutory law. I suggest that Scott implicitly takes this position in *The Heart of Midlothian* by showing how much suffering could be avoided if only the law itself could have been challenged and reconstructed by a wise judge in Effie's case.

The fears of disorder that Scott never quite managed to overcome, along with the support for Union with England that he publicly maintained, lead him to surround proposals for reinventing the law either with humor, as he does by having Mrs. Saddletree articulate the solution, or with threats of rebellion, as he does when he depicts the Porteous rioters carrying out a legal sentence in an illegal manner. His fears, nevertheless, do not make him fetishize the given legal or social code. He shows the notion of a transcendent legal structure, an all-embracing statutory code, as clearly problematic, and he valorizes the judgment of individual human beings in individual cases. The explicit valorization of individual judgment occurs in the novel's denouement, which relies on the discretion of benevolent persons such as the queen and the Duke of Argyle to bring justice, mercy, and sympathy to social relations. Through their adjustments of an abstract legal system, Effie's sentence is mitigated, and within the Duke's jurisdiction of Roseneath, many of the characters have the opportunity to reconstruct their lives.

3

Baillie's Interventions

DEPENDING ON WHAT ONE COUNTS AS A REFERENCE TO CAPITAL PUNISH-ment, one could find allusion to that topic in almost half of the twenty-seven plays Baillie wrote.[1] Executions are staged, albeit not usually carried out, in *Rayner, Henriquez, Witchcraft, Ethwald II, The Bride,* and *The Dream.* Often, their purpose in the play is to illustrate the abuse of power. The acts of vigilantism and persecution central to, respectively, *The Family Legend* and *The Martyr* bring these plays into close association with the first group. Indeed, *The Family Legend* contains a reference to rising water as Helen's "executioner" in a scene showing that character deliberately left to drown on a sometimes submerged rock (3.1.494). Though executions are not dramatized in *The Stripling* or *The Homicide,* the gallows looms figuratively over the thoughts and actions in these plays about characters on trial for capital crimes. It looms likewise over the plot of *The Separation,* which deals with the affective bonds between a murderer and his wife. Though the topic is obviously more suited to tragedy than comedy, passing allusions to execution in comedies such as *The Election* and *The Siege* sometimes serve strategic purposes. In the former, for instance, as I point out in chapter 7, the reference illustrates the speaker's character.

In representing or alluding to executions, Baillie habitually directs attention to the humanity of the prisoner and the inhumanity of punitive justice, creating opportunities for spectators to critique the interactions that define criminality. She exposes the failures in interpretation and sympathy through which social relations disintegrate and, conversely, the successes in those thoughts and feelings through which positive social construction occurs. Often, the plays enact behaviors described in the *Introductory Discourse,* especially in the matter of sympathetically observing the prisoner to learn about the self and others. Most plays involving the problem of capital punishment contain a scene that, in the language of the *Introductory Discourse,* "lift[s] up the roof of [the] dungeon"[2] and enables us

77

to study the thoughts and feelings of the captive, though those thoughts and feelings are not always so profound as Rayner's. In addition, Baillie often pointedly contrives dialogues in which characters ask jailers, confessors, or visitors how the prisoner looks and acts, much as the crowd in *Rayner* eagerly listened to one person's account of an execution he had witnessed. In fact, a discussion between servants in *The Stripling* echoes the language in which the clown in *Rayner* expressed his desire to learn to watch executions. When one servant returns from visiting his employer in prison, the other asks for a detailed description of the prisoner's appearance, because, he says, "I wants hugely to know how he looks, and how / he demeans himself upon it." His coworker replies that "he demeans himself like a man," and together the servants express sympathy for their employer and blame others for leading him astray (1.2.553). With such scenes and dialogues, Baillie's playwriting *performs* her *Introductory Discourse*, socially animating its structure. She enables spectators to participate in the investigation of human nature and social interaction that would lead, in the terms of the *Discourse*, to a more just and more merciful world.

Though Baillie's plays do have recurrent techniques and themes, they nevertheless show considerable range in the events they treat, the angles of vision they take, and the questions they raise. To give some indication of the extent of Baillie's interventions in problems of criminal justice, I examine four plays—two, *The Dream* and *Henriquez*, from the passions series and two miscellaneous plays, *The Stripling* and *The Homicide*—that are organized around a capital crime and oriented toward developing sympathetic social relations but that present different interpretive challenges to their spectators.

THE DREAM

The Dream, a tragedy on fear in the passions series, presents execution as a frightening practice, but not because of any deterrent effect the example may have on potential lawbreakers. Instead, it is the prisoner himself who is so terrified by the ordeal he faces that he dies on the scaffold before the axe falls on him. What spectators should fear, however, is the abuse of power and obsession with revenge that motivates this sentence, for any notion of justice or humanity is swept aside by hostility toward the criminal. The play challenges spectators to see how arguments for the common good may harbor selfishness, superstition, or fear and to consider whether a more sympathetic view of the criminal might promote greater good.

The plot, set in a fourteenth-century Swiss monastery, begins with an act of scapegoating. Several monks have had a dream, vision, or hallucination in which a figure commands them to get a member of the Imperial army to spend a night at the monastery atoning for some unspecified wrong; if they fail to do so, the plague afflicting the village will spread to the monastery. Eager to interpret this dream as true, the Prior entreats General Osterloo to provide a man, chosen by lot, to perform this penance because, he says repeatedly, "the lives of the whole community depend upon it" (1.2.262). The lot falls to Osterloo himself.

The dream, and the Prior's interpretation and motives, are called into question by the skeptical monk Benedict, who suspects that the vision grew from one monk's bad dream exaggeratedly recounted to suggestible brothers (2.2.266), but spectators need not rely on Benedict alone to evaluate the Prior's decision. The Prior reveals his own character in his treatment of Osterloo. As the plot unfolds, we learn that Osterloo had long ago murdered the Prior's brother because he had stolen the affections of a woman Osterloo loved. The Prior wants revenge for the crime and will be satisfied with nothing less than Osterloo's death. As Benedict tries to moderate the Prior's hostility, spectators see two different ways of responding to wrongdoing.

Osterloo's confession, which the Prior hears in the presence of Brothers Benedict and Jerome as witnesses, is more like a trial or interrogation than a religious ritual. Like the interrogation of Waverley by Melville and Morton in the novel Scott published two years later, the scene shows how an official's bias constructs a prisoner's identity.[3] The Prior is an inflexible judge. Once Osterloo has admitted his guilt, the Prior sees him only as the "murderer." He will not consider the alternative identity of "penitent" that Benedict proposes (2.2.267). The Prior also does not recognize Osterloo's humanity. His lack of sympathy is especially obvious in the scene on the scaffold, where he expresses impatience with the monks who are soliciting remembrances to his soldiers from Osterloo. The Prior states, "angrily" according to the stage direction, "There is too much of this: and some sudden rescue may prevent us" (3.3.275).

Spectators might sympathize with the Prior's loss of his brother if his inhumanity were not so extreme. Urged by Benedict to devise a penalty other than death, the Prior refuses, admitting "I can think of nothing but revenge" (2.2.268). It becomes clear that the Prior uses the idea of the common good for his own narrow ends. Though he claims that the execution of Osterloo will accomplish the atonement required by the vision and thereby save the monastery from the plague, he cares nothing for the danger to the monastery posed by the death within its walls of Osterloo.

Reminded by Benedict that Osterloo's soldiers will hold the monks accountable, the Prior replies only that the monastery's own troops can defend it (269). The Prior lacks sympathy not only for Osterloo and for the other monks but also for the villagers who seek the monks' help. Like all the monks except Benedict, the Prior is reluctant to minister to the sick for fear of catching their disease (2.3.269–70). Even if this portrayal of the monastery as a selfish and self-enclosed society owes a large debt to the anti-Catholic conventions of Gothic fiction, it is on that account no less conducive to value inquiry over the problem of punitive justice. As Beiderwell says of Scott's placing the brutal punishment of treason in the distant past, the attempt at distancing only makes the connection with the present clearer.[4] Benedict's characterization of the Prior as a selfish authority figure quite willing to abuse his power makes him an example of a judge or magistrate most in need of the training in sympathy Baillie's plays provide. *The Dream*, then, follows up on the singling out of legal professionals in the *Introductory Discourse*, though Baillie includes more direct reference to judicial corruption in *The Homicide*. More broadly, *The Dream* encourages spectators to become critical of retributive values and open to the more sympathetic thinking practiced by Benedict.

Benedict serves as something of a sympathy-broker or humanity-monger for Osterloo, though he is a cautious one and therefore one who can open even conservative spectators' minds rather than engage their defenses. In his own words, his motives for taking vows were "misfortunes and disgust of the world, not superstitious veneration for monastic sanctity" (2.3.271). When the Prior remarks that Benedict "hath no zeal for the order" (270) he makes a doubly meaningful statement. In the text of the play, the line refers accurately to Benedict's skepticism about the attitudes and actions of the monks as a group. In wider contexts that the play might call to mind, the line suggests skepticism about any given social order or structure. It suggests a willingness to ask what keeps structures in place and to adjust them when the answer is that they serve selfish ends. In his attitude toward Osterloo, Benedict focuses on Osterloo's repentence rather than his guilt. He does not propose a specific alternative sentence — other than something less than death — for Osterloo; rather, he sees developing Osterloo's penitent identity and reintegrating him into society in penitential terms as the responsibility of the monks. Insofar as they neglect to do so, the monks fail in their duty, in Benedict's eyes, and their failing may appear criminal in the eyes of anyone who defines crime in Baron Hume's terms as "the infringe[ment of] . . . those duties which [a person] owes to the community."[5] Benedict physically displays his disapproval of the monks' treatment of Osterloo by refusing to watch the exe-

cution. The stage directions report that he "turns his back" to the scaffold
(3.3.275). In Benedict, Baillie creates a serious counterpart to the clown
in *Rayner* whose sympathy for prisoners prevents him from watching executions. The clown does not progress from sympathy to critical consciousness, so he wants to learn to conform to his society's norms. Benedict has a highly developed critical consciousness that makes him protest
his society's norms.

With the uncertainty suitable for value inquiry, Benedict does not entirely rule out the possibility of capital punishment for Osterloo. What he
rules out is the possibility that the monks have a right to pass that sentence. In speaking with the Prior, Benedict urges him to leave revenge to
"the laws of the empire" (2.3.269), but in speaking with Leonora, the no-
blewoman who would help Osterloo, he says "it belongs not to us to inflict
the punishment of death upon a guilty soul, taken so suddenly and unpre-
pared for its doom" (271). As spectators connect lines and scenes from the
play with the experiences they call to mind, they may supply antecedents
other than the monks for Benedict's "us" and thus consider whether "it belongs to" a just and humane society to impose such a penalty. One specta-
tor/reader who did so may have been Walter Scott, who found *The Dream*
"extremely powerful."[6] Benedict's scruples about the execution of Osterloo may be seen as an analogue of Jeanie Deans's scruples about the execution of "The Whistler." Leaving aside the abstract and theoretical issue
of whether capital punishment is ever justified, Benedict is convinced—in
the pragmatic and personal terms most compelling to Jeanie Deans, Baillie, Scottish courts, and later interactionists—that it is not justified in Osterloo's case. As a result, he is willing to conspire with Leonora to free Osterloo from the monastery's prison—a plot that fails.

So far, I have considered only symbolic interactions occurring around
Osterloo, those in which he is not a subjective participant. In one way,
that approach exactly reflects what happens in the play and in most
criminal justice proceedings. Osterloo, like most prisoners, loses the ability to affect his fate. He becomes the object of others' interpretations
rather than a subject who joins in the creation of meaning. Such substitution of passive subjection for active or creative subjectivity is one of
the characteristics of the criminal justice system that Addams and Mead
wished to reform. For them, a just society would learn about and respond to the perspective of the lawbreaker,[7] and preceding them, in Baillie's and Scott's time as Farmer has indicated, Scottish courts began to
pay greater attention to the state of mind of the prisoner. In an allusion
that connects *The Dream* to this legal context as well as to Baillie's later
play *The Homicide*, Benedict wants to consider "the frenzy of passion" in

which Osterloo committed the crime, a factor that could mitigate the charge and sentence in a Scottish court.[8] Though it is doubtful from Osterloo's confession of stalking and ambushing his victim that he committed any crime less than murder, the allusion, late in the play (2.3.271), calls attention to how little consideration went into determining Osterloo's fate early in the play.

While Osterloo's thoughts, feelings, and character are irrelevant to those with power over him, they are not irrelevant to others in the play or to spectators. In fact, as a play on the passion of fear, *The Dream* purports to show the rise of that emotion to predominance in Osterloo's character and thus help spectators recognize warning signs of a dangerous condition they might avoid. Like the other plays in the series, it contributes to the legal and social responsibility of controlling one's passions that Hume asserts.[9] It is not, however, immediately apparent how control of fear would prevent the tragedy in this play. If Osterloo had not died of fear on the scaffold, he would not necessarily have remained alive when the Imperial ambassador arrived to offer him the protection of the court and to rebuke the Prior for overstepping the bounds of his authority. The axe is within seconds of falling when Osterloo dies and the ambassador arrives (3.3.275). It would seem more important to curb the jealousy and anger that led Osterloo to murder his rival or the vindictiveness that led the Prior to demand Osterloo's death. The fact that other emotions compete with fear for spectators' attention testifies to the complexity of the play and bears out Baillie's defense of her passion plays against critics' charges that they unrealistically isolate emotions from each other. Working out the perplexities that arise from the operation of fear in this play is part of its interpretive challenge.

One function of fear in the play is to humanize Osterloo. As a military officer with a reputation for harshness (1.2.261) and an admitted murderer, Osterloo has few qualities that elicit sympathy. Spectators whose sympathy logic evokes a "belief in a just world" might well see little difference between the General and the Prior and conclude that the former gets only what he deserves from the latter's sentence. Osterloo's exceptional terror at the thought of execution frees him from the stereotype of the harsh, brave commander and changes his behavior, leading him to ask for the Prior's mercy (2.3.269). This behavior prompts spectators to see him differently and possibly to sympathize with him as some of the monks and officers do. Typically, Baillie brings out this reaction in a dialogue over how the prisoner looks. In this instance, Baillie explicitly links the disruption of stereotype with a new view of humanity as an unnamed monk urges an officer guarding Osterloo to look beneath the badges of office —

the "brazen helmet" or the "woolen cowl"—at the person who is subject to emotion (3.3.274). Earlier in the play, another officer observing Osterloo remarks, "[i]t is a piteous thing to see him so beset" (2.3.269).

The inconsistency between Osterloo's fear of execution and his fearlessness in battle, which the play alludes to repeatedly and illustrates by having Osterloo fight boldly in his attempted escape (3.2.273), gives Baillie the opportunity to emphasize the link between character and circumstances that she posited in the *Introductory Discourse*. In fact, she takes the matter up again, specifically regarding *The Dream*, in the preface to the third volume of passion plays in which *The Dream* appeared. In that preface, Baillie defends her depiction of Osterloo in anticipation of the charge that a demonstrably brave soldier cannot consistently be said to fear death. Baillie argues that what seems inconsistent in terms of essential character is actually consistent in terms of situated behavior. Distinguishing between active and passive courage, Baillie analyzes the soldier's courage as a consequence of his definition of the combat situation[10] as alterable: he fights because he believes he can shape events to his will, and that belief allows him to act without regard to a fear of death. When faced with events that he cannot shape—or that he *believes* he cannot shape—to his will, he becomes logically and consistently fearful. The reciprocal, she says, also obtains. Men of "peaceful habits" who "would have marched with trepidation into battle, have died under the hands of the executioner with magnanimous composure."[11] For Baillie, such passive courage comes from a habit of defining situations by hope: the peaceful man is used to being in apparently unalterable circumstances yet at the last minute devising or benefiting from some strategy that changes them. The peaceful man is actually "better prepared" to bear the doom of a capital sentence because he "has often before, in imagination at least, been in a similar predicament."[12]

This prefatory analysis clarifies Baillie's conceptualization of passion. Emotions may be an essential part of human nature (as Forbes observes[13]), but they develop differently in different people depending on their circumstances. Baillie's interest lies in helping spectators recognize and alter familiar courses of development. Control of fear in situations comparable to *The Dream*, then, would not simply be a matter of transferring a courageous reaction from one setting to another but of learning new ways to deal with perceived threats—ways that replace the soldier's combativeness with a more active approximation of the peaceful man's hope for deliverance.

I wish to make two related points in connection with this preface before returning to the matter of Osterloo's fear. First, Baillie again takes the opportunity to counter gender essentialism by asserting that women facing execution "have always behaved with as much resolution and calmness" as peaceful men;[14] further, she uses the example of Osterloo, a male protagonist, to balance the example of Orra, the female and titular protagonist in her other tragedy on fear, so as not to give the impression that fear is a feminine emotion. My second point concerns Baillie's use of evidence. Her defense of her portrayal of Osterloo is based on what has been "very well ascertained" or what is known by "experience" about the conduct of soldiers and peaceful men and women under the various circumstances at issue. By the disciplinary standards predominating in sociology, Baillie's statements lack credibility because they do not document the means of collecting this data or specify what soldiers and prisoners in what battles or cases were studied. Even many interactionists who would not require quantification of this data would dismiss Baillie's statements unless assured that she was a firsthand observer of specified soldiers and prisoners. Though Baillie may very well have observed executions, she was never in combat. The source of her "experience" must lie in books and conversations, yet the "accuracy" of her depictions of matters she knew only in a secondhand way has been confirmed by those with firsthand knowledge. Byron's notorious comment about the masculinity of Baillie's tragedies[15] exemplifies such confirmation. If Baillie could reach an understanding of persons and positions she could only approach in imagination, she strongly testifies to the equivalence of literary and lived experience. Both prompt interpretive activity that constructs and reconstructs relations between selves and others.[16] Moreover, Baillie's prefatory references to what "has been found by experience"[17] encourage readers to check the assertion from their viewpoint; they thus effectively encourage the relation of private to public experience either by leading to what Denzin would call "epiphanies" in which readers would realize a connection between the two or by leading readers to criticize the assertion as contrary to their experience and then to become more self-conscious about what that experience is and how it relates to others.

In returning to *The Dream*, I shift focus from Osterloo as a subject who experiences fear to death as the object of Osterloo's fear, for that fear depends as much on what he interprets death to be as on how he interprets his ability to alter circumstances. Death may be the ultimately unalterable circumstance, yet there are many ways of defining its meaning. Baille's preface defines Osterloo's fear as a "horror . . . of the awful retributions of another world,"[18] and the scene in the play in which we observe him in his prison cell, trying and failing to obtain some consolation from Brother Jerome (3.1.272–73), gives us further insight into this interpretation. On one hand, Osterloo is preoccupied with the prospect of conscious interaction with people in an afterlife and of not being forgiven by them for his crime: "The dead are there; and what welcome shall the murderer receive from that assembled host?" On the other hand, he imagines an afterlife that is merely a void: "the unknown, the unbounded, the unfathomable" (272). What these two views of the afterlife have in common is a lack of humanity, in both literal and figurative senses. Indeed, Osterloo's reflections on his impending death begin: "Nothing but one short moment of division between this state of humanity and that which is to follow!" (272). The play shows, however, that Osterloo is not living figuratively in a "state of humanity" but in a society in which that quality is largely absent. In fact, one of Osterloo's earliest comments to the Prior when being sentenced to death is "this is inhuman!" (2.3.269). What Osterloo fears is unrelenting retribution. Baillie shows that that is not a supernatural force but an unsympathetic human power that spectators should fear enough to correct.

Along with *The Dream*, Baillie published an additional tragedy on fear, *Orra*, which deserves a brief mention here because it involves superstition, supernaturalism, and injustice, though it has no execution scene. In *Orra*, numerous characters take advantage of the titular protagonist's superstitious fear in attempts to gain their own ends. Specifically, they imprison her in a "haunted" castle to frighten her into agreeing to an arranged marriage. Orra is rescued by the man she really wishes to wed, who appears disguised as a ghost, but the apparition so terrifies her that her mind becomes permanently deranged as a result. Reading through theories of "hauntology," Julie Carlson finds the play indicative of Baillie's deep concern for justice: the ghosts of the past return in the present because the forms of oppression they represent have not been laid to rest.[19] Focusing more on Orra's resultant mental collapse, Frederick Burwick also finds the play haunted by injustice. In his reading, Orra's fate reveals Baillie's familiarity with "aberrational psychology," a topic on which her brother, Dr. Matthew Baillie, was an expert. Baillie's interest was both clinical and humane: she was sensitive to the "devastating" effects of mental illness on those suffering from it as well as those who try, and often fail, to cure them. Orra's affliction is doubly unjust because it is not caused simply by an inexplicable force of nature but by human cruelty.[20]

Burwick's allusion to the failure of Orra's illness to respond to a "moral cure"[21] raises interesting questions about the relation between Baillie's plays and the particular therapy for mental illness known as the "moral cure" or "moral treatment." If, as Rebecca Stern argues, a reaction against the moral treatment can be seen in Victorian sensation fiction, I suggest that it may be plausible to see a favorable response to it in Baillie's plays. The moral treatment in question refers to the therapy pioneered by William Tuke during the 1790s by which the mentally ill were encouraged to practice sane behavior. Asyla were made to look like private homes, and patients were coached through social rituals, such as dining, in the hope that this "social training" would teach them sufficient "self-restraint" to allow them to function outside the institution. In Stern's words, the therapy amounted to "acting classes for the mentally ill."[22] Baillie's goal of teaching spectators to function more sensitively in the world outside the theater and to curb their own rising passions so as not to suffer the fates of the characters in her plays seems an analogous *preventive* therapy. Her plays would reach spectators before their obsessions destroyed their personal and social lives. According to Stern, moral treatment appeared threatening to many in the sane world because it so openly endorsed what we have come to call "performative identity."[23] I need hardly repeat that this concept is also central to Baillie. Stern sees a notable reaction against performative identity in the outcry against (im)personation in Victorian sensation fiction and in the growing influence of biologically based theories of identity.[24] It is tempting to consider the early popularity of moral treatment as a factor in Baillie's own Romantic-era popularity and the backlash against that therapy, with its openness to performativity, as a factor in the decline of Baillie's reputation in Victorian times.

Baillie returns to themes of superstition, mental illness, and justice in her late miscellaneous play *Witchcraft*, which I analyze in chapter 5. In the rest of the present chapter, however, I turn to plays that intervene more directly in the administration of criminal justice.

HENRIQUEZ

In *Henriquez*, a play on remorse in the passions series, the title character kills his best friend because he believes, mistakenly, that his friend and his wife have become lovers. Remorse gradually overwhelms Henriquez, and we see this emotion change his behavior from concealing the crime, to atoning secretly, to confessing publicly and demanding his own execution. We would expect his remorse to unite his society in what Mead called "the emotional solidarity of aggression,"[25] drawing them together in hostility against him as a transgressor of their norms and making them eager to exclude him. Instead, Henriquez's society unites in a desire to pardon him and retain him as a contributing member. The execution is only carried out because Henriquez, before confession, extracted a promise from the king "to let fall the law's unmitigated justice" on the murderer whose name he can reveal (5.1.379). Because Henriquez is an important military officer, the king readily agrees, then tries to void the agreement by telling Henriquez, "The public weal requires thy service; oaths / Adverse to this do not, should not, bind" (380). Henriquez, however, insists that he "soul demands this sacrifice" (380). Glorifying an ideal of justice as retribution, Henriquez and his peers construct his identity as a martyr to that principle and stage his execution as a celebration of his heroism.

In Julie Carlson's reading, this bizarre and disturbing play indicts chivalric values that glorify blood sacrifice to the realm.[26] On that ground alone, it exemplifies Addams's notion that plays can expose received "moral instruction as platitudinous and effete."[27] But *Henriquez* offers further opportunities for value inquiry. Both Henriquez and his society accept a narrow definition of justice as retribution in kind, and they do not alter the notion even when the king verges on seeing that it does not serve social good. Spectators, however, can see devotion to that principle as questionable, for it makes Henriquez's remorse oddly selfish: he becomes more focused on and self-righteous about his commitment to the letter of the law than on atoning for wrongdoing. Instead of criticizing that point of view, the king adopts it, deciding that Henriquez is a "noble malefactor" whose descendants can "proudly" include "the very implements of execu tion" in their coat of arms (5.2.381). The play's exaggerated ennobling of the principle of retribution can prompt spectators to question the value that the characters accept and to consider whether justice might be conceived in any other terms.

The climactic fifth act of the play amounts to a missed opportunity for change, as the characters cling to the old value of justice and their old selves instead of adjusting the situation to accommodate the emerging events by which Henriquez has gone from law keeper, indeed defender of the law, to lawbreaker. The promise Henriquez extracts from the king fixes in place the old structure of meaning, guaranteeing that it will not be altered by the new information. In effect, Henriquez imposes his definition of the situation on everyone involved. Only one character, Henriquez's wife, Leonora, sees how manipulative he is being—"in what *he deems* the right, / He is inflexible," she states—and urges the king to take control of the situation, but the king replies that he cannot command men's wills (381, emphasis added). At one level, such a statement from a monarch conveys a remarkable sense of respect for his subjects, but at another level, it reveals a view of social interaction limited to the dichotomy of commanding or conceding. What spectators should see is that alternatives are needed.

One alternative would be perpetuating the discussion with Henriquez but focusing more clearly on how his service is needed. In the existing discussion, the king only asserts *that* it is needed, presumably in the same terms as in the past, but as a lawbreaker, Henriquez can no longer fill the role of law defender in exactly the same way as he had. If the characters had confronted changed roles and activities, they could have transformed themselves and their society. A passage from Mead on the growth of the social self can help to clarify the nature of the missed opportunity. Mead posits a situation like the one in the play, one in which a new value—social good—has emerged to compete with an old one—punitive justice. In Mead's hypothetical "field," old values "find a spokesman in the old self" while new values "find other spokesmen to present their cases." Mead emphatically states: "To leave the field to the values represented by the old self is exactly what we term selfishness." After elaborating on that term as indicative of ignoring everything except one's "habitual character of conduct," Mead describes the effects of selfishness on the given discussion of values: it makes it "take on the form of the sacrifice of the self or of the others."[28] These terms of sacrifice are exactly the terms in which Henriquez couches his demand to be executed, and as we will see in considering *The Stripling*, *The Homicide*, and *Witchcraft*, sacrifice is as problematic a concept for Baillie as for Mead. As the above essay continues, Mead argues that the value conflict "should not resolve itself into a struggle between selves but into such a reconstruction of the situation that different and enlarged and more adequate personalities may emerge."[29] This process occurs through role-taking and "reflective analysis." It may be helpful to consider this point in Mead's words: "In the reflective analysis, the old self should enter upon the same terms with the selves whose roles are assumed, and the test of the reconstruction is found in the fact that all the personal interests are adequately recognized in a new social situation. The new self that answers to this new situation can appear in consciousness only after this new situation has been realized and accepted."[30] To sum up, Mead states: "Solution is reached by the construction of a new world harmonizing the conflicting interests into which enters the new self."[31] The tragedy of *Henriquez* is that no such solution is even attempted, much less reached.

In practice, the process Mead's essay outlines involves much cognitive, emotional, and interpretive struggle, and Baillie's play does capture the difficulty of responding to emerging events. The drama teems with references to masked identities and concealed information; the characters do not fully know the circumstances they are in, the others they encounter, or even their own motives. Aileen Forbes reads this stress on concealment as part of Baillie's design for the passions series: the series is to reveal the "secret" of human passions, and the example of Henriquez reveals the process by which Henriquez becomes conscious of his passion of remorse and takes on a remorseful identity.[32] We can, however, also read Henriquez's success in so defining himself as a failure in interpreting the situation: it depends on what he does not or chooses not to know.

Misinformation motivates Henriquez's crime, his murder of Don Juan. Henriquez believes an anonymous letter accusing his wife and friend of infidelity, and he assumes that preparations for a meeting between Juan and Mencia are actually preparations for a meeting between Juan and Leonora (1.1,2). Instead of trying to learn more about what may be happening. Henriquez acts as if he understood the situation fully, and he becomes remorseful when he learns that he did not. We might say that Henriquez's crime is a failure of interpretation, for his reflections on what he has done are remarkable in their lack of attention to his motives. The problems of intention and provocation that dominate legal treatments of homicide, as I show in connection with Baillie's play by that title, do not figure in Henriquez's confession of his crime to the king. Henriquez's confession juxtaposes statements about his long-established friendship with Juan—an established interpretation of the situation—with statements about the act he committed that contradicted the given interpretation, but he leaves out the transitional meaning that prompted the act. For example, he states:

> He [Henriquez, speaking of himself in the third person] had a friend,
> . . . whose fost'ring love had been the stay,
> The guide, the solace of his waywad youth,—
> Love steady, tried, unwearied,—yet he slew him.
> A friend, who in his best devoted thoughts,
> His happiness on earth, his bliss in heaven,
> Intwined his image, and could nought devise
> Of separate good,—and yet he basely slew him;
> Rush'd on him like a ruffian in the dark,
> And thrust him forth from life. . . . (5.1.379)

After hearing this account, the king tries to supply the missing motives: "Thou in the frenzy of some headlong passion / Hast acted as a madman" (379). His explanation fits the action presented in the play when Henriquez kills Juan, which is presented by staging that juxtaposes Henriquez's coming to the mistaken conclusion that Juan betrayed their friendship (1.2.264) with his reappearance on stage carrying a bloodstained sword and muttering about "holy justice" and "righteous retribution" (2.1.365). It also evokes terms in which Baron Hume's *Commentaries* describe the "rage and heat of blood" that might cause someone to lose "presence of mind" and commit homicide.[33]

My point is not to defend Henriquez. As we will see in connection with a comparable case of impassioned killing in *The Homicide*, it is unlikely that Henriquez's act would be excused in a judgment informed by Hume's guidelines. My point is to note the absence of the excuse for or any interpretation of the killing of Juan in Henriquez's confession. In fact, when the king supplies this meaning, Henriquez denies it, redefining his behavior in terms of the "brooding thought" and "slow intent" that, as spectators will recall, it did not exhibit. Erasing the interpretive activity by which he moved from law keeping to lawbreaking, Henriquez inserts himself back into a previous situation of friendship, in which his new behavior does not fit. Given his familiarity with only combative or concessive responses, he can conclude only that the deviant behavior must be punished; society must exercise segregative control.

Spectators, of course, can be better judges of the represented actions than the characters. Baillie leaves it to us not to "join the procession" (5.5.385) following Henriquez to the scaffold but to open new social roads through interpretive interaction.

The Stripling

Literary and lived experience combine explicitly in *The Stripling*, which today we might call a "true crime" story. A note to the published text[34] indicates that Baillie based the plot on an incident reported to have occurred in Glasgow. Specifically, the adolescent son of a prisoner awaiting trial for a capital crime killed the only witness who could testify against his father.[35] The note does not say what crime the father committed, but in the play, the crime is forgery, which brings to mind another analogue for this work. I associate *The Stripling* with the Dodd case, the notorious affair in which a clergyman was executed in London in 1777 for forgery, despite Samuel Johnson's efforts to obtain mercy for him.

The case has an unusual connection with Baillie's family, for her uncle John Hunter conducted a medical experiment that tried to resuscitate Dodd's hanged corpse. The purpose of the experiment, which did not succeed, was to test Hunter's hypothesis about the effect of violent death on the "life principle": Hunter surmised that violence at first only suspends life and that quick action might therefore call it back.[36] I know of no reference to Dodd by Baillie, but her interest in the medical research of her uncles and brother,[37] combined with the notoriety of the case, makes it hard to believe that she could have been unaware of Dodd's history. Questions about Hunter's experiment continued to be posed in periodicals during the 1790s and even the 1820s,[38] keeping the case from fading out of popular consciousness.

An analysis of the case by John J. Burke, Jr. points out that Johnson did not like Dodd but intervened because he disapproved of capital punishment for crimes against property; it also points out the prominence of humanitarianism in the case. Both Boswell and Johnson's less famous biographer Sir John Hawkins present Johnson as acting out of "humanity," for which Boswell praises him and at which Hawkins sneers.[39] Since Dodd was not a malicious or habitual criminal but, like Arden in Baillie's play, merely a weak man who forged a promissory note to pay the debts he incurred by his "expensive habits of living" and "licentiousness of manner,"[40] the unyielding severity with which the court prosecuted him seems inexplicable until we consider why forgery was perceived as a dangerous crime during the eighteenth century.

According to Randall McGowan, forgery aroused much anxiety because it was perceived as a threat to the well-being of a commercial nation—one in which public and private interests required trustworthiness in the extension of credit and the payment of debts. Wealth and character were fused (or confused) in promissory notes "whose worth relied upon [the] personal credit and reputation" of the persons who signed them.[41] It had in fact been the increasing participation of private individuals in commercial transactions and the decreasing likelihood that all parties could be personally identified by each other that had prompted early eighteenth-century English legislators to define forgery broadly and punish it severely. They sought a way to know a person's character once and for all, to make sure that official documents represented character accurately, and to curtail any financial transactions—or social interactions—that departed from the norm. Before the forgery act of 1729 (2 Geo. II, c. 25), counterfeiting, altering or misrepresenting financial documents from individuals or private companies were not capital crimes; only forgery involving notes from the Bank of England or other large public companies could result in the ultimate penalty. After 1729, that penalty could be applied to falsely making or using a long list of private notes, bills, deeds and other financial instruments.[42]

From an interactionist perspective, this legal development betrays mistaken notions about the self and social relations. It assumes that character is an essential part of a person—a part that can be fixed in place and that, once fixed, should remain the same irrespective of time and circumstances.

It assumes further that character can be known in the abstract: documentation can substitute for interaction. Such a view of people as static entities could not be farther from an interactionist understanding of them as dynamic beings whose selves are repeatedly altered by encounters with others. Though there is a good deal of continuity in personal interactions, especially with respect to culturally valued character traits, character cannot meaningfully be conceptualized apart from lived experience. Insofar as the English forgery statute was designed to valorize disembodied transactions over personal interactions, it shares the shortcomings of many "grand theories" that seek transcendent solutions for social problems.

Predictably, a more personal and pragmatic approach was taken in Scotland.

In his introduction to the *Commentaries*, Hume singles out the kind of forgery that Baillie's protagonist commits to illustrate how differently Scottish and English systems handle the crime. Arden, Baillie's forger, received from Fenshaw a bill (in the sense of a promissory note) for a hundred pounds to help him (Arden) pay his gambling debts. Needing far more than a hundred pounds, Arden changed the amount to a thousand (3.[no scene divisions].560). For Hume, this kind of case involving "the alteration of bills, promissory-notes and the like, to the prejudice of the acceptor" illustrates the superiority of the declaratory and discretionary powers of Scottish judges. The first Scottish judge recorded to have confronted the crime used his declaratory power to define it and his discretionary power to sentence the offender to transportation. Subsequent cases in Scotland had been handled by common law and received sentences of transportation, but in England, "by certain statutes[, it] is a felony without benefit of clergy." Hume argues that the Scottish approach is both more effective in preventing the proliferation of such offenses because judges can define the criminal nature of a particular act without waiting for a statute to recognize it and more "merciful" to offenders because the early response makes unnecessary the harsh punishments that are usually sought when a statute is passed to halt what is by then perceived as a crime wave.[43]

But Hume does not rule out the use of capital punishment for a different kind of forgery—the counterfeiting of another person's signature on a document to the false signer's advantage, for he sees this deed of "presumptuously assum[ing] the person, and act[ing] in the name of another" (the crime that Dodd committed) as different from altering the amount on a note that bears an authentic signature (the crime that Arden commits).[44] Hume's distinction comes close to interpreting selves and social relations performatively. For him, the more serious crime is imitating someone in interaction; it abuses role-taking by pretending to be the other person rather than responding to the other's gesture. Arguably, altering the terms of a document is less serious, though still a crime, because it does not steal the other's very place in society. For Hume, the solution to the problem of misrepresenting the self is not a uniform or abstract way of "fixing" character but a commitment to better social interaction. While maintaining that capital sentences can be appropriate in some cases, he argues against the routine use of such sentences. Even in cases of forged signatures, the court should consider the peculiarities of every instance and should be free "to accommodate the correction to the whole circumstances of the offender, and the transgression."[45] Had Dodd been tried in Scotland, his life might have been spared by a sympathetic judge who recognized, as Johnson did, that his crime had "no very deep dye of turpitude."[46]

When Baillie was drafting *The Stripling* in 1805, the Scottish-English rivalry over forgery laws was entering a new phase as English legislators were that year drafting a new statute meant to make their country's broad and severe treatment of that crime apply throughout Great Britain.[47] The time was clearly right for a play like *The Stripling*, a play that would encourage an audience of judges, magistrates, and advocates, along with many participants in commerce, to rethink the connection between lived experience and abstract transactions. Dialogue in the play even links the perceived seriousness of forgery with the values of "a commercial country" (1.1.552) and thus makes the tension between material and moral development a perplexing issue.

The play exposes the problem of (con)fusing character with credit through its portrayal of Robinair, the witness against Arden. Robinair, a successful social climber on his way to being a baronet (2.3.559), has more "character and credit" than Arden in this society (2.3.557), but Robinair acknowledges in private that he "live[s] with some credit" in the world by "show[ing] specious sentiments" (2.3.555, 2.1.555). By allowing her audience access to private conversations between Robinair and Bruton, an unwilling confederate whose gambling debts have put him in Robinair's power, Baillie carries out the plan in her *Introductory Discourse* to show what "men are like in the closet,"[48] and in this case, she reveals that Robinair is an ethical counterfeit. He is "mad with [the] prosperity" he has achieved by habitually taking advantage of others' weaknesses (2.3.559). "I will make a man of thee, Bruton," Robinair tells his associate, urging him to join in a scheme to ruin yet another victim. Bruton replies: "Could you restore me to the man I was, when you first took me up, I should ask no better fortune, and take my leave of you for ever" (2.3.559). The example of Robinair shows that documentation cannot replace interaction. A person may acquire a creditworthy reputation yet nevertheless behave dishonestly. Even in the large, complex, commercial metropolis of London, interaction remains the surest guide to knowing who a person is at particular times and in the range of circumstances that comprise social life.

Though spectators might feel relieved when so mean a witness as Robinair is killed, the plot device borrowed from the Glasgow case (according to Baillie's note) raises additional questions about criminal justice. It inverts the deterrent argument for capital punishment. Instead of discouraging others from breaking the law, the harsh sentence actually leads young Arden to commit murder in a desperate attempt to save his father. The stripling has learned the lesson that Samuel Johnson feared would be taught by the use of capital punishment for property crimes. As he wrote in *Rambler 114*, an early plea for declassification, "to equal robbery with murder is . . . to confound . . . the gradations of iniquity, and to invite the commission of a greater crime to prevent the detection of a less."[49] Moreover, in the play, the capital sentence creates additional opportunities for Robinair, before his death, to victimize Arden's family. Robinair plans to testify against Arden in order to revenge himself on Mrs. Arden for rejecting his sexual advances (2.1.555), and he tells her that he will avoid testifying if she will grant him the favors he wants (2.3.557). Though Arden agrees with his wife's refusal on the ground that Robinair probably would not keep his promise, he nevertheless "almost" wishes that she would make this attempt to save him. Overall, the play exposes what Mead later called the "discrepancy between legal justice and social good."[50] The plot of the play, Galsworthy's *Justice*, that Mead praised for its focus on the stated discrepancy involves a harsh, albeit not capital, sentence for forgery.[51] In *The Stripling*, the legal justice, or statutory inflexibility, of the penalty attached to the crime inhibits the social good that might come of treating the offender more sympathetically. With the capital outcome looming, social relations disintegrate, social problem solving stalls, and the social self is sacrificed. These effects are especially apparent in the stripling's self-defeating behavior.

In the Glasgow incident and in the play, the murder of the witness does result in the prisoner's being set free, but it also results in the death of the son. In Glasgow, the son is executed for the crime, and in the play, young Arden is killed while resisting arrest. However desirable the sparing of the father's life may be, his mere release for lack of evidence does nothing to address the problems of his dishonesty, indebtedness, or gambling. His guilt and the financial losses that led to his committing forgery are revealed in a scene that lifts up the roof of the dungeon and lets us witness his confession to his son (3.559–60). In a community with numerous and flexible patterns of interaction, Arden might have received sympathy that would have effected integrative control. Such a result would be consistent with the effects of sympathy in Clark's study: i.e., sympathy can make a rule breaker feel obligated and attached to the community.[52] But the London society to which these characters belong has only segregative control.[53] Furthermore, ironic dialogue questions its conscientiousness in administering the punitive system it uses. In two separate scenes, characters assert that "the innocent will never be condemned" (1.1.552 and 2.2.556). Since spectators are not certain of Arden's guilt until later in the play, the comments heighten the suspense, but their more crucial function is to raise doubts about the premise. The second scene does so explicitly. The line is spoken by one of Arden's jailers, who adds "in this country." In reply, young Arden says, "Ah! were that but certain, he would be / safe" (557). Like the line about Benedict's zeal for the order in *The Dream*, this line invites skepticism about the given social order. Arden is freed, but how well he can function in this society remains doubtful.

The limited, dichotomous pattern of interaction in this society that can only classify Arden as not proven guilty or guilty, at large in the world or excluded from it, is reflected in the socialization of young Arden. The stripling has no role models from whom to learn ways to cope with complicated situations, emotions, and ideas. Young Arden consequently responds emotionally but not cognitively to his father's plight. Knowing of his father's debts, he is not surprised to learn that he is in prison, but, he declares, "I loved him, nevertheless, / And will love him still" (1.3.554). Though his devotion is moving, it also leads him to deny his father's guilt until told of it by Arden himself, and then it leads him to the unethical plan of murdering the witness.

Throughout the play, young Arden's behavior is more a filling of stereotypes than an interacting with people. As much as Baillie's earlier plays that Burroughs finds grappling with the constraints of gender roles,[54] *The Stripling* shows the stunting effects of the limited roles available to young Arden. Aspiring to manhood, he thinks only of being a financial provider or a forceful rule-breaking champion. The former is evident in the conversation he has with his mother when she tells him that his father is in prison. "But what will / become of you till I am old enough to work for / you?" he asks. "Fie on't! I am old enough now: I am / sound of life and limb, and I have spirit enough / to face anything" (1.3.554). The latter emerges in his plan to free Arden, which he announces, without revealing the specifics, with the declaration: "I am more / than myself. The strength of a man thrills along / my new-strung limbs, and with it there is deliverance / for thee" (3.561). Following the murder, he tells his mother, "my father's deliverance is earned," and as he is dying, he repeats, "I have earned him for you, and he will take care of you" (5.3.569). In terms of the gestures he has read in his society, young Arden has fulfilled an adult role, but spectators can see how morally, socially, and personally unfulfilling his notions are.

That young Arden has also accepted the value of punitive justice is evident in his last words: "I have, I fear, offended my great and awful / Father; but I have prayed to Him to punish / and forgive me" (5.3.569). In his first reaction to his son's plight, Arden calls him "my noble sacrificed boy" (569), which introduces a highly problematic concept for Baillie and interactionists. As we will see in *The Homicide* as well as in *Witchcraft*, self-sacrifice is not necessarily positive. Good social relations depend on adjusting a situation so that it can meet the needs of all people involved, not on sacrificing the needs of one so that most others can be met. Mead addresses this point in the essay on the development of the social self that I quoted in connection with *Henriquez*. For Mead and Addams, criminal law reform involved changing the goal of the system from "the elimination of the person" to "the reconstruction [of] social activities," and the subjective participation of the lawbreaker was as vital to that goal as the participation of others in the community.[55] Self-sacrifice, or the voluntary "elimination of a person," does not further the goal of reconstructing selves and societies because it simply affirms old values and oppositions.

The last words of the play, spoken by Arden, consist of exclamations against foolish, selfish and vain behavior, and though they apply most clearly to Arden, whose "vanity and extravagance," "ambition and thirst for distinction," led him to commit the forgery that had such far-reaching consequences, they have some applicability to the stripling, whose eagerness to distinguish himself as an adult in this society led to his futile and foolish act. The ambiguity of the referent invites spectators to evaluate both characters critically but also to see that their shortcomings are the shortcomings of their social world.

THE HOMICIDE

Though set at an unspecified time in "the Imperial City of Lubeck, and at sea," *The Homicide* evokes the preoccupation with that crime in nineteenth-century Scottish courts. Its plot details differences between killing in self-defense and killing with provocation in terms that closely paraphrase Hume's *Commentaries*. The word designating the crime in the title of the play is also the designation of the relevant chapter of Hume's *Commentaries*: it is the general category under which he treats kinds of killing that are distinguished from each other partly by the motivation of the killer. In both the play and the *Commentaries*, the abstraction becomes meaningful only in connection with the symbolic interactions of particular people in particular circumstances. As Farmer has indicated, preoccupation with one kind of killing—culpable homicide, which includes homicide committed when provoked to great passion—increased in Scottish law when courts sought a substitute for the capital crime of murder and when they took a more interventionist stance in promoting socially responsible behavior. Cases of culpable homicide could amount to the trial of the prisoner's state of mind and heart.[56] Baillie's play stages such a case, challenging spectators to determine where the provocation lies. In the process, they must examine the extent to which the construction of crime and punishment varies according to sympathetic, fearful, or selfish attitudes.

Because the plot of *The Homicide* is intricate, I will divide it into segments for purposes of analysis. I treat the portions defining the crime before the portions involving mistaken and corrected identifications of the criminal, though these segments are intertwined in the play.

The Homicide centers on the killing of Baron Hartman by a Danish nobleman, Claudien, in an angry reaction to Hartman's defaming the character of Rosella, for whose love they are rivals. The play does not reveal exactly what was said. It gives us Claudien's account of what happened, along with his interpretation of his behavior. He admits that he did not act in self-defense but argues that Hartman's words amounted to sufficient provocation to justify his response. A comparison of Claudien's account of his crime and Hume's example of such a crime reveals how closely the play and the *Commentaries* coincide.

Claudien recounts his actions twice, first to his friend Van Maurice, then in court. His first account comes immediately after the killing, when distraught and covered with blood, he arrives at Van Maurice's house and exclaims: "He [Hartman] did attack me; from his hand I wrested / The clenched dagger—lunged it in his breast" (1.4.647). When Van Maurice takes this account as a narrative of self defense or at least of a deed done by "provocation," by "reckless, instantaneous impluse" (647), Claudien corrects him:

> Would it had been an instantaneous impulse! . . .
> I at the moment arm'd, he weaponless;
> I was the victor, he upon the ground.
> I might have saved his life, and meant to save it;
> But keen suggestions rush'd, I know not how,
> Like blasts from hell, all nature's virtue searing; . . .
> Athwart my mind they rush'd; and what came after! (647–48)

The arrival of Kranzberg and two "officers of justice" with news of Hartman's death prevents this dialogue from continuing, but when Claudien tells his story again in court, he attaches to it the justification of provocation first supplied by Van Maurice:

> He at the moment lay unarm'd; I, therefore
> Can make no plea of self-defence. But murder
> Deliberately devised, ne'er stain'd these hands:
> And if there be a man in this assembly
> Who loves a virtuous woman — ...
> Let him declare how he should feel on hearing
> Her fair name outraged by a sland'rous tongue. (3.3.663)

As a result of these circumstances, Claudien asks for mercy from the court, which grants it, for the following reasons stated by the judge: "Forasmuch as the murder of Hartman was not a premeditated act, but perpetrated, though unjustifiably, in a moment of provocation and passion; and further, that the criminal hath delivered himself up to justice, making full confession of the crime, we remit the punishment of death, and condemn the Count Claudien of Denmark to perpetual banishment from the city and territories of Lubeck" (663). In short, the court defines Claudien's crime as "culpable homicide" because of his state of mind when he committed it. Like the king in *Henriquez*, they have looked for evidence of what Hume calls *"Dole"* — "that corrupt and evil intention which is essential . . . to the guilt of any crime,"[57] but unlike Henriquez, Claudien has done his best to argue that he acted without criminal intent.

Claudien's account comes very close to the following passage in which Hume elaborates on self-defense by the example of a fight between "John" and "James": "if James, . . . disarms John, and tosses his sword to a distance; and if instead of using this opportunity to escape, or make himself master of John's sword, James shall follow up the accident with repeated thrusts at John, thus disarmed, and kill him; he has at least lost his pretensions to the plea of self-defence, however the case may be as to any other."[58] The other possible plea is culpable homicide, which differs from murder, according to Hume, because the killer "is not actuated by wickedness of heart, or hatred of the deceased, but by the sudden impulse of resentment, excited by high and real injuries, and accompanied with terror and agitation of spirits."[59] In the several paragraphs that follow, part of which I have quoted in chapter 2 in connection with Baillie's *Introductory Discourse*, Hume explains why people should be held accountable for such killings—because self-control of emotion "is a part of every man's duty"—and why they should nevertheless be treated mercifully—because self-control is an ideal to which people aspire rather than a condition they can always sustain; because judgment must consider the frailties of human nature and encourage improvement; and because excessive punishment would discourage prosecution and conviction of the crime.[60]

Claudien's sentence of lifelong banishment may seem inconsistent with this orientation toward mercy, but it is actually consonant with Hume's guidelines about the kinds of provocation that deserve clemency. It is unlikely that Hume or other Scottish judges would share Claudien's view of the adequacy of the insult to Rosella to justify his act. Though proud that the Scottish legal system was on the whole more lenient than the English, Hume was equally proud of its relatively greater severity in the matter of manslaughter. According to Hume, "It is no excuse in our law, that the pannel is in rage and heat of blood, though excited by some rude or contemptuous freedom taken with his person: This passion must be occasioned by some adequate and serious cause, some harm, as well as with present smart and pain of body; so that the sufferer is *excusable* for the loss of his presence of mind, and excess of the just measure of retaliation."[61] In short, homicide is excusable only in "situations, which require a more than ordinary strength of mind, and command of temper to withstand them; not in those where the pride more than the person of the man has been offended."[62] Hume criticizes as too generous a jury verdict of culpable homicide and a judge's sentence of transportation for fourteen years in a case from 1804 that bears some resemblance to the case in Baillie's play. Hume's case details a quarrel between two men, during the course of which one called the other's wife a "whore." Afterwards, both husband and wife followed the accuser. Reaching him first, the wife seized his arm, and he responded by striking her, though not hard enough to make her fall. Seeing this, the husband chased the man and stabbed him fatally with a bayonet.[63] As we can see from Hume's disapproval, he expected judges and juries to give as much weight to the duty of self control as to the recognition of human weakness. For him, the concept of "provocation" was not to be used as a rubber stamp for acquittal, as he believed it was in England; instead each case was to be evaluated for sufficient provocation to warrant loss of self-control.

Baillie's *Homicide* invites spectators to evaluate the provocation in this case, but to do so thoroughly, they cannot stop with Hartman. Behavior is not only a matter of individual character but of combined interactions. Hartman may be the vain, vindictive, and self-important figure he appears to be in the scenes preceding his murder, but he is also deceived by Rosella, who leads him on so as to divert attention from her relationship with Claudien, and manipulated by Kranzberg, who wants to create conflict among Hartman, Rosella, and Van Maurice that he can turn to his own financial advantage. (Kranzberg is a kinship relative of both Hartman and Van Maurice, and he is Van Maurice's heir.) The search for provocation in this play leads back through a chain of selfish, unsympathetic, and deceitful interactions that should prompt us to indict the social relations in this play. Rosella, Claudien, Hartman, and, above all, Kranzberg, are guilty of another kind of culpable homicide recognized by Hume and the Scottish courts—acting "without that caution and circumspection which may serve to prevent harm to others."[64]

Of course, I am applying Hume figuratively here. This concept of neglect was usually applied to careless driving or operation of trains or factory equipment. But, as Farmer argues, the expansion of legal inquiry into areas of omission, along with the analysis of provocation, shows an increased interest in discerning states of mind and directing social relations.[65] In such a context, Baillie's play reminds spectators of the duty of caring for others and helps them anticipate the consequences of negligent behaviors, such as Rosella's toying with Hartman's affections, that do not immediately seem harmful. By making spectators critical of these social relations, it also prompts them to imagine how social relations might become more careful or caring—or, in more Meadian terms, how they might engage more fully in the activity of "minding."

To explore the socially reconstructive aspects of the play, I turn to the segment of the plot involving the arrest and trial of the wrong person. Though Claudien ultimately confesses in court, he does so only after Van Maurice has been convicted and sentenced to die for murdering Hartman. He is thus a less selfish character than Zaterloo in *Rayner,* who does not manage to rise to this level of responsibility as long as doing so would have any adverse consequences for him. Regarding Claudien's conduct, we should recall that Claudien visited Van Maurice and confessed to him that he had killed Hartman. In response, Van Maurice helped Claudien escape from Lubeck by ship. A bloodstained dagger is found at Van Maurice's house, and he is accused of murdering Hartman. Though he could defend himself by exposing Claudien, he feels bound by honor and friendship to keep Claudien's secret, even at the cost of his own life. His feelings and decision to trust in heavenly justice if he cannot trust in earthly courts is revealed in a scene, typical of Baillie's plays, in which we look in the prison at the prisoner.

The play does not valorize Van Maurice's self-immolating behavior. As we have seen in connection with *Henriquez* and *The Stripling,* Baillie is consistently critical of such behavior, for reasons that can be illuminated in terms of Mead's consonant critique, and as we will see in connection with

Witchcraft, she does not valorize Violet's self-sacrifice. Although Van Maurice is certainly trying to think of others before himself, his response is a betrayal of the self. The social self, the minding mind, *engages* with others; it does not lose itself in or destroy itself for them. It deserves self-respect—an idea that is captured in Ardusoffe's (Van Maurice's lawyer's) exhortation, "do justice to yourself" (2.3.653).[66] In the play, that point is made by both Van Maurice's lawyer, who maintains that "death and disgrace must not be incurred from romantic adherence to honour" (2.3.654), and a judge, who criticizes the "romantic pitch" of honor behind Van Maurice's belief that he must respect the confidence of the killer (3.3.661). A century later, Addams voiced similar disapproval of the adolescent who invents a counter-cultural value system and "imagines himself as a stoical hero who mounts the gallows without flinching."[67]

Beyond offering an opportunity to question the value of self-sacrifice, the false imprisonment of Van Maurice occasions some of Baillie's most critical comments about capital punishment, such as this exchange between Van Maurice and Ardusoffe:

Van Mau.	Have you then, in the course of your legal experience, known instances of the innocent suffering death for imputed crimes?
Ard.	I have; even when tried by an impartial judge, and the fair laws of their country.
Van Mau.	But their memory was vindicated afterwards, else you had never been acquainted with such dismal perversion of circumstances.
Ard.	After many years, —nearly the lapse of half a century, it was discovered.

(2.3.653)

Such dialogue moves toward questioning any use of capital punishment on the ground that it may mistakenly kill an innocent person.[68] Furthermore, the play calls attention not only to the possibility of error but to the possibility of corruption, for Kranzberg wants Van Maurice convicted, whether he is guilty or not, so that Van Maurice will lose and Kranzberg gain control of his property (2.1.652). To that end, Kranzberg is rushing the trial so that it will be heard by a judge partial to his interest (2.4.656). Like the Prior in *The Dream*, he does not want any last-minute rescues to interfere with his satisfaction, and also like the Prior, he claims to be acting to remove a threat from the community (2.1.652).

The play stops short of confirming collusion between Kranzberg and the judge. Though the judge grants Kranzberg's request for an immediate trial, he is acting on the belief that Van Maurice tried to escape from prison, and he does not seem to know that Kranzberg arranged for a report of such an attempt specifically because it would accelerate the trial. The judge does, however, seem aware of Kranzberg's character when he tells him "thy humanity equals thy candour" (2.6.657). More clearly than the ambiguously referential words with which *The Stripling* ends, this remark conveys a double meaning. While the *Introductory Discourse* had indicated that judges, advocates, and magistrates need sympathetic curiosity to treat people humanely, *The Homicide* indicates that they also need a highly developed sense of social responsibility to resist the designs of such figures as Kranzberg. The play does not pursue the issue of judicial corruption; rather, it raises a cautionary flag about it, much as does Hume, who devotes most of a chapter to crimes stemming from carelessness or "wilful error" by judges.[69] By not focusing on corruption, the play can glance at other reasons why inhumane attitudes may permeate the legal system. Professionals may become inured to its brutality. Such is the case of the minor official in *The Homicide* of whom Father Francis laments: "Woe is me that human nature should come to this! The pride and spirits of that creature, how, rise on an occasion like this. The condemnation of a fellow-creature creates no other feeling in him, but the enjoyment of increased importance and comparative security!" (3.2.660). Many years before *The Homicide*, Baillie had caricatured such figures in the executioners in *Rayner*. Baillie's work encourages people inside and outside the legal system to look critically at its effects on those who control its practices as well as on those controlled by them.

The conclusion to *The Homicide* showcases—and, I posit, parodies—the deterrent theory of capital punishment—i.e., the belief that capital punishment provides a discouraging example to potential lawbreakers. Before Claudien confesses, the court imposes a death sentence on Van Maurice for the stated reason of making him an example to deter others from a crime perceived as excessively common or troublesome in a community. In this case, Baillie makes the crime wave an increase in murders "among people of noble condition" and the judicial response the "reviv[al] . . . of a law that has been too long laid aside": Van Maurice is to "be broken alive upon the wheel" (3.3.662). If parody is criticism by imitation, then this scene parodies capital sentencing in nineteenth-century courts by imitating the form and justification used but filling that form and rationale with archaic and brutal references. By bringing the past and present together, Baillie invites spectators to associate capital punishment with remote and obsolete attitudes that have no place in an enlightened culture. Like her use of axe-wielding executioners in *Rayner*, her use of this deterrent justification moves punitive justice off the stage of her spectators' present and makes space for them to imagine less brutal alternatives.

The need for an alternative is reinforced in *The Homicide* as well as in *Rayner* by the innocence of the accused. In fact, *The Homicide* suggests that Van Maurice is a scapegoat for a social problem created by elite conflict that the court has not addressed directly. Such a problem is more likely to be solved by preventive interventions that encourage more responsible behavior—interventions such as Baillie's plays, Scott's novels, and Hume's emphasis on the duty to be mindful of others. That capital punishment enacts a version of scapegoating is all the more apparent in *The Homicide* for the presence in that play of a traditional act of scapegoating. The traditional ritual occurs on the ship by which Claudien escapes from Lubeck. When a storm threatens to sink the ship, the superstitious crew conclude that they are being punished for allowing a murderer to sail with them, for they recall hearing Claudien murmur something about killing, and they use that reference to construct an explanation and solution for their predicament: the murderer Claudien must be thrown overboard to save the ship. Though vowing to fight anyone who tries to carry out that sentence, Claudien voluntarily jumps overboard, sacrificing himself for the crew (2.1.651–52).

This scene provides an important parallel between the superstition of the crew regarding Claudien and the rationalization of the court regarding Van Maurice. Both lines of thinking assume that segregative control will preserve their society, and the "primitiveness," as Baillie's spectators would term it, of the former situation comments on the latter. In addition, the scene prepares but disrupts a parallel between Claudien's and Van Maurice's acts of self-sacrifice. Claudien takes a calculated risk of surviving, as he indeed does, managing to swim ashore. He does not "sacrifice" his social self in the manner of Van Maurice. Given the parallels that the scene establishes, it is no wonder that Baillie considered it integral to the drama despite criticism to the contrary. The substantive importance helps to account for her leaving the scene in the play but offering an alternative at the end of the text for use by theater managers who claimed they could not stage the events at sea.[70]

In the end, neither the execution of Van Maurice, who is cleared by Claudien's confession, nor the banishment of Claudien occurs because Claudien and Kranzberg kill each other in a quarrel while still in court. Perhaps no other outcome could so clearly show the futility of the deterrent argument for capital punishment or the need for more integrative social control.

4

The Problem
of Poverty

Contemporary readers are uncomfortable with inequality. We perceive it as a social problem that should be corrected, and consequently most treatments of patriarchal and paternalistic social relations, especially those between rich and poor, are critical of these systems in which a large group of people remain in childlike dependence on a small number of benefactors. The concept of deference, by which the former are expected to show excessive gratitude for the latter, strikes us as degrading, and we read as ironic, disingenuous, or hypocritical the claims that deference captures the feelings that family members have for each other.

Such critical consciousness informs Elaine Hadley's presentation of patriarchy and deference in *Melodramatic Tactics*. She describes the melodramatic mode as a "profoundly reactionary" effort to salvage "a passing deferential society and the status hierarchies such a society nurtured." After establishing that "deferential system[s are] based on sympathetic exchange" between benefactors and dependents, Hadley stresses that "it would be anachronistic" to think of the sympathy involved in such a system as a "personal, spontaneous feeling" or "private emotion"; on the contrary, "sympathy, benevolence, kindness, and respect" were "modes of public and universal behavior, 'social feeling,' that . . . regulated welfare exchange and other forms of cultural interaction."[1] To some extent, Hadley's goal is to correct the anachronism by exposing the impersonality of this mode. She argues that deferential societies are maintained through ritualized social performances in which people of different ranks develop self-consciousness about their interdependence in an unequal system and that deferential societies were replaced by individualized relations in market cultures. Analyzing responses to this socioeconomic change, she contrasts Romantic poetry to the melodramatic mode. On the one hand,

Wordsworth's poem "The Old Cumberland Beggar" privatizes the formerly public, sympathetic feelings: the poem presents an unknowable beggar toward whom others act by consulting their own mental scripts. On the other hand, Dickens's *Oliver Twist*, a novel in the melodramatic mode, tries to bring social relations back into the public sphere.[2]

I approach the "anachronism" of personalizing the emotions of a deferential society in a different way. Following Christensen, I associate anachronism with "unrecognized possibility,"[3] and I see Baillie and Scott working toward societies in which the sentiments imputed to paternalism literally inform and transform all social positions. Though Baillie and Scott did not see inequality itself as a social problem, they did see poverty and oppression as social problems that should not only be relieved but prevented by caring interactions. Given the fact of inequality, Baillie and Scott would make nonelite positions livable and dignified, and they would charge those in elite positions with personal responsibility for those social others. But relations within this transformed system would not consist simply of dependent and benefactor roles. They would consist of mutually dependent roles in which people across ranks contribute to each other's welfare and provide for each other's needs, both in tangible and intangible ways. Scott projects these possibilities in his presentation of the beggar Edie Ochiltree in *The Antiquary*, which I treat later in this chapter in contrast to Wordsworth's "The Old Cumberland Beggar." Baillie projects them in her *Metrical Legend of Lady Griseld Baillie*, whom she presents as a role model of charity for Romantic-era women, and I examine that work in the next chapter. Through the symbolic interactions in these and other works, deference becomes mutual respect. These works open up an ongoing process in which social structure is transformed by a new emotional valuation as much as it is transformed by new cognitive definitions. The ongoing process leads beyond forms that Baillie and Scott could recognize toward those envisioned by Addams[4] and Mead and, beyond them, present-day interactionists.

Baillie and Scott approach this transformation in different ways, though their works share some common elements. Most notably, both are critical of elite behavior that falls short of responsive and responsible ideals, but Scott takes a more incremental and tentative approach to altering existing roles, one consistent with his preference for building onto the castle of law. Scott treats any relatively elite role—from lord of the manner to justice of the peace—in a way that can be illuminated by comparison to Mead's "generalized other."

As the generalized other in the present represents a sort of personification of the community, so this generalized other from the past represents a sort of behavioral legacy from all previous holders of such positions.[5] These predecessors do not determine the actions of future holders, but they show a variety of ways to contribute to the community through the duties associated with the given roles. In imagining her or himself in the place of various predecessors, the present role-taker has the opportunity to consider which ways enhance and which diminish the legacy and to carry forward the positive line. Through such a response, past failures can be avoided while past accomplishments are not only honored but renovated. The social self of the present role-taker develops when she or he reanimates the traditional role within the present community. As I show later in this chapter, this notion of a behavioral legacy is most important in Scott's conceptualization of the public roles of elite members of society, such as the Master of Ravenswood, but it can also apply to Jeanie Deans's performance of her role as minister's wife.

Before leaving this point, I would emphasize the importance of seeing the past generalized other in literally personal terms rather than as a mere abstraction. As I quoted in the introduction, Mead argues that the process of relating to a generalized other, though an abstract thought process, can "at any moment . . . become personal" and dramatic.[6] The social renovation that Scott would effect depends on taking social relations personally, and it is for that reason that the legacy of the past cannot simply be set aside even when the failings of some predecessors are recognized. Renovated social relations must involve respect for all others. Scott reflects this necessity through a deferential attitude toward the past: structures must be repaired, not razed; roles must be refigured, not refused.

Scott's and Baillie's interest in socially responsible roles becomes more meaningful when their work is contextualized with respect to the problem of poverty in their time. Controversies over the administration of the Poor Laws, the system that provided relief for destitute and disabled members of society[7], resounded in England and Scotland during the Romantic era until reforms were legislated for England in 1834 and for Scotland in 1843. Controversy centered on the matter of personal obligation. The old system was based on paternalistic notions of the duty of the elite; the new system, in England, was based on the operation of natural and/or market forces. The old system operated locally and personally; the new, nationally and as impersonally as possible. Scotland never adopted the most extreme new measures but later implemented more modest adjustments to the old system. In the context of struggles over the Poor Laws, Baillie's and Scott's works can be read as interventions that resist depersonalizing forces and turn an obligation to relieve poverty into a challenge to provide for social welfare. After outlining the terms of the Old and New Poor

Laws in England and Scotland, I examine criticisms and constructions of relevant roles in Scott's letters and in *The Bride of Lammermoor*, *The Antiquary*, and the Roseneath section of *The Heart of Midlothian*. In the next chapter, I examine the role model of Lady Griseld Baillie as well as the symbolic interactions between rich and poor in *The Bride of Lammermoor* and Baillie's *Witchcraft*, which according to her note, responds to Scott's representation.

Poor Laws

The Poor Laws operative in England and Scotland during the Romantic period were the retroactively named Old Poor Law, a centuries-old accumulation of statutes and practices. The Old Poor Law was replaced with comprehensively legislated New Poor Laws in England in 1834 and Scotland in 1845, though experimental changes were attempted much earlier.[8] The salient features of the old laws were decentralization, outrelief, and personal responsibility.

In each country, local units—kirk-sessions or parishes—of the national churches assumed responsibility for helping the poor in their jurisdictions. No larger body supervised or coordinated local practices, which thus could vary considerably. Decentralization affected eligibility for relief as much as responsibility for giving it. To be eligible, a person had to be "settled" in a parish. England passed detailed laws about how birth, marriage, and other conditions determined settlement; Scotland used a more informal system of assignment.[9] Money for relief came from voluntary donations as well as from compulsory payment of the poor-rate tax, with the former predominating in Scotland and the latter in England. Relief given usually consisted of a pension or goods to supplement what the pauper received from family or from his or her own work. It was called "outdoor" or "out-relief" in reference to the lodging arrangements of the recipients, who lived with their families or on their own, not in poorhouses or workhouses (which provided "indoor" relief). Anthony Brundage stresses that "kinship networks . . . were an integral part" of the old system, allowing it to minimize costs by restricting the most expensive provision of total indoor relief to people with no alternatives.[10] In less materialistic terms, the reliance on outdoor relief spread responsibility for the welfare of others throughout the community. Personal involvement and responsibility were the features of the old system valorized by its supporters.

If much can be said in favor of the old system, much can be, and has been, said about its faults. Critics in the nineteenth century as well as in our own time have attacked its paternalism, unevenness, and ineffi-ciency.[11] Like the laws against vagrancy that Toby Benis studies in *Roman-ticism on the Road*, the Poor Laws existed as instruments for social control. They allowed elite members of society to dictate the terms on which nonelite members could survive. The Poor Laws did so by restricting eli-gibility for relief. Vagrants, for example, were not eligible for relief, an ex-clusion that reveals anxieties about outsiders and anyone who strayed from conventional living and working arrangements.[12] To receive relief, one had to conform to norms of stability and industriousness. Especially in England, the requirement that one be settled in a parish created hard-ships for people who had traveled in search of work. Sometimes such people were "removed" to their original parishes for help; sometimes, they could petition their parishes for nonresident relief.[13] Begging was con-trolled in the old system in various ways. When funds were low in Scot-land, applicants for relief were sometimes issued licenses to beg; licensed beggars wore badges or blue gowns as a sign of this authorization.[14] In England, pensioners were often forbidden to supplement their income by begging, and to ensure that they could not easily obtain donations if they tried, they were required to wear badges that would announce their parish dependence to anyone they might approach.[15]

The value of work was further reinforced by restrictions on relief for able-bodied people. In Scotland, such people were generally excluded: one had to be "destitute" and "disabled" to be eligible for relief, though, as I address below, those conditions were seldom strictly observed.[16] In En-gland, able-bodied people who were temporarily unemployed or whose wages were inadequate for survival could be eligible for relief.[17] English efforts to impose conditions of employment on anyone capable of working led to the notorious institution of the workhouse. Though out-relief re-mained dominant under the old laws, various parishes tried schemes for indoor relief by which poor workers would make goods that could be sold, thus funding their keep and profiting the community. According to Brundage, such schemes were seldom profitable.[18] Though the harsh con-ditions imposed on the granting of poor relief seem to belie the argument that the old system formed parishes into support networks, the controlling policies were often mitigated by liberal practices. To understand the ef-fects of the old Poor Laws, we must examine the interactions by which some people claimed a right to relief and others assumed an obligation to provide it.

Mitchison stresses that no right to relief existed under Scottish law; relief was provided, rather, out of a sense of obligation.[19] Obligation was likewise the dominant concept behind the old Poor Laws in England, where the church had a "statutory obligation . . . to provide for the indigent."[20] Yet, as Boulton and Hitchcock, King, and Sharpe point out, a right to relief was often inferred from this obligation.[21] As Hitchcock and his collaborators explain, the "legitimacy" of this stratified social system depended in part on the willingness of those with relatively greater wealth to assist those who had less. Since the gap between rate-payers and relief recipients was not always great, the material benefits did not always move in one direction. Rate-payers who fell on hard times could find themselves in need of assistance, so many embraced the "obligation" to provide a social safety for others because they realized the net could catch them too.[22] In examining letters and petitions from people seeking relief, recent researchers note that the applicants often alluded to their history of rate-paying as a reason why they should receive relief from their present difficulties.[23] The discovery of how such interactions, negotiations, and role reversals carried the Poor Laws into lived experience and modified them along the way, in practice if not in theory, is the raison d'etre of the research by Hitchcock, King, Sharpe, Boulton, and a host of other investigators of "history from below." Unless we look in the "places where the rich and poor interacted—where social knowledge was acquired and deployed,"[24] we will fall short in understanding the dynamics of social relations.

The local and personal interactions prevalent under the old Poor Laws and preserved in the new law in Scotland made it possible for people to interpret the laws in ways that modified their harshness. For example, the requirement that persons be "destitute" and "disabled" to qualify for relief in Scotland is harsh in the extreme, and English critics often took their able-bodied inclusions as signs of their system's greater humanity, perhaps balancing Scottish claims to have the more humane criminal justice system, but in Scottish practice, to quote Paterson, "destitution and disability were two very elastic terms." Destitution could be construed as earning insufficient wages for survival; disability included both physical and mental impairments as well as such disabling conditions as being widowed or deserted by a spouse.[25] Of course, nothing in the letter of the law ruled out narrower applications of these terms. Broad and inclusive definitions depended more on the attitudes of people toward each other and toward their interlocking rights and obligations than on the terms dictated by legislation. In a phrase evocative of Scottish criminal law practice, Mitchison states: "the wording of statutes played a relatively small part in the interpretation of the Poor Law."[26] Given that condition, experiences that shape attitudes and interpretive capacities, including experiences of reading fiction and watching plays, are important factors in the construction of a humane social system.

The interactions by which people devise understandings of poverty and charity and experiment with the roles of giver and receiver are evident in the imaginative works by Scott and Baillie that depict encounters between rich and poor characters. These works deserve to be added to the expanded list of sources for learning about the experience of the Poor Laws and of negotiated social systems that Hitchcock, King, and Sharpe propose. For them, crucial sources are the letters, diaries, petitions, and transcripts from trials and examinations that give us the statements of the poor themselves; inventories of household goods also shed light on the way the poor lived.[27] To these, I would add the letters of more highly situated people such as Scott, whose correspondence with John B. S. Morritt (a friend who was a Member of Parliament), Robert Southey, and Joanna Baillie reveals his struggles to come to terms with his obligation to the poor. Further, I would add novels like *The Bride of Lammermoor* and plays like *Witchcraft* that both represent interactions between rich and poor characters and elicit interpretations of them. In effect, the stories and dramas become the imaginative spaces in which people can experiment with new plots and roles and from which they can reform existing social relations. Such transformations are "real" whether or not they are reflected in legislation, for as we saw in the case of the Scottish Poor Laws, the experience of living within that system depended more on how people interpreted the law than on what terms the law dictated in the abstract. If, in practice, laws evolve with people's attitudes, then the interpretive work facilitated by imaginative literature can alter the structure of prescribed and proscribed behaviors in a given society. Ultimately, the administration of the Poor Laws depended on attitudes about mutual responsibility. As reformers called for less personal systems and passed in England the disastrous new law reviled by Dickens among others,[28] Scott and Baillie raised voices for adjustments within the old system that were later echoed in social work. Before turning to Scott and Baillie, it is necessary to say something about the New Poor Law.

The new law passed in England in 1834 inverted or reversed the old one. It replaced local control with a national bureaucracy; it eliminated outdoor relief and made lodging — in effect, incarceration — in the workhouse a requirement for the receipt of assistance; it minimized personal discretion and emphasized the impartiality of the system. Advocates of the new system considered it fairer than the old because it freed the poor from the variable mercies of their local communities and corrected abuses such as favoritism. They also considered the use of the workhouse for social control a good compromise with economists who wanted poor relief eliminated in favor of natural or market forces.[29] If the workhouse were no better than a prison, then people would try every means possible to earn their livings outside of it. The threat of the workhouse would thus deter nonessential applications for relief, reinforce the value of industry, and constrain potentially troublesome segments of the population. Critics of the new approach called it cruel and inhumane. As the odd alliance between Tories and radicals that Brundage and Roberts's record shows,[30] the reasons behind their judgments reflect their attitudes toward social relations. The Tories objected to the loss of local, personal, paternalistic authority; the radicals, to the loss of the "historic rights of the poor."[31] To workers who had depended on out-relief to supplement their wages, the new law was "a seismic shock" that aroused their "anger and disbelief."[32] It generated so much opposition and controversy that Scotland resisted reform until the depression of the textile industry in 1841 made it impossible to cope with the unemployed; the new Scottish law, passed in 1845, was deliberately crafted against the new English model, and thus kept out-relief and local participation in a system that would be gradually centralized.[33]

What is remarkable about the 1834 law for my purposes is its distrust of personal interactions. It subjected people to impersonally determining forces and structures, placing or misplacing confidence in the latter to create and sustain a totally balanced system. This confidence in determining abstractions became the key characteristic of the scientific mindset that dictated social policy and organized disciplinary systems from the late nineteenth to the late twentieth centuries. As we have become disenchanted with this literally dehumanizing approach, it is time to revalue the constructions of social welfare by Scott and Baillie.

SCOTT'S EPIPHANIES

Scott's most direct comments on the Poor Laws appear in letters written between 1817 and 1819, a period generally taken to mark the beginning of serious debate over reforming relief policies.[34] He compares the laws in Scotland and England, much to the latter's disadvantage; criticizes the burden of compulsory poor-rate taxes while favoring voluntary efforts to help the poor; and despite some undeniable condescension and stereotyping, treats poor workers as dignified actors in a mutually supportive community.[35] Scott's attention to helping the able-bodied confirms that the Scottish Poor Laws were interpreted broadly while his sense of the personal responsibility of those providing relief makes a significant entry in the Poor Laws debate. For Scott, if the Poor Laws are ineffective, it is because those in elite positions are not living up to their obligations. Reform, then, should consist of awakening those who could help others to their responsibilities—not just as providers of money but as guardians of a common welfare. According to Scott, "the rich . . . do not in general require to be so much stimulated to benevolence as to be directed in the most useful way to exert it."[36] In lived and literary experience, Scott tried to provide such direction.

Scott carried out his ideas about poor relief by accelerating renovations on his own estate so as to employ thirty people who would otherwise have suffered through a hard winter. He contracted for their labor at a fair rate rather than at the reduced rate typical of work relief proposals because he believed that reduced wages demoralized workers, preventing them from bringing "heart and spirit" to their tasks.[37] In another example, he reports that his own and other parishes set up road improvement projects to employ the poor during hard times, and they did so "with so little ostentation that the people never found out that it was done for the *nonce*." Scott attaches great significance to the latter because, he says, "It is the last of degradation so far as I have been able to observe when the honest and independent labourer has become an object of eleemosynary relief. His proud spirit is broken . . . and he ceases to possess one great impulse to every honourable exertion—self estimation."[38] By hiding the design of elite providers, Scott deprives them of the full measure of deference and gratitude that they might expect from their act. He insists that they focus instead on how they can contribute to the material and immaterial good of the community, helping people not only to survive but to develop self-worth. Scott does not address the problem of inequality itself, which he does not see as a problem, but he would adjust the gaps between ranks and the attitudes with which they approach each other so as to make them closer to the interdependent ideal he finds in Scotland. "[Y]ou English both in high and low degree stand rather too much isolated and too much detached from connections and relationship," he wrote to John B. S. Morritt. The letter continues, "In Scotland men of all ranks but especially the middling and the lower classes are linkd [sic] together by ties which give them a strong interest in each others success in life and it is amazing the exertion which men will make to support and assist persons with whom you would suppose them connected by very remote ties of consanguinity and by no other link whatever."[39] For Scott, the problem of poverty would be eliminated if everyone in society took this personal responsibility for others seriously; doing so would transform the traditional role of the elite from dominant providers to supportive facilitators.

Doubts about the extent to which Scott's thinking redefines the meaning of relationships within a stratified system might be allayed by considering his ideas in light of Randall Collins's work on present-day stratification, deference, and inequality. According to Collins, we can only begin to understand inequality by looking at interaction among people ("microsituational encounters") instead of at structural markers such as income distribution and educational levels ("macrodata"). The latter are misleading, even on a topic that seems so rigid as stratification, because structure depends on interaction for meaning. The "actual experience of stratification in social encounters is highly fluctuating, [and] subject to situational contestation."[40] Collins further argues that even deferential encounters can be dynamic because they involve at least two kinds of power—the power to give orders (deference power or "D-power" throughout his analysis) and the power to get things done (efficiency power or "E-power"). Subordinates may appear to honor D-power while using their E-power for subversion or for the operation of a "shadow hierarchy" that actually does things differently.[41] If we bring this orientation toward looking at stratification and deference in terms of the dynamics of encounters and the meanings of those encounters for the participants to our reading of Scott's letters and novels, we can more readily credit his alteration of elite roles.

A further point about structure is worth making since Collins alludes to the "patrimonial household" in traditional societies, an allusion that brings to mind Scott's castle of law. For Collins, the breakup or abandonment of that household increases opportunities for dynamic encounters. It leaves us, he says in a delightfully unexpected comparison, in the role of adventurers "in an ancient or medieval picaresque story": away from the defining household, identities are shaped only by encounters.[42] For Scott, tearing down or abandoning the patrimonial household is not an option. It must be renovated as a "new old" structure that helps inhabitants redefine their roles within it.[43]

A letter from Scott to Baillie shows his own struggle to come to terms with his role as a provider. "I have," he writes, "limited my other habits of expense very much since I fell into the habit of employing mine honest people." He then describes his feelings while watching "about an hundred children" of those workers at a New Year's Eve gathering on his estate: "I declare to you my dear friend that when I thought the poor fellows who kept these children so neat and well taught and well behaved were slaving the whole day for eighteenpence or twenty pence at the most I was ashamed of the gratitude and of their becks and bows." Despite this embarrassment, he rationalizes his behavior, deciding that the best way to help his community is by making modest employment available to as many people as possible: "[A]fter all, one does what one can and it is better twenty families should be comfortable according to their wishes and habits than half that number should be raised above their situations."[44] However much modern sensibilities may find the latter phrase offensive and agree with Scott's later comment that "all this smells of sad Egotism,"[45] we should suspend judgment long enough to recognize that the gathering was an "epiphany" for Scott. What he describes is a turning point moment that, according to Denzin (as I have documented in chapter 1), links private and public concerns and significantly develops the social self. Scott's more intimate letter to Baillie reveals more clearly than his less confessional correspondence with Morritt and Southey how he reached self-consciousness about his role in the community by responding to the needs of its poorer members.

Scott built a similar epiphany into *The Bride of Lammermoor*, which he published later in the same year that he had confided his own epiphanic experience to Baillie. The symbolic interaction between Lord Ravenswood and the sextant who criticizes the former's father for failing his community by squandering his estate offers the large and comfortable audience for Scott's novels the opportunity to reflect on, interpret, and revitalize their traditional role. The conversation in the novel occurs in a graveyard where the young master of Ravenswood is arranging for the burial of Alice Gray, a longtime family dependent. Through this act itself, Ravenswood is carrying out a traditional responsibility, but he learns more about what he owes the community from the sextant. Mistaking Ravenswood for some distant English relative of the deceased and therefore feeling entitled to speak candidly, the sextant blames the old Lord Ravenswood for failing to care for his dependents: "[H]e loot his affairs gang to the dogs, and let this Sir William Ashton on us, that will gie naething for naething, and just removed me and a' the puir creatures that had bite and soup at the castle, and a hole to put our heads in, when things were in the auld way" (333). When Ravenswood protests that the lord can hardly be blamed for these troubles because he himself suffered the loss of his property and position, the sextant disagrees: "[Y]e winna persuade me that he did his duty, either to himself or to huz puir dependent creatures" (333). The loss of the property itself was an irresponsible act in the sextant's view because the lord treated it as his own to hold or waste as he wished instead of treating it as a community resource entrusted to him. Listening to the sextant's tirade, Ravenswood has an epiphany about the public responsibility attached to private privilege. The narrator describes him as "conscience-struck" by the realization that "the penalties of extravagance extend far beyond the prodigal's own sufferings" (333).

The encounter between Ravenswood and the sextant raises questions about rights and obligations evocative of the Poor Laws debates. Without explicitly treating the latter, the scene suggestively alludes to the "auld way" behind the Old Poor Law and valorizes it by narrative affirmation and character development. Ravenswood's epiphany, like Scott's own in his letter to Baillie, expands the notion of the self by its responses to others; it turns the concept of the mind into the process of minding. By "naturalistic generalization," readers can use the example of Ravenswood for value inquiry in reconsidering the Poor Laws. The interpretive processes by which readers compare Ravenswood's case with parallels in their own experience can stimulate the emergence of new insights into social welfare that might not arise in theorizing about the Poor Laws directly or abstractly or by compiling statistics related to their administration. *The Bride of Lammermoor*, then, can be said to intervene in the Poor Laws debates insofar as it provides a vehicle for discussion of the values at issue. As readers interpret Ravenswood's encounter, the scene can become the source of their own epiphanies.

Despite narrative gestures toward a positive evaluation of the "auld way," the bleak outcome of the novel casts some doubt on their viability. In contrast to the utopian world of Roseneath with which he concludes *The Heart of Midlothian*, Scott sets *The Bride of Lammermoor* in a dystopian world where all social systems and relationships have broken down. Ravenswood does not live to fulfill his social role, and as Burwick points out, the promising marriages and alliances typical of Scott's novels are conspicuously absent from this one. Burwick's reading calls attention to the prosperity of the village of Wolf's-hope, which is due to the mercantilism that freed it from feudal dependence.[46] Though that outcome may appear to reduce valorization of the Lord's role to nostalgia, the novel's portrait of Wolf's-hope exposes a hollowness in its social relations that could be filled by the revival of personally responsible attitudes.

Burwick rightly notes that the villagers "do not begrudge Caleb the food that he has stolen for his master's table in the ruined tower,"[47] but he does not scrutinize the motives behind their acceptance. They are moved by self-interest. The owner of the stolen provisions was furious until informed that they would be consumed not just by the ruined Ravenswood but by the powerful Lord Keeper who was visiting him. Imagining the benefit to rebound on himself if he pays tribute to this budding alliance, he sends more goods for the feast (181–90). Similarly, when the fire at Wolf's-crag sends Ravenswood and the marquis to Wolf's-hope for accommodation, they are well received because the villagers anticipate a "shower of preferment" to reward their hospitality (354). Social relations

in the village move gradually away from the personal attachments lingering, early in the novel, from the old system to the impersonal detachment
exhibited by the boys who can watch the old tower burn with no feeling
for the loss (355–56). Poor relief consists of giving away "ony thing totally uneatable" left from the feast (367). The narrative comment on the
activity of John Girder in entertaining the Marquis's party sums up
social interaction in Wolf's-hope: it amounts to "build[ing] castles in the
air" by "court[ing] favour" through "the expenditure of . . . worldly sub-
stance" (368). *The Bride of Lammermoor* leaves it to readers to reconstruct
social relations that bring personal responsibility back into mercantile society.

An instructive contrast to the dysfunctional social systems in *The Bride
of Lammermoor* can be derived from Scott's earlier novel *The Antiquary*,
which depicts a functional social system animated by the spirit of the Old
Poor Law. That spirit is verbalized in the dialogue between Lovel and
Oldbuck as the latter answers the former's questions about the beggar
Edie Ochiltree. At first, Oldbuck, exasperated by Ochiltree's disturbing
his antiquarian research, calls the beggar "one of the plagues of the country" and adds, "I have been always against poor's-rates and a workhouse — I think I'll vote for them now, to have that scoundrel shut up"
(46). But when Lovel confirms that "[i]n England . . . such a mendicant
would get a speedy check" (47), Oldbuck retracts his condemnation and
explains more carefully who Ochiltree is in this society:

> "[H]e is a sort of privileged nuisance — one of the last specimens of the
> old- fashioned Scottish mendicant, who kept his rounds within a partic-
> ular space, and was the news-carrier, the minstrel, and sometimes the
> historian of the district. That rascal, now, knows more old ballads and
> traditions than any other man in this and the four next parishes. And
> after all," continued he, softening as he went on describing Edie's good
> gifts, "the dog has some good-humour. He has borne his hard fate with
> unbroken spirits, and it's cruel to deny him the comfort of a laugh at his
> betters." (47)

Despite the condescension in Oldbuck's statements, they clearly convey a
sense of Ochiltree as a person, not just a recipient of relief. He is described
as a participant in the community, a resource for it rather than a drain on
it. The fact that he is known and called by name reinforces the sense of
personal relationship asserted here.

Later in the novel, Scott gives us a compatible description of Ochiltree's identity and role in the community from Ochiltree's own point of
view. Ochiltree considers himself "independent"[48] because, in his words,

"I beg nae mair at ony single house than a meal o' meat, or maybe but a mouthfou o't—if it's refused at ae place, I get it at anither—sae I canna be said to depend on ony body in particular, but just the country at large" (117). Moreover, he does not simply accept food from the houses he visits. He helps with chores, sings songs and tells stories, and carries messages and parcels between farms (117). The inclusion of Ochiltree's point of view may do more than the content of his statements to indicate how he is part of a mutually responsible system. Attending to the thoughts and feelings of one in Ochiltree's position implies a degree of respect that complicates the condescension shown earlier in Oldbuck's remarks.

Scott's attention to Ochiltree's viewpoint and performance in social interaction stands in obvious contrast to Wordsworth's presentation of "The Old Cumberland Beggar," for the absence of the beggar's viewpoint from the poem has been its most troubling feature for many readers. Wordsworth seems to reduce the beggar to an object for the benefit of those who encounter him.[49] Elsewhere, I have argued that this implication is an unintended consequence of Wordsworth's interest in studying human relations in ways approaching sociological theory,[50] and the contrast between that aim and what I represent in this study as Scott's interventionist aim can help clarify both. Like classic sociological theorists, Wordsworth's goal is to separate observation from intervention. His poem presents what he can observe about the effect of the beggar in the community. His advocacy of the Old Poor Law is an application that may follow from yet remain distinct from observation.[51] Scott did not aim to separate observation from advocacy. His "Advertisement" to *The Antiquary* presents Ochiltree as his purposeful creation, a composite of mendicants he has encountered and read about (6–11). His purpose may be partly to defend the humanity of the Old Poor Law, which was beginning to be a topic of controversy at the time he wrote the novel, by creating an extraordinarily personable beggar, but the novel goes beyond defending an existing system to calling for its renewal. Ochiltree's personality serves that purpose well. The character is designed to disrupt stereotypical condescension toward such figures or, in Scott's words, to "vindicate Edie Ochiltree's right to the importance assigned him" (11). The difference between Scott's and Wordsworth's beggars reflects the difference between pragmatic and theoretical approaches to social problems.[52]

If Ochiltree receives a degree of respect beyond his position in the given stratified society, he acts toward others with a degree of candor unusual for one in his position. Observing outward signs of deference such as not coming upstairs in Isabella Wardour's house (115), he nevertheless breaches deferential conventions by advising Isabella to treat Lovel more kindly and by inserting himself into Oldbuck's and Wardour's antiquarian affairs. In examining Scott's portrayal of Ochiltree's interactions, it is helpful to recall Collins's argument that deference can, in some situations, be dynamic. Though Ochiltree accepts, even embraces, his subordinate rank, he is not conventionally deferential toward those above him. On the contrary, he uses his "E-power" to undermine them when, for example, he indicates that he built the shelter the antiquarian takes for a Roman camp (43). Ferris, reinforcing Wilt, describes Ochiltree's revelation as a "deflationary counter-reading" probably designed "to tweak the 'book-leared laird.'"[53] Oldbuck and Isabella Wardour likewise accept differences in rank but interact with Ochiltree in ways that reduce their distance from him: Isabella in fact invites Ochiltree upstairs; it is he who refuses to take that liberty, though he takes greater ones in their ensuing conversation.[54] I believe the behavioral inconsistencies stem from Scott's efforts to portray traditional social hierarchies as supportive communities. The more he emphasizes mutually responsible interaction, the more he inevitably adjusts the social structure as a result of them. Again, we see him involved in Zaret's "paradox of innovation," and perhaps in the figure of Ochiltree, whom Malley terms an "anachronism," we also see the catalytic function that Christensen attaches to the term.[55] The implications of the impact of interaction on structure that Scott portrays lead to a conclusion that Scott would not accept, i.e., that activation of the values he endorsed would lead to a more egalitarian society. Fearful of any questioning of stratification itself as a preface to revolution, Scott approached social change as a matter of making traditional structures better. In the process, he constructed a society that did not traditionally exist—the non-deferential hierarchy in *The Antiquary*.

ROSENEATH AS UTOPIA

It is easy to classify Roseneath, or more broadly, the whole of the territory within the jurisdiction of the Duke of Argyle, as a "utopia," an ideal place that does not exist in the "real" world. Despite the geographical specificity of its location on the Frith of Clyde, the island lies "beyond the bounds of ordinary law and civilisation" (406, 410). Highland and lowland Scots coexist in arrangements superintended by Duncan, Captain of Knockdunder, who even tries to dress in combinations of both groups' garments (426–27). With the notable exceptions of Gottlieb, D'Arcy, and Austin, readers usually complain that this representation of "another world" is not a fit conclusion to a novel that deals so powerfully with the given one.[56] I would add that settling for an illusory order seems inconsistent with a plot that struggles against structural containments.

But *is* Roseneath a static utopia that halts the interactionism of the novel? New thinking about utopianism suggests otherwise. According to the scholarship that Michael Wiley has recently applied and developed with respect to William Wordsworth, along with scholarship advanced by Lucy Sargisson, utopia is above all a critical space. Utopia "configures an alternative world in critical relation to the actual world."[57] Its goal is not to fix an alternative in place but to disturb complacency about the world we inhabit. Arising from "dissatisfaction" with what is, it creates a space in which to express discontent with such matters as divisions between private and public spaces, and between self and other, and to consider how they might be reformed.[58] We might say that utopianism performs on a larger scale the adjustment of social relations enacted in the theater and in the Settlement houses. Furthermore, utopianism as Sargisson conceives it shares with symbolic interactionism, and particularly with interpretive interactionism, a commitment to social problem solving: Sargisson calls her work "pragmatic" and cites Mead; Denzin says that a "utopian spirit" leads interpretive interactionists to "imagin[e] and pursu[e]" social change.[59] Following Sargisson in looking at utopias in terms of function rather than form or content, we can see them as imaginative springboards rather than blueprints.[60] Wordsworth's Grasmere may be one such utopia, for as Wiley argues, the pressure of outside problems on the space inside the Vale leads Wordsworth to explore what kinds of social and economic relations people could sustain in nineteenth-century Britain.[61] Roseneath is likewise a functional utopia that allows Scott to explore the kinds of interactions that promote structural flexibility and integrative control.

The social structure of Roseneath consists entirely of the personal relations among its inhabitants. Structure does not solidify around them; rather, it exists as the flow of their interactions. Unlike an order that can be maintained indefinitely by any individuals, Roseneath changes as the participants in the community change: it becomes less "intimat[e] when the Duke is succeeded by his brother because the latter is less personally involved" (462). The duke who presides throughout most of the book is identified by his benevolent actions, not his position of authority. Though he exercises absolute power in this territory, he believes, as he stated to Jeanie during their first meeting, that he does not, as an individual, have power over the law (349).[62] Thus situating himself in a larger social world, he develops a sense of responsibility that prevents him from being tyrannical or self-indulgent. Yet he does not hesitate to exercise his discretionary power over some cases: smuggling is not prosecuted in Roseneath (430).

Despite the duke's importance, the Roseneath section of the novel does not focus on him. It focuses on the interactions of David Deans, Jeanie Deans Butler, and Reuben Butler, and, specifically, on the thought processes by which they make decisions in their daily lives.[63] This topic is somewhat repetitive and anticlimactic as we have already watched them make decisions in the crisis over Effie earlier in the novel. But by extending their problem-solving orientation beyond the crisis and making it characteristic of their approach to other areas of experience, Scott presents it as an alternative to thought processes that predominate elsewhere in the novel and in the world. The latter processes include the reliance on statute, abstraction, and theory determining the course of Effie's trial as well as the short-sighted projections of the Porteous rioters. In Roseneath, discretion adapts principles to circumstances and self-criticism checks self-interest. Thinking comes closest to "minding" in the Meadian sense of that activity. This orientation minimizes conflict and promotes careful interactions. It does not produce a perfect society, but it does indicate how people can live responsibly with each other. Though Jeanie most exemplifies the process, it is important that she is not the sole model. Mindful interacting is a cooperative endeavor among unique individuals, not an abstract behavior pattern identical for all. Readers should not so much imitate Jeanie as evaluate the interactions in which she engages and ask how such behavior connects with their own experience.

Jeanie is more able than her father or husband to think from the point of view of others. This ability allows her to be a "mediating spirit" between the two. Because she recognizes the values, prejudices, and feelings motivating David's and Reuben's stances on various issues, she "excuse[s]" rather than "defend[s]" each to the other, helping them to avoid conflict and to learn to understand each other (450). Though Scott casts Jeanie in a traditional gender role here he does not reduce her to a stereotype.[64] The major events earlier in the novel—her refusal to lie and her devising and carrying out a plan to obtain a pardon for Effie—give her a strong personality. In Roseneath, she transforms the roles of daughter, wife, and mother that she takes in the community more than she merely assumes them. Or, we might say, she treats these roles with their expectations of deference and caregiving as a "generalized other," the term Mead uses for the numerous people who represent the expectations of a community for a particular individual, to which she responds.

Austin precedes me in finding Jeanie's behavior transformative. For Austin, Jeanie's secret acceptance of Effie's money makes her home a site of "clandestine exchange with what should be inadmissible to its boundaries." Through such exchanges, the opposition between private and public, domestic and political is refigured, giving the Roseneath section the purpose of advancing and encouraging critique of those oppositions.[65] In interactionist terms, however, I would stress Jeanie's mindfulness as much or more than her transgressions. She decides to keep the money only after determining that refusing it and/or exposing Effie's secret "would restore no right to anyone, for [Effie] was usurping none," and Jeanie plans to use the money for the good of her family, not herself alone (457–58). Her reasons for not telling Reuben the source of the money she gives him to increase their property holdings include her respect for Effie's and Staunton's privacy and her respect for Reuben's public position: she does not want to create role conflict for him (465–66, 457). For his part, Reuben is satisfied with her assurance that it comes from an honest transaction, and he does not press her for details (465–67). Jeanie and Reuben have brought mutual respect into the traditionally hierarchical relationship of marriage and thus renovated their roles in private life in the manner that Scott projected for a larger social circle as well.

In his role as minister, Reuben tries to balance respect for his father-in-law and other traditional authority figures, such as Knockdunder, in the community with his own theological learning and moral beliefs. He often listens to instead of arguing with David, but he plays backgammon openly because he does not think that indulging in the game is objectionable, though David does (452). He will not punish women for witchcraft, as David still seems to expect, but he is inclined to punish them for deceiving people with promises of fortune-telling; however, when warned by Duncan that publicly correcting one such woman could open the door to her persecution by a mob—a possibility all too reminiscent of the fate of Madge Wildfire—Reuben agrees to make the case a matter for private discussion (457).

David's religious convictions limit his ability to put himself in the place of anyone who does not share his faith, but he does respect each person's conscience (421). And, like Reuben in the fortune-telling incident, he lets "speculative principles" be guided by the "circumstances" of individual people in individual cases. This discretionary judgment allows him to accept the duke's appointment of Reuben as minister to the church despite his abstract objection to patronage: the appointment is acceptable *in this case* if the parishioners also want Reuben to be minister. Though the narrator sometimes gently pokes fun at the tortuousness of David's thinking, there is no mockery in his singling out the "peace-making particle 'if'" in David's acceptance of the ministerial appointment (415–16). It *is* the peace-making and cooperative spirit of their interactions that allows these characters to construct a livable society.

Another important aspect of the thought processes of these characters is the ability to be self-critical. This quality is partly to blame for the tortuousness of David's reasoning: he is sincerely pious and always trying to be sure that he acts for reasons other than mere self-gratification (419). Jeanie possesses the most developed habit of self-criticism, as we see in her reactions to the first letter containing money she receives from Effie. At first, she suspects Effie of "egotism" for flaunting the money and status she has gained through her marriage, but then Jeanie questions her own anger at Effie, wondering if it masks envy (456). The narrative calls attention to her deliberately pausing for reflection, though without as much reference to the religious origin of the practice as Scott had included in an earlier passage when Jeanie paused to pray before her secret meeting with Robertson. In the earlier section, the narrator explains the historical context for her confidence in prayer and provides an alternative view of its benefit: praying usually helps people to act "rather from a sense of duty than from any inferior motive" (144). Foregrounding the secular benefit in the later passage, Scott's presentation of Jeanie's talking herself into more generous feelings for Effie suggests the processes of role-taking and sympathy-giving detailed in Clark's study and has something in common with the deliberative weighing of ideas against each other that Chandler associates with the positive aspects of casuistry.

Chandler indeed points out instances of casuistry in other examples of reasoning in the novel, including David Deans's acceptance of Reuben's appointment as minister.[66] Chandler's study salvages casuistry from the "pernicious" connotations that have grown up around it: in his usage, it denotes a reasoning process of weighing one case against another; it "mediat[es] between the particular and the general[, . . .] circumstance and principle." Chandler reads *The Heart of Midlothian* as weighing a legal case against a moral case and not reaching resolution because moral conduct requires more than cognitive direction.[67] I suggest that Clark's processes of sympathizing supply another dimension to the thinking and feeling in the novel; as Clark stresses, sympathizing is a physical, emotion, *and* cognitive process.[68] In turn, casuistry can help explain the cognitive origin of structural change. In Chandler's words, casuistry creates "a rival normative framework in which the hegemony of the central system comes in for challenge and possible modification."[69] We may find both casuistry and sympathy in Jeanie's thinking about Effie's money. To challenge her envious reaction, Jeanie puts herself in Effie's place; she further weighs Effie's suffering against the consolations Effie has gained from her marriage and wealth. Deciding that the suffering still exceeds any such consolations,

Jeanie decides to sympathize with Effie and to comply with her wishes that she keep the money (456–58).

In Austin's reading, the sympathy Jeanie develops after she moves to Roseneath "reverses" an earlier lack of sympathy evident in her unwillingness to lie for Effie or to admit a kinship with Madge Wildfire.[70] The greatest example of Jeanie's emergent sympathy, however, comes not from her treatment of Effie but from her treatment of "The Whistler," Effie's and Staunton's son whom Knockdunder imprisons and plans to execute for killing Staunton (503–4). By making it possible for "this parricide" to run away, Jeanie, according to Austin, "grant[s] not only freedom but sympathy to a figure who clearly escapes her patronage and control"; furthermore, she defies the "dictates of patriarchy" and thus accomplishes the reorganization of domestic and political spaces in the novel.[71] Though I also take the freeing of the Whistler as an important incident, I find as much discretion as transgression in the act.

What disturbs Jeanie about the Whistler's condemnation is its inhumanity toward "a creature so young and so wretched" and its indifference to his mental and spiritual condition (504–5). In accordance with the emphasis on judging homicide by criminal intent that, as I addressed earlier, preoccupied Scottish courts from Baron Hume's time onward, Effie visits the captive Whistler to ascertain his thoughts and feelings. She plans to argue for mercy and integrative control if "upon conversing with him, she should see any hope of his being brought to better temper" (504). Jeanie's interrogation of the prisoner aims at finding "good in him": that is why she unties him; she is making a gesture of "fair play" to learn whether he will respond in kind (505). By taking the opportunity to flee, he escapes legal justice but perhaps he allows social good to prevail in Roseneath.

As I indicated in chapter 3, I believe that *The Heart of Midlothian* owes some debt to Baillie's *The Dream*. Specifically, Jeanie's reluctance to see the Whistler executed calls to mind Benedict's disapproval of the execution of Osterloo. Though the situation and the characters are more subdued in the novel, Jeanie, like Benedict, wants to redefine the prisoner's identity in penitential terms, and also like Benedict, she disapproves of capital punishment in the given case, not necessarily in general. In the Whistler's case, as in Osterloo's, the only purpose sought through the execution is revenge. That goal is clearly specified by Knockdunder when he rebuffs Reuben's pleas to have the Whistler and the other captives sent for trial to Glasgow or Inverary (504). Compromising so far as to have all but the Whistler sent to court, Knockdunder invokes ancient rights of jurisdiction and the ancient practice of retribution that ally him with the world of Donacha Dhu outside of Roseneath, a world dominated by thoughts and acts of revenge (502–3). Knockdunder's attitude is neither consistent with nor worthy of the mindfulness that had characterized Roseneath, and that inconsistency is especially apparent in his plan to hang the Whistler without fully ascertaining his guilt. The narrative twice calls attention to that lack of certainty: first, the account of the killing is given almost entirely in passive voice and indicates that Staunton "fell, as there was too much reason to believe, by the hand of his son"; secondly, Jeanie reflects not on the murder that the Whistler committed but on "the murder that he had too probably committed" (503–4). These very faint qualifications raise no serious doubts in readers' minds about whether the Whistler committed the act, but they do raise doubts about the attitudes, practices, and judgments emerging in Roseneath. By persisting in the careful minding of others that leads her to try to know the Whistler and inadvertently allow him to escape, Jeanie saves Roseneath from the collective self-righteousness that was closing in on it.

To borrow Austin's notion of the final book reversing earlier ones, I would say that Jeanie's freeing the Whistler exercises the discretionary power that the court should have been free to exercise in Effie's case. Though without self-conscious decision, her characteristic sense of responsibility for others allows her to accomplish the release of a prisoner who has not been proven guilty and whose understanding of his actions she doubts. From the utopian space of Roseneath, Scott deploys this discretionary action against the statutory paralysis in the work's and readers' other worlds, inviting a critical response. Without rejecting punitive justice in general, Scott raises the idea that there may in some cases be greater good[72] and that people must be able and willing to engage personally in pursuing it.

5
Impoverished
Social Relations

"ARE NOT WITCHES ALWAYS OLD AND POOR," ASKS THE SHERIFF IN Baillie's *Witchcraft* (3.2.630), thus defining the situation that shapes the identities of witches. The social construction of the self is a central concern of the play, for as she indicated in an appended note, Baillie wrote *Witchcraft* partly to explore the puzzling behavior, documented in transcripts of witchcraft trials, by which the accused women embraced identities as witches even when doing so led to their execution. Why, Baillie wanted to know, did they derive satisfaction from being accused of witchcraft? In addition to reading trial transcripts, Baillie paid close attention to the scenes involving reputed witches in Scott's *Bride of Lammermoor*, particularly the one in which "the old women, after the division of largess given at a funeral, are so dissatisfied with their share of it, and wonder that the devil, who helps other wicked people willing to serve him, has never bestowed any power or benefits upon them." Baillie's note credits Scott with "com[ing] within one step of accounting for" the behavior in the trial transcripts; it reports her unsuccessful effort to persuade him to write more on the topic, and it presents *Witchcraft* as her own attempt to pursue the topic.[1] But if *Witchcraft* explains why the women on trial and in Scott's novel wanted to be witches, what motive does it assign to them, and what step did Baillie think Scott missed? One answer to the first question is that the women embrace identities as witches in a fantasy of compensation for their powerlessness. Such a maneuver raises questions about the social relations between rich and poor that were fluctuating as changes in the Poor Laws were contemplated. In this chapter, I consider together three texts—Scott's *Bride of Lammermoor*, Baillie's *Witchcraft*, and Jane Addams's narrative of the Devil-Baby at Hull-House—that reveal how mistrustful interactions impoverish social relations. First, however, I look at Baillie's efforts to enrich social relations though the model of Lady Griseld Baillie.

Enriching
Social Relations

Less is known about Baillie's attitude toward the Poor Laws than about Scott's. Her plays give us no Edie Ochiltrees. Her letters supply somewhat contradictory information, though the clearest one, her reply to Scott's letter about his embarrassment over his workers' deference that I quoted in Chapter 4, praises the kinship networks of the traditional Scottish system: "I like much what you tell me of your hogmanae party particularly the young men who work for their Widow mothers & Brothers & sisters. I am pleased & proud of my native land when I think how much she excells this country in filial duty. A man very seldom works for any body here but his own wife & children; and this I believe is the consequence of our poor's laws."[2] Other references are more cryptic. A letter dated November 25, 1834, to Margaret Holford Hodson, alludes to "a change in the political world," footnoted by Slagle as referring to the Poor Law Amendment Act, that will result in "Mrs. Lawrence['s] . . . resum[ing] her importance in the Borough of Ripon"; Baillie adds: "and I hope she will, for, Whig as I am, I could by no means endure the ingratitude of her tenants & liege-men."[3] Though this comment endorses traditional expectations about the attitudes of dependents, it hardly takes a position on the old or new laws. An equally ambiguous reference occurs in a letter to the Andrews Nortons, dated April 4, 1834, alluding to Harriet Martineau's work. Baillie conjectures that "the works she is now engaged in will probably be more useful to us than those which have preceded them, as poors [sic] laws or the effect of poor's [sic] laws come more perfectly under her own observation than matters of political economy."[4] Since this remark suggests that Baillie was not pleased with the *Illustrations of Political Economy* that Martineau began publishing in 1832, she was probably disappointed, despite her speculation, with *Poor Laws and Paupers Illustrated,* as the two works are quite similar.

By 1840, Baillie seems to have lost confidence in kindred responsibility. Writing on May 9 to Elizabeth Fletcher, she expressed frustration with the "degraded state of the Scotch poor and the systematic hardheartedness of the rich," and she voiced hope that "Dr. Alison's book" would be influential in "establishing a poor's rate for Scotland."[5] Though Slagle's footnote conjectures that the book is a reprint of the Rev. Archibald Alison's *Essays on the nature and principles of taste,* I surmise that it is Dr. W. P. Alison's *Observations on the Management of the Poor in Scotland*, published in 1840.[6] In the letter Baillie concurs with Alison that the existing Scottish system cannot handle a large number of impoverished people in an urban, industrial environment. Dating from the time when the depression of the textile industry did indeed force the revision of the old Scottish Poor Law,[7] Baillie's support for a national tax for poor relief is more a response to a crisis than a repudiation of earlier values.

A better sense of Baillie's attitude can be derived from what is known about her own practice of charity, which took a personal approach, and from her comments on Martineau's theoretical discussions, which, as I quoted in the introduction, she compared to steeplechasing.[8] Moreover, her *Metrical Legend of Lady Griseld Baillie* celebrates her ancestor's personal commitment to relieving the sufferings of those left destitute by war and presents her as a role model for Romantic-era women. Wholehearted support for the New Poor Law would not be consistent with any of this material. Baillie's work, rather, evokes the value of the old sense of obligation and looks for ways to implant it in social relations in her own time. Rooted in the past, Baillie's approach branches out toward the future, for it reaches toward the role of the social Settler Jane Addams defined.

The chief means by which Baillie contributed to the material welfare of others was by donating profits from the sale of her works or works she edited specifically for a charitable cause. Significantly, the "cause" tended to be a particular person or family, though she did support more general efforts to end the use of "climbing boys" to sweep chimneys.[9] Profits from *The Family Legend*, for example went to a "Mr. Henderson who was taking care of seven sisters and two brothers"; profits from *A Collection of Poems, Chiefly Manuscript, and From Living Authors*, which Baillie solicited, edited, and published, went to her "needy friend, Mrs. James Stirling."[10] Baillie's material charity was thus closely allied with what might be called her immaterial charity—the social work of writing plays that may contribute to more just and more merciful interactions. The conjunction of writing or editing and charity calls to mind the notion of "vocational philanthropy" that Patricia Comitini imputes to Dororthy Wordsworth. Baillie's charity both converges with and diverges from her contemporary's philanthropy.

Comitini presents vocational philanthropy as a maternalistic counterpart to paternalistic norms and an alternative to the "'associated' philanthropy" by which organizations analogous to "joint stock" companies contributed to the building and maintenance of schools, hospitals, and prisons.[11] Vocational philanthropy is a particular adaptation of the "Lady Bountiful" role by which a woman like Dorothy Wordsworth "maintains a superior benevolent, middle-class position in relationship to the laboring classes . . . because she can articulate their level of material needs and determine their worthiness for personal amelioration."[12] For Comitini, vocational philanthropy literally emerges from Dorothy Wordsworth's journals, which she reads as both creating and recording the identity Dorothy Wordsworth pursued. The journals record her encounters with beggars, for instance, not because she was keeping notes for poems but because she was reflecting on her social responsibilities.[13] Comparing William Wordsworth's poem "Beggars" with Dorothy Wordsworth's journal entries, Comitini finds the poem designed to elicit feeling about "some lost time or landscape" rather than about the "beggars' poverty"; she finds the journal designed to demonstrate "the writer's benevolence and judicious action."[14] Though Comitini does not address "The Old Cumberland Beggar," I would venture to substitute it in the configuration above to further illustrate the Wordsworths' differing purposes: William presents observations about a social environment; Dorothy presents her activity in that environment.

Vocational philanthropy, however, does not consist only of charity toward destitute strangers. The responsibility is a comprehensive commitment to improving the lives of family, neighbors, and self, as well as helping those more distant and less fortunate strangers. Pursuing this calling entailed discovering the true nature of people's needs and meeting them in sometimes material and sometimes intangible ways. Even refusing requests from mocking or deceitful people could be an appropriate response if it meets a need for moral instruction. Vocational philanthropy could include writing or editing for charity, and Dorothy Wordsworth sold a story by subscription to aid the orphaned children of some neighbors. She was adamant, however, that sales must be by private subscription only, so as not to subject the children to undue publicity.[15]

What distinguishes Dorothy Wordsworth's philanthropy from Joanna Baillie's charity, however, is a gender division that Baillie resisted. As Comitini presents it, vocational philanthropy is "a special calling to women to 'love mankind'" and to make the improvement of an extended domestic circle their particular goal.[16] Comitini argues that Dorothy Wordsworth practiced this vocation in her care for her brother and her brother's household, and though that activity was specifically counter-professional, it served an equivalent function in her life as did poetry in his: her journals design "different sites of discursive intervention for herself and for William."[17] Baillie's practices do not fit into these separate sites. Her charity writing and editing are part of her professional, public life. The roles of Lord and Lady Bountiful are one for her: charity is an elite, rather than a gendered, responsibility. In offering Lady Griseld Baillie as a role model, Baillie is not trying to create a separate sphere or role for women but to draw them out of a private, self-enclosed sphere into the social world.

The *Metrical Legend* of *Lady Griseld Baillie* was published in 1821. The work was composed, however, during 1817–1819,[18] the years of rising concern about the Poor Laws and of Scott's most sensitive correspondence with her on that topic. Griseld Baillie epitomizes the privileged person who uses her resources for the good of an extended community. During her youth, those resources were not great. Her family lived in self-imposed exile in The Netherlands to escape religious persecution in Scotland at the time of the civil war. The nineteen-year-old Griseld distinguished herself by returning to Britain to bring out a younger sibling who had been left behind because of his illness when the family fled. After all were successfully settled abroad, Griseld became the principal caregiver in the family, looking after material, intellectual, and spiritual needs. She cooked, sewed, and helped the children with lessons and prayers. Her household attracted other exiles who gathered there for comfort and entertainment. In the words of the legend, Griseld creates a "magic circle" from which she "chace[s] the fiends that vex the human race" (34.754).[19] As a refuge for suffering neighbors and a place for interactions that are constrained elsewhere, Griseld Baillie's household-in-exile is an analogue of the Settlement houses. It is especially suggestive of Hull-House, where poverty and prejudice seemed chased away by Jane Addams's charismatic presence, where immigrants were given access to the Settlers own possessions, and to music, literature, and art. Griseld Baillie and Jane Addams may be said to show us the development of the self as a socially responsive being, of the mind as the act of minding.

Griseld Baillie continued to minister to the needs of an extended community after the Glorious Revolution made it possible for their family to return to their homeland. The next crisis in which we see her act comes with the Jacobite uprisings and subsequent depletions of estates and failures of crops. Griseld, a wealthy widow who disapproved of the Highlander support for the Stuarts, nevertheless provided nonpartisan assistance to any left in "want and distress" by the fighting (53.757). With her resources diminished, she restricted her own consumption so as to stretch provisions as far as possible among her dependents (54.757–58). The legend reports her peaceful death and notes that her tombstone "gives to other days her modest, just renown" (56.758), but that is not the end of the story.

Shifting from past to present, Joanna Baillie directly challenges her readers, especially her young women readers, to use the legend for value inquiry: "And now, ye polished fair of modern times, / If such indeed will listen to my rhymes, / What think ye of her simple, modest worth, / Whom I have faintly tried to shadow forth?" (758) Leading, almost goading, them to compare Griseld Baillie with the role models—"pattern ladies" (758)—available to them in popular culture, she quickly caricatures celebrity singers and dancers, women obsessed with clothes and appearance, and Bluestockings obsessed with ignoring them out of a contrived intellectualism; women whose interactions consist chiefly of flirting and quarrelling (758–59). Dismissing these negative role models, Baillie acknowledges that positive ones do exist in her own time. They are the portion of the "British fair" who have "kindred sympathy" with the legend and who revive Griseld Baillie's spirit in their conduct: "Yea, leagued for good they act, a virtuous band, / The young, the rich, the loveliest of the land, / Who clothe the naked, and each passing week, / The wretched poor in their sad dwellings seek" (759).[20] These passages suggest the commitment to countering "fashion" with "passion" (i.e., turning attention from outward appearances to inner character) that Henderson has found in the *Introductory Discourse* to the plays on the passions.[21] The presence in the poem on Griseld Baillie of explicit criticism of fashionable trends allows us to see continuities in Baillie's work extending from the passion plays through the miscellaneous plays to the metrical legends. All are persistently concerned with fostering socially responsible attitudes in their audiences and with doing so by honing their interpretive capacities. Here, despite the heavy-handed gestures toward the virtuous band and away from the fashionable crowd, the text is not truly prescriptive or proscriptive. Rather, it prompts readers to evaluate the represented behaviors and develop contemporary analogies, both in thought and action. Though Baillie's design on women's social consciences is transparent in the legend, she still carries it out by encouraging interaction with individual cases, not adherence to general theories or principles. The specific praise for women's social work, however, warrants further comparison with Hull-House, for Addams likewise wished to turn young women's minds from careless indulgences to mindful interactions.

In "The Subjective Necessity for Social Settlements," Addams argues that most well-educated women are not directed to respond to the "social claim" on their lives; consequently, they "dissipate their energies in so-called enjoyment."[22] Social Settlements channel these energies into work toward a common welfare. They thus develop the social self while relieving the suffering of the poor and therefore benefit both givers and receivers. On the whole, the personal contacts between the advantaged and disadvantaged people that Settlement life brings together results in widespread solidarity.[23] Because she is interested in social and self-development, Addams finds the Settlement approach to the problem of poverty preferable to the visiting approach derived from the Charity Organization Society. In a lengthy critique of the visiting model, Addams identifies its chief failing as its lack of personal relations.[24] Charity visitors remain distant from the poor. When they enter the homes of those they would help, they bring their abstract assumptions about the virtues of hard work, cleanliness, temperance, and thrift, but they do not take away from their awkward and superficial contact an understanding of why these virtues cannot simply be implemented in the given situations. Such encounters leave visitors baffled and judgmental; hosts, baffled and resentful. Food, clothing, medicine, or other goods may be provided as a result of the visitor's assessment, but giver and receiver remain mysteries to each other. Visitors never learn to respond to others' needs as people or to experience the interdependence of people in society.[25] In contrast, Settlers learn all of those things. As neighbors, they interact with the poor in ways that lead to understanding and trust. When they supply material goods, they do so in the spirit of sharing what they have, which they will discover is characteristic of the way the poor themselves help each other.[26] Because of their personal relationship with the people in need of their assistance, the Settlers give—and receive—more than material aid. They construct a mutually supportive community.

Addams's conviction that social and self-development occur through personal interactions among differently positioned people connects her with Baillie's—and Scott's—revivals of the spirit of the old charitable norms despite other great differences between them. In positing this connection, I do not deny that Addams stands apart from the earlier figures on many other points. For example, Addams understood social improvement in specifically egalitarian and democratic terms that are not part of Scott's or Baillie's agendas. In *Democracy and Social Ethics*, she argues for replacing the "individual code" that inclines people to care exclusively for their own families, businesses, and constituencies with a "social code" that would take them beyond their personal circles. She blames the "family claim" for retarding women's efforts to fulfill the "social claim"—a view that seems to invert the correspondence between helping one's family and helping a larger group in the legend of *Lady Griseld Baillie*.[27] Addams wanted to eliminate charity visiting in favor of social Settlements whereas Baillie embraced the notion of visiting. But for all her insistence on equality, Addams never argued for achieving it by the impersonal, regimented, and regimenting means of the New Poor Laws and COS bureaucracies. On the contrary, she reached back past the bureaucratization that took over with the New Poor Law to tap into the power of personal responsibility inchoate in the Old Poor Law. She would transform the individual code and the family code into the social code, making the larger ministry an expansion of the former. Even in political reform, she would have people transfer the trust they placed in corrupt aldermen to the larger government that could rein in its representatives, but the transfer can only take place if it preserves the personal and direct relations among representatives and constituents. "[W]hat headway," she asks, "can the notion of civic purity . . . make against . . . manifestation[s] of human friendliness."[28] A reformer who works by abstract principle, "who believes that the people must be made over by 'good citizens' and governed by 'experts'" is farther in her eyes from the spirit of democracy than the corrupt alderman, however much she abhorred the latter. Addams's objections to charity visiting center on its embarrassing intrusiveness and impersonality—characteristics that had grown with the bureaucratization of relief programs.[29] But when Baillie alludes to visiting the poor in their own houses, she is alluding to the personal relationship possible under the Old Poor Law. The poor remain in their homes; they have not been institutionalized in workhouses.

By noticing the importance Addams placed on personal interactions, then, it is possible to link her efforts to make society less impoverished, in tangible and intangible ways, with Baillie's and Scott's endeavors to do likewise. Addams and her Romantic-era predecessors lived at opposite ends of a development that joins them in common disapproval. Baillie and Scott looked ahead at the gathering momentum of impersonal and abstract approaches to dealing with human problems; Addams looked back at its accumulated, and in her time still accumulating, force. All three resisted this development by valorizing personal relations. Baillie and Scott believed that their alternative refurbished positive aspects of the past. Addams was inclined to see her alternative as evolving away from the past, which, like her repudiation of De Quincey, shows that her thought was disciplined by the notions of scientific progress dominating knowledge systems in her time.[30] From the vantage point of the twenty-first century that has learned to distrust total institutions and totalizing systems, the possibility of enriching social relations by personal, individual interactions is newly attractive. As I noted in the introduction, social work is increasingly the activity of helping individuals reconstruct their relations with other people in a constraining social structure; it is an attempt to change the ways the structure constrains those least able to adjust it. The prominence of symbolic interactions in social work demands a revaluation of Romantic-era efforts to reconstruct society by that means.

Bewitching
Social Relations

As we have seen, *The Bride of Lammermoor* contains a good deal of criticism
of characters who refuse or neglect their roles as providers for their communities. But it also criticizes recipients of even a meager and grudging
dole when they express dissatisfaction with it. The expectation of gratitude from the poor for inadequate and condescending assistance is perhaps even more troubling to modern readers than the idealizing of elite
providers; nevertheless, the criticism of the poor serves several important
functions for value inquiry. It reflects the fears of theft and homelessness,
analyzed in Benis's study, that complicate relations between people who
have material advantages and people who do not. Such fears have to be
confronted if a supportive community is to be established, for when they
reign unchecked and unexamined, they bewitch social relations, causing
people to demonize and criminalize each other.

In the scene from *The Bride of Lammermoor* that so captured Baillie's
imagination, Scott portrays just such negative interactions. In the context
of the whole novel and of the old poor relief system, he suggests that the
selfishness of the privileged characters is largely to blame for the corresponding selfishness of these most disadvantaged figures. But Scott does
not pursue this suggestion so far as to moderate his criticism of the reputed witches. He dwells, rather, on their refusal to interpret the dole, irrespective of its quality, as a gesture toward community and to find
greater value in being connected to that community than in gratifying
their individual wants. For Scott, the greatest danger to community is
self-contained and self-gratifying behavior, and he indicts it in all social
ranks, even when dong so leads him to require the poor to accept hardship. Fearful of any change that radically disrupts rather than gradually
adjusts the social system, Scott expects individually self-sacrificing behavior from rich and poor alike so that all develop a sense of mutual dependence and responsibility. The emergence of socially responsible selves
at any level held for Scott the promise that the existing social system could
fulfill its potential as a supportive community.

It is, perhaps, the aborted connection between the meanness of the rich
and resentment of the poor to which Baillie refers when she notes that *The
Bride of Lammermoor* "comes within one step of accounting for" the willingness of some women to embrace identities as witches. Though not a supporter of revolution, Baillie was less willing than Scott to accept the collective value of voluntary self-sacrifice. In *Witchcraft*, she goes one step
further than Scott in presenting the attitudes of the witches as a justified

response to the callous treatment they receive from more fortunate people. I suggest that *The Bride of Lammermoor* and *Witchcraft* make complementary investigations into the ways fears and resentments interfere with adequate poor relief. Only by moving beyond superstitions that place some individuals outside of society can the problem of impoverishment be alleviated. To develop this hypothesis, I offer an intertextual reading not only of Scott's novel and Baillie's play but also of Addams's account of the Devil-Baby at Hull-House. As will become apparent, Addams's insights into the correspondence between resentment and superstition, and between voluntary self-sacrifice and social cohesion, can further our understanding of Scott's and Baillie's works. In turn, their differing attitudes toward self-sacrifice can help us see that Baillie may be the most innovative thinker of all.

The reputed witches in *The Bride of Lammermoor* are three aged and infirm "matrons of the village": Ailsie Gourlay is over eighty years old; Annie Winnie is "lame of a leg from some accident"; and the third, called only "Maggie," is described as "paralytic" (320). Given their disabilities, they would be eligible for relief under the old Scottish Poor Law, but the issue in the novel is not regular relief but the extraordinary provision of goods to the villagers in connection with the weddings and funerals of members of the ruling family. We are told by the narrator that "a liberal dole was distributed to the poor" after the wedding of Lucy Ashton and Lord Bucklaw (431) and the wedding party itself was "accompanied with the attendance of both rich and poor," in keeping with the "festive publicity" characterizing such events in the traditional social order (435). Clearly, the aim of the "dole" was to extend the significance of family events to the surrounding community, creating an emotional bond between ranks.

After both the wedding and Lucy's funeral, the women break this community bond by complaining about the amount and quality of the dole as well as about the spirit in which it was given:

> "I hae gotten but five herring instead o' sax, and this disna look like a gude saxpennys, and I daresay this bit morsel o' beef is an unce lighter than ony that's been dealt round; and it's a bit o' the tenony hough, mair by token, that yours, Maggie, is out o' the back sev."
>
> "Mine, quo' she?" mumbled the paralytic hag, "mine is half banes, I trow. If grit folk gie poor bodies only thing for coming to their weddings and burials, it suld be something that wad do them gude, I think."
>
> "Their gifts," said Ailsie Gourlay, "are dealt for nae love of us—nor out of respect for whether we feed or starve. They wad gie us whinstanes

for loaves, if it would serve their ain vanity, and yet they expect us to be as gratefu', as they ca' it, as if they served us for true love and liking." (431–32)

Though this latter statement contradicts the narrator's description of the dole as "liberal," it raises doubts about the extent to which the Ashtons are living up to their traditional obligation, and it points out that stinginess and hypocrisy on the part of the elite breaks the community bond as surely as the ingratitude of their dependents, which the narrator criticizes here. The women are described as "enviously comparing the shares which had been allotted to them" (431). More tellingly, the narrator says that a "mutual hatred betwixt these hags and the rest of mankind had steeled their hearts against all impressions of festivity" (434). Indeed, Annie Winnie admits to preferring funerals to weddings because "there's as large a dole, and folk are not obliged to girn and laugh, and mak murgeons, and wish joy to these hellicat quality, that lord it ower us like brute beasts" (432).

The narrator makes a point of distinguishing between the bitterness of these women and the attitudes of most of their peers; their discontentment was "by no means" shared by "the multitude at large" (434). Irrespective of whether the dole was liberal or scanty, their hostility separates them from the community. Belonging requires a more generous interpretation of the gestures of others, even when such a generous interpretation involves some suppression of disappointment. By foregrounding their own desire for better treatment, they refuse their roles in this society. While a radical novelist could use the characters' pointed criticisms of the dole to indict the social system, Scott uses them to criticize attitudes and behaviors within the system that should be avoided or corrected for that system to function. The novel does not simply dismiss their statements; it tries to investigate their claims and explain their attitudes. It does so by looking at the interactions through which the community identified them as witches and through which they came to embrace that identity.

As is characteristic of Scott's treatments of the supernatural, the treatments of witchcraft in *Lammermoor* include rational explanations juxtaposed with folklore. Scott's penchant for allowing mutually exclusive systems of meaning—folklore and rational explanation, legend and history, invention and documentation—to coexist is among the most puzzling and frequently studied aspects of his work.[31] Regarding the legendary in *The Bride of Lammermoor*, Burwick argues that Scott lets superstition stand along with reason in acknowledgment of the inadequacy of either to account for the causes of events.[32] It follows, then, that allowing "competing" systems to coexist involves both humility and respect: it admits that one's own favored explanation may be less than comprehensive and that an alternative may serve as well, or may have served others as well, in some cases.

Just as Scott forms what I (drawing on Denzin) have called a "behavioral legacy" from the interactions of people who preceded Ravenswood in his role, so he suggests here a notion of an "intellectual legacy." Collective wisdom deserves respect even if it can no longer be fully believed because that attitude is more conducive to positive social relations than is arrogant self-assertion. Scott takes this issue up directly in *Woodstock*, having Markham Everard take such an attitude toward the haunting of the Lodge. Everard refuses to rule out a supernatural explanation even though he strongly suspects human conspirators to be the agents. "I do not deny the existence of preternatural visitations," he tells Rev. Holdenough, "because I cannot, and dare not, raise the voice of my own opinion against the testimony of ages" (1:291–92).[33]

Respect for collective wisdom, however, does not amount to uncritical acceptance for Scott, just as respect for predecessors does not lead to uncritical imitation of the behaviors of all who ever took a given role. The problem of respecting ideas without necessarily believing them might be helpfully approached by asking a version of the question I quoted from Lyman in the introduction: instead of asking whether an idea is true, I ask what it allows the character or the author to do. In Ravenswood's case, recourse to two explanations allows him to work through his perplexity about his encounter with the old women in a way that fosters a sense of community. He adjusts superstition by reason and reason by superstition without destroying either, and he arrives at a provisional understanding that is meaningful in the given situation. On the "rational" side, Ravenswood sees accusations of witchcraft as social constructions: "the hypochondriac habits of those whom age, infirmity, and poverty rendered liable to suspicion" prompt people in a credulous "age and country" to assign supernatural causes to conditions they fear (324). Regarding the willingness of the women themselves to admit to witchcraft, Ravenswood reasons that the threat of torture and death coerces those "confessions which encumber and disgrace the criminal records of Scotland" (324). Ravenswood uses reason to try to overcome his unsympathetic personal reaction to these women, who are, after all, part of this community.

Ravenswood's intellectual negotiation is satisfactory if we see that he is working with competing explanations in pragmatist terms, i.e., as problem-solving devices rather than as abstract principles or theories that must apply to all cases at all times. As long as we recognize, as Scott did, that meaning is constructed and reconstructed in situational encounters, different explanations do not have to be reconciled or settled once and for all. To extend Burwick's comment about the conclusion of *The Bride of Lammermoor*, Scott always "le[aves] the stage set for . . . another drama."[34] Scott's narrators, as well as his characters, negotiate differently with different meaning systems at different times. The narrator in *Woodstock* comments sympathetically on Everard's belief, explaining that, although he was not superstitious, "he had the usual credulity of the times" (1:198). The narrator in *The Bride of Lammermoor* gives a more particular account of the social interactions that surround Ailsie Gourlay with suspicions of witchcraft yet stop short of open accusation and confession. He uses reason to make a less sympathetic judgment.

Gourlay is skilled in herbal medicine and had apparently cured some illnesses, though the narrator calls them "pretended cures" and sees them operating only on the imagination. He implies that a relationship of mutual exploitation deflects confrontations between Gourlay and the neighbors and clergymen who suspect her of witchcraft. They withhold accusations so that they can take advantage of her skill. Even Lady Ashton hires her as a "nurse" for Lucy because she wants her assistance in wearing down Lucy's resistance to the marriage Lady Ashton wants to arrange. For her part, Gourlay "was not indeed fool enough to acknowledge a compact with the Evil One"; she publicly disavows the "occult sciences" she practices "in private" (403). According to the narrative analysis, her flirtation with witchcraft arises from a desire to have more power in society than she could ordinarily achieve. She is one of "those who, steeled by want and bitterness of spirit, were willing to adopt the hateful and dangerous character [of a witch], for the sake of the influence which its terrors enables them to exercise" (402–3). Though the connection between witchcraft and "want and bitterness" could launch a sympathetic analysis, the narrative line turns surprisingly judgmental, finding grounds on which to excuse persecution:

> The worst of the pretenders to these sciences was, that they were generally persons who, feeling themselves odious to humanity, were careless of what they did to deserve the public hatred. Real crimes were often committed under pretence of magical imposture; and it somewhat relieves the disgust with which we read, in the criminal records, the conviction of these wretches, to be aware that many of them merited, as poisoners, suborners, and diabolical agents in secret for domestic crimes, the severe fate to which they were condemned for the imaginary guilt of witchcraft. (403)

This passage could serve equally as a narrative commentary on Meg Murdockson in *The Heart of Midlothian*, for in that novel she is portrayed as a "real" criminal who is hanged as a witch. One spectator is credited with insight into the "real" crime: "this was nae witch," she tells the others, "but a bluidy-fingered thief and murderess" (391).

This unsympathetic treatment of Murdockson and Gourlay is hard to reconcile with the sympathetic treatment of Madge Wildfire, the other "witch" in *The Heart of Midlothian*, until we realize that the narrative judgment consistently condemns self-promotion. Madge—and old Alice, her counterpart in *The Bride of Lammermoor* whom I discuss below—do not assert themselves aggressively against the society in which they live. Their deviance is portrayed as harmless. Murdockson and Gourlay, in contrast, do not accept their roles within the community and are therefore portrayed as threats to the collective whole. But the critical portrayal of these women does not cancel out the critical portrayal of the elite behavior that has embittered them. The criticism of both elite and nonelite characters coexists in the novel like the superstitious and rational explanations of witchcraft itself. Readers can use one to check the other and move beyond blaming one class for social problems to recognizing faults at all levels.

The nature of the threat that Gourlay represents is made clear in the scene that Baillie noted, the scene in which Gourlay and her companions complain about the dole after the funeral. Their dissatisfaction with these provisions repeats their dissatisfaction with the provisions from the wedding, but Gourlay voices a chilling satisfaction with the intangible benefit she believes she derives from Lucy's death. She believes herself to be avenged for the slights she received from the Ashton family. More generally, she advises her companions to interpret the misfortunes of anyone in a wealthy and powerful position as revenge for the suffering of the poor, disabled, and powerless. Countering Winnie's complaint, Gourlay asks:

> can a' the dainties they could gie us be half saw sweet as this hour's vengeance? There they are that were capering on their prancing nags four days since, and they are now ganging as dreigh and sober as oursells the day. They were a' glistening wi' gowd and silver—they're now as black as the crook. And Miss Lucy Ashton, that grudged when an honest woman came near her, a taid may sit on her coffin the day, and she can never scunner when he croaks. And Lady Ashton has hell-fire burning in her breast by this time; and Sir William, wi' his gibbets and his faggots, and his chains, how likes he the witcheries of his ain dwelling-house? (443).

It is this vengeful attitude that welcomes the destruction of a family—or a society—so long as it gratifies personal wishes that the narrative criticizes—and criticizes across social ranks, for the novel allies Gourlay and Lady Ashton, showing their obsession with their own preferment to be socially destructive.

Gourlay's allusion in the above passage to Lucy's "grudg[ing] when an honest woman came near her" refers to Lucy's aversion to Gourlay's presence as her nurse (404). By hiring her to increase pressure on Lucy, Lady Ashton shows a willingness to abuse power and abdicate her social responsibility to care for the well-being of her dependents in order to gratify her own wishes. It is this behavior that the narrator sees as a threat to society. His remark that only Lady Ashton's rank saves her from being suspected of witchcraft by association with Gourlay (403–4) only calls more attention to the association that Scott makes in the novel. Lady Ashton is called "diabolical" in her determination to arrange a marriage that her daughter does not want and in her desire for revenge on her daughter's preferred suitor, Lord Ravenswood, for interfering with her plans. As Gourlay's lack of sympathy and generosity cuts her off from the shared emotions at the community events of weddings and funerals, so Lady Ashton's lack of "sympathy" cuts her off from her family. She is said to treat Lucy's resistance as an angler treats the resistance of a fish or as an attacker treats the resistance of a "beleaguered city" (401). Both Gourlay and Lady Ashton have abdicated their social roles, treat others like objects, and cultivate individual selves that are hostile to all others. Their destructive interactions contrast with the constructive ones by which others attempt to forge livable social relations.

The most relevant contrast is between Gourlay and old Alice, a former servant of the Ravenswoods now dependent on the Ashtons. At least partly because of her age and blindness, Alice is likewise suspected of witchcraft, but unlike Gourlay and her companions, she makes the most of what little she has and is not embittered about her poverty. When Lucy urges her father to order repairs on Alice's house, Alice declines the offer on the ground that the dwelling is adequate for her (52). Lucy's generosity toward Alice and the dialogue with her father in the preceding chapter that points out Lucy's sympathy for "all the old women in the country" (45) offsets the later depiction of her antipathy toward Aisle Gourlay (404). Lucy's shrinking from Gourlay is not a class-specific reaction but a response to Gourlay's designs on her in the given situation.

Despite her acceptance of her poverty, old Alice is not naively unaware of the miserliness and abuses of power surrounding and affecting her. Regarding the rumors that she herself is a witch, she says: "If the usurer, and the oppressor, and the grinder of the poor man's face, and the remover of ancient land-marks, and the subverter of ancient houses, were at the same stake with me, I could say, light the fire, in God's name!" (253) With this statement, Alice implicates the accusers in the "crime" of witchcraft, but her response is not a call for vengeance but for self-sacrifice. The opposite extreme of Gourlay, she maintains a sense of a social whole so strong that she would sacrifice herself if doing so would rid it of people who are undermining it. Her self-sacrificing behavior is both the strength and weakness of a compassionate social system, and it is what Baillie makes problematic in *Witchcraft*.

Witchcraft likewise includes three disadvantaged women who are reputed to be witches, a privileged woman who is diabolical in her selfishness, and a self-sacrificing counterpart, but the symbolic interactions in *Witchcraft* differ from those in *The Bride of Lammermoor*. Whereas Scott introduces his three reputed witches late in the novel, Baillie brings hers into the first act. Their situations and attitudes, and other characters' perceptions of them, are central to the play, and they arouse more sympathy than the *Lammermoor* figures. The wealthy and powerful Annabella poses a comparable threat to others as does Lady Ashton, but the self-sacrificing Violet is a less impassioned social critic than old Alice. Overall, Baillie does more to justify the witches' attitudes, to downplay their menace, and to suggest that more social selves might easily emerge in response to more humane gestures.

According to Dorothy McMillan, the very setting of *Witchcraft*—partly in Paisley—suggests a decision to confront problems of poverty and oppression, for Paisley was a "textile town" that finally succumbed to bankruptcy a few years after the play was published.[35] Though McMillan does not allude specifically to the Poor Laws, her point about the setting calls to mind the fact (which I reported in chapter 4 and earlier in this chapter) that the reform of the Scottish Poor Law was necessitated by the failure of the textile industry. The women who would be witches in the play—Mary Macmurren, Elspy Low, and Grizeld Bane—have no power, family support, or standing within the community. In fact, Grizeld Bane is a recent immigrant "frae far awa' parts" lodging with Mary Macmurren (2.1.622), who also has a mentally impaired son, the "idiot" Wilkin.[36] It is later revealed that Grizeld Bane has come from a mental asylum and that her mind became disturbed as a consequence of her husband's having been executed for murder (5.2.642). Though easily classified as "destitute" and "disabled" and thus eligible for poor relief, the women apparently have received no help from anyone, so in angry desperation, they seek it from the devil.

Going out on a stormy night in hopes of meeting Satan, they express their desires for "revenge" on those who have greater wealth but will not relieve their poverty:

> Ay: the hated anes will pay the cost, I trow
> We'll sit at our good coags of cream, and think
> o' the growling carle's kye wi' their udders lank
> and sapless, and the goodwife greeting ow'r her/kirn. . . .
> They refused us a han'ful' in our greatest need,
> but now it wull be our turn to ha' fou sacks and
> baith cakes and kebbucks at command, while
> their aumery is bare. (1.3.616–17)

Though they say they want power to make others suffer as they are suffering, they make no mention of taking satisfaction in unrelated misfortunes, such as the illness of Lady Dungarren's daughter, which she suspects them of causing. They are thus a less chilling group than the *Lammermoor* women who are pleased by the death of Lucy Ashton. Without approving of the "Robin Hood" ethics (to adapt Jane Addams's descriptor for such thinking[37]) that Baillie's would-be witches express, an audience might easily correlate their resentful wishes with their deprived circumstances and believe that those who failed in their obligation to prevent both deserve more criticism than do these pathetic figures.

When the tryst with Satan does not improve their circumstances, Mary and Elspy turn their anger on Grizeld Bane. They think she has cheated them and kept the power for herself. They are right that "[t]here's power to be had" (2.1.622) but mistaken in attributing it to supernatural beings. As the play makes clear, the power lies with people in higher social ranks. The truly powerful—and diabolical—character in the play is Annabella, who takes advantage of others' credulity for her own ends.[38] Believing herself robbed by Violet of the love of Dungarren, to which she feels entitled, Annabella contrives to have Violet arrested and executed for witchcraft. Suppressing her scruples about framing Violet for bewitching a sick child, Annabella rationalizes that Violet might be guilty of other acts of witchcraft, since she has been observed keeping secret rendezvous; therefore, manufacturing evidence to convict her of that kind of act "is but the sacrifice of truth for right and useful ends" (5.1.637).

By juxtaposing the attitudes and behaviors of the would-be witches and Annabella, the play allows spectators to gauge the relative threats they pose to the community. Clearly, the greater threat comes from Annabella. Baillie further mitigates the witches behavior by having Grizeld catch on to Annabella's scheme and confront her with the comment, "There is not a cloven hoof, nor a horned head of them all, wickeder and bolder than thou art" (5.1.638). However disturbed she may be, Grizeld has a more highly developed social self than Annabella. Commenting on a draft of the play, Scott wrote to Baillie, "your mad witch [is] a sublime creature."[39] In contrast, Annabella is more the "terrible character" Scott envisioned in an earlier letter asking Baillie how she planned to develop the play. "I think a wicked woman desirous of becoming a witch and half believing that she was one would be a terrible character," he wrote.[40] In Baillie's dramatization, Annabella's "wickedness" comes from her individually limited sense of self that prevents her from caring about others. She believes in her right to wield extraordinary and arbitrary power over them. Though not a play in the passions series, *Witchcraft* shows the emotion of revenge developing in Annabella when her "right" to Dungarren is challenged until it overwhelms all other thoughts and feelings. Awaiting Violet's execution, Annabella soliloquizes, "Revenge is sweet; revenge is noble; revenge is natural; what price is too dear for revenge?" (5.1.637).

The play repeatedly prompts spectators to question what they think they know about others.[41] Whereas Scott preserves supernatural explanations as a mark of respect for traditional knowledge that must be adapted rather than demolished, Baillie more pointedly questions the effects of such beliefs, noting that they can be used to harm the innocent. She had even dramatized such effects, as I indicated in chapter 3, in *Orra*. In *Witchcraft*, Annabella's plot nearly succeeds because people do not carefully evaluate the accusation. When torn clothing belonging to Violet is found in the sick child's room, because Annabella put it there, they let their suspicions and prejudices create an explanation for them. Because Violet has been observed going alone out of the village and because her father has been arrested for murder, the villagers conclude that she must be involved in some supernatural plot against them. They are willing to prosecute and execute her to protect themselves from the threat they convince themselves she poses. Violet accurately states, "I am condemned by what honest, though erring men, believed to be the truth" (5.2.638). The play gives spectators alternative information about Violet's activities—i.e., that her secret trips out of the village were to meet her father who has escaped from prison and who is hiding nearby while trying to clear his name. Moreover, it makes them privy to Annabella's scheme, enabling them to see the error of the accusation against Violet. The "hermeneutic challenge" (in the vocabulary I have been borrowing from Haney) of the play, however, is not simply sorting out its complex plot. The challenge lies in figuring out how and why witchcraft seems a satisfactory explanation to the villagers.

Except for the skeptical Dungarren, most of the characters want to believe in witchcraft as a way of explaining undeserved suffering. Lady Dungarren "knows" that her child is bewitched because she does not know how else to account for the illness (1.1.614). Similarly, some villagers gloat over Mary Macmurren's arrest because it gives them someone to blame for their troubles. This wish for a clear explanation and remedy is voiced in such comments as "she'll pay for her pastime now, I / trow, / For a' the milk kye she has witched. / For a' the bonnie bairns she has blasted" (4.1.632). When Mary insists that she never did any of them any harm and asks what makes them rage at her so (632), spectators can answer that question. The villagers are raging at Mary for the same reason she and her companions tried to raise the devil against the villagers: they do not know how else to explain and alleviate their hardships. In their anger, they have imagined themselves trapped in a supernaturally determined structure, which they want to alter by eliminating the supernatural agents behind it. As Violet's accusers miss the human agent behind the crime, so the villagers fail to look for human causes and human solutions for their problems. They fail to see that they could improve their collective situation by interacting differently with each other.

That the villagers are entrapped by their own ungenerous attitudes is made clear in the dialogue between Mary and the clergyman pressing her to confess before her execution. Though previously eager to identify herself as a witch, Mary ultimately will say only that she is what the villagers made her. She asks the clergyman to make a confession for her to repeat after him (5.2.638). Insofar as the villagers lack of charity motivated her experiments with witchcraft and their desire for a scapegoat shapes their perception of her as a witch, Mary Macmurren offers a negative example of the social construction of the self. As spectators see that interactions created the problems in this plot, they can also see that interactions can correct them. By naturalistic generalization, they can carry these insights out of the theater and into their own societies.

Human agency does prevail in *Witchcraft*, as someone comes forward to solve each problem in the plot. Violet's father comes out of hiding to reveal that she left the village to meet him, not Satan; in turn, a witness who can clear him of the murder charge appears. A messenger arriving with news that Parliament has decriminalized witchcraft saves Mary from execution. Though these actions reorganize the characters' positions with respect to each other, they do not necessarily change the fearful and self-protective attitudes that led to the original predicaments. Even more troublingly, the problem of how to deal with Annabella is obviated by Grizeld Bane's killing her, and the resultant problem of how to treat Grizeld Bane is handled by her being returned to the asylum. Purinton reads Grizeld Bane's fate as indicative of scientific control of women, of male physicians pathologizing outspoken women as hysterical just as earlier ministers branded them as witches.[42] Without denying that Bane's fate involves segregative justice, I find its punitive implications complicated by the suggestion of illness. After all, the inclusion of mental illness among "disabilities" and the use of poorhouses, workhouses, and asyla to lodge disturbed people were humane aspects of the Scottish Poor Law, and Scott does present the workhouse as a genuine refuge for his "mad witch" Madge Wildfire.[43] Looking ahead, the use of psychiatric evaluation was one of the major reforms of the justice system that Addams sought.[44] Connected to such trends in legal reform, the plot device of returning Bane to the asylum offers a positive alternative to a criminal trial, and it reinforces the classification of mental illness as a disability. Baillie's support for such a classification is likely in light of Burwick's work (which I noted in connection with *Orra*[45]) on Baillie's familiarity with her brother's medical research.

Irrespective of Bane's fate, the killing of Annabella serves as a plot device that avoids the problem of revealing or not revealing Annabella's crime and projecting ongoing interactions between her and her society. While seeming to allow retribution to overtake Annabella (especially if we join McMillan in seeing Bane as "paradoxically a force for good,"[46] the play significantly does not portray an act of punitive justice by society. Dungarren has the last word, which he uses to turn Annabella's fate into a cautionary tale: "those who have felt the tyranny of uncontrolled passions / will think, with conscious awe, of her end" (5.2.643). The statement applies to more than Annabella, for unchecked fears and self-protectiveness crippled most of the character's social selves and lived experiences, leaving them unable to restructure their society. Classified by Baillie as a tragedy, *Witchcraft* is a tragedy of structural determinism, but it is mitigated by the revival of human agency, however imperfect, in the end.

The play's emphasis on the tragic consequences of deterministic thinking makes Violet's passivity problematic in the play. Though Violet is in many ways a strong and admirable character who defies convention by visiting her outcast father and risks the loss of Dungarren's love by not confiding in him the purpose of her secretive excursions (2.3.623–25), she gives up on positively affecting her relations with others after she has been arrested for witchcraft. In prison, she accedes to the mistaken judgment of the villagers. Generously interpreting their view as both "honest" and "erring," she takes on the identity of a martyr instead of a social critic. Whereas Scott's old Alice would confront her accusers with the nature of their errors (166), Violet asserts her innocence without criticizing those who condemn her (5.2.638). Her generous interpretation of their motives does not help them question their beliefs; instead, it preserves a community consensus that ought to be unsettled by some conflicting ideas. Effective interaction—gestures between Violet's generosity and Dungarren's contempt for the villagers' "senseless idiotical delusion" (4.3.636)—are conspicuously absent from the play. Astute spectators will see the space that Baillie has opened for them and experiment with behaviors to fill it.

Witchcraft calls into question any consensus that would depend on the voluntary acceptance of hardship, such as Violet's martyrdom or the reputed witches' poverty, by some members of the community. Baillie thus takes a more accelerated and transformative approach to social change than does Scott, who proceeds more slowly and cautiously in renovating old structures. Baillie's approach is even more accelerated and transformative than that of Jane Addams, for when confronting a similar problem of superstition in the guise of the Devil-Baby at Hull-House, Addams became caught up in admiration for women who accepted mistreatment for the sake of family unity.

Recounted in both the *Second Twenty Years at Hull-House* and *The Long Road of Woman's Memory*, the story of the Devil-Baby begins with a rumor, widely believed throughout the immigrant communities, that a nonhuman being had been born to a woman whose husband had declared that he "would quite as soon have a devil in the house as" religious pictures—or, in another version, "that he would rather have a devil in the family than another girl."[47] The Devil-Baby was allegedly brought to Hull-House, where neighbors thronged to see him. Seeking to learn why so many people, especially old women, wanted to believe in the Devil-Baby (much as Baillie sought to learn why women would want to be witches), Addams hypothesized that the belief held a promise of justice for those who lived mostly with injustice in their daily lives. At one level, it promises the justice of punishment for the husband's blasphemy or misogyny. At another level, it promises the justice of putting the teller of the tale back into social interaction, giving women something to say to people who usually ignored them.[48] But Addams then calls that hypothesis a "mistake." Instead of concluding that revenge is a primary need or desire, she takes it to be a momentary "cr[y] of pain" masking a more basic and more important need for reconciliation. From that point, she concentrates on conciliating behavior, comparing it to the power of tragedy, the power to make coherence out of the disintegrating pressures of experience.[49]

Addams was struck by the difference between the desire to be heard and the desire to take revenge for being neglected or wronged, and it became the basis for the primary significance she assigned to the Devil-Baby story in *The Long Road of Woman's Memory*—specifically, the significance of showing the "sifting and reconciling power inherent in Memory itself."[50] Though the women Addams listened to identified with the Devil-Baby's mother as an innocent victim of unjust treatment, their "companionship" in suffering did not turn them against their victimizers or society. Their lack of "bitterness" or "resentment" led Addams to conclude that memory can "transmute" the past, turning even dreadful "experiences into that which seems to make even the most wretched life acceptable."[51] The companions in suffering of the Devil-Baby's mother had continued to love their often undeserving families, and they looked back on their life experiences with "an emotional serenity." Even the Devil-Baby story it-self transmutes the events into something acceptable and useful—a cautionary tale and a compensatory fantasy.[52] Though saddened by the suffering that the Devil-Baby seekers revealed to her, Addams is most impressed by the resilience of their goodwill toward others, for from such conciliating attitudes she hoped to shape more sympathetic relations in the world.[53]

Though moving in its praise for women who hold their families together by loving them more than those family members seem to deserve, Addams's seeming acceptance of the voluntary oppression of these women is as troubling as Scott's seeming acceptance of the voluntary oppression of the poor. In each case, the value of the family or community is allowed to repress the development of some of its members. In our own time, efforts to reconstruct society around an "ethics of care" continue to founder on this dilemma, as Erin McKenna's analysis makes clear. According to McKenna, "care" centered systems remain as problematic as "justice" centered systems in their limited conceptualization of the self. Neither adequately conceives of the self as growing in relationships with others, and thus each model locks an independent self into structural relations with others. The justice model generates blame and resentment as it tries to enforce an ideal social contract instead of working with the realities of human relations; the care model depends on self-sacrifice, holding society together by the voluntary oppression of some members.[54] The Devil-Baby account moves from one model to the other. More innovatively, *Witchcraft* breaks through this impasse.

The conciliating behavior in *Witchcraft* is not valorized. Two acts of self-sacrifice occur in the play: Violet's willingness to forgive her executioners for acting on their beliefs and her father's willingness to supply her with an alibi even though his doing so would lead to his own prosecution for a crime. The play passes over these acts as futile and contrives a solution that makes them unnecessary. Baillie's refusal of a stifling consensus calls for further inquiry into the relations between self and others, into the possibility of creating a community that thrives by fostering its members' potential. In sum, Baillie destabilizes the value of consensus itself, opening a space in which to imagine a more interactive society.

6

Landor and
the *Solution* of
Political Contention

WHILE CRIMINAL JUSTICE AND POOR RELIEF BECAME PERPLEXING TOPICS for inquiry during the Romantic era, so too did political representation. Petitions to extend civil rights to Roman Catholics and Protestant Dissenters, as well as calls to change the balance of power in Parliament by redefining boroughs and enfranchising men who owned only modest amounts of property, gained strength over the first decades of the nineteenth century, issuing in the major reforms of the 1820s and 1830s. Irrespective of their views on these specific proposals, Baillie's and Scott's works were caught up in the phenomenon of "popular contention"—to use Charles Tilly's term for the whirlwind of petitioning, protesting, and claims making that swept Britain at this time.[1] Baillie and Scott, I argue, tried to tone down this political clamor and channel its energy toward more broadly social ends. But another writer, Walter Savage Landor, was eager to amplify the din.

Read in the context of this rise in political participation, Landor's *Imaginary Conversations* shed a good deal of light on the intervention of literature in social problems. Specifically, they help us consider what kind of social problem political claims making poses and what kind of solution can be worked out by referring to history. Treating reference to the past as a problem-solving device is a signal trait of symbolic interactionism, and it is one of the most liberating aspects of Mead's thought, for it takes control of the future away from the determining forces of history and gives it to human actors in the present. Though Landor's strategic recreations of the past are less familiar than Scott's, they show the problem and solution from the notably different standpoint of an ardent republican. But placing Landor next to Scott lets us examine more than their representations of

148

history. It challenges us to reflect on how we have constructed their reputations or, to phrase the matter more pointedly, how Romanticists have solved problems in the definition of our field by variously minimizing and maximizing the importance of Landor, Scott, and Baillie.

In this chapter, I examine Landor's *Imaginary Conversations* as a response to popular contention; in the next chapter, I examine Scott's and Baillie's contrasting responses; and in the conclusion, I address the problem of studying Landor, Scott, and Baillie in recent disciplinary history. First, however, I offer a brief orientation to Landor so as to account for his extraordinary commitment to contentious interaction.

A Contentious Life

Like Wordsworth, Coleridge, Southey, and many other writers who came of age in the 1790s, Landor was enthusiastic about the French Revolution. The one work by him with which Romanticists are likely to be familiar is *Gebir*, a poem about its title character's failed attempt to conquer Egypt.[2] Appearing in 1798, it coincided with Napoleon's Egyptian campaign. *Gebir* is sufficiently critical of imperialist ideology to warrant classification as a "Jacobin" poem,[3] though the first edition included a note of praise for Napoleon that Landor reversed in the second edition of 1803. In that year, he also brought out an edition of the poem in Latin, a language in which he wrote and published throughout his career. It has been argued that Landor used Latin strategically to make statements that might have invited legal action if made openly in English.[4] After welcoming the French Revolution and even the rise of Napoleon, Landor became disillusioned by the consul's, to say nothing of the emperor's, self-promotion. He renounced Napoleon, joining the Spanish fight against him in the Peninsular War. For his efforts, he was made an honorary colonel in King Ferdinand's army, but he would not keep the commission because he believed the king's government was not sufficiently constitutional.[5] His experience of this conflict, including his conflicting attitudes toward King Ferdinand, influenced *Count Julian*, his 1812 drama about the struggles of competing leaders for control of Spain.[6]

Contentious in affairs of business as well as in affairs of state, Landor mismanaged the restoration of Llanthony Abbey, where he hoped to live, so badly that he moved to Italy in 1814 to avoid the lawsuits. Living abroad, he became the "ardent and perhaps sometimes unthinking and uninformed advocate of every European movement for reform or revolution."[7] Though he did not fight in Greece, he admired those who did so much that he praised Byron, whom he otherwise disliked, for aiding the cause.[8] Despite this rebelliousness, Landor considered himself a conservative. He explained his position in a *Letter from W. S. Landor to R. W. Emerson* (actually a pamphlet prepared for publication in response to Emerson's statements about Landor in *English Traits*): "I was always a Conservative; but I would eradicate any species of evil, political, moral, or religious, as soon as it springs up. . . . I would not alter or greatly modify the English Constitution. . . . Democracy, such as yours in America is my abhorrence. Republicanism far from it."[9] Landor's position may be understood in terms of the English republican tradition stretching back to the seventeenth-century thinkers who wanted "to restore the ancient constitution," which included greater scope for Parliament than recent monarchs had allowed.[10] Landor, like Scott, was preoccupied with the history of the Civil War, Commonwealth, and Restoration, but his sympathies were on the opposite side. Not surprisingly, Landor admired Milton,[11] who might be seen as a role model for Landor's own writing against tyranny.

By the 1820s, Landor wanted to return to England, and he began taking a new interest in English affairs. He supported Catholic emancipation, despite his prejudices against the Roman Catholic Church, and parliamentary reform, which he believed should have occurred long before his own time.[12] He also began planning a series of *Imaginary Conversations* to be published in England. Though he did not actually move back to England until 1835, Landor did publish the *Conversations* there in five volumes between 1824 and 1829. Landor republished these works with additional conversations in a collected edition in 1846, and continued to compose such pieces, some published during his life and some posthumously, in later years. Ultimately, the *Imaginary Conversations* grew to 156 invented discussions among characters drawn from history.[13] Most of the speakers in the *Conversations* are recognizable political or literary figures (e.g., Julius Caesar, Joan of Arc, Dante, Machiavelli, Queen Elizabeth I, Milton, Rousseau, Benjamin Franklin), though some are not now well known (Bishop Shipley, Arnold Savage, Lord Peterborough) and some are not specifically identified (a Dominican, a Florentine Visitor). Landor and his friend Robert Southey speak in a few, and Landor editorializes in notes to a few others. The historical characters come from all eras between antiquity and the nineteenth century, but the *Conversations* are not sequential or connected by narrative. Each discussion is independent from the others. Except for a volume of *Conversations* among Greeks and Romans published in 1853, Landor did not organize the pieces by speakers, nationalities, or eras as some later editors have done.

That he intended this work to stimulate political discussion is evident from his correspondence and publication plans. A letter he wrote to his friend Walter Birch indicates that the *Conversations* were meant to expose "the conspiracy of kings, first against republics, now openly against all constitutions."[14] His resolve to write the pieces in English and seek an English publisher is itself significant, for its departs from the preference for European languages and publishers he had shown since moving abroad in 1814.[15] Under the circumstances, the *Imaginary Conversations* appear designed to intervene in English politics at a crucial time in the nation's history.

CONTENTION, PAST AND PRESENT

As I noted in chapter 2, the excess of capital statutes with which England struggled during the Romantic era was a mixed legacy from the Glorious Revolution. Though morally problematic, the laws testify to the increasing legislative activity of Parliament.[16] Even though few people today remain attached to a "Whig" view of history as progressive, most view increased parliamentary activity in a positive light because most approve of such counters to the personal power of one authority figure. To some extent, modern political history is still told as a tale of progress toward a participatory goal, with one milestone passed between the Glorious Revolution and the Romantic era, when petitioning became a widespread form of claims making, and another passed during the Romantic era, when popular contention became institutionalized as part of British government. A positive understanding of these developments can be obtained from attention to Zaret's history of petitioning and Tilly's research into popular contention, on which I elaborate below. In retrospect, these accounts present participatory government as a solution to the problem of authoritarianism, and they help us recognize Landor's achievement in working out a consonant solution when the problem was much more novel. In the next chapter, I consider a different construction of the problem and solution.

Tracing the history of petitioning from the Middle Ages, Zaret identifies features of the practice that were transformed during the seventeenth century. Prior to that revolutionary era, petitions served as secular counterparts to prayer: they were the means for subjects to bring grievances before a higher authority; they were "deferential request[s]" for justice, mercy, or charity. Zaret cautions against projecting republican or Enlightenment ideals back onto this practice. Traditionally, petitions did not "criticize specific laws nor imply popular discontent with government"; they did not presume to suggest remedies for their grievances, for solutions came from "the wisdom of the invoked authority."[17] Petitions were not supposed to influence legislation or to be associated with any faction; they were not even supposed to be made public, for "the right to petition did not create a public sphere; it established a privilege for petitioners to communicate directly to those in authority."[18] This tradition of petitioning is consistent with presuppositions that put deference and patronage at the core of politics" and that marginalize "conflict and factions . . . as deviant behavior."[19]

Change in this tradition came about, according to Zaret, when the widespread printing of petitions made possible the formation of "public opinion." This development stems from the 1640s, when changes in court controls over printing broadened access to the press.[20] At that time of civic and religious unrest, all factions took advantage of printing to organize supporters, though most were not comfortable with this practice. The use of printed petitions by seventeenth-century royalists involved them in the "paradox of innovation": the unacknowledged use of a practice (cultivation of public opinion) at odds with their beliefs (deference to authority). Even parliamentarians were wary about arousing public interest in a given agenda. Zaret finds "ambivalence bordering on denial" in petitioners' courting of public opinion as a basis for government; all factions typically "relied on traditional rhetoric to justify their petitions and traditional hierarchical notions to attack petitions by their adversaries."[21] Over time, however, comfort with petitioning grew. Petitions from "private associations of individuals" began to represent grievances against the established government. Petitions were made public—read in churches where congregations could be pressed for signatures, deployed in competing propaganda campaigns, and assembled in collections with "critical commentary." The printing of petitions, Zaret concludes, created public opinion; it gave "dialogic order [to] conflict," allowing people "to interpret conflict between king and Parliament, and subsequently among parliamentary factions, as an ongoing debate."[22] For Zaret, the printed petition is the springboard for the development of republican ideas. I would add it is also the starting point for the practice of popular contention in the later eras that Tilly addresses.

By the Romantic era, the practice of petitioning was joined by the more direct and clamorous method of public protest. Such behavior has been identified by Tilly as prominent in early nineteenth-century British politics and has been interpreted as a factor contributing both to the reforms of the 1820s and 1830s and to the ongoing maintenance of parliamentary government.[23] For Tilly, a correlation exists between the extent to which citizens can make verbal or symbolic claims on government and the extent to which their given government succeeds as a representative system. By examining newspaper accounts of more than 8,000 "contentious gatherings"—defined as meetings in which at least ten people "outside the government gathered in a publicly accessible place and made visible collective claims bearing on the interests of at least one person outside their own number"—in England from 1758 to 1834, Tilly discovered that violent gatherings decreased while nonviolent gatherings increased during the period.[24] According to Tilly, the increase in nonviolent assemblies corresponds to the increasing importance of Parliament in national affairs. Violent gatherings were more common when people sought justice through local squires or patronage systems, for the personal approach to justice in such systems was uneven and therefore sometimes unfair or perceived as unfair. When collective claims could not be even fully articulated much less satisfied, frustration erupted in violence. Nonviolent gatherings be-came more common when people directed their concerns to larger governing bodies with expectations of more uniform treatment. Confident that government would eventually respond to them, people could turn frustration into the verbal and symbolic activities of petitioning, electioneering, or organizing social movements. Popular contention gradually pressured Parliament into recognizing citizens' claims, and by recognizing them, Parliament legitimized popular contention. Popular contention became a norm of government during the nineteenth century.[25]

We need only recall the very different view of the justice of personal discretion and the injustice of statutory rule operating within the Scottish courts to realize how novel and perhaps mistaken popular contention could seem during the period. If the claims of some people were unfairly ignored or denied, it could certainly be argued that failures in personal responsibility within the system should be blamed and corrected. In effect, controversies over the way to claim a place in one's society and over whether to direct that claim to political institutions or to personal authorities involve two different ways of perceiving human interaction. In one, conflict, contention, and opposition are normal; they keep any structure from closing in on people. In the other, conflict is abnormal; it should be precluded by sympathetic adjustments in social relations that keep oppressive structures from developing. To accept political claims making, people must accept contentious interaction. Promoting acceptance of contention is, I posit, the function of Landor's *Imaginary Conversations*. Surprisingly, they promote such acceptance in his present time by locating contention in the past. The logic of such an approach can be discovered by reference to Mead's ideas about the use of the past.

According to Mead, what we call the past is a notion we create in the present to establish meaningful connections between succeeding events. Mead sees activity in the present as depending on a sense of continuity: people assume that what they are doing at any given time follows logically from something that occurred at some previous time. The sense of continuity distinguishes lived experience from a "mere juxtaposition of events." It is the idea of the past that replaces juxtaposition with linkage, allowing us to interpret events. All notions of the past "exten[d] . . . present demand": they result from our "spreading backward what is going on so that the steps we are taking may . . . [appear to] advance [us toward our] goals."[26] We treat this past as a "working hypothesis" about previous events that is valid until something unexpected occurs. The "novel event" breaks the sense of continuity and halts present action. People "repair" the break in the present by incorporating the novel event into the past where its satisfactory location reestablishes continuity and makes activity possible again. The result is a "new past" that becomes acceptable or valid if and for so long as it gives meaning to present pursuits.[27] In short, construction of the past is a problem-solving exercise; it is the removal of some obstacle to forward motion in the path from present to future.

The contentiousness that was by the 1820s a prominent feature of public life broke the continuity of social relations established by familiar patterns of deference to personal authority. This novel event was exceptionally disruptive because of its resemblance to French Revolutionary challenges to political and social order. The association frightened many elite Britons, preventing them from calmly evaluating this new direction in claims making. Instead of looking critically at failings within the existing social structure, they often valorized the structure itself and hoped that fixing it in place would contain social unrest. Fear of revolution, then, was an obstacle in the path of just consideration of popular claims.[28] To remove the obstacle, claims making had to be dissociated from the French Revolution; contention had to be perceived as a normal and long-established mode of interaction. Landor's *Imaginary Conversations* accomplish just such a feat.

First, the *Imaginary Conversations* represent contention as the habitual mode of social life: they show people routinely engaged in discussion of all human affairs, routinely making claims and testing each other's claims on any and every issue.[29] The habit of questioning the authority of any claim is turned into a nonviolent alternative to revolution. Contention checks unwarranted claims, preventing any interest from becoming oppressive. It thereby accomplishes a kind of figurative tyrannicide that preempts violent acts. But secondly, and most crucially, the *Imaginary Conversations* present the habit of contention among historical figures. The rewriting of history changes the perceived dynamics of contention and order. Instead of showing a pattern of deference to authority occasionally broken by contention, it shows a pattern of contention occasionally impeded by deference to authority. Thus incorporated into the past, the contentiousness in Landor's present was no longer a novel and disruptive event. With a sense of contentiousness as normal and viable behavior, fear of revolution could be sufficiently removed for many people to consider political reform. In effect, the *Imaginary Conversations* provided a "new past" for a present marked by increasingly representative government.

To understand how these pieces are involved with popular contention, we must return to Mead's ideas about the past. The *Conversations* rely heavily on what Mead would call the "accepted past," or in the phrase of later interactionists, an "implied objective past."[30] This concept refers to a "consensus about the facts of the past," i.e., it involves our sense of what "*must* have been" in the past for the present to be as we experience it. Though consensus gives facts "situational ontology" rather than transcendent status,[31] we habitually treat facts as if they were absolutes. The *Imaginary Conversations* contain a good deal of material from the "accepted past"—not only because their characters are historical figures that readers know, or could know, from other sources but because they present the characters in plausible settings for their historical referents' time and circumstances. Discussions occur between characters from the same historical eras: meetings are not arranged across centuries; when meetings are chronologically impossible, the timing in question involves months or a few years. The figures also maintain predictable political positions: monarchs do not become republican sympathizers. The outcomes of wars and trials are not changed. Coinciding with much in the "accepted past," the *Imaginary Conversations* raise expectations about accuracy that are usually associated with "non-fiction" prose.

The *Conversations* then violate those expectations by consisting of discussions not otherwise known to have occurred. This invented dimension associates the works with fiction, raising the expectation that the characters' significance lies outside their particular instantiation. In other words, they are expected to reveal something about human nature that does not depend on their historical situations—or even their actual existence. The *Conversations*, however, lack the narrative framework and details of plot and characterization that would ordinarily serve as interpretive guides. They therefore have not been constructed as literary objects comparable to, say, Scott's historical novels. They also lack the focus of allegories, fables, or philosophical dialogues. While they raise issues of sovereignty, civil rights, justice, and power, they do so in a rambling, digressive manner.

Landor deliberately chose this format to approximate the way people actually talk to each other instead of the way philosophers set up dialogues. An *Imaginary Conversation* between Landor and Southey includes criticism of philosophical dialogues. Landor says that he will voice whatever thoughts come into his mind as they talk, adding "as you perceive I have frequently done in my *Imaginary Conversations* and as we always do in real ones." Southey endorses Landor's practice and criticizes dialogues that "collect a heap of arguments to be blown away by the bloated whiffs of some rhetorical charlatan."[32] Despite Landor's distaste for straw men, the *Imaginary Conversations* do not fully stage "real" conversations because they pay little attention to the circumstances in which people interact. Though some allude to a setting or rationale for the characters' meeting, others neglect even those points; the conversation *is* the purpose of the meeting. The *Imaginary Conversations*, therefore, are not fully comparable to Baillie's dramas, which explore situated behavior.

On the whole, the *Imaginary Conversations* seem to be neither fictions interpreting experience nor accounts recording it but a pastiche of allusions and fantasies. Therein lies their strength. It is in this very contradictoriness, where the imagined converges with the accepted, that the contentiousness of Landor's present slips into his history of the past.

Illustrative Conversations

To illustrate Landor's designs, I examine five *Imaginary Conversations* ("Galileo, Milton, and a Dominican," "Marvel [sic][33] and Bishop Parker," "Oliver Cromwell and Walter Noble," "William Penn and Lord Peterborough," and "Lady Lisle and Elizabeth Gaunt") set during the Commonwealth and Restoration eras, a crucial time in the history of republican contentions. These conversations stage inquiries into the problem of authoritarianism, offering contention and claims-making as ways to resist domination and to sustain republican systems. I then look at a conversation set in the more recent (for Landor) past—an 1809 dialogue in which Romilly and Perceval contend over the declassification of capital crimes.

The inquiries are staged on two levels. On a large scale, each conversation treats one theme or issue, such as the justice of regicide ("Oliver Cromwell and Walter Noble") or the integrity of Milton's political conduct ("Marvel and Bishop Parker"). On a smaller scale, each conversation teems with accidental remarks on kings, justice, visions, history, power, and numerous other concepts that add layers of meaning to the discussions and open lines for further investigation. One of the few *Conversations* set in the present, one in which Landor and Southey discuss Milton, offers a good orientation to how the other *Conversations* proceed. Elaborating on how they should conduct their investigation of Milton, Landor says: "Let us be reverent; but only where reverence is due, even in Milton and Shakespeare. It is a privilege to be near enough to them to see their faults: never are we likely to abuse it. Those in high station, who have the folly and impudence to look down on us, possess none of it" (2:168). From the main topic of their discussion, the assessment of Milton's poetry, come offshoots on the obligation to criticize others responsibly and on the incompatibility of arbitrary rank with responsible evaluation of merit. The passage continues with ever more specific evocations of the contradiction between rank and merit—"Do you doubt that the most fatuous of the Georges, whichever it was, thought himself Newton's superior?"—thus making a question about judging Milton's poetry lead to questions about judging and ranking people in society. The problem of unmerited power is never far from the discussion even when the conversations are ostensibly about something else. The passage also suggests that role-taking is vital to Landor's project, though in a way quite different from its connection with sympathy for Baillie or with a behavioral legacy for Scott. For Landor, role-taking has a more sharply critical function. It allows one to come close enough to others to see faults, along with merits, as one interprets their gestures. Role-taking is the alternative to gazing down at others from some distant elevation that Landor associated with monarchies and aristocracies and that he so despised.

No conversation does more to point out the value of contention than "Galileo, Milton, and a Dominican." The conversation occurs when Milton visits Galileo, who has been arrested by the Inquisition, and it focuses on the responsibility of a society's scientists, writers, and philosophers to recognize and resist abuses of power—for their own benefit but also for the benefit of less astute citizens. Metaphors of vision dominate the conversation, making poignant reference to the physical blindness that Galileo suffered by the time of the meeting and that Milton would suffer in the future, but the ability to see also stands for the ability to discern the common good. When Milton laments "that blindness should consummate [Galileo's] sufferings" (2:235), he makes a doubly meaningful statement. At one level, he expresses sorrow at Galileo's having to endure that physical condition above all others. At another level, he makes the figurative blindness of the Inquisition the means of worsening whatever suffering Galileo would have endured with age. The physical reference launches a discussion of the intellectual blindness of those in power and the responsibility of the intellectual visionary.

Blind power, of course, is most explicitly represented in this conversation by the Inquisition, which has placed Galileo in prison or at least under house arrest for discovering things about the universe that might undermine the Church's doctrine and authority. The conversation pointedly raises questions about whether Galileo is in jail or confined at a private estate. The uncertain setting allows Milton to uncover the deceptions of authority, for he sees "house arrest" as doublespeak for "imprisonment" (2:234). The Inquisition is oppressively present throughout this conversation in the person of a Dominican guard who monitors the discussion, interrupting when he hears references to forbidden topics such as theology or literature. He ends the conversation when Milton and Galileo persist in discussing the "obscene" authors Ariosto and Tasso, and he vows that Milton will never be permitted to visit again (2:237).

Before being silenced by the guard, Galileo and Milton discuss the responsibility of educated people to prevent the institutionalization of such power as the Inquisition's. According to Milton, those who support the Inquisition's power over Galileo are as "criminal" as those who actually arrested and tortured him. In a speech suggesting a younger writer's version of "I cannot praise a fugitive and cloistered virtue," Milton wishes that "the learned and intelligent in all regions of Europe" would stop coming out of their "collegiate kennels . . . [to] hunt only for their masters" and instead unite in a disinterested effort to enlighten the world. Then, he predicts, would "the ignorant and oppressive, now at the summit of power, resign their offices" (2:234). Galileo has less confidence in intellectual revolution. Looking ahead to the Commonwealth, he warns: "The spirit of liberty, now rising up in your country, will excite a blind enthusiasm, and leave behind a bitter disappointment. Vicious men will grow popular, and the interests of the nation will be intrusted to them, because they descend from their station, or order, as they say, to serve you" (2:235). Young and idealistic, Milton is sure that "truth will prevail against" the outcome Galileo predicts, but Galileo insists that "in politics, falsehood always" prevails. He describes in detail how the corrupting influence of power operates even on good men, and he reminds Milton that the greatest temptation Christ faced was the temptation to possess wealth and power (2:235).

Galileo and Milton do not resolve this debate because the Dominican enters and forbids them to speak further (2: 235). The lack of resolution, however, makes the conversation much more compelling than any solution that Landor might have devised. Readers must consider both Milton's call for intellectual revolution, which is never retracted, and Galileo's warning that revolutionaries often become versions of the oppressors they overthrew. Taking the roles of both speakers, readers are challenged to respond to both the passion of youth and the voice of experience. As the author of this *Conversation* about intellectual responsibilities, Landor casts himself in the role of a Milton for his own time. In that role, he reissues the call for intellectual revolution and trains readers to answer it, not by dreaming with young Milton of the triumph of sincerity over interest nor by resigning themselves like Galileo to finding justice only in heaven, but by working continually in the present to rein in the acts of authorities who will repeatedly strain the limits of popular control.

Significantly, Landor does not depict Milton as the authority figure he is so widely assumed to have been for the Romantics. Landor's portrayal offers further support for Lucy Newlyn's view that many Romantic writers did not see Milton as simply an authority figure but as someone who was struggling with questions of politics, morality, and religion and whose texts, even *Paradise Lost*, consequently have some open-ended and ambiguous qualities. In their own readings of Milton, Romantic writers were especially sensitive to these qualities, which they developed in their own texts. Thus, Romantic responses to Milton are not simply matters of inversion and defiance on one hand or veneration and emulation on the other but of allusion and development.[34] Landor's "Galileo, Milton, and a Dominican" shows some selective development. Landor bypasses the authoritarian qualities of the poet who justified the ways of God to men; instead, he emphasizes the libertarian qualities of the writer who denounced kings and censors. In Newlyn's terms, Landor might be said to have assimilated Milton's revolutionary potential. In Meadian terms, he has interpreted Milton's revolutionary gestures as signals for him to take up the responsibility of an intellectual in his society, and he has responded by writing the *Imaginary Conversations*.

Landor stages his most extensive treatment of Milton's politics—or more accurately, the political behavior Milton models—in a conversation between Marvell and Bishop Parker. The discussion occurs when Marvell, on his way home from visiting the aged, blind Milton, runs into Parker, who claims to be relieved that the new government of the Restoration is not prosecuting Milton for his role in the Commonwealth. The remark strikes Marvel as at best hypocritical, and he launches a verbal attack on the bishop for leaving Milton's defense to others, a defense that Marvell then eloquently makes.

Despite his distaste for straw men in dialogues, Landor comes close to setting up Parker as such a figure. A note in Landor's own voice reminds readers of the "implied objective" basis for the conversation—the historical antagonism between Samuel Parker, a Presbyterian-turned-Anglican who came to accept any measures that would stabilize the government, and Andrew Marvell, Milton's assistant in Cromwell's government, who saved Milton from prosecution when the Commonwealth ended, served in Parliament during the Restoration, but kept the republican cause alive by writing satires (2:98).[35] Though Parker is clearly a negative example, he still contributes substantially to the conversation. His questions to Marvell raise issues that republican partisans should consider if they are to hold their positions with intelligent conviction. Parker cannot be simply dismissed, but neither can Marvell be simply embraced. By his own admission, Marvell speaks too boldly, forcefully, and quickly; his passion is, again by his own admission, a typical weakness of republicans (2:110–11). Taking Marvell's role helps readers experience the revolutionary's exhilaration, but evaluating it should also yield insights into the value of self-control. Marvell points toward Milton as the best republican role model, one whose enthusiasm was intelligently controlled. Successful contention requires patience and moderation.

Marvell's defense of Milton includes a list of things Milton rejected, things such as hereditary office, the unequal application of laws to people of different ranks, and the dependence of the church on the crown (2:106). Though the list is useful as an inverse republican creed, the most important point in Marvell's defense is his eduction of a guiding principle from Milton's example. Milton "would not recommend any interest in opposition to the people" (2:106). More than just another item on the list, this principle informs all the criticism of legal exemption and aristocratic preferment that Milton made. Milton—and by extension any republican—judges particular practices according to whether they serve the interest of the people. He rejects those things, such as hereditary power, that arguably make government self-perpetuating and self-serving, an end in itself rather than a means to the welfare of all. The spirit of republicanism is better served by continual evaluation and adjustment of laws, offices, and institutions than by codification. The principle makes Milton available as a model to all who share a general republican spirit even if they differ over specific details of administration.

Marvell and Parker's discussion, then, appropriately centers on conduct. Parker accuses Milton of hypocrisy—of professing to be a "republican" yet giving up his "Athenian terms and practices" to serve the usurper Cromwell (2:101–2). Milton even continued to serve Cromwell after the latter reestablished the House of Lords, long an object of Miltons scorn (2:103). By this line of attack, Parker means to mock Milton for changing his mind and losing the courage of his convictions, but Parker is hoist with his own petard. Marvell reminds him that he was once Milton's friend and had once praised Milton's *Defense of the English People* (2:116). In response, Parker hedges that he only admired the "subtilty and Latinity of the prose and says that he would have intervened with the new government on Milton's behalf had Milton asked him to do so (2:116, 98). Unlike the bishop, whom Marvell pegs as loyal only to power (2:116), Marvell remains loyal to his friend and to republicanism. Marvell defends Milton for always upholding "liberty of conscience against the conspiracy of tyranny and fraud" and, in phrases suggestive of Blake, for always working "to liberate and illuminate . . . the manacled human race" (2:101, 106).

Marvell himself models republican behavior by contending so openly with the bishop. Not only does he criticize the bishop's behavior toward Milton and contradict him about Milton's conduct, but he speaks at length against the restored political order. The conversation is too wide-ranging to report in full, but relevant points include an attack on the veneration of Charles I as martyr and saint (2:103), an attack on the hereditary peerage (2.104), and an attack on the criterion of ancestry as a determiner of social distinction. Marvell becomes a dubious model, however, when his emotions take over his judgment. From denunciations couched in vivid, or perhaps lurid, analogies—"as a nocturnal blaze in uncultivated lands collects poisonous reptiles" so monarchy "collects the most vicious of every kind about it"—he rises to impassioned address, bidding the "noxious" form to leave the world: "go, go, thou indivisible in the infernal triad with Sin and Death" (2:110). By speaking so heedlessly, Marvell endangers himself gratuitously, for his arrest under the new laws that, as the bishop reminds him, prohibit such speech and actions (2:110) would not assist a revival of the Commonwealth. Marvell's imprudence stands out in contrast to Milton's consistent recourse to the principle of common good.[36]

The conversation between Marvell and Parker raises questions about the problem of leadership in a system where all citizens are equal and deference is implicitly on Marvell's list of words, including *"privilege"* and *"prerogative"* that *"are manifestos* of injustice" (2:110). Marvell proposes a system in which the role of the wise citizen as counselor would be recognized. Meritocracy would replace aristocracy as those "who have corrected the hearts and enlarged the intellects" of others would receive "higher distinction" than those who have "devised the ruin of cities and societies" (2:105). The scheme to award distinction for social service, which establishes some hierarchy, however, coexists uneasily with the principle of equality, which checks leaders' authority. Though the conversation supports the possibility of combining these two ideas by citing the precedents of such Roman emperors as Cincinnatus and Cato who "lived among the wiser and better citizens, with whom they conversed as equals, and where it was proper (for instance on the subject of literature), as inferiors" (2:112), it does not address the cognitive and emotional facets of such relations. It takes a drama like Baillie's *Constantine Paleologus* to fill in the social dimension and stage the symbolic interactions involved in the relationship between a nonauthoritarian leader and his people.

Landor faces the problem of justly recognizing the merit of all citizens in "Oliver Cromwell and Walter Noble." In this conversation, Noble, a member of Parliament, begs Cromwell to spare the deposed king's life. His argument devolves from his idealistic view of the new government: "History, already too dark with blood, should contain, so far as we are concerned, some unpolluted pages" (1:21). Noble wants Cromwell to set up a new standard of justice for the Commonwealth. Old justice was "one-eyed," seeing only the need for retribution (1:21). New justice should open the other eye to rewards and rehabilitation: it should "not condemn to death him who has done, or is likely to do, more service than injury to society" (1: 22). Noble's point about rehabilitation also anachronistically introduces into this conversation an idea of later penal reformers. In Ruoff's reading, Noble is a "humanitarian," though she implies no specific reference to nineteenth-century reformers by her use of that term.[37] Making a case for the former king's previous and potential service, Noble pleads, "abolish the power of Charles, extinguish not his virtues" (1:22).

Cromwell rejects Noble's argument for integrative control. In his view, the former king's existence constitutes a threat to the Commonwealth: Charles would always plot against it, just as "he would sign [Noble's] death-warrant the day after" Noble set him free (1:22). If he spared Charles, Cromwell would betray the Commonwealth. Cromwell extends the consequences of such dereliction of duty beyond the immediate possibility of a royalist coup. His example would license others to shirk their duties and hence to fail to hold the government together: "Men, like nails," he generalizes, "lose their usefulness when they lose their direction and begin to bend: such nails are then thrown into the dust or into the furnace" (1:23). Republicans cannot be merciful to those who want more than their share of power. Of course, that point applies to Cromwell as well as to Charles.

The conversation ends at an impasse. Noble says that Cromwell is cruel; Cromwell admits that may be so but rebukes Nobel for not leaving such judgments to God (1:23). Typically, such an ending would leave readers to respond to the two positions, but Landor seems to provide some resolution through a note in his own person. According to Landor, "Cromwell was not cruel. Had he been less sparing of the worst blood in the three kingdoms, the best would never have been spilt on the scaffold; and England would have been exempt from the ignominy of Sidney's death, Milton's proscription, the sale of the nation to the second Charles, and the transfer of both Louis" (1:23). At one level, the note decides the argument in Cromwell's favor. It may also reveal a blind spot in Landor's republican vision: Landor could never bring himself to look directly at Cromwell's tyrannies.[38] At another level, the conversation still leaves room for a good deal of interpretation and response. The note vindicates only Cromwell's motives, confirming the speaker's perception (or rationalization) of himself as an instrument of the people, while actually introducing criticism of his actions: had Cromwell been even more unbending than Parliament authorized him to be, he might have done greater good for the Commonwealth. The question of Cromwell's character and the justice of the regicide remains open. The value of the conversation lies in Noble's having called Cromwell to account, a value consistent with Landor's emphasis on republicanism as the limiting of personal authority.

Both Landor and Scott adapted their representations of Cromwell to their views of political contention, and it is useful to compare how their refigurings spread backwards their concerns. Though a comprehensive examination of refigurings of Cromwell lies outside the scope of this study, it is worth noting that Landor and Southey were far from unique in concentrating on Cromwell. After studying many representations of Cromwell over time, Roger Howell finds references to Cromwell well suited to nineteenth-century debates over Parliamentary reform and repeal of restrictions on the civil rights of Catholics and Dissenters as these debates echoed seventeenth-century controversies over the relative power of Church and King. For some later reformers, Cromwell "was 200 years ahead of his time in anticipating the redistribution of parliamentary seats in the 1832 Reform Act."[39] Not surprisingly, then, Cromwell came to embody seventeenth- and nineteenth-century concerns for Landor and Scott.

Like most depictions of Cromwell since soon after the Protectorate itself, Landor's and Scott's participate in what W. A. Speck calls an attempt to make a "usable past"—i.e., "a lesson to be learned to prevent what had gone wrong before going wrong again."[40] The "usable past" is clearly compatible with interactionist ideas about the past as a solution for present problems. As Mead conjectures in *The Philosophy of the Present*, even if we could recover some element from the past that has no relation to the present, "it would not serve us."[41] Usable pasts can admit some complexity in their presentation of people and events, and almost all histories of Cromwell include some concession to a dimension of his character that did not fit the lesson.[42] To Landor's and Scott's credit, they do not simply turn Cromwell into a scapegoat. Ultimately, both find it inappropriate to blame Cromwell alone for his abuses of power. For Landor, the fault is shared by citizens who failed to follow Noble's lead and challenge Cromwell more insistently and repeatedly. For Scott, the fault is shared by all who embrace and promulgate republicanism.

An *Imaginary Conversation* in which William Penn and Lord Peterborough agree that Cromwell was the best leader for his time makes it clearer than does the discussion between Noble and Cromwell himself that Landor holds citizens responsible for their leaders. For Penn and Peterborough, the behavior of any leader, whether king or Lord Protector, depends on the people who allow themselves to be led by him. According to Peterborough, "[t]he king is the work of our hands, we are not the work of his: we existed before him, and shall exist after him: he may do much with us, without us nothing." Penn agrees: "[i]n this thou art wise; and on this secure part of thy wisdom let thy bravery act and rest (1:554). Given his view of the source of leadership, Peterborough refuses to consider Cromwell a "usurper." "If he was one, so is the gentleman I helped to introduce from Holland," concludes Peterborough, alluding to his part in bringing William of Orange to the English throne (1:554). Penn's indulgent opinion of Cromwell rests on Cromwell's having served on the "side" in the war that Penn considers "righteous" — "the side of the sufferer and the oppressed" (1:554). Penn's evaluation continues: "He [Cromwell] is thought to have been a hypocrite for the sake of power; whereas in fact he was sincere, until power by degrees made him a hypocrite. How little then of it should be trusted to any man, when the wisest, and the Bravest, and the calmest are thus perverted by it!" (1:554). Not Cromwell, then, but a system with insufficient checks on personal authority is to blame for abuses of power. Peterborough is all too eager to have the military keep individual leaders in line (1:554), and on that point he and Penn part company, with the conversation turning to other topics.[43]

Scott's indictment of the way of thinking that produces a Cromwell appears most clearly in *Woodstock*, a novel written in 1826–27 when he was most acutely anxious about both personal and political affairs.[44] As D. J. Trela has pointed out, Scott's treatment of Cromwell is remarkably "evenhanded." For Trela, this balanced characterization allows Scott to criticize the disorder "of the times in which [Cromwell] rose to prominence" more than the man himself.[45] If Scott's Cromwell "is at once an ambitious, bloodthirsty tyrant and a self-effacing Christian gentleman reluctantly drawn into battle," it is because he represents "erring humanity" trying to cope with the contradictions of his day. Scott's goal in the novel is to correct the conditions that can produce a Cromwell: he rejects fanaticism and reconciles opposites so that only the line of the moderate Alice and Markham Everard survives.[46] I would add, however, that the complexity of Scott's characterization does not preclude partisan use and that Scott's critique of disordered times and the minds they produce is directed against the republican climate of his own day.

Scott's portrayal of Cromwell exploits some of the more extreme rhetoric of various partisan views. For instance, Restoration rhetoric, as studied by Howell, typically made Cromwell the devil incarnate while Dissenting histories continued to associate him with liberty because of his advocacy of religious tolerance.[47] Scott adapts the former in the haunting of Woodstock: according to Wildrake, who returns from his interview with Cromwell saying that he brings a warrant from the devil (1:149), "goblin or devil was never heard of at Woodstock, until it became the residence of such men as they [the commissioners sent by Cromwell], who have now usurped the possession" (1:227).

Scott reveals the error of placing individual judgment over tradition in Cromwell's final meditation on his own fitness to govern. Why, he wants to know, has he not won the respect and allegiance of "English gentlem[e]n" such as Sir Henry Lee: "Yet what can they see in the longest kingly line in Europe, save that it runs back to a successful soldier [such as himself]? I grudge that one man should be honoured and followed, because he is the descendant of a victorious commander, while less honour and allegiance is paid to another, who, in personal qualities, and in success, might emulate the founder of his rivals dynasty (2:341–42). Conscious of his own merits, Cromwell cannot think of deferring to others. In interactionist terms, he has failed to respond to gestures from the community that invite him to take a leadership role. That role might be described as a "generalized other" previously embodied by kings. The challenge for Cromwell to meet, as for Ravenswood in his taking the role of the Master of Ravenswood, is to emulate only the benevolent qualities of his predecessors: "Earlier, Cromwell had marveled at cavaliers who are, in his words, silly enough to run their necks into nooses and their heads against stone walls, that a man called Stewart, and no other, should be king over them. Fools! are there no words made of letters that would sound as well as Charles Stewart, with that magic title beside them? Why, the word King is like a lighted lamp, that throws the same bright gilding upon any combination of the alphabet, and yet you must shed your blood for a name!" (1:147–48).

In focusing on the emptiness of the sovereign's position, Cromwell misses the interpretive activity that fills any such position with meaning for either republicans or royalists. For republicans, the meaning comes from citizens' authorization, as Penn and Peterborough indicate. For royalists, it comes from respect for the traditional system. Cromwell wants simply to stake his claim to the position, and Scott portrays his preoccupation with his own claim as his error. Yet Cromwell's error is not so much a character flaw as a philosophical one: republican thinking necessarily encourages the assertion of claims as opposed to the acceptance of a subordinate place. Scott reflects this error as confusion in Cromwell's thoughts and speeches.

Scott takes pains, both through narrative assertion and exploitation of the belief that Cromwell was a rambling, dissembling orator, to show Cromwell as confused rather than as hypocritical (1:123–24). This portrayal suggests that Cromwell's religious and political principles were not a cover for his personal ambition; rather, his personal ambition was a consequence of his religious and political principles. Like Landor's Cromwell, Scott's Cromwell tries to define himself as the mere instrument of God's cause (in his own words, "a judge raised up for the redemption of England" instead of "the son of those Kings whom the Lord in anger permitted to reign over her" 2:323), but his willingness to blow up Woodstock shows less care to save the country than to secure his own election. For Scott, this pursuit of an individual claim indeed makes Cromwell "representative of the democracy of England" (1:124). I turn to other aspects of *Woodstock* in the next chapter. In this chapter, more remains to be said about the *Imaginary Conversations*.

Requiring speakers to be always skeptical about each other's motives, to suspect others of always seeking power, and to be quick to prevent them from winning that goal, the *Imaginary Conversations* do little to infuse social relations with sympathy, hesitancy, or respect. Their limited behavioral range makes them strong political works but weak social ones. They do, however, share Baillie's and Mead's disapproval of self-sacrifice, and their portrayals of less contentious characters can arouse readers to claims making on behalf of others and thus encourage social interactions beyond those they represent. A conversation between Lady Lisle and Elizabeth Gaunt epitomizes this effort.

Lisle and Gaunt converse in a Restoration-era prison, where they are awaiting execution for harboring republican fugitives. Their motives for doing so, however, were religious, not political: they believed they should minister to anyone in need of food or shelter. Lisle absolves the jury from blame for condemning her because she did indeed harbor fugitives. Gaunt voices no criticism of her accuser, a fugitive who repaid her kindness by turning her in to the authorities for a reward; instead, she worries about how difficult it must be for him to have his act of betrayal on his conscience (1:386). The value of their nonjudgmental stance is questionable, for it accepts and reinforces the power of the restored monarchy over them. Their statements, however, are not offered for imitation but for evaluation. Lady Lisle's words, which reveal how the judge threatened to convict the jury of treason if they did not find her guilty (1:386), are calculated to provoke in readers the outrage she will not express. The effect of the conversation is to excite oppositional force on behalf of those who will not or cannot speak for themselves.

Some of the *Imaginary Conversations*, such as "Romilly and Perceval" and "Mr. Pitt and Mr. Canning," are set very close to the time in which Landor was writing and refer directly to the reform of Parliament and of the capital statutes. The conversation between Pitt and Canning, in which Pitt expresses a desire to see Canning succeed him as prime minister and advises him on how to fill the office by lying without seeming to and by choosing associates because of their "tractability and connections" (1:347), clearly aims at exposing corruption and deceit and thereby justifying reform. Landor would give readers the penetrating vision that Pitt claims people do not have: "They have keen eyes who can see through all these words [of obfuscation]: I have never found any such, and have tried thousands. The man who possesses them may read Swedenborg and Kant while he is being tossed in a blanket" (1:376). The conversation between Romilly and Perceval comes closer to dealing with criminal justice reform as a social issue; nevertheless, it subordinates that topic to the issue of political corruption and inertia as obstacles to this reform as to all others. Like Baillie's *Stripling*, the conversation raises concerns about the inhumanity of capital punishment for financial crimes. Unlike the play, it does not dramatize the human cost and social effects. It challenges readers to rise to political action more than to social consciousness.

Many of Landor's readers would have personal memories of these two opposite political figures—Romilly, who wanted significant reforms, especially declassification of numerous capital crimes, and Perceval, the reactionary prime minister assassinated in 1812, who opposed almost any reform. Those considering the *Conversations* after Romilly's *Memoirs*, which Baillie read "with interest," were published would know that Romilly discontinued his personal friendship with Perceval because he found it hypocritical to be friendly in private with a person he opposed in public.[48] Though Landor does not set the scene or provide an occasion for their meeting beyond a reference to Romilly's congratulating Perceval on his appointment to office (which dates the meeting to 1809), a statement by Romilly marks the discussion as a private conversation in which the topic of capital punishment is treated "more loosely than . . . in parliament, but more openly and fairly" (1:267). Not incidentally, the comment also insinuates some criticism of the candor of parliamentary debates.

Before introducing the topic of capital punishment, Landor focuses on the problem of corruption in government by having Romilly deflate Perceval's praise for his "immortal" predecessor William Pitt. For Romilly, Pitt's reputation depends on "clubs expressly formed for the purpose of irrigating this precious plant of immortality with port and claret"; Pitt himself, according to Romilly, "came about us like the tide along the Lancashire sands, always shallow, but always just high enough to drown us" (1:265). The conversation thus approaches the topic of capital punishment within the context of statesmanship rather than as a social problem. Romilly wants Perceval to make it his government's priority "to soften the rigour of the penal statutes" (1:266); Perceval cautiously defends the status quo, appearing to lack the vision and will to fathom alternatives.

When Romilly says that "Draco himself did not punish so many with blood as we do" in England, Perceval, instead of focusing on the excessive number of severe sentences, retorts that Romilly can't prove his point about Draco. Moving on to modern crimes, Romilly points out the unjustifiable severity of making forgery and fraudulent bankruptcy punishable by death, for even murder can bring a lesser penalty when not committed out of deliberate malice. Perceval disagrees, claiming that fraudulent bankruptcy "deserves the punishment of death" because it can only be committed by "afore-thought" and "calculation" (1:266). Romilly provides a hypothetical example to the contrary.

"Suppose," he directs, that a modest businessman "from unskilfulness, or the infidelity of his agents, or from a change in the times and in the channels of commerce," faces bankruptcy. Suppose further that the man casts around for some way to protect his family from destitution and decides to hide from his creditors what remains of the money his wife brought to their marriage, reasoning that that money is not part of the business (1:267). Perceval does not argue that the man is malicious or deserving of the death penalty. He simply opines that the man "is much to be pitied: I see no remedy" and asks "What can be done? We are always changing our laws" (1:267). Perceval is willing to let unjust punishment continue because he is unwilling to disturb a prevailing order.

Perceval's statements and question give Romilly the opportunity to expatiate on what can and should be done. His defense of agency over structural determinism is worthy of interactionism: "The greatest evils and the most lasting are the perverse fabrications of unwise policy, but neither their magnitude nor their duration are proofs of their immobility. They are proofs only that ignorance and indifference have have slept profoundly in the chambers of tyranny and that many interests have grown up, and seeded, and twisted their roots, in the crevices of many wrongs. The wrongs in all cases may be redressed, the interests may be transplanted" (1:267). Romilly, however, focuses on political and legal solutions, not social adjustments, despite Perceval's accusation that his (Romilly's) "logic . . . ha[s] been relaxed by [his] philanthropy" (1:267). Romilly's solution is to have a third of a bankrupt person's property protected, by law, from creditors and designated for the use of the person's family so that no one would be tempted to protect assets fraudulently to keep their spouse or children from suffering (1:268).

Though Romilly's proposal clearly follows a philanthropic or humane[49] line of thinking, Romilly claims to be avoiding any argument that will play on Perceval's emotions. Of course, his allusion to the family scenes he will not paint cleverly bring them into the discussion in a roundabout way. More directly, Romilly takes issue with Perceval's disjunction of "logic" and "philanthropy." He professes that he "would appeal to the judgment and the heart together: . . . My argument, if it carried such weight with it as to lay the foundation of law, would render many men more compassionate (which, after all, is the best and greatest thing we can do on earth), and it would render no man fraudulent" (1:267). These words call to mind the aim of creating a more just and more merciful society stated in Baillie's *Introductory Discourse,* but instead of dwelling on the value of improving social relations, from which any legislation may follow, Romilly passes over, parenthetically, the achievement of sympathy in order to focus on legislation.

The conversation ends civilly, with Perceval telling Romilly that his proposal for protecting some family assets does him (Romilly) "honour," though he (Perceval) gives no sign of converting to Romilly's view or actively supporting him (1:268). The conversation does not hold out the hope that people will become more just, merciful, or sympathetic; it holds out the hope that their selfishness and indifference will be checked by contention.

Even from this small sampling, it can be seen how the *Imaginary Conversations* were a problem-solving exercise within the context of parliamentary reform. Breaking the authoritarian narrative of history into episodes of discussion, they created a contentious past that could be continuous with Landor's contentious present and lead to the goal of a more representative government in the future. The exercise was useful even after the landmark date for parliamentary reform (1832), as the success of reform depended on ongoing contention. Hence the reforms of 1832 were greeted almost immediately with calls for further reform, and Landor continued to write, publish, and republish *Imaginary Conversations* into the middle of the century.

Since Landor rewrites history to give contention a power and prominence that it does not have in most other versions, he might be charged with inventing a "mythical past." A "mythical past," according to Maines, Sugrue, and Katovich who educed the concept from Mead, is a fictitious history created to give some group an advantage over others.[50] If all pasts are constructed, however, the line between mythical and legitimate pasts is quite faint. Recourse to an "implied objective dimension" does little to sharpen it. A clearer separation may be made by asking the question I have adapted from Lyman: what does such a past allow someone to do? Mythical pasts allow deception. They are constructed and deployed solely to promote the interest of one group over others.[51] Though the past in Landor's *Conversations* is designed to give an advantage to those favoring republican government over those favoring more authoritarian regimes, it is not an instrument for deceptive self-promotion.

For Landor, contention solved the problem posed by the vagaries of personal authority. For Scott and Baillie, however, contention exacerbated unsympathetic interactions, interfering with care and respect for others. When they spread back their present concerns, the past they create emphasizes temporizing and cooperative behaviors. Their responses to contention are the subject of the next chapter.

$$7$$

Baillie, Scott,
and the *Problem* of
Political Contention

ON THE MATTER OF PARLIAMENTARY REFORM, BAILLIE'S AND SCOTT'S views align with those of their parties, not with each other. Baillie thought the plan was "just" and "reasonable," and she was glad to see people in Scotland becoming "zealous" for it instead of remaining "timidly or rather selfishly pliant" in politics.[1] Her disapproval of mere acquiescence in politics is consistent with the disapproval of self-sacrifice evident in her plays. It does not, however, make her an unqualified supporter of political contention. She disapproved equally of selfish political claims making, which she exposes for criticism in *The Election*, her comedy on hatred. Scott vehemently opposed "the Reform or rather the Revolution bill." Planning to speak against it at a Tory meeting in Selkirkshire, he even prepared a strong text in "no temporising language," but he "pocketed [the] diatribe" instead of reading it when he discovered that others at the gathering had given up on resisting reform and only wanted to quibble about redistricting.[2]

Despite his use of "no temporising language," Scott's pocketing of his protest exhibits the temporizing behavior he advocated in lieu of contention. In the example from the letter, Scott considered what benefit would be derived from speaking out in a way that would not be acceptable to most of the people at the meeting, decided that there would be little or no benefit, and chose not to speak. He conducted himself in a way that let him interact on good terms with the group. He did not, however, change his mind about reform, and his silence in this situation would not preclude his speaking out in others if he perceived some benefit could be derived from his doing so. The restraint he showed in his own disappointment was the restraint he expected from advocates of reform or, indeed, from everyone. By his standards, people should look for ways to make modest and incremental corrections in a system instead of voicing contentious demands.

This behavior has affinities with the conduct by characters in the novels that Chandler analyzes as "deliberation," the careful balancing of one case against another, and that Christensen describes as "equivocation," a mode of survival and negotiation used by people at odds with the ruling power in their state.[3] Asking why Scott developed such a strategy when he did not want to undermine order, Christensen answers with a distinction between "acquiescence" and "consent." The former involves passive acceptance of a condition that cannot be changed immediately; the latter involves active approval of the condition. Exemplified by Waverley, equivocation is a strategy for conservatives who cannot actively support the Hanoverian accession but who also know the Stuarts will not regain control. For Christensen, the strategy meets the needs of people who are waiting for different conditions to emerge in a world that changes through impersonal forces rather than personal agency, a world in which government has become bureaucratic.[4] One need not, however, accept the operation of impersonal forces to recognize the value of equivocation or a similarly named strategy.

Interactionists, particularly present-day interactionists, recognize that structural change can be a long, difficult process, and they take an interest in how people cope with situations to which they do not consent without giving up the idea that human agency can eventually change things.[5] I prefer the term "temporize" for this coping strategy, not only because it occurs in Scott's letter and again in *Redgauntlet* but because it implies a deferring of confrontation.[6] Deferring confrontation takes the opposite approach from the immediate opposition in popular contention, and it has affinities with the situational adjustments Addams and Mead advocated, which depend on taking the time and trouble to "think from all points of view."[7] Such broad consideration can allow for situational adjustments beyond the either-or of victory or defeat. The temporal allusion also calls to mind the adjustment of the past to present needs characteristic of many of Scott's novels and some of Baillie's plays.

In this chapter, I look at the temporizing behavior Scott builds into *Redgauntlet*, a novel published in the same year as the first volume of Landor's *Imaginary Conversations*, as an alternative to contention. I then turn to Baillie's depictions of politics and history. Though I am most concerned with her combination of the two in *Constantine Paleologus* and *The Family Legend*, I begin with her play on contemporary politics, *The Election*, because of its direct concern with contention.

Scott's Temporizing

In *Redgauntlet*, Scott uses temporizing as both a mode of behavior for his characters and a principle of structure and plot. The contentiousness of the characters mirrors the contentiousness of his contemporaries, and the novel shows this mode of behavior as self-defeating, ineffective, or otherwise undesirable while offering temporizing as a more satisfactory strategy. Moreover, it shows Scott's own temporizing approach to history. Scott maintains a deferential attitude toward history even while he creates narratives that reveal the past as an interested invention (or intervention). The fictiveness of the past is an open secret in Scott. He treats it as given, showing that all access to the past is mediated by persons or documents that can never offer complete or completely trustworthy views. Nevertheless, Scott endorses the authority of the history, proceeding *as if* a selected interpretation were trustworthy. Scott asserts authority, implying that those who refuse to follow some guide will be lost in a wilderness of conflicts and skepticism.

The Jacobite conspiracy of the 1760s that figures in *Redgauntlet* is one of the most widely acknowledged examples of Scott's tinkering with history, but while noting the "inaccuracy" of the plot, we should not overlook the "accurate" (i.e., shared by other sources) allusions to the 1760s that balance it. The plot is tied, in Darsie's journal, to provincial agitation against the "present administration," which according to Kathryn Sutherland's note very likely alludes to John Wilkes's newspaper campaign against the Bute ministry and his ongoing efforts "to stimulate London radicalism throughout the 1760s."[8] Bearing out the cliché that politics make strange bedfellows, the Jacobite plot is associated with popular contention against the government.

A further connection between Jacobite and radical agitation occurs during the dinner conversation between Provost Crosbie and Redgauntlet's old comrade, Pate-in-Peril. The Provost "debated with great earnestness upon the stamp act, which was then impending over the American colonies" (245). When he asks his dinner guest, "What do your folk in the country think about the disturbances that are beginning to spunk out in the colonies" over the act, he receives the following surprising and cryptic reply: "Excellent, sir, excellent. When things come to the worst they will mend; and to the worst they are coming" (240). Although Pate-in-Peril's response partly reflects his desire to dismiss the topic so that he can talk about himself, it nevertheless adds to the novel a sense of Jacobite approval of antigovernment agitation, even if it stems from principles different from their own, and a sense of the 1760s as a predominantly contentious time. Significantly, protests over the Stamp Act show both the success and failure of popular contention near the beginning of the period that Tilly defines as its rise. As Sutherland's note points out, agitation against the Stamp Act succeeded in getting it repealed, but it also prompted the passing of a "Declaratory Act" to confirm "Parliament's full sovereignty over the colonies" (451n245).

The insinuated connection between Jacobites and republicans allows Scott to conflate the antigovernment agitation from many times, including the 1820s when Scott was writing *Redgauntlet*, and offer the phenomenon of contention for examination and criticism.[9] In direct contrast to Landor, Scott treats the republican contentiousness that emerged during the seventeenth century as a novel event that disrupted a stable system. He repairs the break in the past by diminishing the consequences of the conflicts. However impossible it may be to undo the events that occurred since 1765, it is possible not to repeat them in the future. It would be possible, in the 1820s, to establish a conceptual or attitudinal continuity with Scott's alternative past, taking deferential relations as a norm and rejecting contentious ones. The assertions of the intervening decades, then, would become aberrant, a break in the normal course of things. Reconnecting with a deferential past would repair that break and allow society, finally, to stabilize itself and build widespread respect onto traditional deference. The most important sign of continuity with the alternative past would be the end of agitation for parliamentary reform.

Abstracted from the novel, Scott's "history lesson" amounts to directions to bow to authority, but within the novel, it is couched in amusing terms that raise readers' anxieties about proceeding without a guide and then win them over to the benefits of trusting someone. From the opening exchange of letters between Darsie and Alan Fairford, through Wandering Willie's Tale, to Darsie's interview with "Father Buonaventure," the novel asks how we can know anyone or anything, and it answers that we must rely on the guidance of some authority.

The opening exchange of letters raises the question of Darsie's identity and recounts his efforts to discover his family tree. First, he wants Alan to lead him on the quest: "make up my history," he begs, using the "lawyer-like ingenuity" that creates a case for a client (17). Alan, however, lacks the time, resources, means, and position to take this lead. When he offers some guidance, it aims at making Darsie take a more practical and realistic approach to his given situation. Moreover, Alan's letters defend his own practical choices and character as much as they criticize Darsie's imaginative bent. Alan's advice makes Darsie defensive, and the two spar with each other throughout their letters over their assessments of each

other's characters and their interpretations of the events they experience.

The exchange between Darsie and Alan might be seen as an epistolary
equivalent to an imaginary conversation between Landor and Southey, an
example of friendly contention between peers. Indeed, Scott implies that
an assumption of parity between them underlies their contentiousness:
their school was "a little republic" where Darsie's "arrogance" was curbed
(14). Alan's Whig convictions are made clear in his account of Herries's
visit to his father. Alan is infuriated by Herries's high-handedness, and he
can "hardly excuse" the elder Fairford "for enduring so much insolence"
and for "never entirely shak[ing] off the slavish awe of the great" learned
in his youth (51). As befits his uncertain identity, Darsie's convictions are
not so sharply defined, but his scorn for tradesmen (15) and his fascina-
tion with romance and sport (passim) foreshadow the aristocratic identity
he eventually assumes. While he does not know his identity, however, he
can contend with Alan on equal terms.

Though their quarrelsomeness is appropriate, friendly, and harmless, it
is useless as a means of discovering what position Darsie should assume in
life. Darsie and Alan can only repeatedly interpret their affairs to each
other: they lack the knowledge of a larger scheme into which Darsie
might fit. Darsie must find a different guide. Had Landor written this exchange, the contention itself could have helped Darsie shape a role model
for his future actions, much as contending with Southey over Milton
shapes Landor's sense of a poetic role model for his time. Contention in
itself is useful, and Landor reinforces the idea in the structure of his work
in which imaginary conversations stand without narrative support. In
contrast, Scott's structure reinforces a sense of contention as inadequate.
Using the letters for just the first third of the novel, Scott switches to om-
niscient narration and comments on the need for authorial guidance in the
process. The letters end because they "can seldom be found to contain all
in which it is necessary *to instruct the reader* for the full comprehension of
the story" (141, emphasis added). Scott's readers are not to be given the
same freedom to interpret as Landor's readers. If readers are to satisfy
their curiosity about Darsie's identity/position, they, like Darsie himself,
are to seek a guide.

The assertion of narrative authority that ends the epistolary portion of
the novel is only the first of several such interventions. Instructions to the
reader appear in several later chapters, especially at junctures in technique or emphasis. The remainder of the novel alternates between omni-
scient narration and excerpts from Darsie's journal. The use of the diary
plays off Darsie's point of view against the narrator's account of what

"really" happened, and it keeps readers dependent on the narrator for information about things outside of Darsie's ken. The diary also further associates contention with unauthorized interpretation. As Jones points out, it is a "repository of contradictory political ideologies."[10] Through the diary, written as a journal-letter to Alan, Darsie continues to quarrel with his friend's criticisms of his imagination. But because Darsie expects other people—people who may have learned the Fairfords' view of him—to find the document, he prepares it to correct any "false estimate" they might have formed about him (218). Scott's presentation, however, inclines readers to look to the narrator for judgments about Darsie's, or anyone's, "real character and disposition" (219) or to deal with such contradictions as Jones notes. Further instructions to the reader accompany the switch from the diary back to the narration of Alan's experiences: a summary of the estimate "the reader ought" to have made of Alan's character (or will have made after reading the summary) effects the transition (226). Narrative authority even overrides the revelation of Darsie's identity in the plot, for when Darsie's lineage as a Redgauntlet is finally revealed, the narrator asserts that he will still call the character "by the name to which the reader is habituated" (334). Although generic convention is no doubt the source of the above narrative comments (and other familiar ones such as "our readers may recollect . . ." and "our history must now . . . instruct our readers of the adventures which befell . . ." [357, 310]), Scott's deployment of an intrusive narrator in this novel creates an authority figure and the expectation that readers will rely on that interpretive guide.

The "Magnum Opus" edition of the novel, prepared as Reformers were in the process of winning their goals, adds even more markers of authority in the form of footnotes. This device, which Scott had used sparingly in his first editions and heavily in the Magnum Opus, clothes his fiction in the guise of history, encouraging readers to trust the "accuracy" of the representation. Robertson notes that annotation was becoming popular in Scott's time, and Scott's footnotes have been the topic of renewed inquiry by Mayer.[11] Footnotes loom large in what Nancy Partner terms the "protocol" of history writing, i.e., the set of conventions that mark a text as "history" even if it includes fictional or imaginary elements. According to Partner, the signal feature of history is not an absence of imaginary elements but the claim that the account is not entirely imaginary. Until scientific methods became dominant in the nineteenth century, histories normally included fictions designed to highlight certain aspects of the presented events and to shape interpretation of them. Conventionally, historians were *supposed to be* interpretive guides: they assumed the authority to direct what people should think about civic affairs, and they usually directed interpretations that would reinforce the ruling powers or maintain cherished traditions.[12]

But even when historians had more license to fictionalize than they have in more recent times, the assumption that they interpreted some given events governed the imaginary aspects of their work. History had to refer to things that people other than the historian could recognize from other sources or from experience in order to fulfill its claim to represent reality.[13] In interactionist terms, it had to deal with, though not necessarily endorse, an "accepted past." History, then, consists of some referential component and an interpretive frame or purpose—with the proportions between these two varying over time. Footnotes and other markers of "verifiability" provide the referential component of the text, the assurance that its interpretation bears on shared experience.[14] By multiplying footnotes in his text, Scott signals an intention to represent reality and asserts a claim to authority to interpret it—even though the content of his notes does not always satisfy the criterion of verifiability.

In Mayer's words, Scott's blending of fiction and history allows his novels to "embody actual research and the lived experience of the historically minded 'Author of *Waverley*.'"[15] Denzin's term "lived textuality"[16] might be aptly substituted to capture the view of Scott as thoroughly immersed in interpretive interaction. His novels display and encourage the kind of relation to the past he tried to perform in his life and works and that he believed was most conducive to community. He relied on history because, like Everard at Woodstock Lodge, he would not "raise [his] voice . . . against the testimony of ages" (149), but he would add his voice in adapting the past to present needs.

It is a strength of *Redgauntlet* that Scott reveals how complex interpretive interaction can be. Even when one is willing to learn from history or from a traditional role model, it can be difficult to identify the right guide. Scott builds discussion of that very issue into Darsie's encounter with Wandering Willie and into "Wandering Willie's Tale." As Darsie, "totally ignorant" of where he is going (100), follows the blind musician through the countryside, Willie asks him, "How do ye ken whether I am honest, or what I am?—I may be the deevil himsell for what ye ken; for he has power to come disguised like an angel of light; and besides, he is a prime fiddler" (101). Because Willie's question is followed by his speculations about the devil, Darsie can avoid answering it and scoff instead at superstition, but the unanswered question haunts the novel.

Most immediately, it lies at the heart of Wandering Willie's tale about his grandfather's descent to hell to obtain from the ghost of Sir Robert

Redgauntlet a receipt to prove that he had paid his rent. Willie's grandfather was driven to desperation by the demands for evidence from Sir Robert's heir. "How am I to believe" that you have paid, asks Sir John (108); reputations for honesty do not count for him: he holds as a "knave amongst us" the person who "tells the story he cannot prove" (109). Sir John is satisfied to have the money, found by following the directions accompanying the receipt, yet he worries about how to interpret Steenie's fantastic tale. Ultimately, interest in protecting his family's reputation leads him to suppress—and to bribe Steenie to suppress—the story of his trip to the underworld. Sir John, Steenie, and the local clergyman conspire to tell whatever versions of it suit their circumstances and allow them to get along with the community as if nothing unusual had happened. Despite the elaborate quest for evidence, no one knows exactly why the money disappeared in the first place or how, supernatural intervention aside, Steenie obtained the receipt and information. The reestablishment of normal relations among the characters rests on belief, interest, and tacit agreement—not on knowledge.

For Scott, the "true" nature of anyone's character, motives, or experience may be unknowable. But instead of worrying about that condition in the abstract, Scott devises a way to live with it in practice. Because people cannot attain certain knowledge, they must trust in tradition and community interest to guide their individual decisions, thoughts, and actions. Ordinarily, people follow these guides by deferring to the civic, religious, and familial authority figures who embody them. Tradition serves community interest. Willie's honesty as a guide may be guaranteed by his association with the bardic legacy that Katie Trumpener has identified as central to Scott's work.[17] Scott's valorization of tradition can so easily serve conservative political ends that it might be construed as a "mythical past" in the sense that Maines, Sugrue, and Katovich use the term,[18] but doing so overlooks Scott's larger social agenda. Political partisans might try to use Scott's work for their own ends, but Scott's own complex representation of his "lived textuality" resists such reductionism.

The resolution of the plot of *Redgauntlet* gives the term "temporize" to the strategy Lilias and Darsie follow with respect to Redgauntlet.[19] Lilias introduces it to discourage Darsie from outright conflict with so superior an opponent: "you may temporize, as most of the gentry in this country do, and let the bubble burst of itself; for it is singular how few of them venture to oppose my uncle directly. I entreat you to avoid direct collision with him" (331). Though Darsie fears that apparent compliance with the Jacobites will land them in trouble with the lawful government, he later comes around to her way of thinking. His decision rests partly on fear of

Redgauntlet ("He had scarce any hope left but in temporizing until he could make his escape, and resolved to avail himself for that purpose of the delay which his uncle seemed not unwilling to grant," 342) and partly on an estimate of the dearth of support for Redgauntlet ("He therefore concluded the enterprise would fall to pieces of itself, and that his best way was, in the meantime, to remain silent" 341). As these quotations make clear, temporizing does not require approval of the authority to which it bows. It is a strategy of putting off conflict, gaining time in which non-combative solutions (escape or the self-destruction of an untenable scheme) may work. Temporizing does not even preclude waiting for military intervention that would completely change a given situation. What temporizing *does* preclude is popular contention. It is an alternative to the continuous checking of authority, the continual adjustments of power relations, favored in republican thinking.

The practice of temporizing, which Lilias and Darsie see as widespread throughout the country, is illustrated by the behavior of the reluctant conspirators whom Redgauntlet would lead to a final Jacobite coup. Without being convinced of King George's legitimacy, these nominal Jacobites have nevertheless gone on with their lives and affairs under his reign (368, 341). When Redgauntlet announces that his nephew and the prince are ready to lead them into action, they are appalled (371). To protect both the stable lives they have built up for themselves and the lingering respect for the Stewart claim, they temporize further. Instead of repudiating the prince and embracing the "real" authority of the king, they attach a condition to their support of Redgauntlet's campaign: they expect the prince to give up his mistress, whose loyalty and discretion they mistrust. The conspirators involve themselves in a contradiction—Zaret's "paradox of innovation"—by dictating the terms on which they will support an absolute monarch, and Scott calls attention to the inconsistency of their position in both the text and in his introduction to the Magnum Opus edition. In the text, Charles Edward himself observes that "conditions can have no part betwixt Prince and subject" and elaborates on his prerogative (337).[20] In the introduction, Scott comments on the unconditional nature of a subject's "duty" to an absolute monarch (8–9). By theorizing that the prince owes his supporters a debt of gratitude and concession to their wishes, the conspirators show that they have been influenced by developing parliamentary norms. Yet they have not embraced contention as a good. They still want to defer to a leader in a hierarchy. This wish is most evident in the way Sir Richard Glendale answers Redgauntlet's question about what the conspirators will do if Charles Edward will not agree to their terms: will they "abandon him to his fate?":

"God forbid!" said Sir Richard, hastily. . . ."I for one will, with all duty and humility, see him safe back to his vessel and defend him with my life against whoever shall assail him. But when I have seen his sails spread, my next act will be to secure, if I can, my own safety, by retiring to my house; or . . . by surrendering myself to the next Justice of the Peace, and giving security that hereafter I shall live quiet, and submit to the ruling powers." (374)

Zaret's analysis of the use of printed petitions by divers seventeenth-century factions can shed light on the predicament of Scott's conspirators. As I indicated in the last chapter, Zaret finds royalists who used petitions to be engaged in a practice (cultivation of public opinion) at odds with their belief (deference to authority). In their "ambivalence" about the practice, they enlisted "traditional rhetoric to justify their petitions and traditional hierarchical notions to attack petitions by their adversaries."[21] If we compare the inconsistency of Scott's conspirators who contend with their prince in support of absolute monarchy, we see that their confusion mirrors the ambivalence that Zaret describes. Scott has captured the force with which many people clung to a deferential model of social organization. The conspirators still perceive themselves as subjects asking for their sovereign's favor even when they are imposing conditions on his reign. They move into the future only because they can deny that they are doing so. Scott's sympathetic portrayal of the conspirators' behavior makes it an analogue for conservative adaptations to parliamentary reform in his own day. Later, he would temporize in this way himself by not delivering his non-temporizing speech at the Tory assembly.[22]

Scott's portrayal of the "paradox of innovation" on the part of the conspirators manages to separate denial of contentiousness from a merely reactionary stance. Such a separation is important for defining a conservative agenda at a time of agitation for parliamentary reform. Scott's conspirators reject the idea that contention should be habitual and normal, the idea at the heart of republican positions, but they can still move forward into the future. In contrast to Redgauntlet, who sees the future as literally determined by the past (186, 212, 338, 399) and who therefore can recognize only a Stewart as king, the conspirators have practiced (practiced but not theorized) a more flexible, interpretive approach to the past. They have approached it according to present needs (or wishes) to take their places in a stable hierarchy.[23] They perceive the contentions of the civil war as having broken that stability in the past, and they repair the break by recovering that system: they would prefer to reconnect with the Stewart line, but when that becomes clearly impossible, they can adapt to the person who will let the whole system in the present most resemble the situation they enjoyed in the past—or believe they enjoyed, for their longing for security in the present may lead them to imagine a more stable past than they (or previous generations) formerly experienced. This constructive recollection reflects Scott's conservative agenda for his own time. As his dedication of the Magnum Opus to King George indicates, he believed that his present needed royalists and that it needed to value deference over contention. He therefore extracts the value of deference from the past, using it as a means to move into the future. He temporizes—i.e., he gains time for that value to take hold of his present society, rescuing it from the grip of contention and allowing for more respectful relations to develop.

Having extracted what he valued from the past, Scott leaves behind the parts that he sees as less crucial or even unnecessary in the present: those parts are the literal identity of the king as a Stewart and a literal allegiance to that line instead of to a whole system. These parts are cast adrift from the present—literally, as Charles Edward and Redgauntlet sail away at the conclusion of the novel.[24] The device of sending away the Stewart prince and his last supporter creates a memorable dismissal of the historical determinism they represent and leaves the novel with the more flexible, usable attitude toward the past represented by the erstwhile conspirators. It also allows Scott to dismiss the contentiousness so valued by his ideological opponents. For conservatives such as Scott, contention amounts to no more than fomenting unrest. This is what Redgauntlet does throughout the novel by his insistence on refighting old battles, remaining always at odds with the Hanoverian monarchy. Despite his literal attachment to the Stewart prince, Redgauntlet is less a loyal subject than a rival leader. He is the charismatic figure who commands the Jacobite faction, and he is willing to disobey the prince's orders to march northward when he believes that his own southward course represents a better battle plan (315). Redgauntlet identifies so literally with the Stewart cause that he sometimes seems to embody it more than the prince. The vindication of the Stewarts certainly looms larger in his mind than the recovery of a stable order. By making Redgauntlet both reactionary and contentious, Scott stigmatizes the value-orientation he most wants to discourage in the present. Contention becomes only a matter of selfish opposition that does not promise a viable future. In contrast, deference, the apparently reactionary stance, emerges as the more flexible and promising attitude.

Scott provides a utopian—or more accurately "uchronian"—representation of a restored monarchy in *Woodstock*, which following Fiona Robertson and Trela, I read as a complex work. For Robertson, the supernatural goings-on raise doubts about the "legitimate" events; for Trela, the fair assessment of Cromwell, along with the acknowledgment of Charles Stewart's vices, moves the novel away from the Tory party line.[25] I would add that the novel may serve as a cautionary tale for conservatives and thus share some of the critical functions of utopian literature addressed in chapter 4. Since it offers more temporal than geographical displacement to create a vantage point from which to criticize the present, I suggest that it be called uchronian.[26] Its blend of fiction and history occurred, literally, at no time, but it is presented as a scenario for a good time that could come about if elite figures would fulfill their responsibility and thus eliminate desires for reform.

The novel makes it clear that, if conservatives are to head off reform, they cannot simply be reactionaries clinging to old ways. The reactionary extremists in the novel—from Sir Henry Lee, who shares something of Redgauntlet's deterministic outlook, to Roger Wildrake, the fool-hardy cavalier—do not have viable agendas for survival. The viable agenda comes from the temporizing Markham Everard, who looks at the tradition in which he was raised with a sufficiently critical eye to see its faults— chiefly, its confusion of personal gratification with aristocratic privilege. Such insights lead Everard even to reject the old regime and become a republican until equally keen awareness of republican foibles leads him back to the conservative fold.

Within the novel, Scott takes the opportunity to correct the elite tendency to use rank for personal advantage instead of for the good of a whole society that includes dependents of lower rank. Scott achieves his critique by opening a uchronian interval within the history of revolutionary events during which even the future king can learn to subordinate his personal desire for Alice Lee to his ethical responsibility toward all his subjects. The Charles Stewart who regains the throne at the end of *Woodstock* is not the historical king but a uchronian one, a monarch who embraces his reign as a familial trust and who saves the country from the independent claims of both Cromwell and Parliament.

Charles learns to be this kind of king in an epiphanic encounter with Alice that in some ways resembles the epiphanic encounter in which Ravenswood learns his traditional responsibilities from the sextant. At first, Charles is willing to abuse his power in order to seduce Alice Lee. Revealing his kingly identity to her, he explains that marriage vows do not apply so strictly in his position as in ordinary ways of life (2:151). His revelation actually works against his immediate object. Alice does not succumb, but neither does she defy his authority. She takes a deferential stance and argues that her refusal of his personal wish is actually consistent with her respect for his higher position. She asks him to think whether seducing her will further his cause of regaining his place in a divinely ordered state, and she asks how she can "reconcile [her] loyalty" with cooperation in "a suit dishonourable to" them both and one that would moreover "diminish his security, even if he were seated upon the throne" (2:155). Alice's temporizing gains time for her to escape from Charles in the immediate situation, and it gives Charles time to learn from her words.

Though Charles is impressed with Alice's behavior ("This must be virtue," he says, 2:158), he does not himself become virtuous at once. Jealous of Everard, he is willing to risk his safety in a duel despite his knowledge that such conduct jeopardizes the entire royalist cause. His encounter with Everard provides the further lesson he needs to separate selfish from benevolent uses of power, the separation that, for Scott, distinguishes the well-ordered hierarchy from the republican state.

As in his encounter with Alice, Charles is at first willing to use his rank to gain his personal ends. When the Rev. Dr. Rochecliffe invokes the Church's authority to prevent the duel, Charles invokes his position as head of the Church to dismiss the argument (2:185). But Charles is moved by Everard's willingness to give up his suit for Alice if Alice wishes him to do so (235–36). To prevent a rift between that couple, Charles reveals his kingly identity and wins deference even from the still-republican Everard. Everard observes the rituals of deference, bowing, uncovering his head, kissing the king's hand, and promises to help the king in any way short of "schemes of actual violence" against the Commonwealth (2:195–99). Everard's focus on what is best for a collective order rather than on his individual preferences provides the second lesson for the king. Charles refrains from using his power over Everard and Alice to gratify his passions for lust and revenge, and reflecting on this restraint, he concludes "that for once in my life, I have acted well" (2:203).

Holding out the promise that those with power can learn to use it benevolently and that temporizing can succeed, as it does for Alice, in checking abuses of power, *Woodstock* encourages readers to solve problems in the present by renovating traditional social relations rather than by contending for new ones.

FROM CONTENTION
TO COOPERATION

The Election has been read both as a subversively feminist play and a politically and dramatically conventional one.[27] My reading falls somewhere in between. I read *The Election* as a play that questions the value of political contention by revealing the social void within the electoral system.[28] Ostensibly, the claims making at the heart of participatory government is claims making on behalf of others.[29] Contentious gatherings express more than their participants' own interests, and elections are contests over who will represent the claims of a constituency. In *The Election*, the candidates and their supporters represent no one but themselves. Contention poisons their social relations, preventing them from sympathizing with each other and from finding ways to adjust to each other's needs. On the whole, *The Election* is an anti- or counter-contentious play. It challenges spectators to look for alternatives to opposition in dealing with each other and to turn political interests into social concerns.

We see the personally and socially limiting effects of contention most clearly in the attitudes of the candidates toward each other and toward the parliamentary office to which they aspire. The Tory candidate Baltimore is consumed by hatred, the passion that the play delineates. At first glance, his hatred seems to set him apart from the Whig candidate Freeman, who keeps trying to share his wealth with the nearly bankrupt Baltimore and who says he "wishe[s] to . . . live in peace with him" (2.3.113), but the two candidates are versions of each other. When we follow clues referring to their physical similarities (1.2.108, 109) and look for emotional similarities, we see that Freeman's favors do not respond to others' needs but impose his money and preferences on them. Neither Freeman nor Baltimore thinks of election to Parliament in terms of taking a public role or fulfilling public responsibilities. They approach it as a private contest, not far removed from the duel to which it regresses in act 5. In short, the development of Baltimore's and Freeman's social selves is impeded by entrapment in party politics. The more socially functional characters—Baltimore's wife, Isabella, and his suggestively named friend, Truebridge—are the least politically engaged.

Baltimore's hatred of Freeman is structurally determined by political and economic circumstances. Baltimore belongs to the declining order of landholding gentry that fears the rise of manufacturers like Freeman. Baltimore accepts this structural determinism. He never considers whether he can alter it in some way. Indeed, he resists his wife's efforts to get him to think critically and self-critically about his opposition to Freeman. When she asks, "Are you sure, Baltimore, that your own behaviour has not provoked him [Freeman] to that opposition?" and "what great harm does all this do you?" he merely expresses frustration at her lack of sympathy for him (1.2.108). Recalling Clark's analysis of the process of sympathizing, we see that Mrs. Baltimore's sense of a "just world" causes her to withhold sympathy from her husband.[30] She does not accept a causal relationship or inevitable correspondence between Freeman's rise and Baltimore's fall. She would prompt Baltimore to define other goods, goals, and positions instead of "throwing away / the last stake of [his] ruin'd fortune on a contested election" (107). Mrs. Baltimore's attitude opens the way for interactions that free social relations from politics and economics. Baltimore's attitude leaves him trapped in the latter structures.

The hollowness of political contention is made even clearer from Baltimore's complaint that he has no "fair occasion of quarrelling" with Freeman (108). He channels the energy he could have used for positive interactions into a search for a real reason to hate Freeman and rejoices when he discovers one in the mistaken belief that Freeman has bought his (Baltimore's) debts so as to press him for payment or put him in jail. When Baltimore *is* arrested for debt, a comic version of the prison scenes Baillie regularly uses to reveal character shows us Baltimore's self-satisfying hatred. He wants to experience the worst possible treatment in prison so as to win sympathy—and the election—from the crowd who will, he supposes, disapprove of Freeman's ruthlessness (5.1.127; 5.2.127).

The suspicion and fear in this political rivalry creates the same kind of oppositional social relations that form between fearful law keepers and lawbreakers. This serious social consequence lies beneath the play's comic references to criminal acts and punitive justice. Baltimore would cast Freeman as a lawbreaker if he could: he looks, unsuccessfully, for evidence that Freeman is a thief, and he even says he'd be willing to be killed by Freeman so that Freeman would hang for the deed (4.1.123). This ironic wish projects a version of the plot Baillie seriously developed in *The Homicide*, the tragedy in which Kranzberg gladly sees Van Maurice tried for a capital crime because his conviction would put his estate in Kranzberg's hands. Further distancing politics from justice or good, the plot of *The Election* is driven by vengeance, though it is Mrs. Freeman, not Freeman himself, who defines that goal for his campaign. Perceiving Baltimore's refusal of Freeman's favors as slights, she presses her husband to "think how you may be revenged upon him" (2.3.113). Mrs. Freeman does in fact resort to dishonest, if not criminal, means to pursue her goal, for it is she who buys Baltimore's debts and contrives his arrest.

As a couple, the Freemans reverse the gender stereotypes represented by the Baltimores. Whereas the latter fulfill expectations that men will act aggressively in the public sphere and women will conciliate in private, the former disrupt those expectations with her aggressive and his conciliating stance. For that reason, I see the play as going beyond even the feminist subversiveness for which Purinton argues. Concentrating on the friendship that develops between Baltimore's wife and Freeman's daughter, Purinton reads the play as positing non-oppositional relationships between women as a counterplot to the masculinist contest for power and possession in the main action.[31] But factoring in the Freemans' behavior, the play unsettles the notion that women's relationships are cooperative and men's contentious. The problem of contention crosses gender lines as well as party lines. If the relationship between Baltimore's wife and Freeman's daughter offers one cooperative model, Truebridge's behavior offers another, albeit a less immediately admirable one.

Early in the play, Truebridge announces his intention of absenting himself during the election and making the most of any outcome: "let the new member be who he will, I am resolved to shake hands cordially with him. It won't do for one who has honours and pensions in view, to quarrel with great men" (1.2.110). His apparent indifference to any principle beyond self-interest does little to endear him to the audience, but because of his nonpartisanship Truebridge becomes an effective mediator later in the play. Despite his initial announcement, he does not pursue his own gain; or, more exactly, he does not pursue it as an end in itself. Instead, he seeks to reconcile Baltimore and Freeman, allowing whatever benefit he may derive from the reconciliation to follow in due course. Truebridge researches and reveals the kinship between Baltimore and Freeman that ends their rivalry. Additionally, he devises a strategy to mitigate Baltimore's passion (4.2.126). Knowing that reasoning with Baltimore about Freeman's merits will make Baltimore all the more determined to hate him, Truebridge takes an indirect approach based on his belief that most people are "incline[d] . . . to the side of the oppressed" (5.2.128), a belief consistent with the *Introductory Discourse*'s assertion about the predominance of kindness in the world.[32] Implementing this strategy, Truebridge voices harsh criticism of Freeman to Baltimore, prompting Baltimore's kinder nature to come to his defense. Truebridge thus elicits a counterpassionate response that keeps Baltimore's hatred from hardening irreversibly, even if Baltimore can make his defense only (according the stage direction) "ironically" (5.2.128). With Truebridge as mediator, the play disrupts not only the opposition between Baltimore and Freeman but also the opposition between self-interest and altruism. Truebridge is neither a self-sacrificing figure nor a politically engaged one. He is *socially* engaged, with a good deal of insight into character, interaction, and the widespread benefits of cooperation. He earns the right to make the play's announcement of "victory" over hatred and to pronounce its final prayer of thanksgiving for the "restor[ation of] a rational creature to the kindly feelings of humanity" (5.4.132–33).

Because he tries to act generously toward his rival, Freeman might seem to be a non-contentious character, but his generosity is subtly domineering. An inept role-taker, he is not mindful of others. Instead of putting himself in Baltimore's place and becoming sensitive to the loss Baltimore feels due to his diminished wealth and status, Freeman ostentatiously "improves" the grounds around both their houses, cutting down trees and diverting a stream; offers financial "advice" based on his success at making a "large fortune"; sends wine for Baltimore's guests and dinner invitations for Baltimore himself, making it clear that he does not expect Baltimore to reciprocate. Then he is baffled by Baltimore's "aversion" (2.3.113–14). With more insight than Freeman, spectators should realize that he is a selfish figure, despite his material generosity, because of his limited imagination of others. He is still contending with Baltimore by imposing his idea of what will satisfy Baltimore's needs; a more cooperative and interactive approach would seek to ascertain Baltimore's perception of his needs.

Since *The Election* is a comedy, the characters' faults and predicaments are correctable. The resolution comes about through two incidents: Freeman falls into a pond and is saved from drowning by Baltimore, who insists that the rescue was a "common office of humanity" and not an act that changes his aversion to Freeman in particular or makes him willing to accept any favors (4.2.125). But when Baltimore is in prison, Freeman does pay off his debts, obtain his release, and throw the election in Baltimore's favor. Though these acts suggest a keener perception of Baltimore's needs and occur in a spirit of reciprocity, they do not effect Baltimore and Freeman's reconciliation. What accomplishes that is the discovery that the two are half brothers.

Slagle justifiably expresses some disappointment with this conventional ending because it changes Freeman's status rather than reconciling Baltimore to the rising middle class,[33] yet the play does not simply restore an old order. If we take structure as dependent on meaning, then the social structure has been changed by the redefinition of the situation. Baltimore and Freeman no longer cast each other in rival roles; each puts himself in the other's place as half brother. And if we ask, following Lyman's questioning lead, what the reconciliation allows the characters to do, we can answer that it allows them to cooperate in seeking social good now that they are no longer contending for political preferment. Taking cooperation rather than contention as the goal of political behavior opens the way to a broader social perspective on political and national situations. To recall an example I gave in the introduction, Mead saw the ability to expand "national selves" and work toward a common goal to be the key to the success of such programs as the World Court. The characters in *The*

Election take a step toward nonpartisan cooperation by expanding their interests beyond their originally selfish goals. Many years later, when Baillie wrote approvingly of Scottish zeal for the Reform Bill, she may have been praising the cooperative spirit needed for Scotland to give up "selfishly pliant" acceptance of English rule in favor of collaboration in shaping their government.

BAILLIE'S
USE OF HISTORY

Though Baillie's works are not so filled with historical detail as Scott's or Landor's, they do sometimes evoke the past to comment on the present. As we have seen, the remote settings of some plays imply that the events and attitudes dramatized do not, or should not, have a place in the nineteenth century. Alternatively, commemorations of historical figures like Lady Griseld Baillie call attention to behavior that might still be emulated. Creating "new pasts" does not predominate in Baillie's approach to social problems, but when she does turn to history, she does so as pragmatically as Landor, Scott, or Mead. For her as for them, no scroll of the past provides access to events as they really were; rather, the consensus of historians provides an "accepted past" on which to base present value inquiry. In the preface to the volume *Miscellaneous Plays*, which contained her historical drama *Constantine Paleologus*, Baillie reflects on the interplay between past events and present imaginings, and she develops a hypothesis about the use of the past.

The preface treats the distinction between history and fiction as performative. History consists of previous events that most people choose to accept, and individuals should respect that consensus. Thus, she writes, "we are not warranted . . . to assign imaginary causes to great public events." Comparing these events to "landmark[s]" that orient "inhabitants of the surrounding country," Baillie insists that their "large and general form must remain unaltered."[34] Removing them, she implies, would be disorienting, or, in Mead's terms, it would deprive us of continuity and leave us with an avalanche of incidents. But the landmarks are not intrinsically meaningful. Their meaning arises from the use people make of them in orienting themselves toward various goals, and each explorer may appropriately customize a landmark for his or her purposes. Developing the metaphor at length, she writes: "he may clothe its rugged sides with brushwood, and hang a few storm-stunted oaks on its bare peaks; he may throw a thin covering of mist on some untoward line of its acclivity, and bring into stronger light the bold storied towerings of its pillared cliffs."[35]

Baillie's directions describe symbolic interaction with an "accepted past," an interpretive response to the "landmarks" of a given culture.

Constantine Paleologus exemplifies this approach. According to the preface, Baillie's interest in this last emperor to defend Constantinople from Turkish conquest arose from her reading of Gibbon's *Decline and Fall of the Roman Empire*. What interests her—and what she imaginatively enhances in the play—is the "generous attachment" between the emperor and the small group of supporters who hold the city by "noble and dignified exertion" as long as they can.[36] Baillie does not change the landmark fall of the city, and though she does add a subplot involving Constantine's wife, Valeria, she does not make it a cause of the main action.[37] The other characters in the play balance Baillie's acceptance of Gibbon with her imaginative enhancements. The rival Turkish leader, Mahomet, "correspond[s] with the character given of him by the historian," though Baillie heightens the contrast with Constantine on which the play depends.[38] Constantine's supporter Justiniani corresponds with Gibbon as well, though Baillie elevates his "sense of honour" over his courage. With Justiani, she pairs an invented character, Rodrigo, who, she says somewhat startlingly in the preface, is a composite of British seamen she admires. Further, the preface cites a novel about a Highland sergeant as the source for another innovation in the historical plot—the invention of Othoric, who exploits Mahomet's superstition to avoid torture.[39]

Especially in the invention of Rodrigo and Othoric, we see the process of "naturalistic generalization" that joins one person's preoccupation and experience with public events, or to put it in terms Baillie used elsewhere, we see the "human propensity" of the storyteller to be "present in imagination to every thing he relates."[40] Baillie imaginatively interacted with Gibbon's text, using it as a landmark to orient herself to the kinds of courageous behaviors that preoccupied her in her more immediate situation. While the allusions to British seamanship and Highland courage suggest that Baillie may have spread backward to the siege of Constantinople suppressed anxieties about the subordination of Scotland, many readers would find it more likely that she spread backward anxieties about the Napoleonic Wars. The play is usually read as a comment on that global conflict.[41] In my reading, the play makes a social comment on politics and history, or more precisely, it invites spectators to question the disjunction between social good and political/historical actions. The challenge of the play lies in interpreting the value of Constantine's behavior, which fails historically and politically while succeeding socially. Problematically, the landmarks of history and politics lead us to gauge success by the outcome of usually violent contention: history celebrates the winners of wars and elections. Yet social experience shows us that more conciliatory interactions create a more livable world. Oppositional relationships create social problems: they pit law keepers against lawbreakers, rich against poor, Tories against Whigs, selves against others. I posit that what Baillie spreads back from the present in her reading of the past is a preoccupation with contention. The play assigns value to the cooperative interactions that succeed in Constantine's society despite their failure to change the larger political and historical structure. By critically examining this situation, the play opens the way for present spectators to change that structure in the future. In such a future, there would be a new past. The landmarks would not be the winning outcomes of battles or elections; they would be exemplary cases of cooperative interactions.

The socially functional behavior in the play occurs in interactions between Constantine and his supporters. The band has been characterized as a homosocial or homosexual group,[42] and in terms of gender stereotypes, Constantine is clearly feminized. Here as elsewhere, I read Baillie's disruptions of gendered expectations as part of a larger interest in disrupting the structural and habitual barriers to sympathetic interactions among people. Even under the siege conditions of the play, Baillie shows that interactions need not be defined by opposition. Though Constantine's band is defined structurally by its opposition to the Turks, among themselves the members do not so much enjoy as regret the "solidarity of aggression." Constantine devotes the times they can gather away from battle to "social rites" that recover peaceful and humane attitudes. Disarmoring for one such gathering, Constantine remarks: "This [helmet] galls me strangely: / Mine armourer, methinks, has better skill, / To mar men's heads than save them" (1.2.449). The ensuing scene develops the contradictory meanings compressed in these lines, showing the intellectual and emotional damage done by the war they are fighting for their physical and national existence. It has, for example, curtailed the writing of Othus, "a learned Greek" (according to the dramatis personae) supporter whose "gentle service of th[e] pen" Constantine would prefer (450). Likewise preferring the judicious and sensible service of other supporters, Constantine wants them to protect themselves from "needless dangers" (450). Instead of preparing for the decisive battle in the play by augmenting hostilities, they hold a ceremony of reconciliation (4.2.465–67). Throughout the play, Constantine calls his supporters "friends" and "brothers" and refuses to "command" them (1.2.450; 2.457; 4.2.465–67). Constantine's respectful gestures toward them call out equally respectful responses from them; in the end, Rodrigo says they served him "for love" (5.1.453).

Constantine would apply this attitude in his dealings with the Turks, with whom he keeps trying to negotiate a treaty (2.3.457), and in his dealings with the citizens of Constantinople, who want him simply to surrender. Their calls for "bread and peace" (2.1.453) must uncannily remind later readers of Addams's pacificist work *Peace and Bread in Time of War*,[43] but their attitude, unlike Addams's or Constantine's, advocates mere acceptance of any ruler who will satisfy their material needs. Constantine is not comparable to Addams as a pacificist. His behavior toward the crowd, however, does further the questioning of contention in the play. Insofar as Constantine uses words rather than physical force to put down this uprising, he demonstrates the positive value of nonviolent over violent opposition, but just as importantly, he moves away from the mere substitution of words for weapons that Othus accepts (1.2.451) and toward the use of them to help opponents see each other's points of view. Instead of responding to them antagonistically, Constantine offers an alternative view of their relationship that adapts the biblical parable of the prodigal son. Casting himself as the forgiving father, and the crowd as erring children, he interprets their withdrawal of support from him as a betrayal of responsibility to an extended family, a betrayal that can nevertheless be forgiven and reversed (2.1.452–53). Though the patriarchal metaphor can be read as demeaning to adult citizens, it is not used condescendingly in this scene. On the contrary, it is used to awaken a sense of adult responsibility toward others in citizens who have regressed to childish self-interest. If the speech, like the outcome of the play as a whole in Friedman-Romell's reading, offers indirect support for British conservatives who saw the state in patriarchal terms, it nevertheless "emphasizes that this form of government requires morality, sacrifice, and personal commitment from leaders and subjects alike, if it is to thrive."[44]

Constantine's refusal to surrender allows us to distinguish between accommodating others through interaction and abandoning one's own point of view. Self-respect and respect for the kind of social relations he tries to enact lead Constantine to hold out against Turkish domination. His resistance stems from his value orientation rather than from his hope for a victory or even for posthumous admiration. A speech to Othus explains his motives in the following terms:

> to sustain in heaven's all-seeing eye,
> Before my fellow men, in mine own sight,
> With graceful virtue and becoming pride,
> The dignity and honour of a man
> Thus station'd as I am, I will do all
> That man may do, and I will suffer all
> . . . that man can suffer.

Startlingly, this speech concludes with a comparison to public execution. Constantine asks, "Shall low-born men on scaffolds firmly tread, / For that their humble townsmen should not blush, / And shall I shrink?" (2.4.457). Rather than romanticizing the criminal, the comparison serves to show Constantine's orientation toward others. He interprets the prisoner's courage as motivated by a desire to spare spectators' feelings, and he models his behavior after the example he fashions. The comparison thus also exemplifies the rationale for watching executions that Baillie constructed in the *Introductory Discourse*—the discovery of what human nature can bear and the application of that discovery in one's own conduct.

A similar respect for self and social relations motivates Valeria's suicide, an act she performs to thwart the Sultan's desire to reduce her to his possession (5.3.477–78). Like Constantine, Valeria succeeds in acting according to her values and beliefs.[45] The parallel between Valeria and Constantine exemplifies Baillie's position, taken in the *Introductory Discourse*, that men and women are capable of the same emotions and actions when similarly circumstanced. Within this play, the parallel contributes to the reassessment of behavior in terms of its social effects rather than its political and historical outcomes. Valeria's act repudiates the determinism that joins her subplot to the main plot of the play. Earlier in the play, Valeria had consulted a fortune-teller in an attempt to learn how the siege would end and was pleased to read a reference to Constantine into the deceptive prophecy that her husband, by whom the conjuror meant the conquering Sultan, would reign (2.3.456). As is typical in Baillie's plays, superstition is used by unscrupulous figures as a means of deceiving and manipulating people. Undeceived by the outcome, Valeria attempts to regain control of her fate, and insofar as she diminishes the Sultan's control over her, she *does* modify the determined outcome. Symbolic interaction may not always effect large and immediate changes, but it can always destabilize structures. In the main plot, Constantine's resistance of the Turks is a resistance of deterministic structures, forces, and thinking. It contrasts with Mahomet's confidence that his victory is fated (3.1.460), and it does undermine Mahomet's control, for it deprives him of one of the things he wants—respectful followers such as Constantine had.

Mahomet's envy of the social relations within Constantine's band is introduced in the middle of the play when Mahoment interrogates Othoric, a mercenary, about his reasons for serving Constantine. Othoric replies that he was bribed by "gen'rous admiration of noble manly virtue" (3.2.462), a reply that leaves Mahomet marveling that his rival "is serv'd by men like these" (463). Mahoment does not understand why he himself does not command similar respect, but the play clearly shows that the reasons lie in his own contempt for his men. He considers them "stupid slaves" and sneaks around eavesdropping on them in the futile hope of hearing praise for himself (4.1.464). After the fall of the city, he tries to enlist Rodrigo and Othus in his service, but they tell him that their allegiance is not transferable (5.3.478).

The final words of the play, spoken by Othus, make the reversal of social and political values explicit: Othus predicts that the Sultan's reign will be troubled by social unrest, and he refigures the defeat of Constantine as a kind of victory:

> think not when the good and valiant perish
> By worldly power o'erwhelm'd, that heaven's high favour
> Shines not on them. — Oh, no! then shines it most.
> For then in them it shews th'approving world
> The worth of its best work.
> And from their fate a glorious lesson springs;
> A lesson of such high ennobling power;
> Connecting us with such exalted things
> As all do feel, but none with such true force,
> Such joy, such triumph, as a dying man. (5.3.478)

The meaning of these statements need not be confined to its otherworldly metaphor, for the play challenges spectators to transform this world by bringing the "lesson" of Constantine's socially constructive behavior into its future.

Baillie's other explicitly historical play, *The Family Legend*, undertakes a comparable reversal of social and political values but openly projects the possibility of such a change taking place in the future of this world. "That day will come," prophesies the Earl of Argyll at the end of the play, after a failed alliance between his clan and the Macleans has ended in bloodshed, when a future generation will "pity, admire, and pardon / The fierce, contentious, ill-directed valour / Of gallant fathers, born in darker times" (5.4.507).

The play takes a landmark Scottish legend as the same kind of "authority" for the given events as Gibbon for the events in *Constantine Paleologus*. Indeed, Bailie's preface to the *Family Legend* uses the word "authority" with reference to the story preserved by the Damer family, which is summarized and separated from Baillie's enhancements of the charcters' motives.[46] The legend orients spectators to the violently contentious history of Scotland. That contentious past has continuity with the contentious present—with its Napoleonic Wars, suppressed conflicts between Scotland and England, and nonviolent but still clamorous political claims making—in which Baillie lived. The play invites spectators to disconnect the present from the contentious political line and connect it instead to the conciliatory social relations envisioned by two of the plays characters, Helen of Argyll and Hubert de Grey.

I suggest that the latter invitation makes the play a bit more challenging than it appears to be from its framing and performance history. Staged in Edinburgh because of Scott's enthusiasm for the play, the performance was deliberately used to promote goodwill between Scotland and England and between descendents of different Scottish factions.[47] In the performance, albeit not in the written text, the clan name "Maclean" was changed to "Duart" so that the representation of violent and unappealing characters would not reflect on their descendents.[48] A prologue by Scott and an epilogue by Henry Mackenzie frame the work as a drama of progress in which the violent Scottish past has given way to the nonviolent British present. In that present, the violent past is so remote and nonthreatening that it can be the subject of historical, aesthetic, or cultural curiosity. The *Waverley* novels Scott would begin publishing four years after *The Family Legend* was first staged share some of its purpose and strategies. Within *The Family Legend*'s progressive plot, however, lies an opportunity to move toward more responsible social relations in the future. That opportunity stems from the attitudes with which Helen and Hubert respond to the clans' activities within the plot. Their attitudes are not the ones that prevail historically or politically, but they are the ones that promise the greatest social change.

Briefly, the plot of *The Family Legend* is as follows: the rival clans of Maclean and Argyle have arrived at a truce sealed by the marriage of Helen, daughter of Argyll, to the chief of Maclean. Maclean's vassals, opposed to the "shameful peace" (1.1.482) and greedy for more power, undermine the alliance by representing Helen as a spy and witch to their weak and superstitious chief. Maclean allows them to carry Helen off to a rocky island where she will be drowned by the rising tide.[49] But Helen's cries are heard, and she is rescued, taken to her father's house, and avenged by her brother, who kills Maclean. The limited scale of the retributive combat is part of the progressiveness of the play. Instead of waging war against the whole rival clan, as would have been the custom in the time before the play, Argyll wants to punish only the people who plotted against Helen; with the others, he still wants to live in peace (5.4.507). His attitude sets in motion progress toward relatively less violent relations, but it does not change the norm of retributive justice or reject the mode of opposition itself.

A different course is envisioned by Helen, who does not want revenge even on the guilty (5.3.505; 5.4.506), and Hubert, who thinks of saving Helen's baby, still held by the Macleans, instead of seeking vengeance (4.2.498; 4.4.501). Hubert is absent until the end of the final conflict because he has gone on that rescue mission. Helen and Hubert envision social relations that respond to wrongdoing with the "pity" Helen feels for Maclean and the wit and will to reorganize rather than contend evident in Hubert's actions. Though *The Family Legend* does not end with the wedding of Helen and Hubert, it implies the suitability of such an event not only by having Hubert bring Helen's child to her but by revealing that the two had been in love before Helen's marriage to Maclean and that they still share feelings for each other that they scrupulously suppressed while Helen was a wife to Maclean (4.4.501; 5.4.507).

The play further suggests Helen as a model for alternative social relations by emphasizing her willingness to marry Maclean (4.1.498). The use of Helen to secure a truce surely enacts, as Adrienne Scullion agues, the patriarchal "plot" in which women are objects for exchange,[50] but Helen's attitude complicates the drama. After her rescue, as her father changes his mind about the wisdom of the marriage and berates himself for being "thoughtless and selfish" in arranging it, Helen contradicts him: "We acted both for good," she says, and reminds him that she agreed "willingly" (4.1.498). Through that marriage, Helen sought the greater good that Jane Addams identified as the "social claim"—"that life which surrounds and completes the individual and family life."[51] Addams argued that the exclusivity of the "family claim" must be broadened to allow women to participate more fully in the world. She saw the "family claim" as particularly limiting for college-educated women, who felt that it closed off opportunities that their schooling had only just opened.[52] If this notion seems far removed from Baillie's play, we may bring it closer by seeing it as a development of Wollstonecraft's arguments for the education of women that Scullion and others have used to contextualize Baillie's work.[53] Helen does act out a version of broadening the family claim into the social claim in her wish to achieve more than personal fulfillment through marriage and in her efforts, after marriage, to promote reconciliation and charity within and between the clans (1.2.485). Moreover, in speaking with her brother, Helen states that she does not regret the marriage. She refuses, she states, to be "like the spoil'd heiress of some Lowland lord" who wastes her time "with poor repining, losing every sense of what she is, in what she has been" (2.1.488).

The historically contentious orientation of Maclean and his vassals prevents the Argyll-Maclean alliance from effecting social change, but the play leaves open the possibility that attitudes like Helen's and Hubert's can change society in the future if spectators realize them.

8
The Problem
of Disciplinarity

Having considered one way of reading the works of Baillie, Scott, and Landor as engaged in social problem solving, I turn to the question of why that way is unusual. Though many factors condition how we do, and do not, read any given works, one factor has posed a significant obstacle to associating literature with social work throughout the twentieth century. That factor is disciplinarity—specifically, the norm of dividing literary from lived experience that served to constitute our separate fields but that also isolated us within our territories. A complicating factor has been the privileging of science within this disciplinary configuration, which organized the "two cultures" hierarchically rather than equivalently. John Guillory has analyzed the pressures involved in this formation and the consequences for studying the literature of any period. It is helpful to call to mind the general trend before looking further at its effects on Romantic-era studies.

Briefly, Guillory explains, every area that would be part of the modern academy had to define a unique object of study. "English," for example, had to define a linguistic or literary object that was different from an historical or a sociological object. At first, it tried to be "philological," studying language by scientific methods that promised to chart and predict change; then, it tried to extend that approach to studying literature, but its charting of literary history was (dialectically) opposed by more aesthetic orientations.[1] Without the pressure of the scientific ideal, the historical approaches might have grown, cooperatively with sociology, into multifaceted investigations of cultural interactions, and in fact, a recent proposal for reviving philology in order to give "foreign" language study a renewed sense of purpose has been made: according to Holquist, a philological approach can and should convey "positive knowledge of other cultures and [foster] a critical stance toward one's own culture."[2] But litera-

197

ture from any time and place became institutionalized as a "resistance to science."[3] Responding to the pressure to define a unique object, scholars in the field tended to abstract literature from cultural situations, to endow it with transcendent qualities, and to generalize about these attributes. The institutionalized study of English, which might be dated from the founding of the Modern Language Association in 1883 (more than twenty years before the founding of the American Sociological Association but only eight before the founding of the *American Journal of Sociology*) shows a gradual narrowing from early historical orientations to later formalist orientations, culminating, famously (or infamously), in The New Criticism. The pattern of disciplinary formation, then, is a pattern of separation, competition, and narrowing.

This pattern shows itself in Romantic-era studies in the creation of a canon of major poets whose work could be valorized for transcendently imaginative qualities. This canon came to epitomize Romanticism, and works by other poets or novelists or dramatists whose works could not so easily be abstracted from the social sphere were treated as less important for an understanding of the period. Thus, Scott's historical novels and Landor's historically oriented *Imaginary Conversations* became objects of study only for those with residual or partisan interests in philological, political, or social approaches. Studies of Scott were dominated by the political aims of Lukacs.[4] Landor studies were dominated by efforts to sort out the political from the literary aspects of the *Imaginary Conversations*, a century-long project I detail in the next section. Studies of Baillie were not directly caught up in theses struggles because Baillie, like other dramatists and women writers, received relatively little consideration at all;[5] however, Baillie's case is related to the problem of separating literary from lived experience insofar as it is a case of the conflict between private and public spheres in which Mellor has contextualized the reception of women writers from this period. Baillie's plays received little attention because their social emphasis placed them far from the canonical center of Romanticism. Not redefined as "mental theater" like the dramas of the canonical poets,[6] Baillie's plays were known only to those with specialized historical interests; they had no "public" presence in the field.

Post-disciplinarity has changed this situation in ways that have greatly affected the study of Baillie and Scott but not yet affected the study of Landor. Considering how and why Landor became unreadable for most of the last century sheds a good deal of light on the processes that defined our objects of study as well as the processes now changing them. In the following section, I look at the fate of Landor in disciplinary history and at his potential as an object for study in a post-disciplinary age. I contrast his status with the status of Scott, who has become a new object for inquiries that specifically play out our disciplinary concerns. Extending such engagement to Landor, I argue, would further understanding of both Scott and Landor as well as of the nature of interpretive interaction through their texts. In the subsequent section, I consider Baillie's fate in disciplinary history as parallel to that of Addams. Both were marginalized by the privileging of abstract objects for study and both are being repositioned in the forefront of post-disciplinary concerns. I return to the problem of Addams's repudiation of De Quincey, showing how it reflects disciplinary pressures that no longer have such force. In conclusion, I argue that Addams and De Quincey, social work and literary studies, can and should now be reunited.

SCOTT AND LANDOR
IN DISCIPLINARY HISTORY

The problem of disciplinarity—which is also a problem of epistemology, of the processes and practices of coming to know anything—might be taken as the predominant concern within Scott studies today and the catalyst for renewed interest in his life and work. Books by Rigney, Chandler, and Christensen, along with articles by Mayer, Maxwell, Malley, Ferris, and Burwick,[7] investigate how he and his readers negotiated the interplay of fact and fiction, historical and contemporary meanings, through his works. In differing ways and degrees, this scholarship shows that the categories of knowledge separated in the twentieth century were not so clearly delineated for Scott and his first readers; that pressures to separate them were nevertheless forming; and that separation did not appear to be, for Scott, a desirable measure but one needing compensatory strategies.

For example, according to Rigney and Mayer, Scott bridged the gap between fiction and history with footnotes that "rooted his story more explicitly in actuality" or that "authenticated" his fiction with reference to other people's experience.[8] This practice joins privately imagined with publicly documented aspects of the work in a way that aims to open the former dimension to readers. Such avoidance of isolation and reaching out to readers is consistent with the sympathy Ferris attributes to Scott and with her argument that he worried about antiquarian pursuits as being socially irresponsible. Scott's readers, from his earliest reviewers to his present-day editors, have continued the practice of adding to these notes, joining the story to concerns outside the text[9] and thus continuing interpretive interactions that incorporate Scott's work into lived experience. The difference between earlier and later interactions, however, is a difference between ease and anxiety with the process.

Examining contemporary reviews and letters, Rigney has determined that Romantic-era readers were comfortable with "hybrid" texts like Scott's historical novels in which elements of personal invention coexist with elements from public records or shared traditions. Indeed, "ramifying readers" added connections to his work by investigating possible sources for characters and scenes. When they quarreled with Scott, they raised objections to particular historical points, such as an alleged slight to their family name or to their Presbyterian beliefs; they did not quarrel over the coexistence of historical elements with invented ones.[10] Clearly, they expected writing and reading to be part of the dynamics of lived experience. According to Rigney, this ease with hybridity changed as history began to imply only collective experience.[11] In other words, it changed as disciplinary expectations narrowed the objects and practices that could be included in any given field. Ease with interpretive interactions that made texts variably and personally part of their readers' experiences gave way to a suspicion of such personal and situated knowledge. Instead of hybrids and springboards to social understanding, Scott's texts came to be perceived as fractured and self-referential: they were literary narratives with some historical elements but were not fully or productively engaged with the "real" world.[12]

Coming full circle, the view of Scott's texts as fractured rather than hybrid is now a source of discomfort, as is evident from the scholarly attention now devoted to explaining and justifying the combination of fiction and history in Scott's work. Not fully free from the disciplinary expectations that fiction and history can be or should be separated, works like Rigney's treat the expectations as perplexing and use the example of Scott to work through the problem, enlisting the pre-disciplinary text in the search for post-disciplinary practices.

Scott's novels lend themselves to such applications because of the narrative guidance they provide. For Rigney, the narrative gives "continuity" to events. Readers may not accept the given story, but it is the story that orients them toward the significance of the imagined and historical events and that conditions their selection of analogies from their own experience.[13] To make a similar point in interactionist terms, I would say that narrative gestures toward readers, encouraging interpretive response. It encourages them to dramatize the story as part of their lived experience. Going further, interactionist David Maines has explained all lived experience in terms of narrative. People are socialized to certain culturally dominant behaviors and activities, and they then plot their individual stories along and/or against those narratives. Maines's work is significant for positing a specific—and a specifically literary—link between personal and collective experience and for elaborating on the processes of storytelling by which they become entwined.[14] Moreover, Maines's first example of a collective narrative is a narrative that shaped disciplinary history, and thus it helps to explain the disciplinary pressures that I have described above. Maines posits that our knowledge system has presented us with a collective narrative of the "increasing use and legitimation of quantification and the decreasing legitimation of the human utterance."[15] The narrative began in the seventeenth century, was most widely accepted in the early twentieth century, and became questionable in the late twentieth century. Maines's concern is with how sociologists have plotted their work along this narrative and how he hopes they will learn to change their stories. For example, his analysis of one of the founding studies in sociology, Florian and Znaniecki's *The Polish Peasant in Europe and America* (1918–20), reveals how disciplinary expectations influenced what aspects of the study would be taken as significant and what aspects would be ignored. The parts that counted—literally—as knowledge were the quantified and quantifiable elements. The other parts, including "800 pages . . . in the form of letters, biographies, and other narrative documents," were not seen as significant except as fodder for statistics.[16] Given the shape of the discipline at the time, there was no way to look into this blind spot: in sociology, personal narratives were simply not-knowledge. That such a view now appears mistaken is the result of changes in our disciplinary and epistemic system. For Maines, such changes are leading to "narrative's moment"—a time when different aspects of Florian and Znaniecki's study, and of other studies, can be recognized as knowledge bearing.[17] At this moment, it is becoming possible to relegitimate the human utterance.

Applying the terms of Maines's argument to work outside of sociology allows us to look into some other blind spots. Readings of Scott, for example, have been plotted along the narrative of the delegitimized utterance in two ways. In the overall disciplinary configuration, any reading of Scott belonged in a literary field that had a subordinate place in the whole configuration of knowledge because its object of study was humanly expressive and therefore less credible than material data. Scott, then, could not be cited outside the field as a credible source for social information. Within the field, Scott had to be valued primarily as a novelist, his imaginative and inventive qualities made predominant over his social consciousness or referentiality. Even in readings by and in the line of Lukacs, the social insights facilitated by Scott's work were taken to be insights that Scott and his most sympathetic readers would not recognize.

The pressure of this collective narrative is even greater in the case of Landor, and it was harder to value his *Imaginary Conversations* in literary terms because he offers little in the way of narrative assistance of his own. Whereas Scott's narratives orient readers toward putting elements together and so can help sort out invention from reference, Landor's *Conversations* deliberately withholds narrative guidance, breaking its authority and challenging us to take our own contentions as the main plot. Rising to Landor's challenge is something we ought to be able to accomplish in post-disciplinary studies. How impossible a task it was during the disciplinary era is evident from three attempts, from the 1890s to the 1960s, to create an edition of the *Imaginary Conversations* and to encourage wider reading of them. Each of these attempts, as I describe below, founders in a struggle to separate fiction from history, to create a literary object within the given system or narrative of knowledge.

Efforts to produce an annotated edition of the *Imaginary Conversations* began before the end of the nineteenth century. The aim was to identify and verify the historical elements in the pieces, distinguishing them from the imaginary ones. The first such edition, annotated by Charles G. Crump, appeared in 1891. That Landor and his contemporaries apparently saw no need for such an apparatus has been attributed to their greater erudition: they knew more history than later generations, so they could make the distinctions with less help.[18] Significantly, this hypothesis assumes the value of making the distinction, which shows late rather than early nineteenth-century priorities. As Rigney's research on Scott and his readers has shown, that distinction was not vital to them.

Crump did not strive for exhaustive or even thorough coverage in his annotations. He wished simply "to give just that information without which the reader might fail to feel . . . at home" with the works. The notes stem from a concession to "the gap between the days when literature was written by learned men for learned men and the days now come when literature is written by anybody for everybody else."[19] In keeping with this attitude, Crump glosses the identities of figures he thinks readers may not recognize and explains in a few sentences the works they wrote or deeds they performed that are relevant to the particular conversation.

What I find significant about Crump's annotations is their concern with proving or disproving Landor's accuracy. Even when Crump sees no need to identify the characters or to suspect that Landor got the history "wrong," he makes an effort to confirm the issues and incidents central to the conversation. For instance, on "Steele and Addison," in which the speakers discuss the sale of Steele's furniture to pay his debts, Crump cites a biography of Steele to confirm that the incident occurred. The citation provides double confirmation, as it quotes the biographer who quotes a letter as "the most trustworthy account."[20] When Crump cannot corroborate Landor's representation, he reports the discrepancy. On "William Penn and Lord Peterborough," he states that "Landor is more than usually wrong in his chronology" because allusions in the conversation place the meeting in 1699 when Peterborough is unlikely to have been able to travel to America. After trying and failing to place the meeting in 1682, Crump concludes that the report of Peterborough's visit is probably "apocryphal." He then abruptly constructs the conversation as a literary object: "the conversation is one of Landor's best. The characters are well drawn."[21] Separating fact from fiction is a step in determining how the given object may be studied.

Two purposes are served by Crump's procedure. First, the distinction between fact and fiction, history and literature, is maintained in its own right. The maintenance of this distinction was important to the formation of the modern disciplines. Secondly, the distinction becomes a means of constituting objects for study within separate fields. Facts can be placed outside of literary texts in a supportive but unintrusive background; this area can be made the province of history. The imaginative remainder can become the material for literary study. Having determined that inaccuracies disqualify Landor's work as an historical object, Crump constitutes it as a literary object based, in this instance, on the criterion of characterization. "William Penn and Lord Peterborough" emerges as better than "Steele and Addison" because the speakers are more imaginatively (and less accurately) presented.

Neither Crump nor the later editors I address below succeed fully in constituting the *Imaginary Conversations* as objects for literary study. The connections with the "accepted" or "implied objective" past in the *Imaginary Conversations* overshadow the use of novelistic or dramatic conventions. A great deal of the work must be discounted if the historical material is presumed irrelevant. As Crump's analysis of the dates for Lord Peterborough's trip shows, Landor's departures from record are seldom extreme or obvious. Violations of chronology identified by later editors are even more subtle: Lady Lisle and Elizabeth Gaunt could not have talked in prison, as Landor maintains, because Lisle "was executed more than a month and a half before Elizabeth Gaunt was convicted"[22]; Cromwell would not have advocated regicide so unequivocally in a 1648 conversation as there is evidence of his ambivalence until the end of that year.[23] These findings show that the *Imaginary Conversations* have a complex and intricate relationship to history, but that relationship cannot be explained within a disciplinary or epistemic system that segregates fact from invention.

The observation by one of Landor's later editors that we have avoided studying Landor's works because we cannot easily classify them[24] is true in a way that extends far beyond the literary genres to which the remark refers. Landor's works cross the line between the real and the imagined on which our knowledge system has been based. They defy the very use and value of separate categories for history and literature, lived and invented experience, past and present. They therefore became even more difficult to study in the twentieth century when disciplinary distinctions prevailed.

Two projects were begun in the middle of the twentieth century with the hope that they would lead to a fully annotated modern edition of the *Imaginary Conversations*, though neither editor expected to complete the task her or himself. That expectation is itself significant, showing that the task of annotation had grown into a large and daunting one. In many features, the projects are quite different from each other: the one by Prasher is a dissertation, which necessarily has the aim of demonstrating scholarly ability as well as exciting interest in Landor; the other is a volume of selected *Conversations* prepared by an established scholar (Proudfit) to make Landor accessible to colleagues, students, and other readers of nineteenth-century literature. Despite these differences, both Prasher and Proudfit regard Crump as an important predecessor whose annotations are not sufficient for modern needs, and both define their tasks in terms of sifting fact from fiction.

According to Prasher, the greatest challenge in editing the *Imaginary Conversations* is tracking down Landor's sources and determining what he knew about the figures and topics covered.[25] Because of the amount of research involved, Prasher annotates only eight *Conversations*; her selection of the first eight in the first volume Landor published allows her project to lay the foundation for a systematic revisiting of the works. The dissertation consists of three volumes: the first reviews the composition and criticism; the second gives the texts and variants of the eight conversations; the third provides the annotations. In reviewing scholarship on Landor, Prasher ranges over ways in which the *Imaginary Conversations* have been attached to literary conventions or genres, but she finds that the ties do not hold well: Landor was not primarily interested in characterization; he "was not influenced to any great extent by the dialogue tradition."[26] Prasher's annotations are exhaustive, providing elaborate glosses on the persons and issues involved in or referenced in the eight conversations. Her notes identify Landor's departures from historical records and thus shape the conversations for study within a divided disciplinary and epistemic system. Insofar as her elaborations often dwell on literary issues (such as how Landor's making Elizabeth I wish to be remembered favorably develops what we know about her character[27]), they add to efforts to construct the *Imaginary Conversations* as an object for study within a literary field.

Contrasting with Prasher's multivolume work, Proudfit's consists of a single, medium-sized book. It contains the texts and notes for eight conversations from Landor's third volume (1829) chosen "to present a broad sampling" of the whole. The motive for the volume is Proudfit's "belief that an annotated edition of Landor's prose [will] make his acquaintance both possible and pleasurable to a much more extensive audience than he has enjoyed in the past. To that end, Proudfit strives to provide the information that modern readers "need" to comprehend Landor's references.[28]

Proudfit goes beyond Crump or Prasher in constituting the *Imaginary Conversations* as an object for literary study, and he does so by emptying the historical component of significance. One of the best examples comes from his introduction to "Lucullus and Caesar." After stating that Landor's portrayal of Lucullus's character seems more positive than portrayals in historical sources and that the conversation alludes to events subsequent to the given date of the meeting, he concludes that the discrepancies do not matter: "Landor's Romans are creatures of his own desire, and in no way are they meant to be accurate historical representations. . . . Landor's interest in creating an air of historical exactness is that of the dramatic artist rather than the scholarly historian, for he makes little attempt to present an accurate chronology" (17).[29]

Proudfit's conclusion constructs the topic as a literary object based on dramatic criteria, but it raises questions about the "need" he asserted for knowledge of the historical dimension.

In considering Prasher's and Proudfit's studies as unsuccessful attempts to organize scholarship on Landor, I mean no criticism of their impressive, thoughtful, and enthusiastic works. They *did* succeed in studying Landor within the limits of the disciplinary and epistemic system of the modern academy, but they did not reach their own stated goals of encouraging widespread interest in Landor and in prompting completion of a comprehensively annotated edition of the *Imaginary Conversations*. A glance at the 1998 Oxford *Literature of the Romantic Period: A Bibliographical Guide* shows how little work on the *Imaginary Conversations* follows Prasher and Proudfit: it simply states that an earlier bibliography—prepared by Super in 1966—still provides adequate coverage of work on Landor's prose.[30]

I believe that this state of affairs reveals how important and pervasive the assumed distinction between lived and invented experience has been across the disciplines. Prasher and Proudfit take it for granted that we *must* be able to distinguish between Landor's facts and fictions, though they do not explain why we must be able to do so. In retrospect, we can see that the distinction was a condition for studying Landor within the prevailing system, and the limited success of those studies shows how strongly disciplinary norms influence what we know. Study of the *Imaginary Conversations* could not go very far forward because the construction of that work as a topic to know was problematic within the given system. Now that the system itself no longer dominates our thinking, it ought to be possible to look at the *Imaginary Conversations* in a different way.

In the previous chapter, I posited an alternative way of reading the *Conversations* by locating them in the lived experience of political contention. Instead of trying to authenticate the historical elements or valorize the imaginary ones, I asked a version of the question I quoted from Stanford Lyman in the introduction to this study: what did the *Imaginary Conversations* allow Landor to do and how did they allow him to do it? My analysis provided the following answers: they allowed him to intervene in British politics during a crucial period for parliamentary reform; they allowed him to model behavior conducive to the kind of reformed, republican government he advocated, behavior marked by the habitual questioning of authority; and they allowed him to reconcile advocacy of political reform with fear of revolutionary implications and thus to overcome an obstacle to change erected by memories of the excesses and tyrannies devolving from the French Revolution. To explain these answers, I put the *Imaginary Conversations* back into the political-historical context from which previous inquiries took them. Specifically, I argued that the work participates in the rise of popular contention that Charles Tilly has identified as a catalyst for parliamentary reform. This argument takes the concept of conversation as the most significant feature of the work; in other words, the fact that speakers are talking to each other is at least as important as anything they say.[31] Looking at Landor's situation with respect to reform, I discovered why political change was problematic for him and other former revolutionaries, and drawing on Mead's ideas about uses of the past, I examined how Landor's interaction with history offered a solution to the problem. This reading illustrates how meaning emerges when literary and lived experience can be joined.

BAILLIE, ADDAMS, AND DE QUINCEY

When Baillie's and Addams's stories are plotted along the collective narrative of the delegitimized utterance, they appear to be versions of each other. As Deegan and others have shown, pre-disciplinary sociology included reformist aims and respected women practitioners along with men; Addams had a place within that integrated configuration of social studies. It was the institutionalization of sociology within the modern academy that divided social theory from social work, male scientists from women caregivers.[32] In parallel, to quote Mellor, "women participated fully in the public sphere"—or, as she revises the location, the social sphere, during the Romantic era.[33] Baillie had a place within the theatrical and literary culture of her time until, in Burroughs's words, twentieth-century "canonizers" dismissed closet drama and centered the field on purportedly transcendent poetry.[34] It was the institutionalization of English in the modern academy that put Baillie and many other writers outside of readers' notice. This maneuvering enabled both sociology and literary studies to organize themselves around unique inquiries and to plot themselves along the collective narrative: sociology legitimated scientific methods and delegitimated the personal engagements of social work; Romanticists legitimated imaginative poetry and delegitimated more directly referential poems, dramas, and novels.

Each field is now plotting the stories of Addams, Baillie, and other formerly excluded or minor figures[35] *against* (rather than along) the collective narrative. Addams, Martineau, and others are recognized as founders of sociology by scholars dedicated to reconstructing the discipline; Baillie is being read, studied, and performed by scholars equally committed to disciplinary change. Though sociologists' interests in narrative and drama and Romanticists' interests in social relations, situations, and activities have moved these two groups of scholars closer together, I suggest we could go further in collaboration on cultural inquiry by more freely exchanging ideas between us. I have tried to engage in such an exchange in this study by sensitizing the concept of symbolic interaction and applying it to readings of Baillie, Scott, and Landor. In this final section, I examine how the assumption that literary and lived experience must be separated conditions Addams's (mis)reading of De Quincey, and I conclude that the social function of his work for her can now be affirmed. Moreover, I propose that De Quincey's concept of the "involute" be used more freely by scholars in any field concerned with the process by which readers use texts to work through perplexities in their experience.

The passages from Addams I consider in this section are quoted in the opening frame of my introduction. To recap, they are Addams's account, from *Twenty Years at Hull-House*, of how she began her career in social work by turning from books to deeds. She traces her "conversion" to a moment when she rode through London on a bus and, feeling helpless to relieve the poverty around her, compared herself to De Quincey, helpless to shout a warning about a runaway mail-coach until he recalled warning lines from the *Iliad*. By analogy, Addams's concludes that she, her well-read schoolmates, and De Quincey have all been "lumbering their minds with literature,"and she vows to change her conduct in the future.[36] This account has been taken at face value even in recent studies of Addams by Lengermann and Niebrugge-Brantley and Elshtain.[37] It has not, to my knowledge, been remarked on at all by scholars of De Quincey, yet it is a remarkable misreading of the text that changes from laudanum to literature the cause of his slowness to shout a warning and changes from help to hindrance the effects of recalling the *Iliad*.

Drawing on Maines, I read Addams's account as her attempt to plot her personal experience—her story—along a collective narrative inherited from De Quincey. But I also draw on an additional concept that is not part of the narrative inquiry developed by Maines but that is part of the literary criticism devised by De Quincey and recently recovered for use by Frederick Burwick. I refer to the concept of the "involute." As Burwick explains, "involutes" are "personal links" between lived and textual experiences that readers form in their minds and that they can in turn apply in interpreting other texts or events.[38] I suggest that involutes may serve as problem-solving devices, helping readers grapple with perplexities arising in situations subsequent to their reading, and I believe that the passage from De Quincey was such an involute for Addams. Her misreading, I argue, reflects a conflict with a collective narrative represented by De Quincey and lodged as "involute" in her mind. According to that narrative, literary and other cultural pursuits lead to social good. That plot was credible to De Quincey and to other Romantic-era figures, but it was losing credibility in Addams's time as competing narratives valorizing empirical and scientific methods emerged. Preoccupied with the dearth of social good, caught between competing narratives, and needing to validate settlement work in the eyes of readers of her memoir, Addams retold De Quincey's story as a way of responding to her culture's changing view of literature. Her repudiation, however, is at odds with the habitual reliance on literature evident in her work as well as in the story of her conversion itself. My analysis of Addams's perplexity and how she uses De Quincey to work through it recovers the socially productive value of De Quincey's text that Addams, in her situation, had to deny. I look first, however, at the concept of the involute.

According to Burwick, an involute consists of a "personal link" between a reader's lived experience and some aspect of a text that is forged in the reader's mind. Involutes are produced by "vicarious impulse"—the tendency to refer characters, situations, and ideas in a text back to oneself, to take a text as cognitively and emotionally stimulating "in a way very similar to actual experience."[39] Indeed, De Quincey does not really distinguish between textual and actual experiences, for he finds all experience to be composite.[40] In his words, "far more of our deepest thoughts and feelings pass to us through perplexed combinations of *concrete* objects, pass to us as *involutes* (if I may coin that word) in compound experiences incapable of being disentangled, than ever reach us *directly*, and in their own abstract shapes."[41] Once "lodge[d] within the mind," involutes "may perform an exegetical or hermeneutic function, rendering concrete the vague abstractions of a text"[42] —or, I would add, of a perplexing lived experience.

An example of the operation of an involute for De Quincey can be found in the reference to the shout from the *Iliad* in his essay on *The English Mail-Coach*, the memoir/historical-political essay/prose poem/fantasy published in three installments in 1849 in *Blackwood's Edinburgh Magazine* and subsequently revised for the *Collected Writings*.[43] The essay selects events from De Quincey's own past—some trips he took on the mail-coach during his student years, his opium habit—and from the national past—the introduction of the mail-coach in 1784, the social status of its passengers, its service in circulating news from the Napoleonic Wars, especially news of Waterloo—and emplots them in a sequence that shows him swept up by forces beyond his control (the coach, politics, opium), yet coping with them as heroically as possible because of his intellectual and interpretive acumen.[44] In the portion relevant to Addams, De Quincey tells how the mail-coach once got literally out of the control of its sleepy driver and how De Quincey coped with the situation. His success depends on his using a passage recollected from his reading to interpret and to guide his conduct in his present situation.

The main incident in this portion of the story is the appearance of another coach in the path of the runaway mail-coach. Since the lovers in the other coach are oblivious to the danger, De Quincey must either control the mail-coach or warn the lovers to get out of its way. In telling what happened, De Quincey foregrounds his own point of view, elaborating on and justifying his perceptions and reactions. Acknowledging that he was slow to realize what was happening and inept in his first attempts to respond, he attributes his paralysis to his drug addiction: he admits to taking laudanum as the mail-coach was setting out, and the cumulative effect of his addiction left his "frail, opium-shattered self" capable of little exertion.[45] When he does recognize the danger, he tries first to take the reins from the sleeping driver and to sound the guard's horn, but he cannot grasp the one or reach the other.[46] After these failures, he realizes that his only recourse is shouting to the lovers, and he thinks of the *Iliad* because the volume necessary to convey the warning seems of an epic size beyond his powers. Or perhaps he thinks first of the *Iliad* and from that memory derives the idea of shouting as a recourse. In either case, thought of the poem *helps* him to act. Here is how he tells that portion:

> Strange it is, and to a mere auditor of the tale might seem laughable, that I should need a suggestion from the *Iliad* to prompt the sole resource that remained. Yet so it was. Suddenly I remembered the shout of Achilles, and its effect. But could I pretend to shout like the son of Peleus, aided by Pallas? No: but then I needed notthe shout that should alarm all Asia militant; such a shout would suffice as might carry terror into the hearts of two thoughtless young people and one gig-horse.[47]

De Quincey's reference to the *Iliad* illustrates the functioning of an involute. The literary passage had been impressed on his mind from previous reading. When he subsequently found himself in perplexing circumstances, he was able to draw on it for interpretive purposes — to figure out what he could do to solve a problem. The involute helped him draw an analogy between the remembered, textualized situation and his present situation, and that analogy suggested to him a response to his immediate perplexity. The literary experience became part of his lived experience; it was as real, as productive of knowledge and action, as a lived experience.

De Quincey's analogy between himself and Achilles is not simplistically imitative behavior but complexly responsive behavior that shares some of the characteristics of role-taking. De Quincey does momentarily put himself in the place of the epic warrior whose shout can turn the Trojans' horses, but he does not thereby retreat into fantasy, develop delusions of grandeur, or otherwise lose sight of his immediate difficulty. Rather, he becomes self-consious about his capabilities and viable responses through the analogy with Achilles. He uses it to interpret his own situation, constructing the self who can overcome the frailty and sluggishness in his initial characterization and who can act to save those in danger. De Quincey acquires a heroic identity by plotting his story against the *Iliad*; he reaches self-consciousness through identifying with Achilles, and the effects of that development are as real as if he had reached self-consciousness through interacting with another living person. His example is consistent with Mead's notions of role-taking, which allow for identification with mythic or generalized others in the process of the social development of the self, and with David Novitz's generalizations about the narrative construction of personhood as including the imagination of the self as a fictional character.[48] De Quincey's reading is clearly not an aesthetic experience isolated from his lived experience; the two are linked by the involute that allows him to interpret the one by the other.

So far, I have addressed how the involute was useful to De Quincey after it had been lodged in his mind. A question remains as to why that passage from the *Iliad* would have been lodged in De Quincey's mind at all. The process of involution is not really predictable, though Frederick Shilstone has analyzed it according to modern psychological understandings of episodic and semantic, long-term and short-term, memory.[49] As Burwick says, involutes are formed by "vicarious impulse"[50]: they depend on the reader's circumstances, preoccupations, and associations, and their existence as involutes cannot truly be recognized until they are used exegetically. Like the events selected from the past for narrative emplotment, they acquire their meaning from their use in the present story.[51] It is through interpretive activity, prompted by other associations and circumstances, that involutes become realized. Awareness of circumstances and preoccupations crucial to a reader, however, can help us to account for likely involutes. Likely involutes are saturated with meaning from a collective narrative in the reader's culture. They are portions of texts or whole texts that offer readers opportunities to come to terms with prevalent values, ideals, and standards in their societies. The *Iliad* was such a text in De Quincey's society: it was part of a narrative of cultural achievement into which he very much wanted to fit his story.

Though the collective narrative that Maines explains as the "decreasing legitimation of the human utterance" and the increasing legitimation of impersonal measure[52] began before De Quincey's time, it had not yet in his time reached the extreme proportions it ran to by Addams's era. Command of Greek literature was still the mark of an educated man during the Romantic era and a plausible basis for claims to a socially respectable position. De Quincey experienced the early emergence of new valuations of knowledge and was attracted to political economy, as McDonagh has detailed,[53] but he was excessively proud of his ability as a classics scholar and made his accomplishments in Greek central to his identity. When he presents himself in his *Confessions of an English Opium-Eater*, he takes every opportunity to call attention to his excellence in Greek at school, his qualifications as a "corrector of Greek proofs," and even his recourse to Greek when attempting to speak to the Malay.[54] In foregrounding these episodes, he fits his life story into a collective narrative in which the human utterance is still the basis for knowledge and values, a narrative in which he and many of his contemporaries could still believe. Regarding the concept of believability, Maines points out that groups develop and control criteria for believing or disbelieving any given story, and if an individual account does not meet the criteria, the group rejects the account.[55] Balancing the story of his transgressive activity as an opium-eater with the narrative of his respectable activity as a scholar, De Quincey draws on the lingering power of this narrative of cultural privilege; as he uses it to prop up his own identity, he lends support to the social organization it represents.[56]

Awareness of the importance of classical learning in De Quincey's circumstances and associations makes it easy to see why the *Iliad* would be an involute for him and why it figures in *The English Mail-Coach*. Drawing on the *Iliad*, De Quincey assures himself—and his readers—that his interpretive skills make up for his physical shortcomings and that those skills have valuable applications. Through the involute, De Quincey constructs a story that justifies his perceptions and reactions and that inserts him into a larger narrative in which his skills are culturally privileged. *The English Mail-Coach*, then, shares what has been taken as the "point" of most of De Quincey's writings—the purpose of forging his identity as a literary critic, of showing himself as a superior interpreter of the people he met, the writers he read, and the events he observed.[57] Echoing the shout of Achilles, De Quincey affirms the meaning of the human utterance—and of his own human utterances—in his time and place. Though he is swept up by forces he cannot fully control, he can mitigate their effects by the powers of interpretation that show him how to make a limited response. In the case of the mail-coach incident, his shout does not entirely prevent the accident, but it does lessen its severity, for it reaches the other driver in time for him to move the coach to the side and thus to suffer an oblique rather than a direct collision.[58] For De Quincey, recourse to literature was crucial for coping with the perplexities of lived experience.

As the passage from the *Iliad* served as an involute for De Quincey in his account of the mail-coach incident, so does the passage from De Quincey serve as an involute for Addams in her account of the founding of Hull-House. Her reading has lodged that passage in her mind, where it stays until she dislodges it to interpret a puzzling situation and work out the perplexity. In using the involute, Addams makes significant alterations to De Quincey's account that show the blending of the personal and the collective in her concerns. While literature clearly remained productive of knowledge and action in Addams's own experience, it had lost so much legitimacy in the collective view of her contemporaries that stories of its efficacy were no longer believable. To construct her identity and plot her conduct in that context, Addams ends up denying the value of the very "literary suggestion" she is using to reach her decision.

Turning from De Quincey's version to Addams's version, the difference in the interpretation of events leaps out. Addams portrays the activity of recalling the *Iliad* as a struggle to disentangle it from memory, but for De Quincey, who had so much invested in his identity as a classics scholar, the thought came "suddenly." To Addams, the literary suggestion impedes activity. In the process of inverting its value, she omits reference to the failure of direct action (the attempts to seize the reins and blow the horn) for which, in De Quincey, the literary suggestion compensates as well as to the laudanum that De Quincey blames for his initial paralysis.[59] De Quincey's account has become part of Addams's present concerns about what "we" —i.e., she and her educated contemporaries whose pursuit of culture seemed socially irresponsible — "were doing." Through the involute, she constructs an analogy that helps her concretize the behavior she had found vaguely and generally troubling. Specifying literature as the source of the problem, the analogy also suggests a solution, albeit the imperfect one of repudiating literature.

Addams did not get this negative view of literature from De Quincey or from her own reading experiences, which were, as this engagement with De Quincey testifies, richly productive of knowledge and action for her. The negative view of literature comes from the collective narrative of the delegitimation of the human utterance, which was by Addams's time becoming the intellectual equivalent of a runaway mail-coach — a powerful force speeding toward collision with any nonquantifiable epistemologies in its path. As Maines points out with respect to the work of Addams's contemporaries Florian and Znaniecki, the narrative aspects of *The Polish Peasant* could not then be recognized, even by Florian and Znaniecki, as knowledge-bearing aspects of the study.[60] Addams's disjoining of literature from knowledge and action in her reading of De Quincey should be seen as part of this collective delegitimation.

Addams's plotting of her story against this collective narrative also shows a use of narrative to manage conflict and attain consensus. The "point" of Addams's narrative should be understood in terms of the purpose of *Twenty Years at Hull-House* for which she devised it. According to her preface, she wrote the memoir to justify Settlement work — to defend Settlements from a "charge of superficiality" as well as to defend herself from biographies-in-progress "that made life in a Settlement all too smooth and charming."[61] An effective defense depended on her separating her own and other Settlers' work from the self-indulgent cultivation of esoteric experiences that led her contemporaries on their cultural pursuits. Though Addams's own experience testifies to the fact that reading is not necessarily self-indulgent, escapist, or incompatible with social interaction, her awareness of the trivialization of literary culture in her society made literary models unsuitable for her goal. A dominant notion of literature as aesthetic masters her story,[62] preventing her from fully exploring the real effects of textualized encounters but enabling her to fit the Settlement story into a collective narrative valuing measurable, tangible, immediate actions over the elusive effects of words.

What Addams rejects is not the literary but the disciplined version of the literary, the version that confines it to private reflection. Her collective narrative, however, had no terms in which to make plausible the distinction between the two. De Quincey could construct a valuable identity for himself as an interpreter; Addams could not. She could not even fully believe in that part of his story. To present herself and other Settlers as serious and socially engaged workers, Addams had to distinguish them from aesthetic escapists, which she could most easily, memorably—and ironically—do through a literary allusion. Her characterization of herself and Settlement workers as not-De Quinceys illustrates both Ezzy's point that, given a limited number of acceptable narratives through which to interpret the self, "most people tend to adopt the culturally given plots" and Novitz's point that "whenever people wish to have their narrative identities praised and taken seriously, they try to project them normatively."[63] Addams's approach suggests an attempt to build consensus though narrative, to develop a collective identity for Settlement workers that would give them credibility in their society.

However much Addams conceded to normative distrust of literature in her memoir of Hull-House, she carried out her work there as if she had never repudiated literature. A glance at both scholarship on Addams and at her own words reveals how closely she worked with, in, and through literary modes. She has been credited with taking a narrative approach to sociology and with cultivating a model of knowledge based on literary creativity rather than scientific method.[64] She has been compared to George Eliot and Flannery O'Connor; she has been "place[d] . . . among modernist writers who explore states of consciousness."[65] She made drama an integral part of reform work and value inquiry at Hull-House.[66] In an article that provides another example of the functioning of an involute, she explained the Pullman strike through an extended analogy with *King Lear*.[67] She even wrote a compelling analysis of how reading can influence social interaction, an analysis that dovetails with notions of the involute in its attention to the interplay of literary and lived experience:

> [C]onfidence sometimes comes to the more literate person when, finding himself morally isolated among those hostile to his immediate aims, his reading assures him that other people in the world have thought as he

does. Later when he dares to act on the conviction his own experience has forced upon him, he has become so conscious of a cloud of witnesses torn out of literature and warmed into living comradeship, that he scarcely distinguishes them from the like-minded people actually in the world whom he has later discovered as a consequence of his deed.[68]

It is ironic that such insights into how reading facilitates social engagement should appear in the same work as the disclaimer "while I may receive valuable suggestions from classic literature, when I really want to learn about life, I must depend on my neighbors."[69] Addams's practice does not support the conclusion that learning through reading is inferior to learning through other means; the conclusion, however, shows the impact of modern disciplinarity on her thinking.

I would go so far as to say that the division between literary and lived experience that prevailed throughout much of the last century contributed to social problems because it diminished our ability and willingness to incorporate symbolic resources in social programs and mobilize them for social change. The division distanced Romanticists from the rich legacy of social engagement we inherit from the writers of that era. But as we enter the post-disciplinary age, I draw an optimistic conclusion. We are ready to reunite Addams with De Quincey, lived with literary experience. I have undertaken this study in order to make some contribution toward that end. By reading the works of Baillie, Scott, and Landor as symbolic interactions that assist social problem solving, I have repositioned them where we might more easily notice and respond to their gestures—gestures that direct readers to construct new social relations, try out new social roles, and adapt contentious or temporizing strategies in problematic situations. During the age of disciplinarity, the legacy of literary engagement was lodged like an involute in our minds. In the post-disciplinary age, we can draw on that involute to give new meaning to human utterance.

Notes

PREFACE

1. Norman K. Denzin, "Social Work in the Seventh Moment," *Qualitative Social Work* 1 (2002): 25–38.

2. Paul Hamilton, *Metaromanticism: Aesthetics, Literature, Theory* (Chicago: University of Chicago Press, 2003); David P. Haney, *The Challenge of Coleridge: Ethics and Interpretation in Romanticism and Modern Philosophy* (University Park: Pennsylvania State University Press, 2001); Frederick Burwick, *Mimesis and Its Romantic Reflections* (University Park: Pennsylvania State University Press, 2001).

3. Joanna Baillie, *The Dramatic and Poetical Works* (1851; repr., Hildesheim, Germany: Georg Olms, 1976), 4.

4. Charles Tilly, *Popular Contention in Great Britain, 1758–1834* (Cambridge: Harvard University Press, 1995); *Roads from Past to Future* (Lanham, MD: Rowman and Littlefield, 1997).

5. David R. Maines, "Narrative's Moment and Sociology's Phenomena: Toward a Narrative Sociology," *Sociological Quarterly* 34 (1993): 17–38.

CHAPTER 1. INTRODUCTION

1. Jane Addams, *Twenty Years at Hull-House*, ed. and intro. by James Hurt (1910; repr., Chicago: University of Illinois Press, 1990), 43.

2. Jerome J. McGann, *The Romantic Ideology: A Critical Investigation* (Chicago: University of Chicago Press, 1983).

3. Thomas De Quincey, *The English Mail-Coach*, in *The Collected Writings of Thomas De Quincey*, ed. David Masson (1854; repr., New York: AMS Press, 1968), 13:313–14.

4. Marilyn Butler, "Repossessing the Past: the Case for an Open Literary History," in *Rethinking Historicism: Critical Readings in Romantic History*, ed. Marjorie Levinson et al., 82, (Oxford: Blackwell, 1989).

5. Addams, *Twenty Years*, 61–62, 221–26.

6. David R. Maines rightly takes issue with the phrase "lived experience" as a redundancy" (*The Faultline of Consciousness: A View of Interactionism in Sociology* [New York: Aldine de Gruyter, 2001], 5), but it reflects culturally ingrained practices of distinguishing some experience as "lived" from other experience that is aesthetic or "literary" that are only now being superseded. To have a convenient and familiar way to refer to the dis-

tinction I address and challenge, I retain the phrase, often pairing it with the phrase "literary experience" throughout this study. For comparable reasons, I also sometimes use the phrase "situated behavior," though I accept Maines's observation that "situationless conduct is unknown among human beings," (3).

7. The landmark study in which C. P. Snow identified the "two cultures" remains important for an understanding of the problem (*The Two Cultures and a Second Look: An Expanded Version of The Two Cultures and the Scientific Revolution* [Cambridge: Cambridge University Press, 1969]). Two recent studies that address the Romantic-era experience of a cultural divide are Maureen McLane's *Romanticism and the Human Sciences* (Cambridge: Cambridge University Press, 2000), which analyzes the struggle between poetic and utilitarian discourses to be the representative discourse of humanity (1–42), and Philip Connell's *Romanticism, Economics and the Question of "Culture"* (Oxford: Oxford University Press, 2001), which analyzes how emotional and literary responses to change struggle with rationalistic and scientific ones to define how political economy will assess the human condition (1–12).

8. Jane Addams, *The Long Road of Woman's Memory*, ed. and intro. by Charlene Haddock Siegfried (1916; repr., Urbana: University of Illinois Press, 2002), 4.

9. Jean Bethke Elshtain corroborates that Addams "was ambivalent about" her interest in fiction, though she does not address the problem of disciplinarity (*Jane Addams and the Dream of American Democracy* [New York: Basic Books, 2001], 28–29). Dorothy Ross argues that Addams based her ideas about social relations on a model of "literary production" instead of a model of "scientific experiment," and since most "university sociologists" privileged science, most therefore "discount[ed] Addams's model of social knowledge" ("Gendered Social Knowledge: Domestic Discourse, Jane Addams, and the Possibilities of Social Science," in *Gender and American Social Science: The Formative Years*, ed. Helene Silverberg, 248–49, 254 [Princeton: Princeton University Press, 1998]). Ross does not analyze Addams's reading of De Quincey, to which I return in my conclusion. In her examination of discrepancies between Addams's published account of her experiences in *Twenty Years at Hull-House* and her private account of those experiences in letters and diaries, Victoria Bissell Brown notes that the later published work dismisses the earlier "belief in art's uplifting power" evident in the private documents (*The Education of Jane Addams* [Philadelphia: University of Pennsylvania Press, 2004], 146). Despite this insight, Brown does not analyze Addams's reading of De Quincey. Even Katherine Joslin, who treats Addams primarily as a writer capable of turning the people she met and the events she lived through into symbols that serve the purposes of her texts, pays little attention to Addams's engagement with De Quincey. She notes only that the mailcoach serves Addams as a metaphor for artistic "transport" away from social action (*Jane Addams, a Writer's Life* [Urbana: University of Illinois Press, 2004], 95).

10. Nigel Parton and Patrick O'Byrne, *Constructive Social Work: Toward a New Practice* (New York: St. Martin's Press, 2000); Kathleen Gallagher, *Drama Education in the Lives of Girls: Imagining Possibilities* (Toronto: University of Toronto Press, 2000).

11. Shannon Jackson, *Lines of Activity: Performance, Historiography, Hull-House Domesticity* (Ann Arbor: University of Michigan Press, 2000), 8–9.

12. My review of *The Challenge of Coleridge* (in *ANQ* 15 [2002]: 41–44) offers more detailed reflections on this work.

13. The term Hamilton *does* privilege for Schiller's procedure is "temporize," by which he means perpetually deferred realization, (*Metaromanticism*, 27). Though this usage has some consonance with my analysis of Scott's temporizing, my selection of the term, for reasons given in chapter 7, is independent of Hamilton's.

14. This comment does not imply that scholarship on Baillie has not taken strides toward recovering and interpreting her work. The investigation I propose is possible because Catherine Burroughs (*Closet Stages: Joanna Baillie and the Theater Theory of British Romantic Women Writers* [Philadelphia: University of Pennsylvania Press, 1997]), Anne K. Mellor ("Joanna Baillie and the Counter-Public Sphere," *Studies in Romanticism* 33 [1994]: 559–67), and Marjean D. Purinton (*Romantic Ideology Unmasked: The Mentally Constructed Tyrannies in Dramas of William Wordsworth, Lord Byron, Percy Shelley, and Joanna Baillie* [Newark: University of Delaware Press, 1994]; "The Sexual Politics of *The Election*: French Feminism and the Scottish Playwright Joanna Baillie," *Intertexts* 2 [1998]: 119–30; "Socialized and Medicalized Hysteria in Joanna Baillie's *Witchcraft*," *Prism(s): Essays in Romanticism* 9 [2001]: 139–56) have opened up lines of inquiry into Baillie's social situation and the social implications of her work and because Judith Bailey Slagle has prepared an insightful biography (*Joanna Baillie: A Literary Life* [Madison, NJ: Fairleigh Dickinson University Press, 2002]) and edition of Baillie's letters (*The Collected Letters of Joanna Baillie*, ed. Judith Bailey Slagle, 2 vols. [Madison, NJ: Fairleigh Dickinson University Press, 1999]). While I was writing this manuscript, Baillie scholarship moved into new territory with the publication of a volume of essays edited by Thomas Crochunis, *Joanna Baillie: Romantic Dramatist* (London: Routledge, 2004), devoted to her work. I am pleased that I was able to take account of many essays from this collection in my study.

15. Richard Maxwell proposes that Scott be considered "proto-sociological" because of his preference for inclusive classification over linear progression, but Maxwell associates this preference with Durkheim ("Inundations of Time: A Definition of Scott's Originality," *ELH* 68 [2001]: 419–68). He thus projects Scott into a different kind of sociology than I propose here or in my earlier study, *The Possibilities of Society: Wordsworth, Coleridge, and the Sociological Viewpoint of English Romanticism* (Albany: State University of New York Press, 1997). In that study, I contrast the "sociological viewpoint" and research orientation of the canonical English Romantic poets with the political focus and conservative political agenda of Scott. My attention to Scott is brief and intended mainly to highlight differences. The present study gives me the opportunity to explore how Scott's conservative agenda is also transformative: to protect the paternalistic relations he idealizes, he had to envision them in ways that modified rather than reified existing social systems. The investigation I undertake here is possible because of the turn in Scott studies—evident especially in scholarship by James Chandler, *England in 1819: The Politics of Literary Culture and the Case of Romantic Historicism* (Chicago: University of Chicago Press, 1998); Catherine Jones, *Literary Memory: Scott's Waverley Novels and the Psychology of Narrative* (Lewisburg, PA: Bucknell University Press, 2003); Ann Rigney, *Imperfect Histories: The Elusive Past and the Legacy of Romanticism* (Ithaca: Cornell University Press, 2001); Ina Ferris, "Pedantry and the Question of Enlightenment History: The Figure of the Antiquary in Scott," *European Romantic Review* 13 (2002): 273–83; Shawn Malley, "Walter Scott's Romantic Archaeology: New/Old Abbotsford and *The Antiquary*," *Studies in Romanticism* 40 (2001): 233–51; and Robert Mayer, "The Illogical Status of Novelistic Discourse: Scott's Footnotes for the Waverley Novels," *ELH* 66 (1999): 911–38—toward analyzing the disciplinary and epistemic tensions in his work. Jones associates Scott's work with the "historical sociology" of the Scottish Enlightenment, but the term is not meant to project it into later disciplinary formations as much as to separate it from the Whig ideology prominent in eighteenth- and nineteenth-century historiography (*Literary Memory*, 77–78). The broader approach of those contrary historians may, of course, set a precedent for later efforts to study society without reducing it to politics.

16. Baillie, *Letters*, 299. Slagle's biography of Baillie deals sensitively with her friendship with Scott, but the nature of the biography does not permit extensive analysis of works. Slagle's approach is a welcome change from earlier works, such as Hesketh Pearson's *Walter Scott: His Life and Personality*, intro. by Allan Massie (1954; repr., London: Hamish Hamilton, 1987), that paired them for the purpose of constructing Scott's superiority. Without reference to Scott, Victoria Myers calls for more careful study of what being a Whig meant to Baillie ("Joanna Baillie's Theatre of Cruelty," in Crochunis, *Joanna Baillie*, 107n9).

17. In addition to the developments in Baillie scholarship I note above, theatrical interest in her work has even led to the staging of *Count Basil*, never performed during Baillie's lifetime, in both academic and nonacademic settings. A section edited by Catherine Burroughs in a recent number of the *European Romantic Review* (15 [2004]: 351–86) contains reflections on the performance at the 2003 conference of the North American Society for the Study of Romanticism.

Both the *European Romantic Review* and *Studies in Romanticism* have recently devoted special issues to Scott (respectively, Bruce Beiderwell, ed., *Romantic Enlightenment: Sir Walter Scott and the Politics of History*, European Romantic Review 13, no. 3 [2002]: 223–346 and Ian Duncan et al., eds., *Scott, Scotland, and Romantic Nationalism*, Studies in Romanticism 40, no. 1 [2001]: 1–152). Scott's novels are being newly edited in a controversial project by Edinburgh University Press, which aims to present the first versions of the texts rather than the revised versions from the "Magnum Opus" edition that has long been standard. The rationale for the Edinburgh edition is explained in the general introduction (repeated in each novel) by the general editor, David Hewitt (e.g., "General Introduction," in *The Antiquary*, by Sir Walter Scott, ed. David Hewitt [Edinburgh: Edinburgh University Press, 1995], xiii–xvii); reservations about the project are expressed by Nicola Watson in her Introduction to *The Antiquary* (Oxford: Oxford University Press, 2002), xxviii–xxix. Because Scott's reflexivity is important to my understanding of his work, I cite texts based on the Magnum Opus edition throughout my study.

There are no comparable developments in Landor scholarship; I address the reasons for and implications of that lack in chapter 8.

18. Walter Scott, *The Bride of Lammermoor*, Caledonian Edition of The Works of Sir Walter Scott, (Boston: Houghton Mifflin, 1913). Further references to the novel will be given parenthetically in the text.

19. Anne K. Mellor, *Mothers of the Nation: Women's Political Writing in England, 1780–1830* (Bloomington: University of Indiana Press, 2000), 101.

20. Baillie, *Letters*, 305; Scott, *The Letters of Walter Scott 1787–1834*, ed. H. J. C. Grierson, 2:320 (London: Constable, 1932–37; repr., New York: AMS Press, 1971).

21. For analyses of the construction of "the Scottish Enlightenment," see Paul Wood, "Introduction: Dugald Stewart and the Invention of 'the Scottish Enlightenment,'" in *The Scottish Enlightenment: Essays in Reinterpretation*, ed. Paul Wood, 1–35 (Rochester: University of Rochester Press, 2000), and John Robertson, "The Scottish Contribution to the Enlightenment," in the same volume, 37–62.

22. Ian Ward, "The Jurisprudential Heart of Midlothian," *Scottish Literary Journal* 24 (1997): 25–39.

23. Mary Louise Pratt, "President's Column: 'The New Humanities,'" *MLA Newsletter* 35, no. 3 (2003): 3–4.

24. Jerome Christensen, *Romanticism at the End of History* (Baltimore: Johns Hopkins University Press, 2000), 11. Though with less enthusiasm than Christensen, Hamilton also notes the value of anachronism as "imaginary space." Particularly in the conflations

of Jacobites and Jacobins, Cameronians and Whigs, Hanoverians and Tories in Scott's
Waverley novels, anachronisms serve "as alternatives to historical explanation, or as
places staging the fanciful interregnum between accredited historical discourses"
(*Metaromanticism*, 130).

25. Some interactionists do maintain a separation. Even David R. Maines, whose
groundbreaking work on narrative I address in chapter 8, is wary of "literary criticism"
because of its "endless interpretive regress" (*The Faultline of Consciousness*, 168–69). Of
course, Romanticists should know, especially in light of Haney's and Burwick's works,
that literary criticism does not have to be caught in that vicious circle.

In asserting that interactionism does and should fold lived and literary experience into
each other, I follow a line of thinking advanced by Norman Denzin, whose *Symbolic Interactionism and Cultural Studies* (Oxford: Blackwell, 1992) calls for recognition of the textual
nature of social reality. He has developed this position in additional studies, such as *Interpretive Interactionism*, 2nd ed. (Thousand Oaks, CA: Sage, 2001) and *Interpretive Ethnography* (Thousand Oaks, CA: Sage, 1997). *Symbolic Interaction and Cultural Studies* enlists the
aesthetic in the processes of interpreting and criticizing lived experience by drawing on
Dewey's rather than Kant's version of that concept. In that pragmatist line, aesthetic experience was never so fully disjoined from cognition, ethics, and sociality. As Denzin
summarizes, aesthetic experience "create[s] an integration or interaction of the self with
th[e] aesthetic object and the environment": the "object produces a form of resistance; it
challenges our past understandings and taken-for-granted meanings" (101). As Romanticists struggle with the Kantian legacy, we would do well to keep in mind that there are
other versions of the aesthetic and that, as Isobel Armstrong has argued, alternative versions can still be recovered and created (*The Radical Aesthetic* [Oxford: Blackwell, 2000]).
Regarding the specific conjunction of literary and lived experience in interpretive interactionism, Denzin proposes replacing the notion of "lived experience" with "lived textuality" because all knowledge, including what we know of other people, involves interpretation (*Interpretive Ethnography*, 33). Compatibly, Douglas Ezzy argues that both
written and lived experience lack "intrinsic meaning" and become "completed composi-
tions in their reading" ("Theorizing Narrative Identity: Symbolic Interactionism and
Hermeneutics," *Sociological Quarterly* 39 [1998]: 243), and Joseph R. Gusfield studies
"human action as creating meanings that can be understood 'as if' they were literary
texts." Gusfield remarks that the founders of "symbolic" interaction ought to have paid
more attention to the "poetic side of language and meaning" and ought to have felt more
kinship with "the humanities [which] had been wrestling with problems of meaning for
decades" ("A Journey with Symbolic Interaction," *Symbolic Interaction* 28 [2003]: 125).
The gaps he identifies are, I posit, the effect of the disciplinary divide in which I have introduced Addams's ambivalence toward literature and to which I return in my conclusion.

26. Denzin, *The Research Act: A Theoretical Introduction to Sociological Methods*, 3rd ed.
(Englewood Cliffs, NJ: Prentice Hall, 1989), 9, 15; *Interpretive Interactionism*, 84.

27. David A. Snow remarks on the widespread agreement about Blumer's importance
in defining symbolic interactionism and refers to his work as the "Rosetta Stone" and
"canonical basis" for this way of knowing ("Extending and Broadening Blumer's Conceptualization of Symbolic Interactionism," *Symbolic Interaction* 24 [2001]: 368).

28. Herbert Blumer, *Symbolic Interactionism: Perspective and Method* (1969; repr., Berkeley: University of California Press, 1998), 89.

29. Denzin, *Symbolic Interactionism and Cultural Studies*, 62–63; Gusfield, "Journey,"
131–35; Stanford M. Lyman, *Civilization: Contents, Discontents, Malcontents, and Other*

Essays in Social Theory (Fayetteville: University of Arkansas Press, 1990), 243–49. I deal with the conflict between problem solving and theory building in more detail in "Joanna Baillie at Hull-House: A Working Hypothesis for Disciplinary Reform," *Studies in Symbolic Interaction* 27 (2004): 113–49.

30. *Annual Review of Sociology* 19 (1993): 61–87.

31. Maines, *Faultline*, 1–2, 6.

32. Joane Nagel (program director, National Science Foundation Sociology Program), quoted in unsigned interview, "Joane Nagel Joins NSF Sociology Program," *Footnotes: American Sociological Association Newsletter* 30, no. 8 (2002): 3.

33. Joseph A. Kotarba and John M. Johnson, "Introduction: Postmodern Existentialism," in *Postmodern Existential Sociology*, ed. Joseph A. Kotarba and John M. Johnson (Walnut Creek, CA: AltaMira Press, 2002), 6–8.

34. Denzin, *Symbolic Interactionism and Cultural Studies*, 161–71; *Interpretive Interactionism*, 1–25.

35. Mary Jo Deegan, *Jane Addams and the Men of the Chicago School, 1892–1918* (New Brunswick, NJ: Transaction Press, 1988), 105–21, 210–11, 7–13, 273.

36. Ibid., 2–3, 309–28.

37. Denzin, *Interpretive Interactionism*, 2; *Symbolic Interactionism and Cultural Studies*,167; "Social Work," 28–34. Much recent scholarship aims at recovering other forms of predisciplinary sociology and using them as predecessors to authorize a more interventionist turn in the current field. Especially important lines of research involve the recovery of women founders and feminist methods (e.g., Patricia Madoo Lengermann and Jill Niebrugge-Brantley, *The Women Founders: Sociology and Social Theory, 1830–1930* [Boston: McGraw-Hill, 1998]; Susan Hoecker-Drysdale, *Harriet Martineau: First Woman Sociologist* [Providence, RI: Berg, 1992]), "liberation sociology" (Joe R. Feagin and Hernán Vera, *Liberation Sociology* [Boulder, CO: Westview Press, 2001]), and narrative sociology (Maines, "Narrative's Moment"). Though I allude to some of these lines of research where applicable throughout, a full analysis is beyond the scope of this study.

38. Numerous other government programs, private philanthropic groups, political interest groups, and religious groups provided services that can be classified as social work. I focus on the COS and Settlement Movement, however, because of their prominence, their competitive relationship with each other, and their relevance for symbolic interactionism. Insights into the larger network of charitable and social service providers can be gained from Michael J. Moore, "Social Work and Social Welfare: The Organization of Philanthropic Resources in Britain, 1900–1914," *Journal of British Studies* 16 (1977): 85–104; F. David Roberts, *The Social Conscience of the Early Victorians* (Stanford, CA: Stanford University Press, 2002); F. M. L. Thompson, ed. *The Cambridge Social History of Britain*, vol. 3, *Social Agencies and Institutions* (Cambridge: Cambridge University Press, 1990); and Camilla Stivers, "Settlement Women and Bureau Men: Constructing a Usable Past for Public Administration," *Public Administration Review* 55 (1995): 522–29.

39. The activities of the COS are presented in a positive light by Gertrude Himmelfarb, *Poverty and Compassion: The Moral Imagination of the Late Victorians* (New York: Knopf, 1991) and in a skeptical light by Lauren M. E. Goodlad, "Character and Pastorship in Two British 'Sociological' Traditions: Organized Charity, Fabian Socialism, and the Invention of New Liberalism," in *Disciplinarity at the Fin de Siècle*, ed. Amanda Anderson and Joseph Valente (Princeton: Princeton University Press, 2002).

40. Mina Carson, *Settlement Folk: Social Thought and the American Settlement Movement, 1885–1930* (Chicago: University of Chicago Press, 1990), 8–9.

41. Jackson, *Lines of Activity*, 14.

42. Addams, *Twenty Years*, 57.

43. Jane Addams, *Democracy and Social Ethics*, ed. and intro. by Charlene Haddock Siegfried (1902; repr., Urbana: University of Illinois Press, 2002), 17; *Twenty Years*, 182.

44. Addams, *Democracy*, 16.

45. Addams, *Twenty Years*, 94.

46. Jackson, *Lines of Activity*, 11.

47. Standish Meachum, *Toynbee Hall and Social Reform, 1880–1914: The Search for Community* (New Haven: Yale University Press, 1987); Jackson, *Lines of Activity*, 5–18. Himmelfarb also defends Toynbee Hall for its humanizing effects on residents who would otherwise have only abstract ideas about the poor, though she does so without a sense of the interactive or performative nature of settling and without interpreting it as social change (*Poverty and Compassion*, 233–43).

48. Jackson, *Lines of Activity*, 203–47.

49. Baillie, *Works*, 387.

50. Baillie, *Letters*, 12.

51. Baillie, *Works*, 10–11.

52. Denzin, *Symbolic Interactionism and Cultural Studies*, 27–28; Blumer, *Symbolic Interactionism*, 17–18. Though Richard Lachmann, whose work I introduce below (see note 71), does not identify himself with interactionism, his definition of "structures" as "artifacts of past chains of agency" (*Capitalists in Spite of Themselves: Elite Conflict and Economic Transitions in Early Modern Europe* [Oxford : Oxford University Press, 2002], 14) is compatible with interactionist thinking. The coincidence affirms Maines's thesis about the widening circle of interactionism's influence in sociology (*Faultline*, 1–2).

53. Blumer, *Symbolic Interactionism*, 18.

54. Snow, "Blumer's Conceptualization," 373.

55. Blumer's objection to "attitude as an explanation of human action" refers chiefly to attitude measurement studies that treat the concept as a determining tendency. He does not object to other uses of "attitude" that treat it as developing within a situation (*Symbolic Interactionism*, 93–100). The term "attitude" also has a specialized meaning in theater history. According to Greg Kucich, it refers to a "mode of performance art" in which an actor strikes poses that capture emotional states. This practice of striking attitudes was popular during the late 1700s, as was the practice of staging *tableaux vivants* of historical scenes. Kucich credits Baillie with combining the practices: her plays are filled with scenes that show both individual emotion and "communal relations" ("Joanna Baillie and the Re-staging of History and Gender," in Crochunis, *Joanna Baillie*, 117–18). Juxtaposing Blumer's and Kucich's points, I see an interactionist orientation in Baillie's theatrical technique: she treats attitudes as developing within situations.

56. William I. and Dorothy S. Thomas, *The Child in America: Behavior Problems and Programs* (New York: Knopf, 1928), 572.

57. Stanford Lyman, *Postmodernism and a Sociology of the Absurd: And Other Essays on the "Nouvelle Vague" in American Social Science* (Fayetteville: University of Arkansas Press, 1997), 29. Studying what meaning allows an actor to do does not rule out locating that meaning in competing contexts and, for later interactionists, evaluating moral implications.

58. Baillie, *Works*, 11.

59. Ibid., 5, 2.

60. Ibid., 2.

61. Frederick Burwick, "Competing Histories in the Waverley Novels," *European Romantic Review* 13 (2002): 261–71; Fiona Robertson, *Legitimate Histories: Scott, Gothic, and the*

Authorities of Fiction (Oxford: Clarendon Press, 1994). The studies by Chandler, Christensen, Ferris, Malley, Maxwell, and Mayer have been cited above.

62. George Herbert Mead, "The Nature of the Past," in *Selected Writings of George Herbert Mead*, ed. Andrew Reck (1932; repr., Chicago: University of Chicago Press, 1964).

63. Mead, "Past," 350–52; *The Philosophy of the Present*, ed. A. E. Murphy with a preface by John Dewey (1932; repr., Chicago: University of Chicago Press, 1980), 9–12.

64. Maxwell, "Inundations of Time," likewise finds Scott's sense of social structure at odds with politics and history, though he works with a different sense of social structure from mine.

65. Christopher A. Whatley, *Scottish Society, 1707–1830: Beyond Jacobitism, Towards Industrialisation* (Manchester, UK: Manchester University Press, 2000).

66. Carol Gilligan, *In a Different Voice: Psychological Theory and Women's Development* (Cambridge: Harvard University Press, 1982). My placement of Scott in this company is less startling than it might at first appear in light of Ina Ferris's study of how gender associations pivoted around the *Waverley* novels, a study that thus shows how unstable gender hierarchies are (*The Achievement of Literary Authority: Gender, History, and the Waverley Novels* [Ithaca, NY: Cornell University Press, 1991]). At its first appearance, *Waverley* made a "manly intervention" in the literary field: from *Waverley* on, it became more usual to regard the novel as serious, masculine literature rather than as lighter feminine fare (79, 1–14). During the late Victorian era, however, another "curious migration of gender" had occurred, again "entangl[ing Scott] in female signs" (237). As realism became valued over romance, Scott was "relegated to the lowly, unliterary sphere inhabited by children and women and mere storytelling[; he was] expelled from the literary space for fiction that his own novels had helped forge" (238).

67. Erin McKenna, "The Need for a Pragmatist Feminist Self," in *Feminist Interpretations of John Dewey*, ed. Charlene Haddock Siegfried, 156 (University Park: Pennsylvania State University Press, 2002).

68. Roberts, *Social Conscience*, 2, 15–16.

69. Lindsay Farmer, *Criminal Law, Tradition and Legal Order: Crime and the Genius of Scots Law, 1747 to the Present* (Cambridge: Cambridge University Press, 1997); Paul Turner Riggs, "Scottish Criminal Law and Procedure in the Nineteenth Century" (PhD diss., University of Pittsburgh, 1997); Baron David Hume, *Commentaries on the Law of Scotland Respecting Crimes*, with a supplement by Benjamin Robert Bell (1797, 1844; repr., Edinburgh: Law Society of Scotland, 1986). Scott's admiration for Hume is documented by David Hewitt, "*The Heart of Midlothian* and 'the People,'" *European Romantic Review* 13 (2002): 299–309, and by Jones, who even posits that the Waverley novels can be read as a "map of the law" according to Hume, at least insofar as Hume stresses the need for a grounding in legal history. Jones concentrates on Scott's efforts to master legal history along with other remnants of the past in *Redgauntlet* (*Literary Memory*, 108–10).

70. Bruce Beiderwell, *Power and Punishment in Scott's Novels* (Athens: University of Georgia Press, 1992), ix; James Kerr, *Fiction Against History: Scott as Storyteller* (Cambridge: Cambridge University Press, 1989), 11–12.

71. Throughout the study, I prefer the term "elite" over terms of social "class" because it captures the complexity of material and cultural privilege, which does not fit neatly into the categories of "class." According to Richard Lachmann's award-winning study of "elite conflict" and social change, an "elite" is any "group of rulers with the capacity to appropriate resources from nonelites and who inhabit a distinct organizational apparatus" (*Capitalists*, 9). Instead of seeing society as controlled by a monolithic "ruling class," Lachmann sees it shaped by coexisting groups of elites. Conflict among elites can create

opportunities for nonelites to gain advantages and thus can precipitate social change (8–14). Scott's work, I suggest, aims at shaping various elites into responsible custodians of their resources.

72. My position on Scott's restructurings lies somewhere between Malley's and Ferris's. For Malley, Scott's reuse and recontextualizaiton of old objects "erase[s]" and "destroys" the original meaning to create something else ("Walter Scott's Romantic Archaeology," 241). For Ferris, Scott would be reluctant to see the recreations of history as "something different," though he would acknowledge that old pieces can be "put together to form a new whole" ("Pedantry," 277). I am wary of Malley's inclusion of destruction in the process, as I think Scott strove for the "co-existence" that Malley later mentions in connection with the interpretations of history in *The Antiquary* ("Walter Scott's Romantic Archaeology," 246). I would go so far as to say that the composite structure may indeed be different from any of its analogues, though Scott may not have been able to confront the implications of differences if they threatened his sense of social cohesion.

73. David Zaret, "Petitions and the 'Invention' of Public Opinion in the English Revolution," *American Journal of Sociology* 101 (1996): 1500.

74. Cf. Christensen's reading of *Waverley* as showing the operation of liberal bureaucracy despite Scott's views (*Romanticism at the End of History*, 153–75); my sense of Scott's paradoxically new structures is, however, generally more positive.

75. Roberts, *Social Conscience*, 16.

76. Burroughs, *Closet Stages*, 8–13, 16. For additional analyses of theatrical struggles and gender roles, see Mellor, "Joanna Baillie and the Counter-Public Sphere"; Kucich, "Re-Staging of History and Gender"; Thomas Crochunis, "Joanna Baillie's Ambivalent Dramaturgy," in Crochunis, *Joanna Baillie*, 168–86; Ellen Donkin, *Getting Into the Act: Women Playwrights in London, 1776–1829* (London: Routledge, 1995); and Tracy Davis and Ellen Donkin, eds., *Women and Playwrighting in Nineteenth-Century Britain* (Cambridge: Cambridge University Press, 1999).

77. Denzin, *Interpretive Interactionism*, 3. Romanticists are more likely to be familiar with concepts of performativity from the work of Judith Butler, especially since Butler's ideas figure in Burroughs's analysis of Baillie (*Closet Stages*, 16–18, 117–18). My emphasis on earlier versions of the performative self in interactionism is not meant to displace Butler but to add to our understanding of anti-essentialist ways of conceptualizing identity and accounting for behavior. Indeed, Denzin cites Butler when making points about performativity in *Interpretive Interactionism* (13, 20) and in his more recent "Call to Performance," which charges interactionists with using performative studies to unsettle existing identities and structures and to evoke new ones (*Symbolic Interaction* 28 [2003] 187–207). Because he now valorizes the performative mode as more immediate, urgent, and compelling than textual studies, Denzin's "manifesto" can read disconcertingly like a retraction of his earlier emphasis on textual interpretation (in works listed above in note 25). But *engaged* writing, reading, and interpreting still figure in the performative mode; what is rejected is *disengaged* "textualism" and reductive or totalizing narrative mastery. For commentary on this "Call," see Andrea Fontana, "Norm Denzin and the Windmills of Morality," *Symbolic Interaction* 28 (2003): 209–16.

78. Baillie, *Works*, 9, emphasis added.

79. Aileen Forbes, "'Sympathetic Curiosity' in Joanna Baillie's Theater of the Passions," *European Romantic Review* 14 (2003): 33, 39. Two additional works—by Alan Richardson and Adela Pinch—are relevant for insights into these strains of essentialism and constructionism: contextualizing Baillie with respect to "the emergent biological psy-

chologies of [her] time," Richardson argues that Baillie took a "holistic approach to mind-body relations" ("A Neural Theatre: Joanna Baillie's 'Plays on the Passions,'" in Crochunis, *Joanna Baillie*, 132); though dealing mainly with writers other than Baillie, Pinch argues comprehensively for the passions as socially constructed (*Strange Fits of Passion: Epistemologies of Emotion, Hume to Austen* [Stanford, CA: Stanford University Press, 1996]).

80. Dmitri N. Shalin, "George Herbert Mead" in *The Blackwell Companion to Major Social Theorists*, ed. George Ritzer (Oxford: Blackwell, 2000), 319.

81. Blumer, *Symbolic Interactionism*, 8–9; George Herbert Mead, *Mind, Self, and Society from the Standpoint of a Social Behaviorist*, ed. and intro. by Charles W. Morris (Chicago: University of Chicago Press, 1934), 145–46, 253–54.

82. Blumer, *Symbolic Interactionism*, 12–13, 76.

83. Hans Joas, *G. H. Mead: A Contemporary Re-examination of His Thought*, trans. Raymond Meyer (Cambridge: MIT Press, 1997), 135.

84. Shalin, "George Herbert Mead," 320.

85. Ibid., 321.

86. George Herbert Mead, "1914 Lectures in Social Psychology" in *The Individual and the Social Self: Unpublished Work of George Herbert Mead*, ed. and intro. by David L. Miller, 97 (Chicago: University of Chicago Press, 1982).

87. Addams, *Democracy*, 8.

88. Mead, "1914 Lectures," 100.

89. Addams, *Twenty Years*, 222–23.

90. Ibid., 223–24.

91. George Herbert Mead, "The Psychology of Punitive Justice" (1917–18), in Reck, *Selected Writings*, 217. Mead's example of relying on a play to confront injustice brings to mind George Bernard Shaw's scathing assessment of why people respond to dramatic models more readily than to living examples: it is because drama reaches the consciousness of jaded spectators "to whom real life means nothing" ("Preface," in *Mrs. Warren's Profession* in *Complete Plays and Prefaces*, vol. 3 [New York: Dodd, Mead, 1962], 7). Shaw's explanation overlooks the complexity of self-protective impulses than can turn people away from others' suffering, but his—and Mead's and Addams's—awareness of the power of drama to alter those defenses is significant for understanding the connection between drama and social change. Opportunities to experiment with role-taking in provisional or controlled environments—such as the theater, or the closet or the Settlement that Burroughs and Jackson, respectively, describe—mitigate the threat inherent in the unfamiliar. Once spectators have experimented with the unfamiliar roles inside the theater, they can continue to shape them outside of it since the distinction between "staged" and "lived" experience is illusory: all experience involves the performance and adaptation of social roles.

92. George Herbert Mead, "The Genesis of the Self and Social Control" (1924–25) in Reck, *Selected Writings*, 285.

93. Haney, *Challenge of Coleridge*, 162, 224.

94. In a related generic expansion, Elaine Hadley treats melodrama as both a literary and behavioral mode that can be played out in novels such as *Oliver Twist* (*Melodramatic Tactics: Theatricalized Dissent in the English Marketplace, 1800–1885* [Stanford: Stanford University Press, 1995]). I draw on Hadley's work in chapter 4. Generic expansions are also evident within symbolic interactionism as narrative sociology has emerged as an acceptable model for research. I deal with some aspects of narrative sociology in chapter 8.

95. Denzin, *Interpretive Interactionism*, 7.

96. An example of a different kind can be found in Addams's reading of De Quincey, for it was her sense of a necessary distinction between literary and lived experience that led her to reject him. To hasten the disappearance of that now obsolescent distinction, I reverse Addams's rejection at the end of this study.

97. Chandler, *England in 1819*, 323.

98. Mead, *Mind, Self, and Society*, 150–56.

99. George Herbert Mead, "The Social Self" (1913) in Reck, *Selected Writings*, 147.

100. Mead, "Genesis of the Self" 290.

101. Mead, "Social Self," 146–47.

102. Deegan, *Jane Addams and the Men*, 114.

103. Addams, *Democracy*, 98–120.

104. Baillie, *Works*, 1–2, 4.

105. Addams, *Democracy*, 8–9; *Twenty Years*, 36.

106. Mead, "Genesis of the Self," 292.

107. Ibid., 292–93.

108. Denzin, *Interpretive Interactionism*, 34–37, 39, 2.

109. Baillie, *Works*, 4.

110. Throughout their studies, Farmer and Riggs mention the pragmatic character of Scottish law; for connections between pragmatism and symbolic interactionism, see Denzin, *Symbolic Interactionism and Cultural Studies*, 5–8, 123–38 and my article "Joanna Baillie at Hull-House,"124–26.

111. Anthony J. Blasi focuses on Mead and Adam Smith ("George Herbert Mead's Transformation of His Intellectual Context" in *The Tradition of Chicago Sociology*, ed. Luigi Tomaoi, 154–56 [Brookfield, VT: Ashgate, 1998]); Shalin offers a more comprehensive contextualization of Mead's thought, ranging from American pragmatism to German idealism ("George Herbert Mead," 308–14). Mead's ideas about role-taking, the social self, and human agency have numerous affinities with Keats's notions of "soul-making," the "camelion poet," and the flexibility of romance, which I address in *The Possibilities of Society*, 152–60, 172–75.

112. Cornel West, *The American Evasion of Philosophy: A Genealogy of Pragmatism* (Madison: University of Wisconsin Press, 1989), 209.

113. Amanda Anderson and Joseph Valente, "Introduction: Discipline and Freedom," in Anderson and Valente, *Disciplinarity*, 4.

114. I elaborate in chapter 8 on the particular notion of "hybridity" advanced by Ann Rigney in *Imperfect Histories*. Without reference to Rigney, Kucich sees a certain hybridity in Baillie's works insofar as they combine literary and historical, domestic and national, emotional and dispassionate elements. Her strategic combinations warrant, he argues, associating her with feminist historiographers who use such blends to move private and affective concerns into the center of the public sphere. Kucich considers feminist historiography a "social intervention" not only because it repositions women with respect to politics but because it changes traditional ways of thinking about what constitutes public affairs and the historical field ("Joanna Baillie and the Re-Staging of History and Gender,"109–13).

115. Chandler, *England in 1819*, 207.

116. Scott quoted in David Hewitt, "*The Heart of Midlothian* and 'the People,'" 303.

117. Dealing also with Scott's relationship with Baron Hume, Jane Millgate notes that the description of the law as a rebuilt castle occurs earlier, and with respect to English law, in Blackstone's *Commentaries* ("Scott and the Law: *The Heart of Midlothian*," in *Rough Justice: Essays on Crime in Literature*, ed. Martin L. Friedland, 110–11n13 [Toronto: Uni-

versity of Toronto Press, 1991]). In accenting features of Scottish law here and throughout this study, I do not mean to deny consonances with the English system; rather, I wish to work with the point of view of Scottish sympathizers for whom the construction of difference, according to my research, was important.

118. Works by Frederick Burwick ("Joanna Baillie, Matthew Baillie, and the Pathology of the Passion" in Crochunis, *Joanna Baillie*, 48–68), Karen Dwyer ("Joanna Baillie's *Plays on the Passions* and the Spectacle of Medical Science," *Studies in Eighteenth-Century Culture* 29 [2000]: 23–46), Dorothy McMillan ("'Dr.' Baillie" in *1798: The Year of the* Lyrical Ballads, ed. Richard Cronin, 68–92 [New York: St. Martin's Press, 1998]), Marjean Purinton ("Socialized and Medicalized Hysteria") and Alan Richardson ("Neural Theatre") place Baillie within the context of the medical research of her day, in which her uncle and brother were prominently involved. Victoria Myers places Baillie's work within the context of English legal controversies over "jury competence" and mitigation of punishment, though she hesitates to attribute any direct legal knowledge to Baillie, arguing instead that Baillie's knowledge would have come indirectly from the "aesthetic and moral publications of her fellow Scots Adam Smith and Lord Kames" that deal with topics of primitive justice and revenge ("Joanna Baillie: Speculations on Legal Cruelty," *The Wordsworth Circle* 35 [2004]: 1).

119. Dwyer, "Spectacle of Medical Science," 38, 45–46n63; Myers, "Speculations on Legal Cruelty," 12–13.

120. Baillie, *Letters*, 945.

121. Baillie, *Works*, 4.

122. Hume, 1:239, 233.

123. Hoecker-Drysdale, *First Woman Sociologist*; "Harriet Martineau," in Ritzer, *Blackwell Companion*, 53–80.

124. Baillie, *Letters*, 945. Though Baillie's letter does not specify Martineau's book by title, Slagle's editorial note gives good reason for identifying it as *Society in America*, not merely because of the dates of the publication and the letter but because, in a previous letter to the same correspondent (927), Baillie indicated a desire to read that work based on Norton's review (945n90).

125. George Herbert Mead, "The Working Hypothesis in Social Reform" (1899) in *Selected Writings*, 5.

126. Charlene Haddock Siegfried, "Introduction to the Illinois Edition," in *Democracy and Social Ethics*, by Jane Addams, xxii–xxxi. If perplexity is seen as analogous to curiosity in Baillie's *Introductory Discourse*, then curiosity loses many of the negative, voyeuristic implications that figure in Cox's, Forbes's, and Myers's readings of her works. Forbes and Myers emphasize terminological and conceptual tensions within the *Discourse* itself, which I specify in note 16 of the next chapter. Jeffrey Cox emphasizes a tension between the moral directions given by the *Discourse* and the opportunities for voyeuristic indulgence presented by the plays ("Staging Baillie," in Crochunis, *Joanna Baillie*, 151–56). For a balanced, wide-ranging study of curiosity apart from Baillie's work, see Barbara Benedict's *Curiosity: A Cultural History of Early Modern Inquiry* (Chicago: University of Chicago Press, 2001).

127. Baillie, *Works*, 13; Denzin, *Interpretive Interactionism*, 47, 99.

128. Denzin, *Interpretive Interactionism*, 99, 47, 64.

129. Ibid., x, 2; cf. Gusfield: "[W]e take what we *believe to be* the role of the other and assume the 'other' will respond in terms of our *interpretation*" ("Journey," 130, emphasis added).

130. Haney, *Challenge of Coleridge*, 45.

Chapter 2.
The Problem of Criminal Justice

1. The most extensive linkages are forged in Myers, "Theatre of Cruelty," but connections are also made in Peter Duthie, "Introduction," *Plays on the Passions,* by Joanna Baillie, ed. Peter Duthie, 11–57 (Peterborough, ON: Broadview Press, 2001), Forbes, "Sympathetic Curiosity"; and Richard Incorvati, "Sympathy and the Social Order: The Politics of Emotional Relationships from Hume to Wordsworth" (PhD diss., University of North Carolina at Chapel Hill, 2001).

2. For historical research into the attitudes of such crowds, see V. A. C. Gatrell, *The Hanging Tree: Execution and the English People, 1770–1868* (Oxford: Oxford University Press, 1994), 56–105.

3. Baillie, *Works,* 4.

4. Beiderwell, *Power and Punishment,* 27.

5. Gatrell, *Hanging Tree,* 21–22, 321–38; David Lieberman, *The Province of Legislation Determined: Legal Theory in Eighteenth-Century Britain* (Cambridge: Cambridge University Press, 1989), 199–215.

6. Farmer, *Criminal Law,* 34–36; Riggs, "Scottish Criminal Law," 13–14; Hume, *Commentaries,* 1:5–13. For a more comprehensive treatment of the complexity of the law in Scotland following the Act of Union, see David M. Walker, *A Legal History of Scotland* (Edinburgh: W. Green, 1988), especially volume 5. Though it was "frequently left in doubt" whether and to what extent English laws applied in Scotland, Walker concludes that "the Union . . . had . . . certainly not assimilated the criminal law [of Scotland] to that of England" (5:327, 536).

7. Regarding willingness to sympathize, see Gatrell, *Hanging Tree,* 250–54, 332–33, and Roberts, *Social Conscience,* 280–82; regarding intentionality, see Farmer, *Criminal Law,* 149–60.

8. Jane Addams, *The Second Twenty Years at Hull-House* (New York: Macmillan, 1930) 304–19.

9. Candace Clark, *Misery and Company: Sympathy in Everyday Life* (Chicago: University of Chicago Press, 1997).

10. Baillie, *Letters,* 690.

11. Myers, "Speculations on Legal Cruelty," 22.

12. Ibid.

13. John Sutherland, *The Life of Walter Scott: A Critical Biography* (Oxford: Blackwell, 1995), 49–60, 232–33, 345–46.

14. Beiderwell, *Power and Punishment,* 17–21, ix–x.

15. Beiderwell, *Power and Punishment,* and Myers, "Speculations on Legal Cruelty," situate Scott's and Baillie's works with respect to English but not Scottish debates over capital punishment. I draw on scholarship on the Scottish system published after Beiderwell's study. Of course, I make comparisons with the English system, for the two were often compared in partisan arguments about the superiority of either culture. A comparative orientation is also useful given Scott's and Baillie's own experiences of dual Scottish and British identities and their writing for audiences in both Scotland and England.

16. Gatrell, *Hanging Tree,* 7–9.

17. Hume, *Commentaries,* 1:10–11.

18. Lieberman, *Province of Legislation,* 13–14, 199.

19. Ibid., 200–1; Riggs, "Scottish Criminal Law," 12–14, 194, 208.

20. Gatrell, *Hanging Tree,* 197.

21. Ibid., 203–8; Peter King, *Crime, Justice and Discretion in England, 1740–1820* (Oxford: Oxford University Press, 2000).

22. Lieberman, *Province of Legislation*, 209–15.

23. Without reference to the Scottish system, Peter King argues that the English system was effectively discretionary because its pretrial procedures encouraged accusers and accused to reach compromises that would avoid formal prosecution (*Crime*, 82–93), its juries often declined to convict (233–34), and its judges routinely reprieved prisoners they had just sentenced or supported prisoners' petitions for mercy (261, 297–330, 355). Without denying that discretion can be found in English legal proceedings, I emphasize discretion as a component of Scottish law because of the Scottish perception of their system as uniquely discretionary and their deployment of that concept in contrasting Scottish and English cultures. These rival legal constructions are illuminated by Farmer and Riggs. The perception of the Scottish legal system as uniquely discretionary persists to this day: it is reiterated, for example, by Peter Duff and Neil Hutton in their "Introduction" to a study of contemporary *Criminal Justice in Scotland*, ed. Peter Duff and Neil Hutton, 1–6 (Burlington, VT: Ashgate, 1999). For a matter of controversy concerning discretion in English law, see below (chapter 6, note 48).

24. Hume published additional *Commentaries on the Law of Scotland respecting Trial for Crimes* in 1800 and supplementary notes to both the 1797 and 1800 two-volume sets in 1814. He revised and incorporated all the materials into the two-volume *Commentaries on the Law of Scotland, Respecting Crimes*, published in 1819. He made minor revisions to an edition printed in 1829. The final edition that remains the standard for this work was prepared by Benjamin Robert Bell in 1844. The Law Society of Scotland provided for reprinting in 1986, and I cite that reprint throughout. The publication history I summarize in this note is supplied in the "Introduction to the 1986 Reprint" (Hume, *Commentaries*, 1:1–7).

25. Farmer, *Criminal Law*, 21–39.

26. Ibid., 45–49; Riggs, "Scottish Criminal Law," 13–17; Hume, *Commentaries*, 1:12. Farmer and Riggs usually coincide on points about what Hume said and what happened in practice. They differ in interpreting the significance of these points and practices. Farmer's is a polemical book aimed at provoking current Scottish readers to confront their "mythical past" (37). (Farmer's use of this phrase for what he considers a self-deceiving standpoint has affinities with the interactionist concept of a "mythical past" as a deliberately deceptive construct, which I address at the end of chapter 6.) Riggs's dissertation takes Hume's statements and the tradition of his authority more as givens for the procedures he is describing in detail, though he does present Scotland's practices in opposition to England's. Riggs's purpose is to show how the Scottish legal system adapted to the overload of cases it received due to the growth of both urban populations and dedicated police forces. Adaptation was facilitated, Riggs argues, by the system's discretion and flexibility. Sometimes in English use, "discretion" could refer to the monarch's ability to pardon a sentenced criminal.

27. Riggs, "Scottish Criminal Law," 12–14, 90, 153; Hume, *Commentaries*, 1:187.

28. Riggs, "Scottish Criminal Law," 91, 100.

29. Hume, *Commentaries*, 1:13.

30. The system could be biased against political radicals. Though Farmer (*Criminal Law*, 44) and Riggs ("Scottish Criminal Law," 120n105) pass over this point, Andrew Melrose dwells on the "inequity and infamy of the sedition trials" of the 1790s ("Writing 'The End of Uncertainty': Imaginary Law, Imaginary Jacobites and Imaginary History in Walter Scott's *Heart of Midlothian* and *Redgauntlet*," *Scottish Literary Journal* 25 [1998]:

41). Hamilton addresses the tensions between law and politics with respect to both the treason trials and Scott's representation—or, pointedly, his failure to represent—in *Waverley* the execution of Fergus Mac-Ivor for treason (*Metaromanticism*, 134–36).

31. Riggs, "Scottish Criminal Law," 12, 99–103.

32. This pattern has become almost synonymous with the landmark study in which Michel Foucault identified it (*Discipline and Punish: The Birth of the Prison*, trans. Alan Sheridan [New York: Random House-Vintage, 1979]). For philosophical reflections on this trend, see Ferenc Hörcher, "Beccaria, Voltaire, and the Scots on Capital Punishment: A Comparative View of the Legal Enlightenment," in *Scotland and France in the Enlightenment*, ed. by Deidre Dawson and Pierre Morère, 305–30 (Lewisburg, PA: Bucknell University Press, 2004).

33. See, for example, John Mullan, *Sentiment and Sociability: The Language of Feeling in the Eighteenth Century* (Oxford: Clarendon Press, 1988); J. G. Barker-Benfield, *The Culture of Sensibility: Sex and Society in Eighteenth-Century Britain* (Chicago: University of Chicago Press, 1992); and Pinch, *Strange Fits*. The most extensive treatment focused on Baillie is in Myers, "Theater of Cruelty." Though sympathy is not usually taken to be a predominant concern of Scott's, Ferris, in "Pedantry," makes a case for its importance in understanding Scott's ideas about history, antiquarianism, and community; Evan Gottlieb deals with it in connection with *The Heart of Midlothian* ("'To Be at Once Another and the Same': Walter Scott and the End(s) of Sympathetic Britishness," *Studies in Romanticism* 43 [2004]: 189–207.) I suggest that the term "respect" may be more generally suitable for Scott's approach to human relations, and for reasons that will become clearer in subsequent analyses, I usually focus on respectful attitudes in Scott's work. I consider Gottlieb's argument more specifically in chapter 4.

34. Clark, *Misery and Company*, 100–01, 46–49.

35. Ibid., 21.

36. Ibid., 48.

37. Ibid., 39, 42, 88.

38. Addams, *Twenty Years*, 36.

39. Jane Mansbridge, "The Making of Oppositional Consciousness," in *Oppositional Consciousness: The Subjective Roots of Social Protest*, ed. Jane Mansbridge and Aldon Morris, 4–16, 18nn11, 14 (Chicago: University of Chicago Press, 2001).

40. Jeff Goodwin, James M. Jasper, and Francesca Polletta, "Introduction," in *Passionate Politics: Emotions and Social Movements*, ed. Jeff Goodwin, James M. Jasper, and Francesca Polletta, 1–23 (Chicago: University of Chicago Press, 2001).

41. Clark, *Misery and Company*, 57.

42. Gatrell, *Hanging Tree*, 250–54.

43. Ibid., 226, 285.

44. Ibid., viii, 332–33, 418–19.

45. Gatrell is reluctant to credit humanity mongering with much force before the 1830s (*Hanging Tree*, viii), but extending its influence back seems warranted by evidence ranging from references to Samuel Johnson's humane efforts in the Dodd case (which I take up in chapter 3), through Baron Hume's attention to "reason and humanity" (*Commentaries*, 1:37), to the continuities between Romantic and Victorian concerns with humanity that Roberts displays in his chapters on humanitarianism and philanthropy (*Social Conscience*, 229–331). Roberts describes these two concepts in a way that clarifies how humanitarianism could have the "pervasive" and "powerful," albeit "not wholly dominant [,] role in the near abolition of the death penalty" with which he credits it (280).

According to Roberts, philanthropists formed associations, societies, and institutions and worked in coordinated ways toward particular goals that were often tied to religious or legislative agendas. Humanitarians were more "diffuse" in their methods and goals. Usually working apart from any organization and independently of any theory, they mobilized "direct and spontaneous compassion for the suffering of the exploited and the oppressed" (260–61). Humanitarian efforts could thus appeal to and enlist people with differing religious and political beliefs. They could make the issue of criminal justice more of a social than a political one.

Roberts indicates that humanitarianism had its critics: philanthropists often disapproved of humanitarians' emotional emphasis (260). Consonantly, Myers indicates that some reformers did not want their arguments for criminal law reform confused with merely emotional appeals ("Speculations on Legal Cruelty," 9). Humanitarians did, nevertheless, manage to influence legal attitudes, practices and sentences.

46. Gatrell, *Hanging Tree*, 497.

47. Ibid., 416.

48. Riggs, "Scottish Criminal Law," 99–107, 48; cf. Farmer: "By the late 1830s, theft was no longer in practice a capital crime in Scotland." Farmer also notes the small number of capital sentences in Scotland (*Criminal Law*, 119, 44n103).

49. Quoted in Riggs, "Scottish Criminal Law," 119n93.

50. Farmer, *Criminal Law*, 43, 38, 153–54.

51. Hume, *Commentaries*, 1:37.

52. Farmer, *Criminal Law*, 153.

53. Hume, *Commentaries*, 1:239.

54. Ibid., 1:240, 233.

55. Farmer, *Criminal Law*, 149–60, 158.

56. See, for example, Andrew Lincoln, "Conciliation, Resistance, and the Unspeakable in *The Heart of Midlothian*," *Philological Quarterly* 79 (2000): 69–90; Melrose, "Imaginary Law"; Millgate, "Scott and the Law"; and Ward, "Jurisprudential Heart of Midlothian."

57. Clark, *Misery and Company*, 199–224, 199.

58. Clark maintains, however, that integrative control cannot simply replace segregative control because leniency works only if the threat of punishment is real (*Misery and Company*, 224).

59. Mead, "Psychology of Punitive Justice," 217, 220–21. Mead's statements epitomize two of what I have called "signal traits" of interactionism — an orientation toward problem solving over theory building and toward personal relations over abstractions.

60. Mead, "Psychology of Punitive Justice," 222–23, 227, 230–39.

61. Ibid., 227.

62. Ibid., 230–39.

63. Addams, *Second Twenty Years*, 310, 311–14, 319, 335, 329–33.

64. Harriet Martineau, *A History of the Thirty Years' Peace*, 4 vols. (1849–50; repr., Shannon: Irish University Press, 1971).

65. For Scott's position on Peterloo, see *Letters*, 5:485–87.

66. Since line numbers are not given for the plays in Baillie's *Works*, I give citations by act, scene, and page number. From here on, citations to the plays will appear parenthetically within the text. Line numbers also do not appear in the reprints of her first editions (Joanna Baillie, *A Series of Plays*, 1798, 1802, 1812, ed. Donald Reiman, 3 vols. [1798, 1802, 1812; repr., New York: Garland, 1977]; *Miscellaneous Plays*, ed. Donald Reiman, [1804; repr., New York: Garland, 1977]).

67. The dialogue may serve mainly to reveal Jane's exaggerated devotion to her brother—or, following Burroughs's reading, her ideal of her brother (*Closet Stages*, 119–29). In Myers's reading, however, De Monfort's "private" death is the equivalent of a mitigated sentence: he is spared public execution after he has been subjected to a trial of character in the play ("Speculations on Legal Cruelty," 22).

68. Gatrell, *Hanging Tree*, 416.

69. My reading here diverges from Myers and Forbes. Myers argues that Baillie pairs sympathy with curiosity to acknowledge and explore the ways in which sympathy can mask a cruel voyeurism and desire to control others ("Theatre of Cruelty," 90). For Forbes, the pairing uses sympathy to overcome shame about curiosity and thus become free to explore human passion ("Sympathetic Curiosity,"40).

70. Baillie, *Works*, 2.

71. Mead, "Psychology of Punitive Justice," 217. For an analysis of the "slippage" between the officially solemn rituals of sentencing and execution and the mocking "counter theatre of the condemned," see King, *Crime*, 334–52.

72. Myers draws a different conclusion than I do about this aspect of the *Discourse*. She argues that Baillie's goal is "to uncover the dimension of cruelty in government power and the collusion of the public in that cruelty" ("Theatre of Cruelty," 100).

73. Baillie, *Works*, 4.

74. Hume, *Commentaries*, 1:21.

75. Ibid., 1:239, emphasis added.

76. Ibid.

77. Because a sense of the difficulty of perceiving likeness between the self and others figures in arguments by Forbes ("Sympathetic Curiosity"), Myers ("Speculations on Legal Cruelty," "Theatre of Cruelty") and Jeffrey Cox ("Staging Baillie") about the contradictory tendencies in Baillie, I should note why I do not find so much contradiction in this difficulty. It is because I follow Denzin in seeing all others as essentially unknowable ("In social life there is only interpretation," *Interpretive Interactionism*, 2) and in finding that interpretive condition as conducive to more, rather than less, respectful relations (as I commented at the end of the introduction). To be sure, interpreters can confuse their experiences with those of others and either accidentally or deliberately impose their views on others, and Denzin acknowledges and indicts such insensitivity (3). But genuine interactionism corrects and minimizes insensitivity toward others. Acknowledging the interpretive nature of any knowledge of others requires one to avoid dispossessing them of their own personhood. For an additional argument about respectful relations built on the acknowledgment of incommensurability, see Lorraine Code, "Rational Imaginings, Responsible Knowings: How Far Can You See From Here?" in *Engendering Rationalities*, ed. Nancy Tuana and Sandra Morgen, 261–82 (Albany: State University of New York Press, 2001).

78. Baillie, *Works*, 4; Addams, *Twenty Years*, 36. Considering Baillie's emphasis on kindness, cf. Addams's views of the predominance of kindness in human relations stressed by Lengermann and Niebrugge-Brantley in *Women Founders*, 79.

79. Michael Gamer, *Romanticism and the Gothic: Genre, Reception, and Canon Formation* (Cambridge: Cambridge University Press, 2000).

80. In *The Dream*, which I examine in the next chapter, Baillie creates a character, the monk Benedict, who does go beyond his community's conditioning and refuses to watch an execution.

81. Denzin, *Interpretive Interactionism*, 47, 99.

82. Baillie, *Works*, 13.

83. Carrying forward the argument about the symbolic nature of all experience that I have been pursuing, my phrasing here deliberately overrides any distinction between the play and nontheatrical events.

84. Gatrell, *Hanging Tree*, 99–100, 109–96, 272–79.

85. Denzin, *Cultural Studies*, 100–102.

86. Studies by Andrea Henderson ("Passion and Fashion in Joanna Baillie's 'Introductory Discourse,'" *PMLA* 112 [1997]: 198–213) and Gamer (*Romanticism and the Gothic*) offer further insights into the complexity of Baillie's (and Scott's) connections with popular culture. It seems important to stress the possibility of mixed motives and multiple effects since Terence Allan Hoagwood ("Elizabeth Inchbald, Joanna Baillie, and Revolutionary Representation during the 'Romantic' Period," in *Rebellious Hearts: British Women Writers and the French Revolution*, ed. Adriana Craciun and Kari E. Lokke, 293–316 [Albany: State University of New York Press, 2001]) casts doubt on the sincerity of reformist aims in Baillie's work and Baillie scholarship.

87. Hume, *Commentaries*, 2:481–82; Gatrell, *Hanging Tree*, 298.

88. Baillie, *Works*, 105.

89. As Maureen A. Dowd points out, remote historical settings could also be used to disguise the revolutionary potential of a drama's ideas. Such was the case with the medieval setting of Schiller's *Die Räuber*, with which Baillie's work was associated ("'By the Delicate Hand of a Female': Melodramatic Mania and Joanna Baillie's Spectacular Tragedies," *European Romantic Review* 9 [1998]: 471–72). For analyses of Baillie's connections with German melodrama and British national tradition, see Dowd (469–500) and Gamer (*Romanticism and the Gothic*, 24, 140–60).

90. Dowd, "Delicate Hand," 478.

91. Ohio's act of sabotage was so widely regarded as absurd by contemporary readers that Baillie commented on it in a preface to the second edition of the *Miscellaneous Plays*. Though conceding that the logistics were "not happily conceived," she is not much troubled by the awkwardness. The method, she states, "might easily be changed into any other in which Ohio is still made the agent, by any person who should be willing to bring the play before an audience" (*Works*, 386). Baillie's comment openly invites readers to practice the processes of analogizing and reflecting she describes in the *Introductory Discourse* (*Works*, 13): they are to imagine similar scenes that they judge less absurd and insert them into the play. I take Baillie's directions as reinforcing both my sense that she wanted to promote value inquiry and my sense of connection between the plays in the passions series and the miscellaneous plays. I take it also as reinforcing the conclusion by which Cox resolves his sense of a tension between didacticism and voyeurism in Baillie's works. Specifically, he concludes that Baillie was open to the contingencies of performance and therefore did not author(ize) stable texts ("Staging Baillie," 160) — or limit her meaning to a reductive lesson.

92. Mead, "Psychology of Punitive Justice," 222.

93. Burroughs quotes the phrase in an article title, though she focuses on De Monfort's always being outside of polite culture rather than his awakening horror at the consequences of his having killed Rezenvelt ("'Out of the Pale of Social Kindred Cast': Conflicted Performance Styles in Joanna Baillie's *De Monfort*," in *Romantic Women Writers: Voices and Countervoices*, ed. Paula R. Feldman and Theresa M. Kelley, 223–35 [Hanover, NH: University Press of New England, 1995]).

94. Baillie, *Works*, 389.

95. In Mead's words, "The moral question is not the one of setting up a right value against a wrong value; it is a question of finding the possibility of acting so as to take into

account as far as possible all the values involved" (*The Philosophy of the Act*, ed. and intro. by Charles W. Morris et al. [Chicago: University of Chicago Press, 1938], 465).

96. Percy Bysshe Shelley, "On the Punishment of Death: A Fragment," in *Complete Works of Percy Bysshe Shelley*, ed. Roger Ingpen and Walter E. Peck, 6: 85–90 (London: Ernest Benn, 1926–30; New York: Gordian Press, 1965) "Preface" to *The Cenci*, in *Shelley's Poetry and Prose*, ed. Donald H. Reiman and Sharon B. Powers, 238–42 (New York: W. W. Norton, 1977).

97. William Wordsworth, *Poetical Works of William Wordsworth*, ed. Ernest de Selincourt and Helen Darbishire, 4:135–41 (Oxford: Clarendon Press, 1952–59).

98. For Wordsworth's phrase, see *Letters of William and Dorothy Wordsworth: The Later Years, Pt. 4, 1840–53*, rev. ed. by Alan G. Hill (Oxford: Oxford University Press, 1988), 292. Also see Sharon M. Setzer, "Precedent and Perversity in Wordsworth's *Sonnets upon the Punishment of Death*," *Nineteenth-Century Literature* 50 (1996): 428.

99. William H. Galperin, *Revision and Authority in Wordsworth: The Interpretation of a Career* (Phildelphia: University of Pennsylvania Press, 1989), 238–41.

100. Baillie, *Works*, 4.

101. Ward, "Jurisprudential Heart of Midlothian," 27.

102. Beiderwell, *Power and Punishment*, 73, 66.

103. I say "rule" rather than "law" breaker because Effie did not commit the infanticide of which she is accused. She does, however, violate expectations by not cooperating fully in proceedings that could exonerate her.

104. Beiderwell, *Power and Punishment*, 17–21, ix–x.

105. Farmer, *Criminal Law*, 23–27. Farmer further analyzes the function of the declaratory power in allowing Scotland to define its own community standards since it could not, given the Union, define its own national ones (45–56); Riggs credits the declaratory power with enabling Scotland to deal with social change ("Scottish Criminal Law," 17).

106. Hume, *Commentaries*, 1:12.

107. These effects are drawn from my exposition of Clark earlier in this chapter.

108. Ward, "Jurisprudential Heart of Midlothian," 32–33.

109. Here and throughout, page references to *The Heart of Midlothian* appear parenthetically in the text. The edition used is the Oxford World's Classics, ed. with an intro. by Claire Lamont (Oxford: Oxford University Press, 1999).

110. Ward, "Jurisprudential Heart of Midlothian," 32.

111. Since England prided itself on its common law tradition in contrast to the continental penchant for theorizing (Lieberman, *Province of Legislation*, 215), there is some paradox and/or irony involved in any criticism of England for slighting common law. Melrose takes a different view of Scott's legal position, arguing that he rejects the old Scottish legal tradition that includes Baron Hume and favors a new approach represented by Erskine and Wallace ("Imaginary Law," 40–41). I find it hard to reconcile Melrose's thesis with Scott's open admiration for Hume.

112. Marie Hockenhull Smith reaches a consonant conclusion, though surprisingly, she does not draw on Baron Hume to support it ("How Can ye Criticise What's Plain Law, Man?': The Lawyer, the Novelist, and the Discourse of Authority" in *Law and Literature: Current Legal Issues 1999*, vol. 2, ed. Michael Freeman and Andrew D. E. Lewis, 239–62 [Oxford: Oxford University Press, 1999]). Noting that the judge's failure "to use his discretion to interpret the Scottish penal statute against child-murder narrowly to avoid convicting an innocent woman" represents a decision in favor of the "rule of law" and that such severity was advocated by neither Blackstone nor Bentham, Smith generalizes: "contemporary theoretical discourse on the development of the law allowed,

indeed required, a more active contribution from the judge" (254–55). She then offers a Bakhtinian interpretation of why the judge errs: he takes the words of the statute as fixed conveyors of meaning in all situations whereas he should recognize it as a "historically unique utterance"; he should then adapt it to the uniqueness of Effie's case (255–56). Smith's only reference to Hume is as the probable source for the character Ratcliffe in the novel (259).

113. Lincoln, "Conciliation," 69.

114. Additionally, the portrayal of the Porteous rioters is significant for being more concerned with social and legal than with political contexts. After examining Scott's portrayal of crowds in the *Heart of Midlothian*, David Hewitt maintains that Scott minimizes the political implications of the Porteous uprising by framing his description in legal terms drawn from Hume's *Commentaries*. The Porteous rioters form more of a "mob" expressing anger at a particular injustice than a treasonous group defying the given system of laws and lawmaking. Scott thus avoids projecting back onto this gathering a later political consciousness of people's rights, though he does accelerate the development of such a political consciousness as the characters, especially Jeanie, reflect on the event in terms of Scottish responses to English authority. Contrastingly, D'Arcy believes that the lynching of Porteous encodes a criticism of the terms of Anglo-Scottish Union by making the "supposedly unique distinguishing features of post-Union Scotland" ineffective in maintaining order: the mob ignores Butler's plea that they spare Porteous in the name of those features of law and religion ("*The Heart of Midlothian* and 'the People,'" 32).

115. Beiderwell sees Meg Murdockson and Madge Wildfire as a "parallel" pairing with Wilson and Porteous (*Power and Punishment*, 72).

116. Mead, "Psychology of Punitive Justice," 227.

117. Hume, *Commentaries*, 1:37. Though Jeanie certainly should not be thought inhumane, her attitude toward Madge may be seen as more mixed or complex in light of Lincoln's and Carolyn F. Austin's comments on its self-interested aspects: according to Lincoln, Jeanie wants to keep Madge alive as a source of information about Effie's baby, an interest for which Lincoln faults her ("Conciliation," 85); according to Austin, Jeanie pays insufficient attention to Madge because she fail[s] to realize "the near-familial relationship" between them ("Home and Nation in *The Heart of Midlothian*," *SEL, 1500–1900* 40 [2000]: 627).

118. However critical one may be about workhouses in other contexts (an issue that I take up later in connection with the Poor Laws), they could be refuges for the mentally ill. In connection with his reading of Madge Wildfire as a displaced figure of Scott's desire to rebel against England, Lincoln documents early efforts to create separate refuges for prostitutes and the mentally ill ("Conciliation," 81–82). The treatment of the mentally ill—especially the "moral treatment" on which I comment in chapter 3— is also a significant issue in Baillie's *Orra* and *Witchcraft*. I address those plays in chapters 3 and 5.

119. This preoccupation had a recent (in Scott's time) analogue in the treason trials of the 1790s, which were, as John Barrell's study has brought to light, dominated by the concept of "constructive treason" (*Imagining the King's Death: Figurative Treason, Fantasies of Regicide, 1793–1796* [Oxford: Oxford University Press, 2000], 40–41).

120. For Hume's phrasing, see *Commentaries*, 1:196.

121. Melrose quotes the passage as evidence of Scott's disapproval of the law, though the implications he develops refer to the thesis I indicate in note 111 above.

122. Hume, *Commentaries*, 1:240–43, 244.

Chapter 3.
Baillie's Interventions

1. To obtain the total of twenty-seven, I count the two parts of *Ethwald* as two plays.

2. Baillie, *Works*, 2.

3. Walter Scott, *Waverley*, ed. Andrew Hook (London: Penguin, 1972). Scott pays extended attention to the different ways in which Melville and Morton construe the charge of treason against Waverley, showing how their backgrounds and outlooks influence their judgments. Major Melville, a military man preoccupied with duty and public order, is predisposed to find Waverley guilty and to want him punished; Mr. Morton, a clergyman inclined to look for good in people, thinks that Waverley's guilt is not proven and, even if it were, that Waverley deserves mercy because of the "moral motive" behind his actions (252). The predispositions of both men limit their interpretations of Waverley's case, though Melville's view is the narrower of the two. As Waverley rightly asks him, "what does it avail me to answer you? . . . You appear convinced of my guilt, and wrest every reply I have made to support your own preconceived opinion" (248), or in Beiderwell's words, "Waverley becomes what Melville thinks he is" (*Power and Punishment*, 16). According to Beiderwell, Scott brings in a more "pragmatic" character to mediate between Melville and Morton in deciding Waverley's fate. With flexibility and tact, Colonel Talbot decides that "the execution of Waverley would serve no purpose" because Waverley is not a committed rebel; execution should be reserved for characters like Fergus Mac-Ivor, who do threaten social order (17–19). Talbot's mediation, of course, is limited by his acceptance of punitive justice.

4. Beiderwell, *Power and Punishment*, 19.

5. Hume, *Commentaries*, 1:21.

6. Scott, *Letters*, 3:36.

7. I hasten to add that "responding to" does not mean "affirming"; reducing response to affirmation is a topic of inquiry and criticism in *Henriquez*.

8. I take up this matter in the section on *The Homicide* where I show parallels between Baillie's text and Hume's *Commentaries*.

9. Hume, *Commentaries*, 1:239.

10. I use this phrasing (and similar phrasing, occasionally, on subsequent pages) to call to mind the interactionist concept of the "definition of the situation," which I introduced in chapter 1.

11. Baillie, *Works*, 229.

12. Ibid.

13. Forbes, "Sympathetic Curiosity," 33.

14. Baillie, *Works*, 229.

15. Lord Byron, *Byron's Letters and Journals*, ed. Leslie Marchand, 5:203 (Cambridge: Harvard University Press, 1976).

16. Baillie's achievement also supports the notion that respectful relations are based on an acknowledgment of the unknowability others (on which I commented in note 77 to chapter 2). It was Baillie's interpretation of experiences she did not share that won Byron's admiration.

17. Baillie, *Works*, 229.

18. Ibid.

19. Julie Carlson, "Baillie's *Orra*: Shrinking in Fear," in Crochunis, *Joanna Baillie*, 207–15.

20. Burwick, "Pathology of the Passions," 51–53, 61–65.

21. Ibid., 64.

22. Rebecca Stern, "'Personation' and 'Good Marking-Ink': Sanity, Performativity, and Biology in Victorian Sensation Fiction," *Nineteenth-Century Studies* 14 (2000): 37.

23. Ibid., 36.

24. Ibid., 38–44.

25. Mead, "Psychology of Punitive Justice," 230.

26. Julie Carlson, "Remaking Love: Remorse in the Theatre of Baillie and Inchbald," in *Women in British Romantic Theatre: Drama, Performance and Society, 1790–1840*, ed. Catherine Burroughs, 292–95 (Cambridge: Cambridge University Press, 2000).

27. Addams, *Twenty Years*, 223.

28. Mead, "Social Self," 148.

29. Ibid.

30. Ibid.

31. Ibid., 149.

32. Forbes, "Sympathetic Curiosity," 44–45.

33. Hume, *Commentaries*, 1:248.

34. *The Stripling* was published as a miscellaneous play in the 1836 volume, but information in Slagle's biography of Baillie suggests that it was drafted as early as 1805. Specifically, Slagle identifies the young actor whom Baillie alludes to in a note about casting the title role as William Henry West Betty, a "child actor" reaching celebrity "around 1805" (*Life*, 262n71). Slagle's attention to the play (262–63), like Burroughs's (*Closet Stages*, 88, 113) centers on theatrical issues.

35. Baillie, *Works*, 551.

36. Jessie Dobson, "John Hunter and the Unfortunate Doctor Dodd," *Journal of the History of Medicine and Allied Sciences* 10 (1955): 377.

37. Recall notes 118 and 119 to chapter 1.

38. Dobson, "John Hunter and the Unfortunate Doctor Dodd," 373–76.

39. John J. Burke, Jr., "Crime and Punishment in 1777: The Execution of the Reverend Dr. William Dodd and Its Impact upon His Contemporaries," in *Executions and the British Experience from the 17th to the 20th Century: A Collection of Essays*, ed. William B. Thesing, 59–75 (Jefferson, NC: McFarland, 1990). Gatrell cites Hawkins but believes that class-based sympathy and solidarity rather than humanitarianism motivated efforts on behalf of Dodd (*Hanging Tree*, 293).

40. James Boswell, *Life of Johnson*, ed. R. W. Chapman, intro. by Pat Rogers (1791; repr., Oxford: Oxford University Press, 1980), 828.

41. Randall McGowan, "From Pillory to Gallows: The Punishment of Forgery in the Age of the Financial Revolution," *Past and Present* 165 (1999): 115. Cf. Margot C. Finn, *The Character of Credit: Personal Debt in English Culture, 1740–1914* (Cambridge: Cambridge University Press, 2003).

42. McGowan, "From Pillory to Gallows," 111, 128.

43. Hume, *Commentaries*, 1:12.

44. Ibid., 1:140.

45. Ibid., 1:159.

46. Boswell, *Life of Johnson*, 834. My speculation about the outcome of Dodd's trial in a different venue is inspired by a comment in one of the sources Dobson quotes: in a 1794 issue of the *Aberdeen Journal*, a writer imagines that Hunter managed to revive Dodd, who was then sent to live in Scotland ("John Hunter and the Unfortunate Doctor Dodd," 373). Though there is no warrant for taking this statement to imply that Dodd could live in Scotland because of that country's less Draconian approach toward sentencing forgers, it is tempting to do so.

47. As I indicated above in note 6 to chapter 2, quoting Walker's *Legal History of Scotland*, uncertainty existed about the force of English laws in Scotland. Some statutes, however, contained clauses specifying their applicability. A clause in the forgery act of 1729 (2 Geo. II, c. 25) specified that it did *not* apply to Scotland; a clause in the forgery act of 1805 (45 Geo. III, c. 89) made it apply throughout Great Britain. The texts of both acts can be found, respectively, in *Statutes at Large from Magna Charta, to the Thirtieth Year of King George the Second Inclusive, 1225–1757* (London: T. Baskett, 1758): 4:708 and *Statutes at Large from Magna Charta, to the End of the Eleventh Parliament of Great Britain, Anno 1761.* (Cambridge: J. Bentham, 1762-1807): 45:1118-22.

48. Baillie, *Works*, 5.

49. Johnson, Samuel. *The Rambler*, ed. W. J. Bate and Albrecht B. Strauss, in *The Yale Edition of the Works of Samuel Johnson*, ed. John H. Middendorf, 4:241–47 (New Haven: Yale University Press, 1969.)

50. Mead, "Psychology of Punitive Justice," 217.

51. John Galsworthy, *Plays. Second Series: The Eldest Son, The Little Dream. Justice* (New York: Scribner's, 1913).

52. Clark, *Misery and Company*, 199–224.

53. Baillie's play does not explore the treatment of debtors whose only misdeed is indebtedness. The use of debtors' prisons suggests a preponderance of segregative control, though Margot Finn's detailed examination of that phenomenon in England points out that such incarceration was sometimes regarded as a way to protect spendthrifts from their own habits and that charitable attitudes toward debtors did exist as countertrends within commercial society (*Character of Credit*, 109–195). As Walter Scott's fear of prosecution for bankruptcy testifies, Scotland was not exceptionally lenient toward debtors, but it did institutionalize sanctuary for non-criminal debtors at Holyrood Abbey. Scott considered seeking that protection when one of his creditors became impatient with the arrangements for repayment (*Letters* 10:302–03). On the treatment of debtors and the administration of Holyroodhouse, see Walker, *Legal History of Scotland*, 5:609–14.

54. Recall the beginning of the section on "Performing Selves and Societies" above in chapter 1.

55. Mead, "Psychology of Punitive Justice," 239; cf. Addams, *Second Twenty Years*, 304–7, 333–42.

56. Farmer, *Criminal Law*, 149–60. Myers makes a related point in connection with trials in England. Because the court expected to carry out capital sentences only against habitual criminals who could serve as the best deterrent examples, the trial for the given offense often turned into a trial of the prisoner's "entire life" ("Speculations on Legal Cruelty," 7).

57. Hume, *Commentaries*, 1:21.

58. Ibid., 1:225.

59. Ibid., 1:239.

60. Ibid., 1:239–40.

61. Ibid., 1:248.

62. Ibid., 1:249.

63. Ibid., 1:248–49n2.

64. Ibid., 1: 233.

65. For details, see above, chapter 2.

66. Baillie's *Introductory Discourse*, with its reference to "respect[ing] ourselves, and our kind" as an effect of sympathetic curiosity (*Works*, 4) lays a foundation for the equivalence between respect for self and others that she builds on in her plays. To some extent,

Scott builds on a similar foundation in the Roseneath section of *The Heart of Midlothian* (which I examine in chapter 4). Integral to that section are Jeanie's attempts to satisfy her own conscience (i.e., maintain her self-respect) while respecting the wishes of others—especially Effie's wishes that Jeanie keep secret her (Effie's) identity and benefit from the money that she (Effie) sends. Jeanie decides to keep the secrets when she figures out how to do so without compromising her self-respect. Jeanie's keeping of Effie's secret thus differs from Van Maurice's keeping of Claudien's because her behavior is not self-destructive. The fact that Jeanie considers her own needs in making her decision may account for readings such as Austin's that find a hint of wrong doing in Jeanie's secretiveness ("Home and Nation," 631–32). What looks like selfishness may come closer to self-respect when we factor in the balancing of needs that Jeanie accomplishes. Though *The Heart of Midlothian* shows reservations about self-sacrifice, Scott's next novel, *The Bride of Lammermoor,* is much more willing to attach positive value to that concept. As I show in chapter 5, Baillie goes much further than Scott or even Addams in questioning the ethics of self-sacrifice.

67. Addams, *Second Twenty Years*, 309–10.

68. As I note in chapter 6 in connection with Landor's imaginary conversation between Romilly and Perceval over reform of the Criminal Code, some opponents of reform believed that mistaken executions of innocent people should be understood as the necessary sacrifice of individuals for collective good. Baillie's *Homicide* invites criticism of that line of thinking.

69. Hume, *Commentaries*, 1:xi.

70. Though the criticism and response are presented in terms of technical staging, the substantive parallels further account for the scene's importance. Problems of representationality in connection with this scene have been addressed by Colin Harris, "The Place of the Page: Dramatic Discontinuity in Joanna Baillie's *The Homicide*" (paper presented at the conference of the North American Society for the Study of Romanticism, New York, August 1–5, 2003).

CHAPTER 4.
THE PROBLEM OF POVERTY

1. Hadley, *Melodramatic Tactics*, 11, 17, 97.

2. Ibid., 15–19, 24–30, 114–32.

3. Christensen, *Romanticism at the End of History*, 11; and see above, chapter 1, note 24.

4. The pattern I project seems all the more likely in light of the pattern in Addams's approach to social work traced by Victoria Bissell Brown in *The Education of Jane Addams*. Placing Addams at an intellectual starting point not far from Baillie and Scott, Brown posits that Addams's approach grew out of elite stewardship into democratic empowerment.

5. Though Hadley does not allude to role-taking, she does describe a similar process by which self-consciousness in a deferential society "was actually constituted through the hierarchical relationship and mutual feelings . . . [in] theatrical exchanges," and she argues that personification could be effectively used in eighteenth-century poetry because "personified faculties and attributes . . . were seen to be immanent in society and thus, in turn, present in any individual inhabiting that society" (*Melodramatic Tactics*, 17). Unlike interactionists, however, she treats social development as dependent on traditional structures.

My concept of a behavioral legacy draws not only on Mead's generalized other but also on Denzin's concept of legacy. Reflecting on the history of interpretive inquiry and methods, Denzin concludes: "Each of the earlier historical moments is still operating in the present, either as legacy or as a set of practices that researchers still follow or argue against." Consequently, the present teems with paradigms for investigation or transformation (*Interpretive Ethnography*, 19). I read Scott as responding to the past as legacy rather than blindly following or resisting it.

6. Mead, "Social Self," 147.

7. There were also private institutions devoted to charity and philanthropy, partly because government was perceived as unequal to or unsuitable for the task. See Roberts, *Social Conscience*, 375–95.

8. Anthony Brundage explains that singular and plural references to both the old and new legislation vary according to context (*The English Poor Laws, 1700–1930* [New York: Palgrave, 2002], 7). Following his practice, I let context determine my usage throughout.

9. Brundage, *Poor Laws*, 10; Audrey Paterson, "The Poor Law in Nineteenth-Century Scotland" in *The New Poor Law in the Nineteenth Century*, ed. Derek Fraser, 171–72 (London: Macmillan, 1976).

10. Brundage, *Poor Laws*, 14; Rosalind Mitchison, *The Old Poor Law in Scotland: The Experience of Poverty, 1574–1845* (Edinburgh: Edinburgh University Press, 2000), 105–10.

11. The unevenness and inefficiency of a system that operated by personal relations at local levels made Harriet Martineau one of the most outspoken critics of the old system. Convinced that the old system was riddled with abuses (*History*, 2:313–14, 485–89), she worked zealously for reform in the ways on which I elaborate below in note 29. Martineau's dissatisfaction with local relief and local justice mirrors the dissatisfaction that Tilly identifies as a driving force behind parliamentary reform. I address that topic in chapter 6.

12. Toby R. Benis, *Romanticism on the Road: The Marginal Gains of Wordsworth's Homeless* (New York: St. Martin's, 2000), 5–6.

13. Brundage, *Poor Laws*, 10, 25.

14. Mitchison, *Old Poor Law*, 98; Paterson, "Poor Law," 173; Scott, in the "Advertisement" to *The Antiquary* printed with that novel, elaborates on the practices of begging. I cite the Oxford World's Classics edition, ed. Nicola J. Watson (Oxford: Oxford University Press, 2002), 5–11. Subsequent references to the novel will appear parenthetically in the text.

15. Jeremy Boulton, "Going on the Parish: The Parish Pension and Its Meaning in the London Suburbs, 1640–1724," in *Chronicling Poverty: The Voices and Strategies of the English Poor, 1640–1840*, ed. Tim Hitchcock, Peter King, and Pamela Sharpe, 34–35 (New York: St. Martin's, 1997).

16. Paterson, "Poor Law," 171, 178; Mitchison, *Old Poor Law*, 96–97.

17. Brundage, *Poor Laws*, 27.

18. Ibid., 11–12.

19. Mitchison, *Old Poor Law*, 47.

20. Boulton, "Going on the Parish," 21.

21. Ibid.; Tim Hitchcock, Peter King and Pamela Sharpe, "Introduction" in *Chronicling Poverty*, Hitchcock, King, and Sharpe, 10.

22. Hitchcock, King, and Sharpe, "Introduction," 10.

23. Boulton, "Going on the Parish," 27; Pamela Sharpe, "'The bowels of compation': A Labouring Family and the Law, c. 1790–1834" in Hitchcock, King, and Sharpe, *Chronicling Poverty*, 92.

24. Hitchcock, King, and Sharpe, "Introduction," 1, 4.

25. Paterson, "Poor Law," 185.

26. Mitchison, *Old Poor Law*, 96.

27.Hitchcock, King, and Sharpe, "Introduction," 4–5.

28. Hadley focuses on Dickens's deployment of the melodramatic mode against the New Poor Law (*Melodramatic Tactics*, 77–132).

29. Advocates of the New Poor Law included Harriet Martineau, who wrote at the request of Lord Brougham several volumes of stories meant to convince a working-class audience of the advantages of the new system. These volumes, *Poor Laws and Paupers Il-lustrated*, first published in 1833–34, along with an earlier (1832–34) set of *Illustrations of Political Economy*, also designed to reconcile working-class readers to the operation of market forces, have been recently (2001) republished in a new edition with an introduc-tion by Caroline Franklin. Franklin remarks on the "chilling rigour [of] Martineau's sup-port for the new laws," though pointing out that the *Poor Laws* stories soften her earlier commitment to an "extreme *laissez-faire* position" opposed to any relief ("Introduction," in *Illustrations of Political Economy, Taxation, Poor Laws and Paupers* by Harriet Martineau, ed. Carolyn Franklin, [Bristol: Thoemmes, 2001], 1:xvii).

It is hard to reconcile Martineau's support of the New Poor Law with the identifica-tion of a need for greater sympathy across social ranks that she attached to her account of Peterloo (*History*, 1:324) or with revisionist histories of sociology that credit her with making a sympathetic attitude a prerequisite for social research (Lengermann and Niebrugge-Brantley, *Women Founders*, 34). It is hard, that is, until we think in terms of disciplinarity. However sympathetic, Martineau was caught in the rising tide of science and theory. As Hoecker-Drysdale explains in her article on Martineau for *The Blackwell Companion to Major Social Theorists*, Martineau "subscribed to a broadly conceived science of society, a science which, in her view, would offer the key to understanding societal change and the 'uncertainties of the age'" (54). The abstraction in her works that re-minded Baillie of "steeple hunting" (*Letters*, 945) evidences her theoretical bent. Though her theory may very well differ from that of other founding sociologists, as Lengermann and Niebrugge-Brantley maintain (*Women Founders*, 40), she nevertheless takes a theo-retical rather than pragmatist approach to studying social relations and conditions. In contrast, Baillie's resistance to theory may make her dramas of situated behavior more radical analogues than Martineau's didactic tales of the operation of principles for the combination of sociology with social work that revisionists are now trying to envision.

30. Brundage, *Poor Laws*, 68–69; Roberts, *Social Conscience*, 289.

31. Brundage, *Poor Laws*, 68.

32. Hitchcock, King, and Sharpe, "Introduction," 3–14.

33. Mitchison, *Old Poor Law*, 185–215.

34. Brundage, *Poor Laws*, 45; R. A. Cage, *The Scottish Poor Law, 1745–1845* (Edinburgh: Scottish Academic Press, 1981), 111.

35. The relevant passages can be found in Scott's *Letters*, 4:414–15, 446–48, 456–58, 494–96; 5: 114–15, 286–88.

36. Ibid., 4:448.

37. Ibid., 4:446–48.

38. Ibid., 5:114–15.

39. Ibid., 4:456.

40. Randall Collins, "Situational Stratification: A Micro-Macro Theory of Inequal-ity," *Sociological Theory* 18 (2000): 19–20.

41. Ibid., 34–35.

42. Ibid., 39.

43. Though Malley (from whose title I take the "new old" phrase) and I differ over the extent to which destruction is involved in reconstruction, our ideas about the goal of rebuilding are compatible. I also see a link between my notion of Scott's redefining the role of inhabitants and the "solution" to the "problem" of "how to live in time" that Maxwell finds in *Guy Mannering*: "The solution is to define a present connected with the past but possessing its own vivid, focused identity"; the outcome is "an inhabitable present" that is related to the past but, since Mannering's tower is not finished, does not replicate the past ("Scott's Originality," 450–51).

44. Scott, *Letters*, 5:287.

45. Ibid.

46. Burwick, "Competing Histories," 264, 267, 270.

47. Ibid., 267.

48. Reference to Ochiltree's independence calls to mind Benis's comments on the relative freedom of the Old Cumberland Beggar compared to those pressed into national service, as shown in the Salisbury Plain poems (*Romanticism on the Road*, 118).

49. For an extensive treatment of this topic, see James Averill, *Wordsworth and the Poetry of Human Suffering* (Ithaca: Cornell University Press, 1980).

50. Hewitt, *Possibilities of Society*, 83.

51. For an alternative reading of Wordsworth as engaged from as early as the first *Lyrical Ballads* volume in an explicit critique of utilitarian plans to rationalize the Poor Laws, see Scott Boehnen, "The Preface to *Lyrical Ballads*: Poetics, Poor Laws, and the Bold Experiments of 1797–1802," *Nineteenth-Century Contexts* 20 (1997): 287–311. Boehnen cleverly imagines Wordsworth writing "The Last of the Flock," "Goody Blake," and other poems as answers to Bentham's request for information for a chart categorizing types of paupers receiving relief (287–88). Further, he reveals how Wordsworth's language in the *Preface* co-opts the language of utilitarianism to make the poet emerge as the more capable leader of plans for reform (292–303). Boehnen's thesis about Wordsworth's early involvement in Poor Laws controversies might seem superseded by Connell's argument that the connection between the "Old Cumberland Beggar" and Poor Law reform was made retrospectively through the Fenwick Note; however, Connell's point is not that Wordsworth was unconcerned about the Poor Laws during the 1790s but that controversies over the Poor Laws did not then pit humanitarians against political economists as the later debates came to do (*Romanticism, Economics, and the Question of "Culture,"* 22–25). Boehnen and Connell both aim to show how familiar readings of Wordsworth underestimate the social effects that can follow from poetry and miss the complexity of the poet's social and political engagement because they automatically impose aesthetic limits on his work. However divergent our particular interpretations of Wordsworth may be, I join Boehnen and Connell in wanting to reinterpret the relationship between the aesthetic/poetic and the social.

52. In reading Scott as avoiding a theoretical stance, I am not necessarily at odds with Ina Ferris, who argues that in the struggle between the generalizing mode of history and the particularizing mode of antiquarianism played out in *The Antiquary*, Scott ultimately sides with history. According to Ferris, Scott's choice stems from a commitment to "public discourse" that shapes knowledge to a community's needs ("Pedantry," 278). Antiquarians, with their concentration on the minutiae of their findings, lack sufficient sympathy with the community to shape and share their knowledge effectively. Historians, with their ability to generalize, make their knowledge available for social applications (281–82).

Clearly, Ferris and I both read Scott as concerned about social responsibility. The difference in our evaluations of generalization is disciplinary. Within the historical fields she considers, generalization emerged as the more socially engaged mode. In the early history of sociology, generalization—or more precisely, abstraction—held a similar promise, the promise of seeing society as more than a collection of individuals or a synonym for church or state (Hewitt, *Possibilities of Society*, 1–12). But there are blind spots within every perspective and method, and as sociologists became aware of what classic theory did not allow them to see, interest arose again in the individual and the particular. Ferris and I thus align Scott with different disciplines at different time periods, and our respective endeavors, along with Malley's placement of Scott with respect to the development of archaeology and Maxwell's placement of him between sociology and political history, reveal as much about present-day sensitivity to how knowledge is formed as about Scott.

53. Ferris, "Pedantry," 277.

54. For a more skeptical reading of the interactions in *The Antiquary*, see Katie Trumpener, *Bardic Nationalism: The Romantic Novel and the British Empire* (Princeton: Princeton University Press, 1997), 120–25, 157; her analysis, however, can convey the impression that Isabella compels Ochiltree to remain outside during their conversation.

55. Malley, "Walter Scott's Romantic Archaeology," 246; Christensen, *Romanticism at the End of History*, 11.

56. Clare Lamont, "Introduction," in *The Heart of Midlothian*, by Walter Scott, ed. Clare Lamont, xix (Oxford: Oxford University Press, 1999). Though he is critical of the ending, Chandler sees the problem as a lack of closure and attributes it to the case form, in which one set of deliberations leads to another (*England in 1819*, 309–10, 320). For Jones, "the utopian logic of the fourth book is both created and undermined by genre memory," i.e., by the evocation of various literary associations from which Scott has tried to turn history into an idyll (*Literary Memory*, 69–74). Gottlieb's reading challenges the notion that Scott meant Roseneath to be an ahistorical idyll. On the contrary, he argues, it shows that the communities that Scott had begun projecting with the conclusion of *Waverley* do not cohere by means of sympathy but by more instrumental relations: Roseneath is sustained by smuggling, bribery, and the "machiavellian *realpolitik*" of Knockdunder ("'To Be at Once Another and the Same,'" 198–200). Gottlieb's reading may actually be classified as a positive one because he sees the shattering of the sympathetic ideal as a step toward imagining more realistic models for English-Scottish relations. A critically positive reading is also ventured by Julian Meldon D'Arcy. In finding the Roseneath section a perfect fit with the rest of the novel, D'Arcy means that it consistently follows up on political criticisms introduced earlier and makes an ironic comment on the benefits of the Union ("Roseneath: Scotland or 'Scott-land'? A Reappraisal of *The Heart of Midlothian*," *Studies in Scottish Literature* 32 [2001]: 26–36). Austin's reading and mine, as will become apparent in this section, are more optimistic about what happens in Roseneath.

57. Michael Wiley, *Romantic Geography: Wordsworth and Anglo-European Spaces* (New York: St. Martin's Press, 1998), 44.

58. Lucy Sargisson, *Utopian Bodies and the Politics of Transgression* (London: Routledge, 2000), 2–4.

59. Ibid., 2; Denzin, *Interpretive Interactionism*, 26; cf. "The Call to Performance," which credits performing with opening "a positive utopian space where a politics of hope can be imagined" (196).

60. Lucy Sargisson, *Contemporary Feminist Utopianism* (London: Routledge, 1996), 1–5; *Utopian Bodies*, 3. The revaluing of utopia may have something in common with the revaluing of the classic sociological concepts of *Gemeinschaft* and *Gesellschaft* by Jean-Luc Nancy on which Gottlieb draws. In this revaluing, *Gemeinschaft* is not posited as an organic precursor to *Gesellschaft* but as the fantasy of organic unity invented in *Gesellschaft* and projected back from it. To live contentedly in *Gesellschaft*, people must reject the fantasy of *Gemeinschaft* ("'To Be at Once Another and the Same,'" 202). I suggest that the process of rehabilitating utopia—or *Gemeinschaft*—is more consonant with Scott's tendency to rework rather than give up on inherited concepts. Gottlieb reaches a similar conclusion about Scott, writing that *The Heart of Midlothian* "suspend[s] a final decision" about the organic ideal (204). I consider other reworkings of *Gemeinschaft* and *Gesellschaft* in *The Possibilities of Society*, 61–87.

61. Wiley, *Romantic Geography*, 48.

62. Chandler takes up the problem of "equality before the law" in a hierarchical system as it relates to events in *The Bride of Lammermoor*, treating it as an "inconsistency" in conservative politics (*England in 1819*, 343–47). I suggest that what is inconsistent in terms of political structure may be less so in terms of social relations informed by respect for a whole community. In keeping with the "hat[r]ed [of] political factions" that, according to Ward, led Scott to embrace Toryism as "a way of life, not a political creed" ("Jurisprudential Heart of Midlothian," 27), Scott's narrator makes a point of describing the duke as "soaring above the petty distinctions of faction, his voice . . . raised, whether in office or opposition, for those measures which were at once just and lenient" (344). Interestingly, the last phrase echoes the "more just, more merciful" combination in Baillie's *Introductory Discourse* (*Works*, 4).

63. Insofar as I take decision-making processes as the focus of this section of the novel, my reading shares some elements with Chandler's, which takes the deliberations of casuistry as central to the entire work. We diverge, however, in the ways we define, contextualize, and exemplify the thought processes. Chandler does not examine the Roseneath section in detail.

64. Many readers, following Judith Wilt's lead in *Secret Leaves: The Novels of Walter Scott* (Chicago: University of Chicago Press, 1985), are critical of Scott's portrayal of Jeanie. Austin ("Home and Nation") takes a more positive view.

65. Austin, "Home and Nation," 631; 621–22, 631–32.

66. Chandler, *England in 1819*, 311–12, 317.

67. Ibid., 209, 310–20.

68. Clark, *Misery and Company*, 36.

69. Chandler, *England in 1819*, 309.

70. Austin, "Home and Nation," 632.

71. Ibid., 632–33. An alternative reading of the freeing of the Whistler is advanced by Gottlieb, for whom it represents the failure of sympathy as a means to improve social relations. Freed, the Whistler continues to be at odds with and outside of "proper" society ("'To Be at Once Another and the Same,'" 201–2).

72. The narrator comments to this effect regarding the Porteous rioters who avoided prosecution and lived prosperous lives: "The forbearance of the magistrate was in these instances wise, certainly, and just; for what good impression could be made on the public mind by punishment, when the memory of the offence was obliterated, and all that was remembered was the recent inoffensive, or perhaps exemplary, conduct of the offender?" (484).

CHAPTER 5.
IMPOVERISHED SOCIAL RELATIONS

1. Baillie, *Works*, 613.

2. Baillie, *Letters*, 385.

3. Ibid., 649.

4. Ibid., 930.

5. Ibid., 1199.

6. Ibid., 1199n230; on W. P. Alison, see Paterson, "Poor Law," 174, 212n3.

7. Mitchison, *Old Poor Law*, 185–215.

8. Baillie, *Letters* 945.

9. Slagle, *A Literary Life*, 164.

10. Ibid., 136–37, 165.

11. Patricia Comitini, "'More Than Half a Poet': Vocational Philanthropy and Dorothy Wordsworth's *Grasmere Journals*," *European Romantic Review* 14 (2003), 309–10. Roberts corroborates this use of "philanthropy" as institutional; he contrasts it with humanitarianism which was "diffuse" and individualistic (*Social Conscience*, 260).

12. Comitini, "More Than Half a Poet," 308.

13. Ibid., 309.

14. Ibid., 318.

15. Ibid., 308–11.

16. Ibid., 308. Addams's work can be fit more easily than Baillie's into gendered divisions of knowledge. For instance, some scholars interpret Addams's pragmatism as distinctly feminist: in contrast to Dewey's and Mead's focus on scientific experiments and rational decisions, Addams's version focuses on ordinary or domestic experience and caring intervention (Deegan, *Jane Addams and the Men*, 304; Ross, "Gendered Social Knowledge," 239–40, 248–49; Siegfried, "Introduction [to *Democracy*]," xxxiii and "Socializing Democracy: Jane Addams and John Dewey," *Philosophy of the Social Sciences* 29 [1999]: 221). This distinction, however, is clearly a matter of emphasis in some contexts and should not obscure the commitment to problem solving that Addams and Mead share. Whether or not Addams was a gender essentialist remains controversial. According to Deegan, "Addams thought that women were biologically superior to men because of their maternal instincts. She practiced, then, a female chauvinism based partly on a biological explanation (*Jane Addams and the Men*, 242). In contrast, Siegfried argues that Addams did not accept the idea of an "essential feminine nature," though she did think women had unique experiences ("Introduction [to *Memory*], xiii). Ross notes Addams's early belief in essential feminine qualities such as intuition but sees her as later moving toward an "androgynous" ideal ("Gendered Social Knowledge," 239, 252). Perhaps Addams's view is not entirely consistent, but she was clearly more inclined than Baillie to give preferential status to women's reactions and perceptions as such. For Mead's affinities with feminism, see Mitchell Aboulafia, "Was George Herbert Mead a Feminist?" *Hypatia* 8 (1993): 145–58.

17. Comitini, "More Than Half a Poet," 313, 317.

18. Slagle, *A Literary Life*, 156–57.

19. Citations in my text give stanza and page number from Baillie's *Works*; the lines are unnumbered. The numbered stanzas of the *Legend* appear between unnumbered opening and closing sections (cited by page number only) that enclose the story from the past within the frame of Baillie's present interest.

20. The quoted lines are followed by ones referring to the gratitude of the poor in line with the expectations expressed in Baillie's letter to Hodgson (*Letters*, 649).

21. Henderson, "Passion."

22. Addams, *Twenty Years*, 70–72.

23. Ibid., 72–76.

24. Power struggles between competing charitable agencies could turn reference to personal and impersonal approaches into weapons. In her analysis of the competition between the COS and the Fabians, Goodlad notes that the COS touted its visiting model as personal but exposes that claim as an implied criticism of the "impersonal" state system the Fabians wanted ("Character and Pastorship," 239–45).

25. Addams, *Democracy*, 11–34.

26. Ibid., 17–18; Addams, *Twenty Years*, 75–76.

27. Baillie's *Family Legend*, however, which I examine in chapter Seven, shows how family and social claims can be at odds.

28. Addams, *Democracy*, 105.

29. Ibid., 117. For a broad treatment of the trend toward bureaucracy and the polarization it effected, see Stivers, "Settlement Women."

30. On the whole, it is more accurate to distance Addams's way of thinking from science, as Ross does most fully, than to draw her close to it, yet Brown notes Addams's youthful enthusiasm for experiment and nature study as an alternative to religious conformity (*Education*, 84–86). That inclination has affinities with Mead's enthusiasm for science, which he defined in anything but abstract and quantifiable terms. Taking scientific method as the most promising tool for social problem solving and adapting it from physical to social applications, Mead ironically transformed it into dramatic experience. What he valued about science was the performance of research, the scientist's willingness to examine all possible ways to solve a problem or reach a goal — even if some of those ways violate "the taboos of institutions that we have regarded as inviolable" ("Scientific Method and the Moral Sciences," [1923] in Reck, *Selected Writings*, 262–65).

In keeping with her concentration on Addams as a writer, Joslin examines Addams's characterization of the charity worker and other figures as examples of "literary cross-dressing" through which she sought the right guise and voice to assume before her audience. For Joslin, Addams evolves from charity visitor to social worker to writer, with the latter having the greatest "authority" as an observer, mediator, and recorder, though this authority is exercised through Bakhtinian dialogism rather than by a domineering narrative voice (*Writer's Life*, 62–68). Joslin's presentation shows how Addams's identity as a writer can be embraced by post-disciplinary readers, but it does not confront the problem of why the writer as social authority was unavailable to Addams as a conscious identity and unacceptable within the modern disciplinary system.

31. This aspect of Scott's work is treated by (among others) Burwick, "Competing Histories," Rigney, *Imperfect Histories*, and Mayer, "Illogical Status." The latter two concentrate on the tensions between literary conventions and historical forms, such as footnotes. I address these tensions in chapters 7 and 8.

32. Burwick, "Competing Histories," 261.

33. This and subsequent references to the novel that appear parenthetically in the text are to Walter Scott, *Woodstock*, Caledonian Edition of the Works of Sir Walter Scott, 37–38 (Boston: Houghton Mifflin, 1913).

34. Burwick, "Competing Histories," 271.

35. Dorothy McMillan, "Unromantic Caledon: Representing Scotland in *The Family Legend*, *Metrical Legends*, and *Witchcraft*," in Crochunis, *Joanna Baillie*, ed. by Crochunis, 83.

36. The term "idiot" appears in the dramatis personae. *Witchcraft* contains many Scottish dialect terms. Susan Bennett reads the use of dialect as evidence of Baillie's insight into language as a factor in status differences; moreover, she sees Baillie's use of dialect as a deliberate substitution of the local, particular and gendered for the universalism conventionally expected in tragedies. The substitution "suggests that women playwrights made attempts to challenge in public the representation of hegemonic cultural codes expressed in those genres which had hitherto been claimed by men for their own (serious) concerns" ("Genre Trouble: Jonna Baillie, Elizabeth Polack—Tragic Subjects, Melodramatic Subjects," in Davis and Donkin, *Women and Playwrighting*, 228–30). McMillan also comments on the use of dialect and prose in the play, pointing out that Baillie eliminates status differences by having all the characters speak alike ("Unromantic Caledon," 84). Recalling (from the previous chapter) that hard times could easily reverse the positions of rate-payers and recipients of relief, we might interpret Baillie's linguistic leveling as nudging her audience toward recognizing themselves in the poor.

37. Addams, *Democracy*, 110.

38. My phrasing overlaps somewhat with that of Cox: "the truly destructive figure is the beautiful, cultured Annabella," who is "the true 'witch' in the play" ("Staging Baillie," 157).

39. Scott, *Letters*, 10:425.

40. Ibid., 10:262.

41. With apparent similarity, Cox states that the play "revolves around errors of perception" ("Staging Baillie," 157), but his argument develops along different lines from mine. Specifically, he reads *Witchcraft* as a successful example of Baillie's using spectacle to turn her audience from cruel voyeurism toward moral judgment. Spectators learn to distrust the appearances of guilt and innocence and acquire more insightful "moral vision" (158).

42. Purinton, "Socialized and Medicalized Hysteria," 148.

43. Reference to Mitchison corroborates that attempts at providing institutional care for the "lunatic" poor were made under the Old Poor Law, though she points out that the quality of care was often not very high (*Old Poor Law*, 170–72). Administration of programs for "lunatics" began to be separated from administration of the Poor Laws during the 1840s in England and the 1850s in Scotland (Brundage, *Poor Laws*, 99; Paterson, "Poor Law," 189).

44. Addams, *Second Twenty Years*, 310–11.

45. See above, chapter 3, note 20.

46. McMillan, "Unromantic Caledon," 85.

47. Addams, *Memory*, 3–4.

48. Ibid., 18–21, 10, 15–16.

49. Ibid., 34, 21, 28.

50. Ibid., 23.

51. Ibid., 33–48, 2.

52. Ibid., 52, 24, 27–45.

53. The larger significance of that hope becomes more apparent in light of Joslin's reading of *The Long Road of Woman's Memory* as Addams's defense of her pacifism during World War I, the time she composed the book. In the context of the war, the Devil-Baby story and the other examples of "transmuted" suffering in the volume promise that myth can "build a community" and "forestall destruction"; they promise that the "immigrant experiment in North America" need not "end with a reprise of European hatreds" (*Writer's Life*, 173–77).

54. McKenna, "Pragmatist Feminist Self," 133–45.

CHAPTER 6.
LANDOR AND THE *SOLUTION*
OF POLITICAL CONTENTION

1. Tilly, *Popular Contention*. Legislative issues affected Scotland as well as England since Scotland, which had not retained its own parliament along with its own legal system after the union of the two countries, was represented in the English Parliament.

2. For recent treatments of *Gebir*, see Simon Bainbridge, *Napoleon and English Romanticism* (Cambridge: Cambridge University Press, 1995); Richard Cronin, *The Politics of Romantic Poetry: In Search of the Pure Commonwealth* (New York: St. Martin's Press, 2000); Mohammed Sharafuddin, *Islam and Romantic Orientalism: Literary Encounters with the Orient* (New York: St. Martin's Press, 1994).

3. Cronin, *Politics*, 79–80.

4. Titus Bicknell, "*Calamus Ense Potentior Est*: Walter Savage Landor's Poetic War of Words," *Romanticism on the Net* 4 (November 1996), http://users.ox.ac.uk/~scat0385/landor.html.

5. R. H. Super, *Walter Savage Landor: A Biography* (New York: New York University Press, 1954), 11–16, 63–67, 85–90.

6. Diego Saglia, *Poetic Castles in Spain: British Romanticism and Figurations of Iberia* (Amsterdam: Rodopi, 2000) includes analysis of *Count Julian*.

7. Super, *Landor: A Biography*, 154.

8. R. H. Super, "Landor and the 'Satanic School,'" *Studies in Philology* 42 (1945): 806–8.

9. Walter Savage Landor, *Complete Works of Walter Savage Landor*, ed. by E. Welby and S. Wheeler, 12:195–96 (London: Chapman and Hall, 1927–36).

10. The quoted phrase is from David Wootton, who argues that even the Levellers were not democrats ("Leveller Democracy and the Puritan Revolution" in *Cambridge History of Political Thought 1450–1700*, ed. J. H. Burns and Mark Goldie, 412–42 [Cambridge: Cambridge University Press, 1991]); on the English Republican tradition more broadly, see Blair Worden, "English Republicanism," in Burns and Goldie, *Cambridge History of Political Thought*, 443–48, and "Milton's Republicanism and the Tyranny of Heaven," in *Machiavelli and Republicanism*, ed. Gisela Bock, Quentin Skinner, and Maurizio Viroli, 227–34 (Cambridge: Cambridge University Press, 1990).

11. Super, *Landor: A Biography*, 26.

12. Ibid., 222–23.

13. I take my final count from the table of contents in *Imaginary Conversations of Walter Savage Landor with Bibliographical and Explanatory Notes by Charles G. Crump*, (London: J. M. Dent, 1891). Because there is some doubt about the authorship of a few other conversations attributed to Landor by twentieth-century editors (according to R. H. Super's overview of scholarship on "Walter Savage Landor," in *The English Romantic Poets and Essayists*, ed. C. W. Houtchens and L. H. Houtchens [New York: New York University Press, 1966], 228), I exclude them from my total. A reprint shows that the collected edition of 1846 contained 124 *Imaginary Conversations* (*Works of Walter Savage Landor*, 2 vols., [1846; repr., London: Chapman and Hall 1868].

14. The letter, dated May 3, 1824, is quoted in Alice Lavonne Prasher, "Walter Savage Landor's *Imaginary Conversations*: A Critical Edition of the First Eight Conversations in Volume One. (with) *Imaginary Conversations of Literary Men and Statesmen*. The First Volume. 1824" (PhD diss., Northwestern University, 1966), 109. Landor's letters have not been collected into a reliable edition.

15. R. H. Super, *The Publication of Landor's Works* (London: The Bibliographic Society, 1954), 26.

16. Lieberman, *Province*, 13–14, 199.

17. Zaret, "Petitions," 1510, 1516, 1514.

18. Ibid., 1513–15, 1517.

19. Ibid., 1508, 1517.

20. Ibid., 1526.

21. Ibid., 1533–35.

22. Ibid., 1524–25, 1519, 1529, 1530.

23. Tilly, *Roads*, 217–44. Though my allusions to "popular contention" evoke the title of Tilly's landmark study of the topic, I cite his points from his reworking of the research in *Roads* because that version is more sharply focused for my purposes than the versions in either *Popular Contention* or *Stories, Identities, and Political Change* (Lanham, MD: Rowman and Littlefield, 2002). I address Tilly's rapprochement with storytelling in note 14 to chapter 8.

24. Tilly, *Roads*, 223–28. Tilly does not overlook such violent occurrences as Peterloo; he treats them, rather, as numerically rare within an overall pattern of decreasing violence.

25. Ibid., 235–42.

26. Mead, "Nature of the Past," 346–49.

27. George Herbert Mead, "History and the Experimental Method," in *George Herbert Mead on Social Psychology*, ed. Anselm Strauss, 323–24 (1938; repr., Chicago: University of Chicago Press, 1977); "Nature of the Past," 350–52; *Philosophy of the Present*, 9–2, 29–30. I have streamlined Mead's ideas considerably here. For a more extensive treatment, see Maines, *Faultline*, 37–54, and the article jointly authored by David Maines, Noreen M. Sugrue and Michael A. Katovich, "The Sociological Import of G. H. Mead's Theory of the Past," *American Sociological Review* 48 (1983): 161–73.

28. The association between reform and revolution is explicitly stated in Scott's letter to Lockhart dated 17 March 1831 (*Letters*, 11:487–88), which I quote in the next chapter.

29. Chandler comments that *Imaginary Conversations* may evidence "a new culturally exemplary role given to conversation in this period" (*England in 1819*, 282n13), but he does not elaborate further on Landor.

30. Mead, *Philosophy of the Present*, 29–30; Maines, Sugrue, and Katovich, "Mead's Theory of the Past," 164.

31. Maines, Sugrue, and Katovich, "Mead's Theory of the Past," 164.

32. Landor, *Works*, 2:58–59. Hereafter, citations to the *Imaginary Conversations* will appear parenthetically within the text. Except when otherwise indicated, I cite the *Imaginary Conversations* from the reprint of the 1846 *Works of Walter Savage Landor* (first referenced above in note 13 to this chapter), which maintains Landor's organization of the material. My preference for this first collected edition is shared by scholars who have most recently edited selections of Landor's work; for statements of their positions, see Prasher, "Walter Savage Landor's *Imaginary Conversations*," 2–10, 54; Charles L. Proudfit, "Introduction," in *Selected Imaginary Conversations of Literary Men and Statesmen, by Walter Savage Landor*, ed. Charles L. Proudfit, xx–xxii (Lincoln: University of Nebraska Press, 1969); Keith Hanley, "Introduction," in *Selected Poetry and Prose of Walter Savage Landor*, ed. Keith Hanley, xl–xli (New York: Persea, 1981).

33. The conversations reflect some of Landor's peculiar spellings, such as the single "l" in "Marvel." Except when quoting, I use the standard "Marvell." On Landor's advo-

cacy of spelling reform, see Charles L. Proudfit, "Landor's Hobbyhorse: A Study of Romantic Orthography," *Studies in Romanticism* (1968): 207–17.

34. Lucy Newlyn, Paradise Lost *and the Romantic Reader* (Oxford: Clarendon, Press, 1993), 2–7.

35. *The Dictionary of National Biography*, ed. Leslie Stephen and Sidney Lee (Oxford: Oxford University Press, 1959–60) gives a concise account of Parker's career (15:272–75); Marvell's own shifting allegiances are well explained by Blair Worden in "Andrew Marvell, Oliver Cromwell, and the Horatian Ode," in *The Politics of Discourse*, ed. K. Sharpe and S. Zwicker, 147–80 (Berkeley: University of California Press, 1987).

36. Landor repeats this contrast between Milton and Marvell in two conversations between them written after the first collected edition. Upon being informed by Marvell that many "zealots" think Milton has grown "lukewarm" with the Restoration, Milton replies, "better to be lukewarm than to boil over" ("Milton and Marvel" in the Crump edition, 5:37, cited above in note 13). In these conversations, both speakers criticize monarchy and prelacy.

37. A. Lavone Ruoff, "Landor's Conception of the Great Leader," *The Wordsworth Circle* 7 (1976): 44.

38. Perhaps because he always saw Cromwell in contrast to Napoleon, Landor always defended Cromwell's integrity. An essay giving "Opinions of Caesar, Cromwell, Milton, and Buonaparte" published among Landor's "Minor Prose Pieces" in the first collected edition gives a comparative analysis from Landor's own point of view (2:457–60). Ruoff finds the contrast between a cruel Cromwell and a humanitarian Nobel more clearly drawn and convincing than I do ("Leader," 44–45).

39. Roger Howell, "'Who Needs Another Cromwell?': The Nineteenth-Century Image of Oliver Cromwell," in *Images of Oliver Cromwell: Essays for and by Roger Howell, Jr.*, ed. R. C. Richardson, 99 (Manchester: Manchester University Press, 1993); "'That Imp of Satan': The Restoration Image of Cromwell," in the same volume, 71; see also "Cromwell, the English Revolution and Political Symbolism in Eighteenth-Century England," in the same volume, 33–47.

40. W. A. Speck, "Cromwell and the Glorious Revolution," in Richardson, *Images of Oliver Cromwell*, 48.

41. Mead, *Philosophy of the Present*, 29–30.

42. Speck, "Cromwell," 56–60.

43. The other topics include capital punishment, about which Penn upbraids: "Ye defend the violence done by system, and punish by the gallows the same violence done by poor wretches incapable of reflection; done perhaps from want of food, perhaps from neglect of education, criminal not in the robber, but in the ministers of the prince. If power is ever righteously to be exercised by one state toward another, it is in taking away the means of injustice and cruelty from the administrators, and in restoring to the people their rights" (1:555).

44. Sutherland, *Life of Walter Scott*, 300, identifies the given years as marked by anxiety.

45. D. J. Trela, "Sir Walter Scott on Oliver Cromwell: an Evenhanded Royalist Evaluates a Usurper," *Clio* 27 (1998): 195–96, 205.

46. Ibid., 7, 10.

47. Howell, "Political Symbolism," 33–34; "Imp of Satan," 69–70; "Nineteenth-Century Image," 102.

48. Baillie, *Letters*, 690; maddeningly, Baillie does not say what interested her about the *Memoirs*. Coleman Phillipson, whose *Three Criminal Law Reformers: Beccaria, Bentham,*

Romilly (1923; repr., Montclair, NJ: Patterson Smith, 1970), is an undisguised tribute to the reformers it treats, defends Romilly's effort to reconcile private and public morality from charges that it maintains too fine a distinction (324), but I wish to call attention to another aspect of Phillipson's study that bears on the terms of my own. To contrast Romilly's position on declassification with the conservative line, Phillipson uses speeches and writings by Romilly and William Paley to construct an "imaginary conversation" (though he does not use that term) between them. His presentation touches on discretionary power and self-sacrifice. Discretion, in this dialogue, refers to the power to pardon after a sentence has been passed, not to the more extensive power in the Scottish court. Sacrifice, for Paley, is an acceptable, if unintended, consequence of the great number of capital sentences given in England, which Paley defends. Answering Romilly's concern about the number leading to the execution of innocent or not maliciously motivated people, Paley replies that pardons should prevent that outcome; when they do not, the unfairly executed people have made an acceptable sacrifice for the sake of public order. Perhaps this point (which I anticipated in note 68 to chapter 3) helps to explain the wariness about self-sacrificing behavior so prominent in Baillie's plays.

49. Perceval's use of the term "philanthropy" for Romilly's thinking brings to mind Roberts's categorization of philanthropy as institutional and humanitarianism as individual (*Social Conscience*, 231–95). Though Perceval seems to have chosen the best term for a legislator's frame of reference, I add "humane" here both because Roberts admits some categorical overlap and because humanity mongering was so closely associated with criminal law reform.

50. Maines, Sugrue, and Katovich, "Mead's Theory of the Past," 164, 167–68. As I remarked in chapter 2, this reference to a "mythical past" is independent of Farmer's (*Criminal Law*, 37), though each has affinities with the other.

51. Ibid., 164, 170.

CHAPTER 7.

BAILLIE, SCOTT, AND THE *PROBLEM*
OF POLITICAL CONTENTION

1. Baillie, *Letters*, 924–25.

2. Scott, *Letters*, 11:487–88.

3. Chandler, *England in 1819*, 208–12; Christensen, *Romanticism at the End of History*, 171–72.

4. Christensen, *Romanticism at the End of History*, 172–75.

5. This point calls to mind Lyman's (*Civilization*, 243–49) and Denzin's (*Symbolic Interactionism and Cultural Studies*, 62–63) explanations of how symbolic interactionism treats structure and agency, which I addressed in the introduction.

6. My elaboration of "temporizing" from Scott should, as I projected in note 13 to Chapter 1, differentiate my use of the term from Hamilton's use with respect to Schiller.

7. Mead, *Lectures in Social Psychology*, 100.

8. Kathryn Sutherland, "Introduction, Notes," in *Redgauntlet*, by Sir Walter Scott, ed. Kathryn Sutherlan, 447n207d (Oxford: Oxford University Press, 1985). Further references to this Oxford World's Classics edition (based on the Magnum Opus) of *Redgauntlet* appear parenthetically in the text. The "American" spelling of "temporize" appears in this edition.

9. Both Jones and Melrose connect *Redgauntlet* to events of the 1820s. For Jones, the appearance of Prince Charles Edward Stuart in Scotland in the novel during the

1760s encodes the visit of King George IV to Scotland in 1822. Pointing out that Scott helped to superintend the latter visit, Jones reads *Redgauntlet* as playing out the conflicts between old and new loyalties, old and new laws, brought back from memory by the royal visit. She concludes that the novel, like the visit, encourages "the social organization of forgetting which supports the power of the established government" (*Literary Memory*, 127, 101–28). In a rather surprising reading arguing that *Redgauntlet* "rescues" Scottish law from the taint of the sedition trials, Melrose proposes a different kind of conflation. He conflates the return of the Pretender with the return of Thomas Muir, who was convicted of sedition and sent to Australia for fourteen years.

Chandler deals with a different kind of contention—the balancing of "rival" cases and tales—in the content and structure of *Redgauntlet* (*England in 1819*, 217–19).

10. Jones, *Literary Memory*, 122.

11. Robertson, *Legitimate Histories*, 145–46; Mayer, "Scott's Footnotes."

12. Nancy F. Partner, "Historicity in an Age of Reality-Fiction" in *A New Philosophy of History*, ed. Frank Ankersmit and Hans Kellner, 26–31, 35 (Chicago: University of Chicago Press, 1995).

13. Ibid., 33.

14. Ibid., 22–23.

15. Mayer, "Scott's Footnotes," 922.

16. Denzin, *Interpretive Ethnography* 33.

17. Alternatively, Jones associates Wandering Willie with the feudal past that the novel aims to forget (*Literary Memory*, 115–17).

18. Maines, Sugrue, and Katovich, "Mead's Theory of the Past," 164. Recall the exposition above at the end of chapter 6.

19. Jones extends the term to cover Alan Fairford's behavior as well. On the whole, she sees Alan and Darsie as versions of each other and both as autobiographical projections of Scott as a young law student (*Literary Memory*, 126, 110). Though she notes the process of temporizing, she does not sensitize the concept as I do.

20. Cf. Christensen's analysis of the irrelevance of the consent of the governed in monarchy with respect to *Waverley* (*Romanticism at the End of History*, 172–73).

21. Zaret, "Petitions," 1533–35.

22. Scott, *Letters*, 11:488 (as I quoted at the beginning of this chapter).

23. Without implying the Meadian terms I evoke here, Fiona Robertson argues that Scott uses present forms, including the popular form of Gothic terror, to approach the past in *Redgauntlet*, and she sees Scott as promoting flexible adaptations (*Legitimate Histories*, 255, 12). Robertson's and my readings seem a bit more optimistic than Jones's, which emphasize the obliteration of folk memory by progress (*Literary Memory*, 128).

24. As Fiona Robertson puts it, Scott has used the literary convention of the Gothic to exorcise the threatening aspects of the past and move safely and successfully into the present (*Legitimate Histories*, 246–62).

Though the casting adrift of what does not suit present needs might seem at odds with Scott's other metaphor for adapting past and present, i.e., the building onto the castle of law, I do not see the two as irreconcilable. Casting adrift does not amount to destruction. It still allows those elements to survive just as the addition onto the building allows for the survival of old rooms.

25. Robertson, *Legitimate Histories*, 270–73; Trela, "Scott on Oliver Cromwell."

26. Uchronianism is much less studied than utopianism—at least among anglophone scholars. A search of the *MLA Bibliography* on December 15, 2003 yielded no results for "uchronia" but eight for the French form "uchronie." The results reflect the importance of Louis-Sébastien Mercier's *L'An 2440*, a 1770 imagination of what society would be like

if a revolution transformed the old (then current) regime, which Gregory Ludlow takes as the inaugural text of the type ("Imagining the Future: Mercier's *L'An 2440* and Morris' *News from Nowhere*," *Comparative Literature Studies* 29 [1992]: 20–38). An independent website (*Uchronia: The Alternative History List http://www.uchronia.com*) maintained by Robert B. Schmunk, however, includes an annotated bibliography of thousands of uchronian works. None by Scott are listed. My point is not to propose adding them; I do not wish to classify Scott as a uchronian or utopian writer. Rather, I wish to associate his more subtle manipulations of time and place with the critical functions of utopian literature and thereby distance them from simple nostalgia or endorsement of a given past.

27. Purinton, "Sexual Politics"; Slagle, *Literary Life*, 97.

28. Though *The Election*, which appeared in the second volume of the plays on the passions published in 1802, was written well before the reform controversies of the 1820s in which I have situated *The Imaginary Conversations* and *Redgauntlet*, it is still appropriate to place it in a developing trend of popular contention. The trend as Tilly demarcates it emerges in the eighteenth century (*Roads*, 223–38).

29. Tilly, *Roads*, 223.

30. See the section on "Legal Justice, Social Good, and Sympathy" above in chapter 2.

31. Purinton, "Sexual Politics," 120.

32. Baillie, *Works*, 4.

33. Slagle, *Life*, 97.

34. Baillie, *Works*, 390–91.

35. Ibid., 391.

36. Ibid., 390.

37. Specifically, she rejects the idea of making "a romantic passion for Valeria the cause of Mahomet's besieging the city" (*Works*, 391); I am reminded of Byron's rejecting jealousy as a motive in the plot of *Marino Faliero* (*Lord Byron: The Complete Poetical Works*, ed. Jerome J. McGann, 4:301–3 [Oxford: Clarendon Press, 1986).

38. In a less picturesque description of imaginative interaction with history than she develops in her "landmark" metaphor, Baillie compares historical figures to outlines that we fill, thereby inevitably "heightening or diminishing the general effect" (*Works*, 390).

39. Ibid.

40. Baillie, preface to *Metrical Legends*, *Works*, 706.

41. Exemplary readings include Beth H. Friedman-Romell, "Staging the State: Joanna Baillie's 'Constantine Paleologus,'" in Davis and Donkin, *Women and Playwrighting*, 151–73; Hoagwood, "Revolutionary Representation"; Kucich, "Re-staging of History and Gender."

42. Friedman-Romell, "Staging the State," 153.

43. Jane Addams, *Peace and Bread in Time of War* (New York: Macmillan, 1922).

44. Friedman-Romell, "Staging the State," 170.

45. I am baffled by Hoagwood's dismissal of this strategic act as a capitulation to patriarchy ("Revolutionary Representation," 309). More consonant with my own reading is Kucich's analysis of the death of Valeria as a plea for social change. Concentrating on the staging of a tableau in which "a small band of Constantine's surviving followers, male and female, gather round her in loving support," the scene "dissolves the conventional regulations of military and gender behavior": it "stop[s] history on stage" and calls for criticism and revision of its course and values. Returning to the scene with a more skeptical eye, Kucich does question its effectiveness, for he notes that the change is predicated upon Valeria's "self-destruction" ("Re-staging of History and Gender,"125–26). I

am less skeptical about the success of Valeria's act because I see it as self-determining: it alters the fate that history would impose on her. I am reminded of William D. Brewer's interpretation of the death of Euthanasia in Mary Shelley's *Valperga*. Instead of seeing Euthanasia as a failure because she did not bring about political change, Brewer sees her as a success because she controlled her passions, rejected merely selfish goals, and pursued rational enlightenment throughout her life ("Mary Shelley's *Valperga*: The Triumph of Euthanasia's Mind," *European Romantic Review* 5 [1995]: 144). As Brewer makes clear, success need not be measured only by tangible effects; in fact, Jackson's study of Hull-House "reformance" is predicated on valuing its less tangible achievements. Interestingly, Brewer believes that *Valperga* was influenced by Baillie's ideas about the passions and the need to control them, though the link he posits is between Castruccio's and Ethwald's ambition (135) rather than between Euthanasia and Valeria.

46. Baillie, *Works*, 479–81.

47. Dorothy McMillan elaborates on the tensions between Scottish and British identities in Baillie's lifetime (and in Baillie's own life) as a context for the play ("Unromantic Caledon," 75–79). Though agreeing that the play was meant to bring factions together, Cox points out that the staging may have undermined the intent since Scott included in the cast members of a military unit whose charge had been "to coerce the Highland poor into the army" ("Staging Baillie,"163).

48. Scott, *Letters*, 2:253–54.

49. With an allusion to the tide as Helen's "executioner," the play can be contextualized with respect to the problem of criminal justice as well as to the problem of political contention. In the former context, the play shows a fearful society—for the vassals fear a loss of their identity from the alliance—constructing a criminal identity for Helen, drawing together in the "solidarity of aggression" against her, and protecting themselves from the perceived threat through segregative control.

50. Adrienne Scullion, "Some Women of the Nineteenth-century Scottish Theatre: Joanna Baillie, Frances Wright and Helen MacGregor," in *History of Scottish Women's Writing*, ed. by Douglas Gifford and Dorothy McMillan, 163 (Edinburgh: Edinburgh University Press, 1997).

51. Addams, *Democracy*, 41.

52. Ibid., 40–42.

53. Scullion argues for the relevance of Wollstonecraft to *The Family Legend* ("Some Women," 163); for her relevance to other plays, see Purinton (*Romantic Ideology Unmasked*, "Sexual Politics") and Mellor ("Counter-Public Sphere").

Chapter 8. The Problem of Disciplinarity

1. John Guillory, "Literary Study and the Modern System of the Disciplines," in Anderson and Valente, *Disciplinarity*, 19, 26–33.

2. Michael Holquist, "Why We Should Remember Philology," *Profession*, 2002, 79.

3. Guillory, "Literary Study," 35.

4. For the trajectory of scholarship on Scott from its nadir at the start of the twentieth century through its Lukacsian phase to its ramifications in the later twentieth century, see Fiona Robertson, "Walter Scott" in *Literature of the Romantic Period: A Bibliographical Guide*, ed. Michael O'Neill, 227–33 (Oxford: Clarendon Press, 1998). Ferris (in *Achievement*) provides a more specialized history of the rise of Scott's reputation during the Romantic era to his "expulsion" from the Victorian canon.

5. An annotated bibliography of editions, biographies, and critical studies of Baillie's work from her lifetime to the present day, prepared by Ken Bugajski ("Joanna Baillie: An Annotated Bibliography") appears in Crochunis, *Joanna Baillie*, 241–312.

6. Richardson, "Neural Theatre," addresses in detail how Baillie's works converge with and diverge from "mental theatre."

7. For introductory references to these studies, see notes 15 and 61 to chapter 1.

8. Rigney, *Imperfect Histories*, 43; Mayer, "Scott's Footnotes," 919.

9. Rigney, *Imperfect Histories*, 43–44; Mayer, "Scott's Footnotes," 923.

10. Rigney, *Imperfect Histories*, 35–55.

11. Ibid., 54–56.

12. Ibid., 15–20, 54–56.

13. Ibid., 28–30.

14. In describing the link as "literary," I do not overlook Maines's reservations about the self-involvement of some forms of literary criticism, which I mentioned in note 25 to chapter 1. Rather I use the term with confidence that most forms of literary criticism are or can become socially involved.

Though Maines is not alone in developing and practicing narrative sociology, I single out his work because it has been groundbreaking and influential; moreover, Maines's landmark article, "Narrative's Moment," deals explicitly with problems of disciplinarity. The additional work on narrative—by Ezzy, "Theorizing Narrative Identity," and by Novitz and Polletta, who are cited below (notes 48 and 62, respectively)—on which I draw reflects the growing attention to narrative in studies of the self and social change. For an overview of the trend, see Joseph E. Davis, "Narrative and Social Movements: The Power of Stories," in *Stories of Change: Narrative and Social Movements*, ed. Joseph E. Davis, 3–29 (Albany: State University of New York Press, 2002).

It is a sign of the strength of the narrative trend that Tilly has come to find the concept of stories meaningfully applicable, with certain qualifications, to his own research on politics and social movements. In *Stories, Identities, and Political Change*, Tilly concedes that he has resisted this trend, and he still finds narrative insufficient to explain social experience because he believes it relies too much on the intentions of individual actors (5, 25–42, 73–74). Though arguing for the importance of "nonstory" explanation, Tilly concludes that "identity claims and their attendant stories constitute serious political business," and he includes "creative interaction" among the ways that "stories and identities produce their effects" (207, 210–11, 209). Tilly identifies his work with "relational realism" rather than with symbolic interactionism, but he notes an affinity between relational realism and American pragmatism (72), to which interactionism is also connected. Tilly's rapprochement with storytelling may be an example of the movement of other sociologies toward interactionism for which Maines argues in *Faultline*. Tilly's affinity with interactionism and its affirmation of Maines's argument are remarked on by Irwin Deutscher, "Little Theories and Big Problems: Chicago Sociology and Ethnic Conflicts," *Symbolic Interaction* 27 (2004): 452.

15. Maines, "Narrative's Moment," 19.

16. Ibid., 19–20.

17. Ibid., 17–19; cf. *Faultline*, 163–65.

18. Crump, "Introduction," in Crump, *Imaginary Conversations*, 1:xxvi; Proudfit, "Introduction," in Proudfit, *Selected Imaginary Conversations*, xvii.

19. Crump, "Introduction," in Crump, *Imaginary Conversations*," 1:xxvii, xxvi.

20. Crump, ed., *Imaginary Conversations*, 4:352n1.

21. Ibid., 3:9n1.

22. Proudfit, *Selected Imaginary Conversations*, 85n.

23. Prasher, "Critical Edition," 683–85.

24. Proudfit, "Introduction," xx.

25. Prasher, "Critical Edition," 4.

26. Ibid., 71–74, 107.

27. Ibid., 762.

28. Proudfit, "Introduction,"*Selected Imaginary Conversations*, xx, xix–xx, xvii.

29. George J. Becker precedes Proudfit in foregrounding biographical connections between Landor and his characters ("Landor's Political Purpose," *Studies in Philology* 35 [1938]: 446–55). Becker's argument, that the speakers are "mouthpieces" for Landor's own political statements (454), uses an expressive criterion to make the *Conversations* an object for study, but this approach is problematic for several reasons. It does not make the *Conversations* amenable to study in the modern literary field because it defines them, at best, as a form of the personal essay and thereby leaves them in the gray area of nonfiction prose. Even if the approach were more effective, it would succeed only by discounting a good deal of the works: monarchical characters do not speak for Landor, and sometimes characters whose separate statements echo those Landor made elsewhere contradict each other in their discussions. Finally, the approach must assume that Landor's prefatory note to the *Conversations*, directing readers "to avoid a mistake in attributing to the writer any opinions in this book but what are spoke under his own name" (*Works*, 1:1), is simply disingenuous.

30. Robert Morrison, "Essayists of the Romantic Period," in O'Neill, *Literature of the Romantic Period*, 341.

31. As I noted in chapter 6 (note 29), Chandler remarks but does not elaborate on Landor's work as significant because it foregrounds conversation (*England in 1819*, 282n13).

32. Deegan, *Jane Addams and the Men*, 1–3, 191–233; Lengermann and Niebrugge-Brantley, *Women Founders*, 1–21.

33. Mellor, *Mothers of the Nation*, 2–3, 6–7.

34. Burroughs, *Closet Stages*, 14.

35. The notion of "minority" introduces a subplot in the disciplinary story. Romanticists have long discriminated among "major" and "minor" writers, considering the latter as inferior to the former yet superior to writers on the edge or outside of the canon. Bracketing the newly prominent category of the "marginal" as different from the "minor," Margaret Russett, in a study of De Quincey's status, argues that "majority and minority are mutually constitutive categories" (*De Quincey's Romanticism: Canonical Minority and the Forms of Transmission* [Cambridge: Cambridge University Press, 1997], 3–4).

36. Addams, *Twenty Years*, 43.

37. For fuller comments on this matter, see above, chapter 1, note 9.

38. Frederick Burwick, *Thomas De Quincey: Knowledge and Power* (New York: Palgrave, 2001), 90.

39. Ibid., 89.

40. De Quincey may have written some of his works, especially those on the "fine art" of murder, to explore, challenge, or mock Kantian distinctions between the aesthetic and the empirical (see Josephine McDonagh, *De Quincey's Disciplines* [Oxford: Oxford University Press, 1994], 121–51; Burwick, *De Quincey*, 67–87). As I stated in the introduction, it is just this problem of the supposed exclusivity of aesthetic experience that is now being confronted in the scholarship of Haney, Hamilton, Burwick, and Denzin and that I have treated throughout this study as a tenacious but mistaken distinction between lived and literary experience.

41. Quoted in Burwick, *De Quincey*, 89.

42. Burwick, *De Quincey*, 90.

43. Though Burwick treats the mail-coach narrative, he connects it with De Quincey's interest in ekphrasis (*De Quincey*, 112–41); he does not develop an argument about its use of involutes. Burwick's examples of De Quincey's involutes center on his Shakespeare criticism and his use of one set of text-based experiences—his reading of the *Arabian Nights* and of newspaper accounts of murders—to interpret another—the knocking on the gate in *Macbeth* (88–111).

The revised version of the *Mail-Coach* was probably the one most readily available to Addams. Checking the revised version in David Masson's edition (*The Collected Writings of Thomas De Quincey* [New York: AMS Press, 1968], 13:270–330) against the now pre-ferred original version in Grevel Lindop's volume (*Confessions of an English Opium-Eater and Other Writings* [Oxford: Oxford University Press, 1998], 183–233), I have found that the passages relevant to Addams remain unchanged except for one phrase. To come as close as possible to the standard reading experience in Addams's time, I cite the revised text from Masson throughout. I address the changed phrase in note 59 below.

44. Here and throughout, I make liberal use of the elements of narrative defined by Maines (especially in "Narrative's Moment" and in "The Storied Nature of Health and Diabetic Self-Help Groups," *Advances in Medical Sociology* 2 [1991]: 185–202), i.e., narra-tive exhibits a selection of events from the past and an emplotment of those events in time and in ways that imply causality and convey a point.

45. De Quincey, *Writings*, 13:306, 313.

46. Ibid., 13:313.

47. Ibid., 13:314.

48. Mead, *Mind, Self, and Society*, 152–60; David Novitz, "Art, Narrative, and Human Nature," in *Memory, Identity, Community: The Idea of Narrative in the Human Sciences*, ed. Lewis P. Hinchman and Sandra K. Hinchman, 143–60 (Albany: State University of New York Press, 1997).

49. Frederick W. Shilstone, "Autobiography as 'Involute': De Quincey on the Thera-pies of Memory," *South Atlantic Review* 48 (1983): 20–34.

50. Burwick, *De Quincey*, 89.

51. Maines, "Narrative's Moment," 21.

52. Ibid., 19.

53. McDonagh, *De Quincey's Disciplines*.

54. De Quincey, *Confessions*, ed. Lindop, 6–7, 24, 56–57.

55. Maines, "Storied Nature," 198–99; "Narrative's Moment," 25–29.

56. The use of this cultural narrative for De Quincey is not far from the use of a "her-itage narrative" for members of a rural Pennsylvania community threatened by develop-ment. As Maines and coauthor Jeffrey C. Bridger explain in their analysis of the latter use, emplotments of selected episodes from the community's past helped residents con-struct a rural, developer-resistant identity for the community in its present ("Narratives, Community and Land Use Decisions," *Social Science Journal* 29 [1992]: 363–80).

57. Maines emphasizes that stories have a "point": they are purposeful plottings ("Narrative's Moment," 21). This view of De Quincey as preoccupied with forming his identity has been developed at length by Russett, *De Quincey's Romanticism*; cf. Burwick, *De Quincey*, 34–42.

58. De Quincey, *Writings*, 13:314–17. The mail-coach is often taken as a vehicle for De Quincey's commentary on government policies (Russett, *De Quincey's Romanticism*, 74–76; Burwick, *De Quincey*, 132–35). In a political reading, De Quincey's plotting of ac-

cident mitigation into the story may have helped him manage anxieties about the imperiousness of the Tory party he supported.

59. Adams's omission of the opium is surprising since De Quincey's claims for the mind-altering effects of the drug had so fascinated her when she read his *Confessions of an English Opium-Eater* during her school days that she and some classmates once tried to replicate them (*Twenty Years*, 28–29). Moreover, the revised version of the mail-coach narrative (which, as I indicated above, is the version Addams's most likely read) calls more attention to De Quincey's opium habit than did the original. Though both versions coincide in reporting the taking of laudanum at the start of the journey, the revised version contains a subsequent reference to "my frail opium-shattered self" (*Writings*, 13:313); the original version refers only to "my single self" (in *Confessions*, ed. Lindop, 221).

60. Maines, *Faultline*, 163–64.

61. Addams, *Twenty Years*, 2.

62. My sense of Addams's story being mastered by a concept from a culturally dominant narrative extends from Francesca Polletta's analysis of protest narratives being infiltrated by concepts dominant in the culture that the protesters want to change ("Contending Stories: Narrative in Social Movements," *Qualitative Sociology* 21 [1998]: 424–25).

63. Ezzy, "Narrative Identity," 247–48; Novitz, "Art, Narrative, and Human Nature," 154.

64. Lengermann and Niebrugge-Brantley, *Women Founders*; Deegan, *Jane Addams and the Men*; Ross, "Gendered Social Knowledge."

65. Elshtain, *Dream of American Democracy*, 31–32; Joslin, *Writer's Life*, 172.

66. Jackson, *Lines of Activity*; Hewitt, "Joanna Baillie at Hull-House."

67. Addams, "A Modern Lear," in *The Jane Addams Reader*, ed. Jean Bethke Elshtain, 163–76 (New York: Basic Books, 2001).

68. Addams, *Memory*, 43.

69. Ibid., 4.

Bibliography

Aboulafia, Mitchell. "Was George Herbert Mead a Feminist?" *Hypatia* 8 (1993): 145–58.

Addams, Jane. *Democracy and Social Ethics*. Edited with an introduction by Charlene Haddock Siegfried. 1902. Reprint, Urbana: University of Illinois Press, 2002.

———. *The Long Road of Woman's Memory*. Edited with an introduction by Charlene Haddock Siegfried. 1916. Reprint, Urbana: University of Illinois Press, 2002.

———. "A Modern Lear." In *The Jane Addams Reader*, edited by Jean Bethke Elshtain, 163–76. 1912. Reprint, New York: Basic Books, 2001.

———. *Peace and Bread in Time of War*. New York: Macmillan, 1922.

———. *The Second Twenty Years at Hull-House*. New York: Macmillan, 1930.

———. *Twenty Years at Hull-House*. Edited with an introduction by James Hurt. 1910. Reprint, Urbana: University of Illinois Press, 1959.

Anderson, Amanda, and Joseph Valente. "Introduction. Discipline and Freedom." In Anderson and Valente, *Disciplinarity*, 1–15.

———, eds. *Disciplinarity at the Fin de Siècle*. Princeton: Princeton University Press, 2002.

Armstrong, Isobel. *The Radical Aesthetic*. Oxford: Blackwell, 2000.

Austin, Carolyn F. "Home and Nation in *The Heart of Midlothian*." *SEL, 1500–1900* 40 (2000): 621–34.

Averill, James. *Wordsworth and the Poetry of Human Suffering*. Ithaca: Cornell University Press, 1980.

Baillie, Joanna. *The Collected Letters of Joanna Baillie*. Edited by Judith Bailey Slagle. 2 vols. Madison, NJ: Fairleigh Dickinson University Press, 1999.

———. *The Dramatic and Poetical Works*. 1851. Reprint, Hildesheim, Germany: Georg Olms, 1976.

———. *A Series of Plays*. Edited by Donald Reiman. 3 vols. 1798, 1802, 1812. Reprint, New York: Garland, 1977.

———. *Miscellaneous Plays*. Edited by Donald Reiman. New York: Garland [1804], 1977.

Bainbridge, Simon. *Napoleon and English Romanticism*. Cambridge: Cambridge University Press, 1995.

Barker-Benfield, J. G. *The Culture of Sensibility: Sex and Society in Eighteenth-Century Britain*. Chicago: University of Chicago Press, 1992.

Barrell, John. *Imagining the King's Death: Figurative Treason, Fantasies of Regicide, 1793–1796*. Oxford: Oxford University Press, 2000.

Becker, George J. "Landor's Political Purpose." *Studies in Philology* 35 (1938): 446–55.

Beiderwell, Bruce. *Power and Punishment in Scott's Novels*. Athens: University of Georgia Press, 1992.

———, ed. *Romantic Enlightenment: Sir Walter Scott and the Politics of History*. Special issue, *European Romantic Review* 13, no. 3 (2002): 223–346.

Benedict, Barbara M. *Curiosity: A Cultural History of Early Modern Inquiry*. Chicago: University of Chicago Press, 2001.

Benis, Toby R. *Romanticism on the Road: The Marginal Gains of Wordsworth's Homeless*. New York: St. Martin's Press, 2000.

Bennett, Susan. "Genre Trouble: Joanna Baillie, Elizabeth Polack—Tragic Subjects, Melodramatic Subjects." In Davis and Donkin, *Women and Playwrighting*, 215–32.

Bicknell, Titus. "*Calamus Ense Potentior Est*: Walter Savage Landor's Poetic War of Words." *Romanticism on the Net* 4 (November 1996), http://users.ox.ac.uk/~scat0385/landor.html.

Blasi, Anthony J. "George Herbert Mead's Transformation of His Intellectual Context." In *The Tradition of Chicago Sociology*, edited by Luigi Tomasi, 149–78. Brookfield, VT: Ashgate, 1998.

Blumer, Herbert. *Symbolic Interactionism: Perspective and Method*. 1969. Reprint, Berkeley: University of California Press, 1998.

Boehnen, Scott. "The Preface to *Lyrical Ballads*: Poetics, Poor Laws, and the Bold Experiments of 1797–1802." *Nineteenth-Century Contexts* 20 (1997): 287–311.

Boswell, James. *Life of Johnson*. Edited by R. W. Chapman. Introduction by Pat Rogers.1791. Reprint, Oxford: Oxford University Press, 1980.

Boulton, Jeremy. "Going on the Parish: The Parish Pension and Its Meaning in the London Suburbs, 1640–1724." In Hitchcock, King, and Sharpe, *Chronicling Poverty*, 19–46.

Brewer, William D. "Mary Shelley's *Valperga*: The Triumph of Euthanasia's Mind." *European Romantic Review* 5 (1995): 133–48.

Bridger, Jeffrey C., and David R. Maines. "Narrative Structures and the Catholic Church Closings in Detroit." *Qualitative Sociology* 21 (1998): 319–40.

Brown, Victoria Bissell. *The Education of Jane Addams*. Philadelphia: University of Pennsylvania Press, 2004.

Brundage, Anthony. *The English Poor Laws, 1700–1930*. New York: Palgrave, 2002.

Bugajski, Ken A. "Joanna Baillie: An Annotated Bibliography." In Crochunis, *Joanna Baillie*, 241–312.

Burke, Jr., John J. "Crime and Punishment in 1777: The Execution of the Reverend Dr. William Dodd and Its Impact upon His Contemporaries." In *Executions and the British Experience from the 17th to the 20th Century: A Collection of Essays*, edited by William B. Thesing, 59–75. Jefferson, NC: McFarland & Co., 1990.

Burns, J. H., and Mark Goldie, eds. *The Cambridge History of Political Thought, 1450–1700*. Cambridge: Cambridge University Press, 1991.

Burroughs, Catherine B. *Closet Stages: Joanna Baillie and the Theater Theory of British Romantic Women Writers*. Philadelphia: University of Pennsylvania Press, 1997.

———. "'Out of the Pale of Social Kindred Cast': Conflicted Performance Styles in Joanna Baillie's *De Monfort*." In *Romantic Women Writers: Voices and Countervoices*, edited by Paula R. Feldman and Theresa M. Kelley, 223–35. Hanover, NH: University Press of New England, 1995.

———, ed. "Producing Joanna Baillie." *European Romantic Review* 15 (2004): 351–86.

Burwick, Frederick. "Competing Histories in the Waverley Novels." *European Romantic Review* 13 (2002): 261–71.

———. "Joanna Baillie, Matthew Baillie, and the Pathology of the Passions." In Crochunis, *Joanna Baillie*. 48–68.

———. *Mimesis and Its Romantic Reflections*. University Park: Pennsylvania State University Press, 2001.

———. *Thomas De Quincey: Knowledge and Power*. New York: Palgrave, 2001.

Butler, Marilyn. "Repossessing the Past: the Case for an Open Literary History." In *Rethinking Historicism: Critical Readings in Romantic History*, edited by Marjorie Levinson et al., 64–84. Oxford: Blackwell, 1989.

Byron, Lord. *Byron's Letters and Journals*. Edited by Leslie Marchand. 12 vols. Cambridge: Harvard University Press, 1973–82.

———. *Lord Byron: The Complete Poetical Works*. Edited by Jerome J. McGann. 8 vols. Oxford: Clarendon Press, 1980–92.

Cage, R. A. *The Scottish Poor Law, 1745–1845*. Edinburgh: Scottish Academic Press, 1981.

Carlson, Julie. "Baillie's *Orra*: Shrinking in Fear." In Crochunis, *Joanna Baillie*, 206–20.

———. "Remaking Love: Remorse in the Theatre of Baillie and Inchbald." In *Women in British Romantic Theatre: Drama, Performance and Society, 1790–1840*, edited by Catherine Burroughs, 285–310. Cambridge: Cambridge University Press, 2000.

Carson, Mina. *Settlement Folk: Social Thought and the American Settlement Movement, 1885–1930*. Chicago: University of Chicago Press, 1990.

Chandler, James. *England in 1819: The Politics of Literary Culture and the Case of Romantic Historicism*. Chicago: University of Chicago Press, 1998.

Christensen, Jerome. *Romanticism at the End of History*. Baltimore: Johns Hopkins University Press, 2000.

Clark, Candace. *Misery and Company: Sympathy in Everyday Life*. Chicago: University of Chicago Press, 1997.

Code, Lorraine. "Rational Imaginings, Responsible Knowings: How Far Can You See From Here?" In *Engendering Rationalities*, edited by Nancy Tuana and Sandra Morgen, 261–82. Albany: State University of New York Press, 2001.

Collins, Randall. "Situational Stratification: A Micro-Macro Theory of Inequality." *Sociological Theory* 18 (2000): 17–43.

Comitini, Patricia. "'More Than Half a Poet': Vocational Philanthropy and Dorothy Wordsworth's *Grasmere Journals*." *European Romantic Review* 14 (2003): 307–22.

Connell, Philip. *Romanticism, Economics and the Question of "Culture."* Oxford: Oxford University Press, 2001.

Cox, Jeffrey. "Staging Baillie." In Crochunis, *Joanna Baillie*, 146–67.

Crochunis, Thomas C. "Joanna Baillie's Ambivalent Dramaturgy." In Crochunis, *Joanna Baillie*, 168–86.

———, ed. *Joanna Baillie: Romantic Dramatist*. London: Routledge, 2004.

Cronin, Richard. *The Politics of Romantic Poetry: In Search of the Pure Commonwealth*. New York: St. Martin's Press, 2000.

Crump, Charles G. "Introduction." In Crump, *Imaginary Conversations*, ix–xxvii.

———, ed. *Imaginary Conversations of Walter Savage Landor with Bibliographical and Explanatory Notes by Charles G. Crump*. 6 vols. London: J. M. Dent, 1891.

D'Arcy, Julian Meldon. "Roseneath: Scotland or 'Scott-land'? A Reappraisal of *The Heart of Midlothian*." *Studies in Scottish Literature* 32 (2001): 26–36.

Davis, Joseph E. "Narrative and Social Movements: The Power of Stories." In *Stories of Change: Narrative and Social Movements*, edited by Joseph E. Davis, 3–29. Albany: State University of New York Press, 2002.

Davis, Tracy, and Ellen Donkin, eds. *Women and Playwrighting in Nineteenth-Century Britain*. Cambridge: Cambridge University Press, 1999.

Deegan, Mary Jo. *Jane Addams and the Men of the Chicago School, 1892–1918*. New Brunswick, NJ: Transaction Press, 1988.

Denzin, Norman K. "The Call to Performance." *Symbolic Interaction* 28 (2003): 187–207.

———. *Interpretive Ethnography: Ethnographic Practices for the 21st Century*. Thousand Oaks, CA: Sage, 1997.

———. *Interpretive Interactionism*. 2nd ed. Thousand Oaks, CA: Sage, 2001.

———. "Social Work in the Seventh Moment." *Qualitative Social Work* 1 (2002): 25–38.

———. *Symbolic Interactionism and Cultural Studies: The Politics of Interpretation*. Oxford: Blackwell, 1992.

———, ed. *The Research Act: A Theoretical Introduction to Sociological Methods*. 3rd ed. Englewood Cliffs, NJ: Prentice Hall, 1989.

De Quincey, Thomas. *Confessions of an English Opium-Eater and Other Writings*. Edited by Grevel Lindop. 1821, 1849. Reprint, Oxford: Oxford University Press, 1998.

———. *The English Mail-Coach*. In *The Collected Writings of Thomas De Quincey*, 1854. Reprint, edited by David Masson. New York: AMS Press, 1968. 13:270–330.

Deutscher, Irwin. "Little Theories and Big Problems: Chicago Sociology and Ethnic Conflicts." *Symbolic Interaction* 27 (2004): 441–59.

Dobson, Jessie. "John Hunter and the Unfortunate Doctor Dodd." *Journal of the History of Medicine and Allied Sciences* 10 (1955): 369–78.

Donkin, Ellen. *Getting Into the Act: Women Playwrights in London, 1776–1829*. London: Routledge, 1995.

Dowd, Maureen A. "'By the Delicate Hand of a Female': Melodramatic Mania and Joanna Baillie's Spectacular Tragedies." *European Romantic Review* 9 (1998): 469–500.

Duff, Peter, and Neill Hutton. "Introduction." In Duff and Hutton, *Criminal Justice*, 1–6.

———, eds. *Criminal Justice in Scottland*. Burlington, VT: Ashgate, 1999.

Duncan, Ian, Ann Rowland, and Charles Snodgrass, eds. *Scott, Scotland, and Romantic Nationalism*. Special issue, *Studies in Romanticism* 40, no. 1 (2001): 1–152.

Duthie, Peter. "Introduction." In *Plays on the Passions*, by Joanna Baillie, edited by Peter Duthie, 11–57. Peterborough, ON: Broadview Press, 2001.

Dwyer, Karen. "Joanna Baillie's *Plays on the Passions* and the Spectacle of Medical Science." *Studies in Eighteenth-Century Culture* 29 (2000): 23–46.

Elshtain, Jean Bethke. *Jane Addams and the Dream of American Democracy*. New York: Basic Books, 2001.

Ezzy, Douglas. "Theorizing Narrative Identity: Symbolic Interactionism and Hermeneutics." *Sociological Quarterly* 39 (1998): 239–52.

Farmer, Lindsay. *Criminal Law, Tradition and Legal Order: Crime and the Genius of Scots Law, 1747 to the Present*. Cambridge: Cambridge University Press, 1997.

Feagin, Joe R., and Hernán Vera. *Liberation Sociology*. Boulder, CO: Westview Press, 2001.

Ferris, Ina. *The Achievement of Literary Authority: Gender, History, and the Waverley Novels*. Ithaca: Cornell University Press, 1991.

———. "Pedantry and the Question of Enlightenment History: The Figure of the Antiquary in Scott." *European Romantic Review* 13 (2002): 273–83.

Fine, Gary Alan. "The Sad Demise, Mysterious Disappearance, and Glorious Triumph of Symbolic Interactionism." *Annual Review of Sociology* 19 (1993): 61–87.

Finn, Margot C. *The Character of Credit: Personal Debt in English Culture, 1740–1914*. Cambridge: Cambridge University Press, 2003.

Fontana, Andrea. "Norm Denzin and the Windmills of Morality." *Symbolic Interaction* 28 (2003): 209–16.

Forbes, Aileen. "'Sympathetic Curiosity' in Joanna Baillie's Theater of the Passions." *European Romantic Review* 14 (2003): 31–48.

Foucault, Michel. *Discipline and Punish: The Birth of the Prison*. Translated by Alan Sheridan. New York: Random House-Vintage, 1979.

Franklin, Carolyn. "Introduction." In *Illustrations of Political Economy, Taxation, Poor Laws and Paupers*, by Harriet Martineau. Edited by Carolyn Franklin. 13 vols. 1832–34. Reprint, Bristol: Thoemmes, 2001.

Friedman-Romell, Beth H. "Staging the State: Joanna Baillie's 'Constantine Paleologus.'" In Davis and Donkin, *Women and Playwrighting*, 151–73.

Gallagher, Kathleen. *Drama Education in the Lives of Girls: Imagining Possibilities*. Toronto: University of Toronto Press, 2000.

Galperin, William H. *Revision and Authority in Wordsworth: The Interpretation of a Career*. Philadelphia: University of Pennsylvania Press, 1989.

Galsworthy, John. *Plays. Second Series: The Eldest Son. The Little Dream. Justice*. New York: Scribner's, 1913.

Gamer, Michael. *Romanticism and the Gothic: Genre, Reception, and Canon Formation*. Cambridge: Cambridge University Press, 2000.

Gatrell, V. A. C. *The Hanging Tree: Execution and the English People, 1770–1868*. Oxford: Oxford University Press, 1994.

Gilligan, Carol. *In a Different Voice: Psychological Theory and Women's Development*. Cambridge: Harvard University Press, 1982.

Goodlad, Lauren M. E. "Character and Pastorship in Two British 'Sociological' Traditions: Organized Charity, Fabian Socialism, and the Invention of New Liberalism." In Anderson and Valente, *Disciplinarity*, 235–60.

Goodwin, Jeff, James M. Jasper, and Francesca Polletta. "Introduction." In *Passionate Politics: Emotions and Social Movements*, edited by Jeff Goodwin, James M. Jasper, and Francesca Polletta, 1–23. Chicago: University of Chicago Press, 2001.

Gottlieb, Evan. "'To Be at Once Another and the Same': Walter Scott and the End(s) of Sympathetic Britishness." *Studies in Romanticism* 43 (2004): 189–207.

Guillory, John. "Literary Study and the Modern System of the Disciplines." In Anderson and Valente, *Disciplinarity*, 19–43.

Gusfield, Joseph R. "A Journey with Symbolic Interaction." *Symbolic Interaction* 28 (2003): 119–39.

Hadley, Elaine. *Melodramatic Tactics: Theatricalized Dissent in the English Marketplace, 1800–1885*. Stanford: Stanford University Press, 1995.

Hamilton, Paul. *Metaromanticism: Aesthetics, Literature, Theory*. Chicago: University of Chicago Press, 2003.

Haney, David P. *The Challenge of Coleridge: Ethics and Interpretation in Romanticism and Modern Philosophy*. University Park: Pennsylvania State University Press, 2001.

Hanley, Keith. "Introduction." In *Selected Poetry and Prose of Walter Savage Landor*, edited by Keith Hanley, xiii–xxxii. New York: Persea, 1981.

Harris, Colin. "The Place of the Page: Dramatic Discontinuity in Joanna Baillie's *The Homicide*." Paper presented at the conference of the North American Society for the Study of Romanticism. New York, August 1–5, 2003.

Henderson, Andrea. "Passion and Fashion in Joanna Baillie's 'Introductory Discourse.'" *PMLA* 112 (1997): 198–213.

Hewitt, David. "General Introduction." In *The Antiquary* by Walter Scott, edited by David Hewitt, xiii–xvii. Edinburgh: Edinburgh University Press, 1995.

— — —. "*The Heart of Midlothian* and 'the People.'" *European Romantic Review* 13 (2002): 299–309.

Hewitt, Regina. "Joanna Baillie at Hull-House: A Working Hypothesis for Disciplinary Reform." *Studies in Symbolic Interaction* 27 (2004): 113–49.

— — —. "On Reconciling Past and Future: Some Effects of Landor's *Imaginary Conversations*." *Studies in Symbolic Interaction* 24 (2001): 273–97.

— — —. *The Possibilities of Society: Wordsworth, Coleridge, and the Sociological Viewpoint of English Romanticism*. Albany: State University of New York Press, 1997.

— — —. Review of *The Challenge of Coleridge*, by David P. Haney. *ANQ* 15 (2002): 41–44.

Himmelfarb, Gertrude. *Poverty and Compassion: The Moral Imagination of the Late Victorians*. New York: Knopf, 1991.

Hitchcock, Tim, Peter King, and Pamela Sharpe. "Introduction." In Hitchcock et al. *Chronicling Poverty*, 1–18.

— — —, eds. *Chronicling Poverty: The Voices and Strategies of the English Poor, 1640–1840*. New York: St. Martin's Press, 1997.

Hoagwood, Terence Allan. "Elizabeth Inchbald, Joanna Baillie, and Revolutionary Representation during the 'Romantic' Period." In *Rebellious Hearts: British Women Writers and the French Revolution*, edited by Adriana Craciun and Kari E. Lokke, 293–316. Albany: State University of New York Press, 2001.

Hoecker-Drysdale, Susan. "Harriet Martineau." In Ritzer, *Blackwell Companion*, 53–80.

———. *Harriet Martineau: First Woman Sociologist*. Providence, RI: Berg, 1992.

Holquist, Michael. "Why We Should Remember Philology." *Profession*, 2002, 72–79.

Hörcher, Ferenc. "Beccaria, Voltaire, and the Scots on Capital Punishment: A Comparative View of the Legal Enlightenment." In *Scotland and France in the Enlightenment*, edited by Deidrew Dawson and Pierre Morère, 305–30. Lewisburg, PA: Bucknell University Press, 2004.

Howell, Roger. "Cromwell, the English Revolution and Political Symbolism in Eighteenth- Century England"; "'That Imp of Satan': The Restoration Image of Cromwell"; "'Who Needs Another Cromwell?' The Nineteenth-Century Image of Oliver Cromwell." In *Images of Oliver Cromwell: Essays for and by Roger Howell, Jr.*, edited by R. C. Richardson, 33–47; 63–73; 96–107. Manchester: Manchester University Press, 1993.

Hume, Baron David. *Commentaries on the Law of Scotland, Respecting Crimes*. 2 vols. Supplement by Benjamin Robert Bell. 1797, 1844. Reprint, Edinburgh: Law Society of Scotland, 1986.

Incorvati, Richard. "Sympathy and the Social Order: The Politics of Emotional Relationships from Hume to Wordsworth." PhD diss., University of North Carolina at Chapel Hill, 2001.

Jackson, Shannon. *Lines of Activity: Performance, Historiography, Hull-House Domesticity*. Ann Arbor: University of Michigan Press, 2000.

Joas, Hans. *G. H. Mead: A Contemporary Re-examination of His Thought*. Translated by Raymond Meyer. Cambridge: MIT Press, 1997.

Johnson, Samuel. *The Rambler*. Edited by W. J. Bate and Albrecht B. Strauss. Vols. 3–5 of *The Yale Edition of the Works of Samuel Johnson*, edited by John H. Middendorf. New Haven: Yale University Press, 1958–).

Jones, Catherine. *Literary Memory: Scott's Waverley Novels and the Psychology of Narrative*. Lewisburg, PA: Bucknell University Press, 2003.

Joslin, Katherine. *Jane Addams, a Writer's Life*. Urbana: University of Illinois Press, 2004.

Kerr, James. *Fiction Against History: Scott as Storyteller*. Cambridge: Cambridge University Press, 1989.

King, Peter. *Crime, Justice and Discretion in England, 1740–1820*. Oxford: Oxford University Press, 2000.

Kotarba, Joseph A., and John M. Johnson. "Introduction: Postmodern Existentialism." In *Postmodern Existential Sociology*, edited by Joseph A. Kotarba and John M. Johnson, 3–14. Walnut Creek, CA: AltaMira Press, 2002.

Kucich, Greg. "Joanna Baillie and the Re-staging of History and Gender." In Crochunis, *Joanna Baillie*, 108–29.

Lachmann, Richard. *Capitalists in Spite of Themselves: Elite Conflict and Economic Transitions in Early Modern Europe*. Oxford: Oxford University Press, 2002.

Lamont, Clare. "Introduction." In *The Heart of Midlothian*, by Walter Scott, edited by Clare Lamont. Oxford: Oxford University Press, 1999.

Landor, Walter Savage. *Works of Walter Savage Landor*. 2 vols. 1846. Reprint, London: Chapman and Hall, 1868.

———. *Complete Works of Walter Savage Landor*. Edited by E. Welby and S. Wheeler. 16 vols. London: Chapman and Hall, 1927–36.

Lengermann, Patricia Madoo, and Jill Niebrugge-Brantley. *The Women Founders: Sociology and Social Theory, 1830–1930*. Boston: McGraw-Hill, 1998.

Lieberman, David. *The Province of Legislation Determined: Legal Theory in Eighteenth- Century Britain*. Cambridge: Cambridge University Press, 1989.

Lincoln, Andrew. "Conciliation, Resistance, and the Unspeakable in *The Heart of Midlothian*." *Philological Quarterly* 79 (2000): 69–90.

Ludlow, Gregory. "Imagining the Future: Mercier's *L'An 2440* and Morris' *News from Nowhere*." *Comparative Literature Studies* 29 (1992): 20–38.

Lyman, Stanford M. *Civilization: Contents, Discontents, Malcontents, and Other Essays in Social Theory*. Fayetteville: University of Arkansas Press, 1990.

———. *Postmodernism and a Sociology of the Absurd: And Other Essays on the "Nouvelle Vague" in American Social Science*. Fayetteville: University of Arkansas Press, 1997.

Maines, David R. *The Faultline of Consciousness: A View of Interactionism in Sociology*. New York: Aldine de Gruyter, 2001.

———. "Narrative's Moment and Sociology's Phenomena: Toward a Narrative Sociology." *Sociological Quarterly* 34 (1993): 17–38.

———. "The Storied Nature of Health and Diabetic Self-Help Groups." *Advances in Medical Sociology* 2 (1991): 185–202.

Maines, David R., and Jeffrey C. Bridger. "Narratives, Community and Land Use Decisions." *Social Science Journal* 29 (1992): 363–80.

Maines, David, Noreen M. Sugrue, and Michael A. Katovich. "The Sociological Import of G. H. Mead's Theory of the Past." *American Sociological Review* 48 (1983): 161–73.

Malley, Shawn. "Walter Scott's Romantic Archaeology: New/Old Abbotsford and *The Antiquary*." *Studies in Romanticism* 40 (2001): 233–51.

Mansbridge, Jane. "The Making of Oppositional Consciousness." In *Oppositional Consciousness: The Subjective Roots of Social Protest*, edited by Jane Mansbridge and Aldon Morris, 1–19. Chicago: University of Chicago Press, 2001.

Martineau, Harriet. *A History of the Thirty Years' Peace*. 4 vols. 1849–50. Reprint, Shannon: Irish University Press, 1971.

———. *Illustrations of Political Economy, Taxation, Poor Laws and Paupers*. Edited by Carolyn Franklin. 13 vols. 1832–34. Reprint, Bristol: Thoemmes, 2001.

Maxwell, Richard. "Inundations of Time: A Definition of Scott's Originality." *ELH* 68 (2001): 419–68.

Mayer, Robert. "The Illogical Status of Novelistic Discourse: Scott's Footnotes for the Waverley Novels." *ELH* 66 (1999): 911–38.

McDonagh, Josephine. *De Quincey's Disciplines*. Oxford: Oxford University Press, 1994.

McGann, Jerome J. *The Romantic Ideology: A Critical Investigation*. Chicago: University of Chicago Press, 1983.

McGowan, Randall. "From Pillory to Gallows: The Punishment of Forgery in the Age of the Financial Revolution." *Past and Present* 165 (1999): 107–40.

McKenna, Erin. "The Need for a Pragmatist Feminist Self." In *Feminist Interpretations of John Dewey*, edited by Charlene Haddock Siegfried, 133–59. University Park: Pennsylvania State University Press, 2002.

McLane, Maureen. *Romanticism and the Human Sciences: Poetry, Population, and the Discourse of the Species*. Cambridge: Cambridge University Press, 2000.

McMillan, Dorothy. "'Dr.' Baillie." In *1798: The Year of the* Lyrical Ballads, edited by Richard Cronin, 68–92. New York: St. Martin's Press, 1998.

———. "Unromantic Caledon: Representing Scotland in *The Family Legend*, *Metrical Legends*, and *Witchcraft*." In Crochunis, *Joanna Baillie*. 69–86.

Meacham, Standish. *Toynbee Hall and Social Reform, 1880–1914: The Search for Community*. New Haven: Yale University Press, 1987.

Mead, George Herbert. "The Genesis of the Self and Social Control." (1924–25). In Reck, *Selected Writings*, 267–93.

———. "History and the Experimental Method." In *George Herbert Mead on Social Psychology*, edited by Anselm Strauss, 319–27. 1938. Reprint, Chicago: University of Chicago Press, 1977.

———. *Mind, Self, and Society from the Standpoint of a Social Behaviorist*. Edited with an introduction by Charles W. Morris. Chicago: University of Chicago Press, 1934.

———. "The Nature of the Past." (1929). In Reck, *Selected Writings*, 345–54.

———. "1914 Lectures in Social Psychology." In *The Individual and the Social Self: Unpublished Work of George Herbert Mead*, edited with an introduction by David L. Miller. Chicago: University of Chicago Press, 1982.

———. "Philanthropy from the Point of View of Ethics." (1930). In Reck, *Selected Writings*, 392–407.

———. *The Philosophy of the Act*. Edited with an introduction by Charles W. Morris et al. Chicago: University of Chicago Press, 1938.

———. *The Philosophy of the Present*. Edited by A. E. Murphy. Preface by John Dewey. 1932. Reprint, Chicago: University of Chicago Press. 1980.

———. "The Psychology of Punitive Justice." (1917–18). In Reck, *Selected Writings*, 212–39.

———. "Scientific Method and the Moral Sciences." (1923). In Reck, *Selected Writings*, 248–66.

———. "The Social Self." (1913). In Reck, *Selected Writings*, 142–49.

———. "The Working Hypothesis in Social Reform." (1899). In Reck, *Selected Writings*, 3–5.

Mellor, Anne K. "Joanna Baillie and the Counter-Public Sphere." *Studies in Romanticism* 33 (1994): 559–67.

———. *Mothers of the Nation: Women's Political Writing in England, 1780–1830*. Bloomington: University of Indiana Press, 2000.

Melrose, Andrew. "Writing 'The End of Uncertainty': Imaginary Law, Imaginary Jacobites and Imaginary History in Walter Scott's *Heart of Midlothian* and *Redgauntlet*." *Scottish Literary Journal* 25 (1998): 34–44.

Millgate, Jane. "Scott and the Law: *The Heart of Midlothian*." In *Rough Justice: Essays on Crime in Literature*, edited by Martin L. Friedland, 95–113. Toronto: University of Toronto Press, 1991.

Mitchison, Rosalind. *The Old Poor Law in Scotland: The Experience of Poverty, 1574–1845*. Edinburgh: Edinburgh University Press, 2000.

Moore, Michael J. "Social Work and Social Welfare: The Organization of Philanthropic Resources in Britain, 1900–1914." *Journal of British Studies* 16 (1977): 85–104.

Morrison, Robert. "Essayists of the Romantic Period." In O'Neill, *Literature of the Romantic Period*. 341–63.

Mullan, John. *Sentiment and Sociability: The Language of Feeling in the Eighteenth Century*. Oxford: Clarendon Press, 1988.

Myers, Victoria. "Joanna Baillie: Speculations on Legal Cruelty." *The Wordsworth Circle* 35 (2004): 123–27.

———. "Joanna Baillie's Theatre of Cruelty." In Crochunis, *Joanna Baillie*, 87–107.

Nagel, Joane. "Joane Nagel Joins NSF Sociology Program." Unsigned Interview. *Footnotes: American Sociological Association Newsletter* 30, no. 8 (2002): 3.

Newlyn, Lucy. Paradise Lost *and the Romantic Reader*. Oxford: Clarendon Press, 1993.

Novitz, David. "Art, Narrative, and Human Nature." In *Memory, Identity, Community: The Idea of Narrative in the Human Sciences*, edited by Lewis P. Hinchman and Sandra K. Hinchman, 143–60. Albany: State University of New York Press, 1997.

O'Neill, Michael, ed. *Literature of the Romantic Period: A Bibliographical Guide*. Oxford: Clarendon Press, 1998.

Partner, Nancy F. "Historicity in an Age of Reality-Fiction." In *A New Philosophy of History*, edited by Frank Ankersmit and Hans Kellner, 21–39. Chicago: University of Chicago Press, 1995.

Parton, Nigel, and Patrick O'Byrne. *Constructive Social Work: Toward a New Practice*. New York: St. Martin's Press, 2000.

Paterson, Audrey. "The Poor Law in Nineteenth-Century Scotland." In *The New Poor Law in the Nineteenth Century*, edited by Derek Fraser, 171–93. London: Macmillan, 1976.

Pearson, Hesketh. *Walter Scott: His Life and Personality*. Introduction by Allan Massie. 1954. Reprint, London: Hamish Hamilton, 1987.

Phillipson, Coleman. *Three Criminal Law Reformers: Beccaria, Bentham, Romilly*. 1923. Reprint, Montclair, NJ: Patterson Smith, 1970.

Pinch, Adela. *Strange Fits of Passion: Epistemologies of Emotion, Hume to Austen*. Stanford: Stanford University Press, 1996.

Polletta, Francesca. "Contending Stories: Narrative in Social Movements." *Qualitative Sociology* 21 (1998): 419–46.

Prasher, Alice Lavonne. "Walter Savage Landor's *Imaginary Conversations*: A Critical Edition of the First Eight Conversations in Volume One. (with) *Imaginary Conversations of Literary Men and Statesmen*. The First Volume. 1824." PhD diss., Northwestern University, 1966.

Pratt, Mary Louise. "President's Column: 'The New Humanities.'" *MLA Newsletter* 35, no. 3 (2003): 3–4.

Proudfit, Charles L. "Landor's Hobbyhorse: A Study of Romantic Orthography." *Studies in Romanticism* 8 (1968): 207–17.

———. "Introduction." In Proudfit, *Selected Imaginary Conversations*.

———, ed. *Selected Imaginary Conversations of Literary Men and Statesmen, by Walter Savage Landor*. Lincoln: University of Nebraska Press, 1969.

Purinton, Marjean D. *Romantic Ideology Unmasked: The Mentally Constructed Tyrannies in Dramas of William Wordsworth, Lord Byron, Percy Shelley, and Joanna Baillie*. Newark: University of Delaware Press, 1994.

———. "The Sexual Politics of *The Election*: French Feminism and the Scottish Playwright Joanna Baillie." *Intertexts* 2 (1998): 119–30.

———. "Socialized and Medicalized Hysteria in Joanna Baillie's *Witchcraft*." *Prism(s): Essays in Romanticism* 9 (2001): 139–56.

Reck, Andrew, ed. *Selected Writings of George Herbert Mead*. Chicago: University of Chicago Press, 1964.

Richardson, Alan. "A Neural Theatre: Joanna Bailie's 'Plays on the Passions.'" In Crochunis, *Joanna Baillie*. 130–45.

Riggs, Paul Turner. "Scottish Criminal Law and Procedure in the Nineteenth Century." PhD diss., University of Pittsburgh, 1997.

Rigney, Ann. *Imperfect Histories: The Elusive Past and the Legacy of Romantic Historicism*. Ithaca: Cornell University Press, 2001.

Ritzer, George, ed. *The Blackwell Companion to Major Social Theorists*. Oxford: Blackwell, 2000.

Roberts, F. David. *The Social Conscience of the Early Victorians*. Stanford, CA: Stanford University Press, 2002.

Robertson, Fiona. *Legitimate Histories: Scott, Gothic, and the Authorities of Fiction*. Oxford: Clarendon Press, 1994.

———. "Walter Scott." In O'Neill, *Bibliographical Guide*, 221–45.

Robertson, John. "The Scottish Contribution to the Enlightenment." In Wood, *Scottish Enlightenment*. 37–62.

Ross, Dorothy. "Gendered Social Knowledge: Domestic Discourse, Jane Addams, and the Possibilities of Social Science." In *Gender and American Social Science: The Formative Years*, edited by Helene Silverberg, 235–64. Princeton: Princeton University Press, 1998.

Ruoff, A. Lavonne. "Landor's Conception of the Great Leader." *The Wordsworth Circle* 7 (1976): 38–50.

Russett, Margaret. *De Quincey's Romanticism: Canonical Minority and the Forms of Transmission*. Cambridge: Cambridge University Press, 1997.

Saglia, Diego. *Poetic Castles in Spain: British Romanticism and Figurations of Iberia*. Amsterdam: Rodopi, 2000.

Sargisson, Lucy. *Contemporary Feminist Utopianism*. London: Routledge, 1996.

— — —. *Utopian Bodies and the Politics of Transgression.* London: Routledge, 2000.

Schmunk, Robert B. *Uchronia: The Alternative History List.* 15 Dec. 2003. http://www. uchronia.com.

Scott, Walter. *The Antiquary.* Edited by Nicola J. Watson. Oxford: Oxford University Press, 2002.

— — —. *The Bride of Lammermoor.* Caledonian Edition of the Works of Sir Walter Scott. Boston: Houghton Mifflin, 1913.

— — —. *The Heart of Midlothian.* Edited by Claire Lamont. Oxford: Oxford University Press, 1999.

— — —. *The Letters of Sir Walter Scott 1787–1834.* Edited by H. J. C. Grierson. 12 vols. London: Constable, 1932–37. Reprint, New York: AMS Press, 1971.

— — —. *Redgauntlet.* Edited by Kathryn Sutherland. Oxford: Oxford University Press, 1985.

— — —. *Waverley.* Edited by Andrew Hook. London: Penguin, 1972.

— — —. *Woodstock.* Caledonian Edition of the Works of Sir Walter Scott. Boston: Houghton Mifflin, 1913.

Scullion, Adrienne. "Some Women of the Nineteenth-century Scottish Theatre: Joanna Baillie, Frances Wright and Helen MacGregor." *History of Scottish Women's Writing*, edited by Douglas Gifford and Dorothy McMillan, 158–78. Edinburgh: Edinburgh University Press, 1997.

Setzer, Sharon M. "Precedent and Perversity in Wordsworth's *Sonnets upon the Punishment of Death*." *Nineteenth-Century Literature* 50 (1996): 427–47.

Shalin, Dmitri N. "George Herbert Mead." In Ritzer, *Blackwell Companion*, 302–44.

Sharafuddin, Mohammed. *Islam and Romantic Orientalism: Literary Encounters with the Orient.* New York: St. Martin's Press, 1994.

Sharpe, Pamela. "'The bowels of compation': A Labouring Family and the Law, c. 1790–1834." In Hitchcock, King, and Sharpe, *Chronicling Poverty*, 87–108.

Shaw, George Bernard. "Preface." *Mrs. Warren's Profession. Complete Plays with Prefaces.* Vol. 3. New York: Dodd, Mead, 1962.

Shelley, Percy Bysshe. *Complete Works of Percy Bysshe Shelley.* Edited by Roger Ingpen and Walter E. Peck. 10 vols. London: Ernest Benn, 1926–30. Reprint, New York: Gordian Press, 1965.

— — —. *Shelley's Poetry and Prose.* Edited by Donald H. Reiman and Sharon B. Powers. New York: W. W. Norton, 1977.

Shilstone, Frederick W. "Autobiography as 'Involute': De Quincey on the Therapies of Memory." *South Atlantic Review* 48 (1983): 20–34.

Siegfried, Charlene Haddock. "Introduction to the Illinois Edition." In *Democracy and Social Ethics*, by Jane Addams, edited by Charlene Haddock Siegfried, ix–xxxviii. Urbana: University of Illinois Press, 2002.

— — —. "Introduction to the Illinois Edition." In *The Long Road of Woman's Memory*, by Jane Addams, edited by Charlene Haddock Siegfried, ix–xxxiv. Urbana: University of Illinois Press, 2002.

— — —. "Socializing Democracy: Jane Addams and John Dewey." *Philosophy of the Social Sciences* 29 (1999): 207–30.

Slagle, Judith Bailey. *Joanna Baillie: A Literary Life*. Madison, NJ: Fairleigh Dickinson University Press, 2002.

Smith, Marie Hockenhull. "'How Can ye Criticise What's Plain Law, Man?': The Lawyer, the Novelist, and the Discourse of Authority." In *Law and Literature: Current Legal Issues 1999*, vol. 2, edited by Michael Freeman and Andrew D. E. Lewis, 239–62. Oxford: Oxford University Press, 1999.

Snow, C. P. *The Two Cultures and a Second Look: An Expanded Version of The Two Cultures and the Scientific Revolution*. Cambridge: Cambridge University Press, 1969.

Snow, David A. "Extending and Broadening Blumer's Conceptualization of Symbolic Interactionism." *Symbolic Interaction* 24 (2001), 367–77.

Speck, W. A. "Cromwell and the Glorious Revolution." In *Images of Cromwell: Essays for and by Roger Howell, Jr.*, edited by R. C. Richardson, 48–62. Manchester: Manchester University Press, 1993.

Statutes at Large from Magna Charta, to the End of the Eleventh Parliament of Great Britain, Anno 1761. 46 vols. Cambridge: J. Bentham, 1762–1807.

Statutes at Large from Magna Charta, to the Thirtieth Year of King George the Second, Inclusive, 1225–1757. 6 vols. London: T. Baskett, 1758.

Stephen, Leslie and Sidney Lee, eds. *The Dictionary of National Biography*. 22 vols. Oxford: Oxford University Press, 1959–60. Stern, Rebecca. "'Personation' and 'Good Marking-Ink': Sanity, Performativity, and Biology in Victorian Sensation Fiction." *Nineteenth-Century Studies* 14 (2000): 35–62.

Stivers, Camilla. "Settlement Women and Bureau Men: Constructing a Usable Past for Public Administration." *Public Administration Review* 55 (1995): 522–29.

Super, R. H. "Landor and the 'Satanic School.'" *Studies in Philology* 42 (1945): 793–810.

———. *The Publication of Landor's Works*. London: The Bibliographic Society, 1954.

———. "Walter Savage Landor." In *The English Romantic Poets and Essayists*, edited by C. W. Houtchens and L. H. Houtchens, 221–53. New York: New York University Press, 1966.

———. *Walter Savage Landor: A Biography*. New York: New York University Press, 1954.

Sutherland, John. *The Life of Walter Scott: A Critical Biography*. Oxford: Blackwell, 1995.

Sutherland, Kathryn. "Introduction." In *Redgauntlet*, by Walter Scott, edited by Kathryn Sutherland. Oxford: Oxford University Press, 1985.

Thomas, William I., and Dorothy S., *The Child in America: Behavior Problems and Programs*. New York: Knopf, 1928.

Thompson, F.M.L., ed. *The Cambridge Social History of Britain*. Vol. 3, *Social Agencies and Institutions*. Cambridge: Cambridge University Press, 1990.

Tilly, Charles. *Popular Contention in Great Britain, 1758–1834*. Cambridge: Harvard University Press, 1995.

———. *Roads from Past to Future*. Lanham, MD: Rowman and Littlefield, 1997.

———. *Stories, Identities, and Political Change*. Lanham, MD: Rowman and Littlefield, 2002.

Trela, D. J. "Sir Walter Scott on Oliver Cromwell: an Evenhanded Royalist Evaluates a Usurper." *Clio* 27 (1998): 195–220.

Trumpener, Katie. *Bardic Nationalism: The Romantic Novel and the British Empire*. Princeton: Princeton University Press, 1997.

Ward, Ian. "The Jurisprudential Heart of Midlothian." *Scottish Literary Journal* 24 (1997): 25–39.

Walker, David M. *A Legal History of Scotland*. 7 vols. Edinburgh: W. Green, 1988.

Watson, Nicola J. "Introduction." In *The Antiquary*, by Walter Scott, edited by Nicola J. Watson. Oxford: Oxford University Press, 2002.

West, Cornel. *The American Evasion of Philosophy: A Genealogy of Pragmatism*. Madison: University of Wisconsin Press, 1989.

Whatley, Christopher A. *Scottish Society, 1707–1830: Beyond Jacobitism, Towards Industrialisation*. Manchester, UK: Manchester University Press, 2000.

Wiley, Michael. *Romantic Geography: Wordsworth and Anglo-European Spaces*. New York: St. Martin's Press, 1998.

Wilt, Judith. *Secret Leaves: The Novels of Walter Scott*. Chicago: University of Chicago Press, 1985.

Wood, Paul. "Introduction: Dugald Stewart and the Invention of 'the Scottish Enlightenment.'" In Wood, *Scottish Enlightenment*, 1–35.

———, ed. *The Scottish Enlightenment: Essays in Reinterpretation*. Rochester, NY: University of Rochester Press, 2000.

Wootton, David. "Leveller Democracy and the Puritan Revolution." In Burns and Goldie, *Cambridge History*, 412–42.

Worden, Blair. "Andrew Marvell, Oliver Cromwell, and the Horatian Ode." In *The Politics of Discourse*, edited by K. Sharpe and S. Zwicker, 147–80. Berkeley: University of California Press, 1987.

———. "English Republicanism." In Burns and Goldie, *Cambridge History*, 443–48.

———. "Milton's Republicanism and the Tyranny of Heaven." In *Machiavelli and Republicanism*, edited by Gisela Bock, Quentin Skinner, and Maurizio Viroli, 227–34. Cambridge: Cambridge University Press, 1990.

Wordsworth, William. *Letters of William and Dorothy Wordsworth: The Later Years, Pt. 4, 1840–53*. Rev. ed. by Alan G. Hill. Oxford: Oxford University Press, 1988.

———. *Poetical Works of William Wordsworth*. Edited by Ernest de Selincourt and Helen Darbishire. 5 vols. Rev. ed. Oxford: Clarendon Press, 1952–59.

Zaret, David. "Petitions and the 'Invention' of Public Opinion in the English Revolution." *American Journal of Sociology* 101 (1996): 1497–1555.

Index